lonely planet

FRANCE'S
BEST TRIPS

38 AMAZING ROAD TRIPS

This edition written and researched by

Jean-Bernard Carillet, Alexis Averbuck, Oliver Berry,
Kerry Christiani, Gregor Clark, Anita Isalska, Catherine
Le Nevez, Hugh McNaughtan, Daniel Robinson, Regis St
Louis, Nicola Williams

SYMBOLS IN THIS BOOK

✓ Top Tips

📖 History & Culture

📷 Essential Photo

⑤ Link Your Trips

👪 Family

🏃 Walking Tour

◯ Tips from Locals

🍷 Food & Drink

✖ Eating

↪ Trip Detour

🌳 Outdoors

🛏 Sleeping

☎ Telephone Number

@ Internet Access

🏊 Swimming Pool

🕐 Opening Hours

📶 Wi-Fi Access

👪 Family-Friendly

P Parking

🥗 Vegetarian Selection

❄ Air-Conditioning

MAP LEGEND

Routes
▬▬▬ Trip Route
▬ ▬ Trip Detour
▬▬ Linked Trip
▬▶ Walk Route
▭ Tollway
▭ Freeway
▭ Primary
▭ Secondary
▭ Tertiary
▭ Lane
▭ Unsealed Road
✕▬ Plaza/Mall
⁙⁙⁙ Steps
⊐⊏ Tunnel
═══ Pedestrian Overpass
▭ ▭ Walk Track/Path

Boundaries
— — International
- - - - State/Province
⌐⌐⌐ Cliff
▬▬ Wall

Population
✪ Capital (National)
◉ Capital (State/Province)
● City/Large Town
• Town/Village

Transport
✈ Airport
⊕ Cable Car/ Funicular
🅿 Parking
⊕ Train/Railway
🚊 Tram
Ⓜ Underground Train Station

Trips
① Trip Numbers
⑨ Trip Stop
🏃 Walking tour
↪ Trip Detour

Route Markers
E44 E-road network
M100 National network

Hydrography
⌇ River/Creek
⌇ Intermittent River
⌇ Swamp/Mangrove
⌇ Canal
⬭ Water
⬭ Dry/Salt/ Intermittent Lake
⬭ Glacier

Areas
░░ Beach
✝✝✝ Cemetery (Christian)
✕✕✕ Cemetery (Other)
▭ Park
▭ Forest
▭ Urban Area
▭ Sportsground

CONTENTS

Normandy & Brittany p95

Paris & Northeastern France p47

Loire Valley & Central France p135

Atlantic Coast p347

Alps, Jura & Rhône Valley p185

Pyrenees & Southwest France p307

Provence & Southeast France p233

Contents cont.

Nice Parasols on Baie des Anges

Provence Lavender fields

WELCOME TO
FRANCE

Iconic monuments, island abbeys, fabulous food, world-class wines – there are so many reasons to plan your very own French voyage.

Whether you're planning on cruising the corniches of the French Riviera, getting lost among the snowcapped Alps or tasting your way around Champagne's hallowed vineyards, this is a nation that's made for road trips and full of unforgettable routes that will plunge you straight into France's heart and soul.

There's a trip for everyone here: family travellers, history buffs, culinary connoisseurs and outdoors adventurers. And if you've only got time for one trip, why not make it one of our eight Classic Trips, which take you to the very best France has to offer. Turn the page for more.

Buckle up, and bon voyage – you're in for quite a ride.

➔

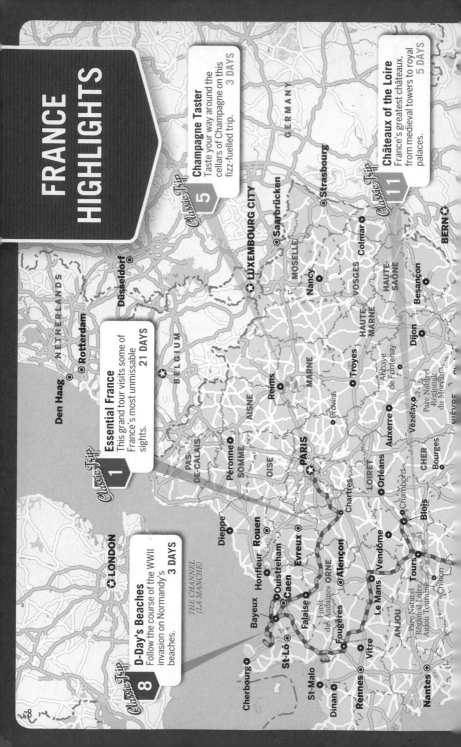

FRANCE HIGHLIGHTS

Champagne Taster
Taste your way around the cellars of Champagne on this fizz-fuelled trip. **3 DAYS**
Classic Trip **5**

Châteaux of the Loire
France's greatest châteaux, from medieval towers to royal palaces. **5 DAYS**
Classic Trip **11**

Essential France
This grand tour visits some of France's most unmissable sights. **21 DAYS**
Classic Trip **1**

D-Day's Beaches
Follow the course of the WWII invasion on Normandy's beaches. **3 DAYS**
Classic Trip **8**

THE CHANNEL
(LA MANCHE)

17
Alpine Adventure
High-country grandeur, from lakeside Annecy to lofty Chamonix.   **6 DAYS**

23
Riviera Crossing
The best beaches, cities, villages and nature along the Med coast.   **4 DAYS**

38
Atlantic to Med
The ultimate south-of-France trip, linking two very different seas.   **10 DAYS**

31
The Pyrenees
Explore the majestic mountain landscape, easily the equal of the Alps.   **7 DAYS**

Classic Trip

ATLANTIC OCEAN
Bay of Biscay
Ligurian Sea
MEDITERRANEAN SEA
Golfe de Beauduc
Golfe de Valencia
ITALY
SPAIN

La Rochelle
Marais Poitevin
Saintes
Cognac
Parc Naturel Régional des Landes de Gascogne
Bordeaux
Biarritz
Pau
Parc National des Pyrénées
ANDORRA LA VELLA
LANDES
GERS
Agen
Sarlat-la-Canéda
Parc Naturel Régional Périgord-Limousin
Limoges
Parc Naturel Régional de Millevaches en-Limousin
Guéret
CREUSE
Montluçon
LOIRE
Lyon
Clermont-Ferrand
Parc Naturel Régional des Volcans d'Auvergne
Parc Naturel Régional Livradois-Forez
Figeac
LOT
Parc Naturel Régional des Causses du Quercy
Albi
TARN
Toulouse
Tarascon-sur-Ariège
Carcassonne
AUDE
Narbonne
Perpignan
Parc Naturel Régional du Haut-Languedoc
Parc Naturel Régional des Grands Causses
Montpellier
Nîmes
Arles
Avignon
PROVENCE
Marseille
Toulon
VAR
Aiguines
Réserve Géologique de Haute-Provence
HAUTES-ALPES
Sestriere
Cannes
Antibes
Nice
MONACO
Valence
ARDÈCHE
Grenoble
ISÈRE
Parc Naturel Régional du Vercors
Bourgoin-Jallieu
Annecy
Geneva
Chamonix
Ajaccio

100 miles
200 km

France's best sights and experiences, and the road trips that will take you there.

FRANCE
HIGHLIGHTS

★

Paris

What is there to say about the City of Light that hasn't been said a thousand times before? Quite simply, this is one of the world's essential cities: sexy, suave and sophisticated. There's a lifetime of experiences here, from the treasures of the Louvre to the cafes of Montmartre – but you'll need nerves of steel to brave the traffic.

Trip

Paris View from in front of Basilique du Sacré-Coeur

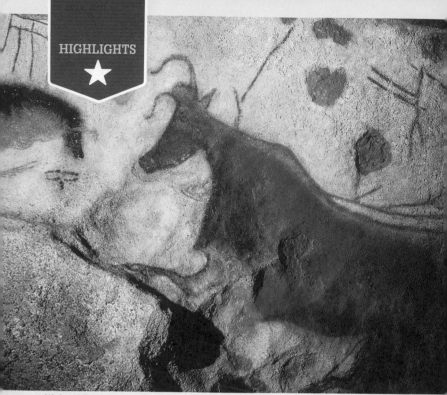

Vézère Valley Prehistoric painting from the Grotte de Lascaux

Vézère Valley

Prehistoric people left an astonishing legacy of paintings and sculptures in the caves of the Vézère Valley. These artworks provide a glimpse into the lives of our ancient ancestors – but opinion is divided on what purpose they served. Were they sacred works imbued with magical significance, or simply prehistoric posters? The truth is, no one knows. Decide for yourself on **Trip 35: Cave Art of the Vézère Valley**.

Trip 35

Mont St-Michel

Perched on an island and connected to the Norman coast by a causeway, this 11th-century abbey is one of France's most recognisable sights. Crowned by spires, ringed by ramparts and thronged by crowds, it looks like it has fallen from the pages of a fairy tale. It's a long climb to the top, but the views are worth every step. We've linked it with other unmissable sights in **Trip 1: Essential France**.

Trip 1

D-Day Beaches

On 6 June 1944 the largest invasion the world has ever seen stormed ashore onto the beaches of Normandy. Now known as D-Day, this audacious assault marked the turning point of WWII, and on **Trip 8: D-Day's Beaches**, you'll see many reminders of the fateful campaign – from the forbidding guns of Longues-sur-Mer to the moving cemetery above Omaha Beach.

Trip 8

Mont St-Michel Island abbey off the Norman coast

BEST ROADS FOR DRIVING

Riviera Crossing Cliff roads and sparkling seas: the drive of a lifetime. **Trip** 23

Gorges du Tarn Drive through a dramatic ravine in the Cévennes hills. **Trip** 28

Route des Vins d'Alsace Meander among vines with views of the Vosges. **Trip** 6

Col de l'Iseran Brave the Alps' highest road pass. **Trip** 17

The Lot Valley Cruise limestone cliffs beside the Lot River. **Trip** 37

The Pyrenees

With their lofty passes and wide-open skies, the Pyrenees have the wow factor. Running along the Franco–Spanish border, they're home to some of the nation's wildest landscapes, and some of its hairiest roads – the closest you'll get to a traffic jam here is finding yourself stuck behind a herd of cows. Take **Trip 31: The Pyrenees** through quiet valleys, traditional villages and mountain-top observatories.

Trip 31

13

Burgundy Vineyard near Beaune

French Riviera

If it's a top-down, open-road, wind-in-your-hair drive you're after, there's only one corner of France that hits the mark, and that's the flashy Riviera. Synonymous with glitz and glamour since the 19th century, it's still one of Europe's most fashionable spots. **Trip 23: Riviera Crossing** twists through hilltop towns and hairpin-bend roads – just remember to pack a camera and a pair of shades.

Trips

BEST TOWNS FOR WINE-LOVERS

Beaune The heart and soul of Burgundy wine. **Trip** 15

St-Émilion Winemakers outnumber residents in this honey-stoned town. **Trip** 38

Bergerac Lesser-known vintages on the edge of the Dordogne. **Trip** 34

Épernay Tour the cellars of Champagne's classic brands. **Trip** 5

Colmar Sip Alsatian wines with a view of the canals. **Trip** 6

15

SHAUN EGAN / GETTY IMAGES ©

Provence The hilltop village of Gordes

Loire Valley Château de Chambord

Hilltop Villages

From red-roofed hamlets to hillside hideaways, France's *villages perchés* will be a highlight of your trip. Most are medieval, and replete with flower-filled lanes, hidden courtyards and quiet squares. Life ticks along at a snail's pace, and there's nowhere better to settle in for a leisurely lunch. **Trip 22: Lavender Route** travels through some of Provence's prettiest.

Trips 6 19 22 36

Châteaux of the Loire

For sky's-the-limit extravagance, don't miss **Trip 11: Châteaux of the Loire**. Constructed by France's aristocratic elite between the 15th and 17th centuries, these lavish mansions were designed to show off their owners' wealth – something they manage to achieve in spectacular fashion. Chambord's the jewel in the crown, but there are many more to visit.

Trip 11

Champagne Vineyards

Let's face it – celebrations wouldn't be the same without a bottle of bubbly. The world's most exclusive tipple is produced on a handful of Champagne vineyards, many of which offer tours and the chance to taste the fruits of their labour. **Trip 5: Champagne Taster** takes in tiny family producers as well as big-name châteaux around Épernay and Reims.

Trip 5

The Camargue

Sprawling across the western edge of
Provence, this huge natural wetland is
a paradise for nature-lovers, with its
population of seabirds, wild horses and
pink flamingos. **Trip 27: The Camargue**
takes a leisurely wander along the back
roads, with plenty of time factored in
along the way to immerse yourself in
the unique cowboy culture.

Trip

Brittany's Coastline

Golden beaches, surf-battered cliffs,
quiet creeks and lonely lighthouses –
Trip 9: Breton Coast is one long parade
of postcard views. Some stretches of
the coastline are busy, while others feel
wonderfully wild and empty – so plan
your route, pack a decent map and just
hit the Breton road.

Trip

(left) **Brittany** Coastal fort dating from the 13th century

(below) **Pont du Gard** Huge Roman aqueduct near Nîmes

Pont du Gard

The scale of this Roman aqueduct is astonishing: 35 arches straddle the 275m upper tier, and it once carried 20,000 cu metres of water per day. View it from beside the Gard River; clamber along the top deck; or arrive after dark to see it lit up in impressive fashion. It marks the start of **Trip 28: Pont du Gard to Viaduc du Millau**, which travels through the Cévennes to another amazing bridge.

Trips 21 28

BEST HILLTOP VILLAGES

Gordes The quintessential Provençal village. **Trip** 22

Vézelay Get spiritual in this ancient pilgrim village. **Trip** 14

St-Paul de Vence Dreamy Med vistas have lured countless artists. **Trip** 23

St-Jean Pied de Port Fortified town overlooking the Spanish border. **Trip** 32

19

IF YOU LIKE...

Camembert World-famous cheese

Art

Impressionist masterpieces, modernist marvels, landmark museums – France's astonishing artistic legacy is guaranteed to be one of the most memorable parts of your trip.

2 A Toast to Art

Inspiring architecture meets cutting-edge art on this trip via the new Louvre-Lens museum, the Centre Pompidou-Metz and Nancy's art nouveau architecture.

7 Monet's Normandy

Cruise through the countryside that inspired the impressionists, finishing with a walk around Monet's own lily garden.

21 Roman Provence

Experience Provence's fantastic Roman legacy, with exceptionally well-preserved ruins integrated into modern cities.

French Cuisine

French food might be synonymous with sophistication, but there's more to this foodie nation than fine dining – there's a whole culinary culture to experience, whether that's guzzling oysters, hunting for truffles, savouring cheeses or buying fresh baguettes from a village *boulangerie* (bakery).

10 Tour des Fromages

Taste your way around Normandy's world-famous cheeses – Camembert, Pont L'Évêque, Livarot and more.

20 Rhône Valley

Fill up on Lyonnaise cuisine in a cosy bouchon (small bistro), then head for Montélimar to indulge in nougat treats.

34 Gourmet Dordogne

For rich French food, there's nowhere like the Dordogne, the spiritual home of foie gras and the black truffle.

Nature

With seven national parks and a host of other protected areas, France's natural landscapes are ripe for outdoor adventure.

13 Volcanoes of the Auvergne

Discover this chain of extinct volcanoes that stretches across much of central France.

17 Alpine Adventure

Hike trails and spot wildlife among the peaks and ski resorts of France's highest mountain chain.

23 Riviera Crossing

Keep your eyes peeled for pink flamingos and wild horses in France's largest wetlands.

26 Corsican Coast Cruiser

Escape the French mainland for a cruise around the wild landscapes and coastline of Corsica, aptly named the île de beauté.

Burgundy Wine tasting

Wine Tasting

If there's one thing France knows about, it's wine. Viticulture has been a cornerstone of French culture for hundreds of years, and the merest mention of the nation's top vineyards makes even hardened sommeliers go weak at the knees.

5 Champagne Taster
Cellars echo to the sound of popping corks on this effervescent adventure through Champagne's hallowed brands.

6 Alsace Accents
Glossy vines and traditional villages form the backdrop to this meander along the Route des Vins d'Alsace.

15 Route des Grands Crus Few regions command more cachet in the wine world than Burgundy. Follow the trail along the Côte de Nuits and Côte d'Or.

Architecture

France has never been shy about showing off its taste for extravagant architecture. Castles and palaces, abbeys and cathedrals – France offers them all, and more.

1 Essential France
From Mont St-Michel to the palace of Versailles, this route explores France's unmissable sites.

11 Châteaux of the Loire
Resplendent châteaux line the banks of the Loire, each one more extravagant than the last.

29 The Cathar Trail
Trek across the parched Languedoc plains, which feature crumbling fortresses and hilltop strongholds.

30 Cheat's Compostela
Tick off churches and cathedrals along the old pilgrim route from Le Puy-en-Velay to St-Jean Pied de Port.

Historic Sites

With a history stretching back several millennia, it's little wonder that France is littered with reminders of its past – both ancient and recent.

4 In Flanders Fields
Take an emotional tour around the battlegrounds and cemeteries of the Great War.

8 D-Day's Beaches
The events of D-Day still resonate along the beaches of Normandy, while museums and memorials provide historical context.

14 Medieval Burgundy
Once an independent duchy, Burgundy is home to marvellous medieval buildings and timeless villages.

21 Roman Provence
Travel back to the heyday of Gaul with an expedition around southern France's Roman ruins.

NEED TO KNOW

CURRENCY
Euro (€)

LANGUAGE
French

VISAS
Generally not required for stays of up to 90 days (or at all for EU nationals); some nationalities need a Schengen visa.

FUEL
Petrol stations are common around main towns and larger towns. Unleaded costs around €1.28 per litre; *gazole* (diesel) is usually at least €0.15 cheaper.

RENTAL CARS
ADA (www.ada.fr)

Auto Europe (www.autoeurope.com)

Avis (www.avis.com)

Europcar (www.europcar.com)

Hertz (www.hertz.com)

IMPORTANT NUMBERS
Ambulance (SAMU) ☏15

Police ☏17

Fire ☏18

Europe-wide emergency ☏112

Climate

Brittany & Normandy
GO Apr–Sep

Paris
GO May & Jun

French Alps
GO late Dec–early Apr (skiing)
or Jun & Jul (hiking)

French Riviera
GO Apr–Jun, Sep & Oct

Corsica
GO Apr–Jun, Sep & Oct

■ Warm to hot summers, mild winters
■ Warm to hot summers, cold winters
■ Mild year-round
■ Mild summers, cold winters
□ Alpine climate

When to Go

High Season (Jul & Aug)
» Queues at big sights and on the road, especially August.

» Christmas, New Year and Easter equally busy.

» Late December to March is high season in Alpine ski resorts.

» Book accommodation and tables in the best restaurants well in advance.

Shoulder (Apr–Jun & Sep)
» Accommodation rates drop in southern France and other hot spots.

» Spring brings warm weather, flowers and local produce.

» The *vendange* (grape harvest) is reason to visit in autumn.

Low Season (Oct–Mar)
» Prices up to 50% lower than high season.

» Sights, attractions and restaurants open fewer days and shorter hours.

» Hotels and restaurants in quieter rural regions (such as the Dordogne) are closed.

Your Daily Budget

Budget: less than €130

» Dorm bed: €18–30

» Double room in budget hotel: €90

» Admission to many attractions first Sunday of month: free

» Lunch *menus*: less than €20

Midrange: €130–220

» Double room in a midrange hotel: €90–190

» Lunch *menus* in gourmet restaurants: €20–40

Top end: more than €220

» Double room in a top-end hotel: €190–350

» Top restaurant dinner: *menu* €65, à la carte €100–150

Eating

Restaurants & bistros Range from traditional to contemporary minimalist; urban dining is international, rural dining staunchly French.

Brasseries Open from dawn until late, these casual eateries are great for dining in between standard meal times.

Cafes Ideal for breakfast and light lunch; many morph into bars after dark.

Price ranges refer to the average cost of a two-course meal:

€	less than €20
€€	€20–40
€€€	more than €40

Sleeping

B&Bs Enchanting properties with maximum five rooms.

Hostels New-wave hostels are design-driven, lifestyle spaces

with single/double rooms as well as dorms.

Hotels Hotels embrace every budget and taste. Refuges and *gîtes d'étape* (walkers' lodges) for hikers on trails in mountainous areas.

Price ranges refer to a double room in high season, with private bathroom, excluding breakfast:

€	less than €90
€€	€90–190
€€€	more than €190

Arriving in France

Aéroport de Charles de Gaulle (Paris)

Trains, buses and RER suburban trains run to the city centre every 15 to 30 minutes between 5am and 11pm; night buses kick in from 12.30am to 5.30am. Fares are €9.75 by RER, €6 to €17.50 by bus and €8 by night bus. Flat fare of €50/55 for 30-minute taxi journey to right /left-bank central Paris (15% higher between 5pm and 10am, and Sundays).

Aéroport d'Orly (Paris)

Linked to central Paris by Orlyval rail then RER (€12.05) or bus (€7.50 to €12.50) every 15 minutes between 5am and 11pm. Or T7 tram to Villejuif-Louis Aragon then metro to the centre (€3.60). The 25-minute journey by taxi costs €35/30 to right-/left-bank central Paris (15% more from 5pm to 10am, and Sundays).

Mobile Phones

European and Australian phones work, but only American mobiles (cells) with 900 and 1800 MHz networks are compatible. Use a French SIM card with a French number to make cheaper calls.

Internet Access

Wi-fi is available at major airports, in most hotels, and at many cafes, restaurants, museums and tourist offices.

Money

ATMs at every airport, most train stations and on every second street corner in towns and cities. Visa, MasterCard and Amex widely accepted.

Tipping

By law, restaurant and bar prices are *service compris* (ie include a 15% service charge), so there's no need to leave a *pourboire* (tip).

Useful Websites

French Government Tourist Office (www.france.fr) Sights, activities, transport and special-interest holidays.

Lonely Planet (www.lonelyplanet.com/france) Travel tips, accommodation, forum and more.

Mappy (www.mappy.fr) Mapping and journey planning.

Opening Hours

Banks 9am–noon and 2–5pm Monday to Friday or Tuesday to Saturday

Restaurants noon–2.30pm and 7–11pm six days a week

Cafes 7am–11pm

Bars 7pm–1am

Shops 10am–noon and 2–7pm Monday to Saturday

For more, see France Driving Guide (p413).

CITY GUIDE

PARIS

If ever a city needed no introduction, it's Paris – a trendsetter, fashion former and style icon for centuries, and still very much at the cutting edge. Whether you're here to tick off the landmarks or seek out the secret corners, Paris fulfils all your expectations, and leaves you wanting more.

Paris Basilique du Sacré-Couer

Getting Around

Driving in Paris is a nightmare. Happily, there's no need for a car. The metro is fast, frequent and efficient; tickets cost €1.80 (day passes €11.15) and are valid on the city's buses. Hire bikes from **1800 Vélib** (http://en.velib.paris.fr) stations; insert a credit card, authorise a €150 deposit and pedal away. Day passes €1.70; first 30 minutes free, subsequent 30 minutes from €1.

Parking

Meters don't take coins; use a chip-enabled credit card. Municipal car parks cost €2 to €3.50 per hour; €20 to €25 per 24 hours.

Where to Eat

Le Marais is one of the best areas for eating out, with its small restaurants and trendy bistros. Don't miss Paris' street markets: Marché Bastille, rue Montorgueil and rue Mouffetard are full of atmosphere.

Where to Stay

Base yourself in Montmartre for its Parisian charm, if you don't mind crowds. Le Marais and Bastille provide style on a budget, while St-Germain is good for a splurge.

Useful Websites

Lonely Planet (www.lonelyplanet.com/paris)

Paris Info (www.parisinfo.com) Tourist-authority.

Secrets of Paris (www.secretsofparis.com) Loads of resources and reviews.

Paris by Mouth (http://parisbymouth.com) Foodie heaven.

Sortiraparis (www.sortiraparis.com) What's on around town.

Trips Through Paris [1]

TOP EXPERIENCES

➡ Eiffel Tower at Twilight

Any time is a good time to take in the panorama from the top of the 'Metal Asparagus' (as Parisians snidely call it) – but the twilight view is extra special (www.toureiffel.fr).

➡ Musée du Louvre

France's greatest repository of art, sculpture and artefacts, the Louvre is a must-visit – but don't expect to see it all in a day (www.louvre.fr).

➡ Basilique du Sacré-Coeur

Climb inside the cupola of this Montmartre landmark for one of the best cross-city vistas (www.sacre-coeur-montmartre.com).

➡ Musée d'Orsay

Paris' second-most-essential museum, with a fabulous collection encompassing originals by Cézanne, Degas, Monet, Van Gogh and more (www.musee-orsay.fr).

➡ Cathédrale de Notre-Dame

Peer over Paris from the north tower of this Gothic landmark, surrounded by gargoyles and flying buttresses (www.cathedraledeparis.com).

➡ Les Catacombes

Explore more than 2km of tunnels beneath the streets of Montparnasse, lined with the bones and skulls of millions of Parisians (www.catacombes.paris.fr).

➡ Cimetière Père-Lachaise

Oscar Wilde, Édith Piaf, Marcel Proust and Jim Morrison are just a few of the famous names buried in this wildly overgrown cemetery (www.pere-lachaise.com).

➡ Canal St-Martin

Join the locals for a walk or bike ride along the towpaths of this 4.5km canal, once derelict but now reborn as a haven from the city hustle.

Lyon Place des Jacobins

LYON

For centuries, Lyon has served as a crossroads between France's south and north, as well as a gateway to the nearby Alps. A commercial and industrial powerhouse for over 500 years, it's now a cosmopolitan and sophisticated city, with some outstanding museums and a notoriously lively nightlife.

Getting Around

Cars aren't much use for getting around Lyon itself. The same €1.80 tickets are valid on all the city's public transport, including buses, trams, the four-line metro and the two funiculars linking Vieux Lyon to Fourvière and St-Just. Day passes cost €5.50.

Parking

As always, parking is expensive, so pick a hotel with a private car park if you're planning on arriving with wheels.

Where to Eat

The classic place to eat in Lyon is a *bouchon* (literally, 'bottle stopper'), a small, cosy bistro that cooks up regional cuisine such as *boudin blanc* (veal sausage) and *quenelles de brochet* (pike dumplings in a creamy crayfish sauce). Afterwards, browse the stalls of the city's wonderful covered market, Les Halles de Lyon.

Where to Stay

Vieux Lyon and Presqu'Île both have a fantastic range of hotels and guesthouses that combine old Lyonnaise architecture with modern style. Croix Rousse is the handiest area for visiting the Roman remains around Fourvière.

Useful Websites

City of Lyon (www.lyon.fr)

My Little Lyon (www.mylittle. fr/mylittlelyon)

Petit Paume (www. petitpaume.com)

Trips Through Lyon

1 20

Lille Place du Général de Gaulle

LILLE

Lille may be France's most underrated major city. This once tired industrial metropolis has transformed itself into a stylish, self-confident city with a strong Flemish accent. Three art museums, lots of stylish shops and a lovely old town make it well worthy of investigation.

Getting Around

Driving into Lille is incredibly confusing, even with a good map; just suspend your sense of direction and blindly follow the 'Centre Ville' signs. Lille's buses and two speedy metro lines run until about 12.30am. Tickets cost €1.40; a Pass' Journée (all-day pass) costs €4.10.

Parking

If you're driving, the best idea is to leave your vehicle at the park-and-ride at **Champ de Mars** (www.transpole.fr; av Cuvier; per 3hr/day €2/4; ⏰24hr, staffed 7am-8pm Mon-Sat) on bd de la Liberté (open from 10am to 6pm or 7pm, closed Saturdays and Sundays, September to March), 1.2km northwest of the centre. It costs €4 a day and includes return travel for five people to central Lille on bus 12.

Where to Eat

Lille's proximity to Belgium has influenced its cuisine. Cosy *estaminets* (Flemish eateries) serve Lillois specialities such as *carbonade* (braised beef stewed with beer, spiced bread and brown sugar) and *potjevleesch* (jellied chicken, pork, veal and rabbit).

Where to Stay

Most hotels are within striking distance of the city centre, but Lille's business focus means many are short on charm. On the plus side, rates drop at weekends.

Useful Websites

Lille Tourisme (www.lilletourism.com)

Trips Through Lille

2 4

NICE

The classic metropolis of the French Riviera, Nice has something to suit all moods: exceptional museums, atmospheric street markets, glittering Mediterranean beaches and a rabbit-warren old town, all bathed in radiant year-round sunshine. With its blend of city grit and old-world opulence, it deserves as much time as you can spare.

Getting Around

The complicated one-way system and heavy traffic can make driving in Nice stressful, especially in the heat of summer. Walking is the easiest way to get around. There's a handy tram line from the train station all the way to Vieux Nice and place Garibaldi; tickets cost €1.50 and are valid on buses.

Parking

Nearly all parking in Nice is *payant* (chargeable) – assuming you manage to find a space. Car parks are usually cheapest (around €2 to €3 per hour, or €17 to €30 per day). All parking meters take coins; car-park pay stations also accept credit cards.

TOP EXPERIENCES

➡ Strolling the Promenade des Anglais

Join sun worshippers, inline skaters and dog walkers on this magnificent boulevard, which runs right along Nice's shimmering seafront.

➡ Musée Matisse

Just 2km north of the centre, this excellent art museum documents the life and work of Henri Matisse in painstaking detail. You'll need good French to get the most out of your visit (www.musee-matisse-nice.org).

➡ Shopping on Cours Saleya

This massive market captures the essence of Niçois life. A chaotic assortment of stalls sells everything from fresh-cut flowers to fresh fish.

➡ Parc du Château

Pack a picnic and head to this hilltop park for a panorama across Nice's red-tiled rooftops.

Nice Quai de Rauba Capeu

Where to Eat

Head for the alleyways of Vieux Nice (Old Nice) for the most authentic neighbourhood restaurants. Don't miss the local specialities of *socca* (chickpea-flour pancake), *petits farcis* (stuffed vegetables) and *pissaladière* (onion tart topped with black olives and anchovies).

Where to Stay

Old town equals atmosphere, but for the best views and classiest rooms you'll want to base yourself near the seafront – the Promenade des Anglais has several landmark hotels. The city's cheapest hotels are clustered around the train station.

Useful Websites

Nice Tourisme (http://en.nicetourisme.com)

Trips Through Nice 23 38

FRANCE
BY REGION

From rugged mountain roads to quiet country lanes, France is a driver's dream. Here's your guide to what each region has to offer, along with suggestions for our top road trips.

Normandy & Brittany

In these charming and varied regions, history buffs head for D-Day beaches; culture-vultures follow the steps of Monet in Giverny and marvel at Rouen's medieval old city; and food-lovers sample cheese, cider, seafood and crepes. For dramatic landscapes, the Breton coast beckons.

Drive the coast on Trip 9

Loire Valley & Central France

The Loire is rightly famous for its châteaux, but there's more here than over-the-top architecture. A world of wine awaits in Burgundy; the region's medieval heritage is a must for history buffs; and volcanic vistas unfold in the Auvergne.

Taste Grand Cru wine on Trip 15

Atlantic Coast

France's wonderfully varied west coast stretches from the vineyards of Bordeaux down to the busy beach towns of Arcachon and Biarritz. The southwest is a stronghold of French Basque culture, while the Dordogne and the Lot Valley offer a dreamy vision of the French countryside.

Hunt for truffles on Trip 34

Paris & Northeastern France

No French trip would be complete without Paris, one of the world's most vital cities. Beyond the capital, explore artistic connections in Nancy, home of art nouveau, tour Alsatian vineyards, visit prestigious Champagne cellars and delve into a war-ravaged past in Flanders.

Quaff Champagne on Trip `5`

Alps, Jura & Rhône Valley

Mountains spiral skywards and the roads get ever higher as you drive through the Alps and the Jura. Brave the slopes and hike the trails, then head into the Rhône Valley for hearty food and postcard-pretty villages.

Enjoy sky-high views on Trip `17`

Provence & Southeast France

Sparkling beaches, glitzy towns, hilltop hamlets, lavender fields: Provence is the stuff of dreams. Cruise the corniches, head inland for Roman ruins and Provençal markets, and if you're feeling adventurous, the wild island of Corsica is only a boat ride away.

Follow the Riviera on Trip `23`

Pyrenees & Southwest France

Straddling the Franco–Spanish border, the valleys and passes of the Pyrenees make for fantastic driving, but you'll need to keep your eyes on the road. Switch to the slow lane in laid-back Languedoc, with its Cathar castles and pilgrims' churches.

Head to the hills on Trip `28`

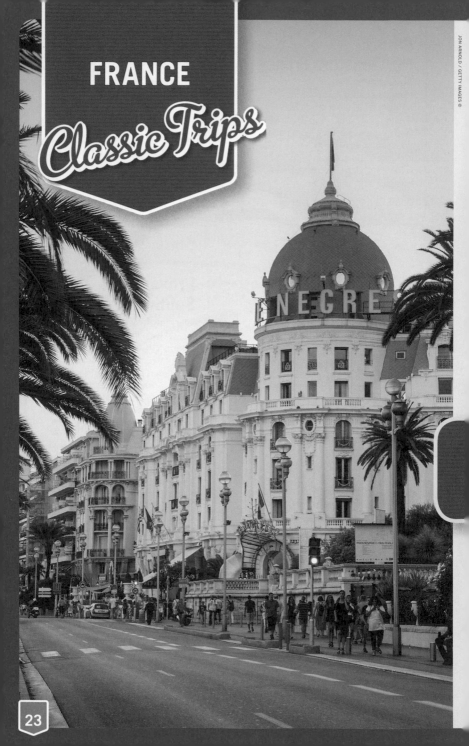

FRANCE

Classic Trips

KAVRAM / SHUTTERSTOCK ©

17

What is a Classic Trip?

All the trips in this book show you the best of France, but we've chosen eight as our all-time favourites. These are our Classic Trips – the ones that lead you to the best of the iconic sights, the top activities and the unique French experiences.

Above: Snow-covered Alps, Chamonix
Left: Promenade des Anglais, Nice

Essential France

1

City to city, coast to coast, this grand tour visits some of France's most unmissable sights. There's some epic driving involved, but this is one trip you won't forget in a hurry.

TRIP HIGHLIGHTS

335 km

Bayeux
Check out the world's longest comic strip

4 Caen
START
⭐ PARIS

2100 km

Chamonix
Savour sky-high views of Mont Blanc

10

• Poitiers

8

Clermont-Ferrand

FINISH
13
• Cannes

1445 km

Sarlat-la-Canéda
Explore the medieval heart of this gorgeous Dordogne town

Gorges du Verdon
Experience France's answer to the Grand Canyon

3060 km

**21 DAYS
3060KM / 1902 MILES**

- - - -

GREAT FOR...

🌳 👪 📖

- - - -

BEST TIME TO GO
April to June

- - - -

📷 **ESSENTIAL PHOTO**

Overlooking the Parisian panorama from the Basilique du Sacré-Coeur.

- - - -

✅ **BEST FOR FAMILIES**

Brave the space-age rides and roller-coaster thrills of Futuroscope.

du Verdon Ravine through Haute-Provence

1 Essential France

This is the big one – an epic trek that travels all the way from the chilly waters of the English Channel to the gleaming blue Mediterranean. Along the way, you'll stop off at some of France's most iconic sights: the château of Versailles, the abbey of Mont St-Michel, the summit of Mont Blanc and the beaches of the French Riviera. *Allez-y!*

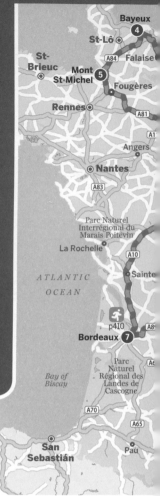

❶ Paris

For that essentially Parisian experience, it's hard to beat Montmartre – the neighbourhood of cobbled lanes and cafe-lined squares beloved by writers and painters since the 19th century. This was once a notoriously ramshackle part of Paris, full of bordellos, brothels, dance halls and bars, as well as the city's first can-can clubs. Though its hedonistic heyday has long since passed, Montmartre still retains a villagey charm, despite the throngs of tourists.

The centre of Montmartre is **place du Tertre**, once the village's main square, now packed with buskers and portrait artists. You can get a sense of how the area would once have looked at the **Musée de Montmartre** (☎01 49 25 89 39; www.museede montmartre.fr; 12 rue Cortot, 18e; adult/child €9.50/5.50; ☺10am-6pm; Ⓜ Lamarck-Caulaincourt), which details the area's bohemian past. It's inside Montmartre's oldest building, a 17th-century manor house once occupied by Renoir and Utrillo.

Nearby, Montmartre's finest view unfolds from the dome of the **Basilique du Sacré-Coeur** (☎01 53 41 89 00; www.sacre-coeur-montmartre.com; place du Parvis du Sacré-Cœur; dome adult/child €6/4, cash only; ☺6am-10.30pm, dome 8.30am-8pm May-Sep, to 5pm

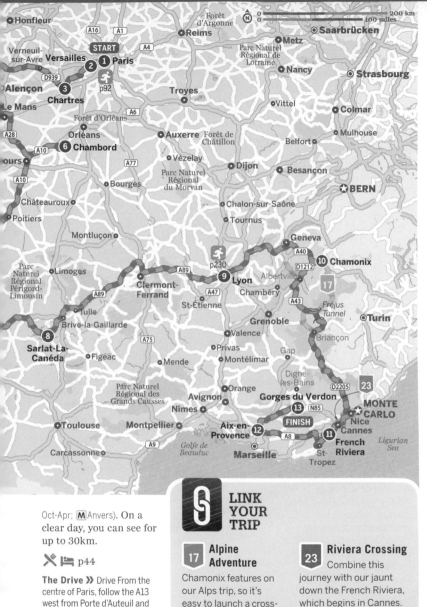

Oct-Apr; **M** Anvers). On a clear day, you can see for up to 30km.

✕ ⌂ p44

The Drive » Drive From the centre of Paris, follow the A13 west from Porte d'Auteuil and take the exit marked 'Versailles Château'. Versailles is 28km southwest of the city.

LINK YOUR TRIP

17 Alpine Adventure

Chamonix features on our Alps trip, so it's easy to launch a cross-mountain adventure from there.

23 Riviera Crossing

Combine this journey with our jaunt down the French Riviera, which begins in Cannes.

37

❷ Versailles

Louis XIV transformed his father's hunting lodge into the **Château de Versailles** (📞01 30 83 78 00; www.chateauversailles.fr; place d'Armes; adult/child passport ticket incl estate-wide access €18/free, with musical events €25/free, palace €15/free; ⏱9am-6.30pm Tue-Sun Apr-Oct, to 5.30pm Tue-Sun Nov-Mar; Ⓜ RER Versailles-Château–Rive Gauche) in the mid-17th century, and it remains France's most majestic palace. The royal court was based here from 1682 until 1789, when revolutionaries massacred the palace guard and dragged Louis XVI and Marie Antoinette back to Paris, where they were ingloriously guillotined.

The architecture is truly eye-popping. Highlights include the **Grands Appartements du Roi et de la Reine** (State Apartments) and the famous **Galerie des Glaces** (Hall of Mirrors), a 75m-long ballroom filled with chandeliers and floor-to-ceiling mirrors. Outside, the vast park incorporates terraces, flower beds, paths and fountains, as well as the **Grand and Petit Canals**.

Northwest of the main palace is the **Domaine de Marie-Antoinette** (Marie Antoinette's Estate; www.chateauversailles.fr; Château de Versailles; adult/child €10/free, with passport ticket free; ⏱noon-6.30pm Tue-Sun Apr-Oct, to 5.30pm Tue-Sat Nov-Mar), where the royal family would have taken refuge from the intrigue and etiquette of court life.

The Drive » The N10 runs southwest from Versailles through pleasant countryside and forest to Rambouillet. You'll join the D906 to Chartres. All told, it's a journey of 76km.

❸ Chartres

You'll know you're nearing Chartres long before you reach it thanks to the twin spires of the **Cathédrale Notre Dame** (www.cathedrale-chartres.org; place de la Cathédrale; ⏱8.30am-7.30pm daily year-round, also to 10pm Tue, Fri & Sun Jun-Aug), considered to be one of the most important structures in Christendom.

The present cathedral was built during the late 12th century after the original was destroyed by fire. It's survived wars and revolutions remarkably intact, and the brilliant-blue stained-glass windows have even inspired their own shade of paint (Chartres blue). The cathedral also houses the Sainte Voile (Holy Veil), supposedly worn by the Virgin Mary while giving birth to Jesus.

The best views are from the 112m-high **Clocher Neuf** (New Bell Tower; Cathédrale Notre Dame; adult/child €7.50/free; ⏱9.30am-12.30pm & 2-6pm Mon-Sat, 2-6pm Sun May-Aug, 9.30am-12.30pm & 2-5pm Mon-Sat, 2-5pm Sun Sep-Apr).

✕ 🛏 p44

The Drive » Follow the D939 northwest for 58km to Verneuil-

VISITING VERSAILLES

Versailles is one of the country's most popular destinations, so planning ahead will make your visit more enjoyable. Avoid the busiest days of Tuesday and Sunday, and remember that the château is closed on Monday. Save time by pre-purchasing tickets on the château's website, or arrive early if you're buying at the door – by noon queues spiral out of control.

You can also access off-limits areas (such as the Private Apartments of Louis XV and Louis XVI, the Opera House and the Royal Chapel) by taking a 90-minute **guided tour** (📞01 30 83 77 88; www.chateauversailles.fr; tours €7, plus palace entry; ⏱English-language tours 9.30pm Tue-Sun).

sur-Avre, then take the D926 west for 78km to Argentan – both great roads through typical Norman countryside. Just west of Argentan, the D158/N158 heads north to Caen, then turns northwest on the N13 to Bayeux, 94km further.

TRIP HIGHLIGHT

➍ Bayeux

The **Tapisserie de Bayeux** (🖉02 31 51 25 50; www.bayeux museum.com; rue de Nesmond; adult/child incl audioguide €9/4; ⊙9am-6.30pm Mar-Oct, to 7pm May-Aug, 9.30am-12.30pm & 2-6pm Nov–Feb) is without doubt the world's most celebrated (and ambitious) piece of embroidery. Over 58 panels, the tapestry recounts the invasion of England in 1066 by William I, or William the Conqueror, as he's now known.

Commissioned in 1077 by Bishop Odo of Bayeux, William's half-brother, the tapestry retells the battle in fascinating detail: look for Norman horses getting stuck in the quicksands around Mont St-Michel, and the famous appearance of Halley's Comet in scene 32. The final showdown at the Battle of Hastings is particularly graphic, complete with severed limbs, decapitated heads, and the English King Harold getting an arrow in the eye.

✕ 🏠 p115

The Drive » Mont St-Michel is 125km southwest of Bayeux; the fastest route is along the D6 and then the A84 motorway.

➎ Mont St-Michel

You've already seen it on a million postcards, but nothing prepares you for the real **Mont St-Michel** (🖉02 33 89 80 00; www. monuments-nationaux.fr; adult/child incl guided tour €9/ free; ⊙9am-7pm, last entry 1hr before closing). It's one of France's architectural marvels, an 11th-century island abbey marooned in the middle of a vast golden bay.

When you arrive, you'll be steered into one of the Mont's huge car parks. You then walk along the causeway (or catch a free shuttle bus) to the island itself. Guided tours are included, or you can explore solo with an audioguide.

The **Église Abbatiale** (Abbey Church) is reached via a steep climb along the **Grande Rue**. Around the church, the cluster of buildings known as **La Merveille** (The Marvel) includes the cloister, refectory, guest hall, ambulatory and various chapels.

For a different perspective, take a guided walk across the sands with **Découverte de la Baie du Mont-Saint-Michel** (🖉02 33 70 83 49; www.decou vertebaie.com; 1 rue Montoise, Genêts; adult/child from €8/5) and **Chemins de la Baie** (🖉02 33 89 80 88; www. cheminsdelabaie.com; 34 rue de l'Ortillon, Genêts; adult/ child from €7.30/5), both

based in Genêts. Don't be tempted to do it on your own – the bay's tides are notoriously treacherous.

🏠 p44

The Drive » Take the A84, N12 and A81 for 190km to Le Mans and the A28 for 102km to Tours, where you can follow a tour through the Loire Valley if you wish. Chambord is about 75km from Tours via the D952.

➏ Chambord

If you only have time to visit one château in the Loire, you might as well make it the grandest – and **Chambord** (🖉info 02 54 50 40 00, tour & show reser- vations 02 54 50 50 40; www. chambord.org; adult/child €11/9, parking near/distant €6/4; ⊙9am-5pm or 6pm; ♿) is the most lavish of them all. It's a showpiece of Renaissance architecture, from the double- helix staircase up to the turret-covered rooftop. With over 440 rooms, the sheer scale of the place is mindboggling – and in the Loire, that's really saying something.

The Drive » It's 425km to Bordeaux via Blois and the A10 motorway. You could consider breaking the journey with stop- offs at Futuroscope and Poitiers, roughly halfway between the two.

➐ Bordeaux

When Unesco decided to protect Bordeaux's medieval architecture in 2007, it simply listed half the city in one fell swoop.

Classic Trip

WHY THIS IS A CLASSIC TRIP
OLIVER BERRY, WRITER

It's an epic in every sense: in scale, views, time and geography. This once-in-a-lifetime journey covers France from every possible angle: top to bottom, east to west, city and village, old-fashioned and modern, coast and countryside. It links together many of the country's truly unmissable highlights, and by the end you'll genuinely be able to say you've seen the heart and soul of France.

Top: Produce market, Aix-en-Provence
Left: Sausages for sale, Sarlat-la-Canéda
Right: Cathédrale St-André, Bordeaux

Covering 18 sq km, this is the world's largest urban World Heritage Site, with grand buildings and architectural treasures galore. Stretch your legs on a walking tour (p410).

Top of the heap is the **Cathédrale St-André**, known for its stone carvings and generously gargoyled belfry, the **Tour Pey-Berland** (place Jean Moulin; adult/child €5.50/ free; ⊘10am-1.15pm & 2-6pm Jun-Sep, 10am-12.30pm & 2-5.30pm Oct-May). But the whole old city rewards wandering, especially around the **Jardin Public** (cours de Verdun), the pretty squares of **esplanade des Quinconces** and **place Gambetta**, and the city's 4km-long **riverfront esplanade**, with its playgrounds, paths and paddling pools.

✕ ⨼ p44, p366

The Drive ≫ Sarlat-la-Canéda is a drive of 194km via the A89 motorway, or you can take a longer but more enjoyable route via the D936.

- - - - - - - - - - - -

TRIP HIGHLIGHT

8 Sarlat-la-Canéda

If you're looking for France's heart and soul, you'll find it among the forests and fields of the Dordogne. It's the stuff of French fantasies: riverbank châteaux, medieval villages, wooden-hulled *gabarres* (flat-bottomed barges) and market stalls groaning with foie gras, truffles, walnuts and

wines. The medieval town of Sarlat-la-Canéda makes the perfect base, with a beautiful medieval centre and lots of lively markets.

It's also ideally placed for exploring the Vézère Valley, about 20km to the northwest, home to France's finest cave paintings. Most famous of all are the ones at the **Grotte de Lascaux** (📞05 53 51 95 03; www.semitour. com; Montignac; adult/child €9.90/6.40, combined ticket with Le Thot €13.50/9.40; ⊙ guided tours 9am-7pm Jul & Aug, 9.30am-6pm Apr-Jun, Sep & Oct, 10am-12.30pm & 2-5pm Nov-Mar, closed Jan), although to prevent damage to the paintings, you now visit a replica of the cave's main sections in a nearby grotto.

The Drive ›› The drive east to Lyon is a long one, covering well over 400km and travelling across the spine of the Massif Central. A good route is to follow the A89 all the way to exit 6, then turn off onto the N89/D89 to Lyon. This route should cover between 420km and 430km.

- - - - - - - - - - - -

❾ Lyon

Fired up by French food? Then you'll love Lyon, with its *bouchons* (small bistros), bustling markets and fascinating food culture. Start in **Vieux Lyon** and the picturesque quarter of **Presqu'île**, then catch the funicular to the top of **Fourvière** to explore the city's Roman ruins and enjoy cross-town views.

Film buffs will also want to make time for the **Musée Lumière** (📞04 78 78 18 95; www.institut-lumiere. org; 25 rue du Premier Film, 8e; adult/child €6.50/5.50; ⊙10am-6.30pm Tue-Sun; Ⓜ Monplaisir-Lumière), where

the Lumière Brothers (Auguste and Louis) shot the first reels of the world's first motion picture, *La Sortie des Usines Lumières,* on 19 March 1895.

✕ 🛏 p45, p229

The Drive ›› Take the A42 towards Lake Geneva, then the A40 towards St-Gervais-les-Bains. The motorway becomes the N205 as it nears Chamonix. It's a drive of at least 225km.

- - - - - - - - - - - -

TRIP HIGHLIGHT

❿ Chamonix

Snuggling among snow-clad mountains – including Europe's highest summit, Mont Blanc – adrenaline-fuelled Chamonix is an ideal springboard for the French Alps. In winter, it's a mecca for skiers and snowboarders, and in summer, once the snows thaw, the high-level trails become a trekkers' paradise.

There are two really essential Chamonix experiences. First, catch the dizzying cable car to the top of the **Aiguille du Midi** to snap a shot of Mont Blanc.

Then take the combination mountain train and cable car from the **Gare du Montenvers** (📞04 50 53 22 75; www. compagniedumontblanc.fr; 35 place de la Mer de Glace; adult/child return €31/26.40; ⊙10am-4.30pm) to the **Mer de Glace** (Sea of Ice), France's largest glacier. Wrap up warmly if you

---

FUTUROSCOPE

Halfway between Chambord and Bordeaux on the A10, 10km north of Poitiers, **Futuroscope** (📞05 49 49 11 12; www.futuroscope.com; av René Monory, Chasseneuil-du-Poitou; adult/child €43/35; ⊙10am-11.15pm Jul, 9am-11.15pm Aug, shorter hours rest of year, closed Jan–mid-Feb) is one of France's top theme parks. It's a futuristic experience that takes you whizzing through space, diving into the ocean depths, racing around city streets and on a close encounter with creatures of the future. Note that many rides have a minimum height of 120cm.

You'll need at least five hours to check out the major attractions, or two days to see everything. The park is in the suburb of Jaunay-Clan; take exit 28 off the A10.

want to visit the glacier's sculptures and ice caves.

✕ 🛏 p205

The Drive ❯❯ The drive to the Riviera is full of scenic thrills. An attractive route is via the D1212 to Albertville, and then via the A43, which travels over the Italian border and through the Tunnel de Fréjus. From here, the N94 runs through Briançon, and a combination of the A51, N85 and D6085 carries you south to Nice. You'll cover at least 430km.

French Riviera The winding coastline

⓫ French Riviera

If there's one coast road in France you simply have to drive, it's the French Riviera, with its rocky cliffs, maquis-scented air and dazzling Med views. Sun-seekers have been flocking here since the 19th century, and its scenery still never fails to seduce.

Lively **Nice** and cinematic Cannes make natural starts, but for the Riviera's loveliest scenery, you'll want to drive down the gorgeous **Corniche de l'Estérel** to **St-Tropez**, still a watchword for seaside glamour. Summer can be hellish, but come in spring or autumn and you'll have its winding lanes and fragrant hills practically to yourself. For maximum views, stick to the coast roads: the D6098 to Antibes and Cannes, the D559 around the Corniche de l'Estérel, and the D98A to St-Tropez. It's about 120km via this route.

The Drive ❯❯ From St-Tropez, take the fast A8 for about 230km west to Aix-en-Provence.

⓬ Aix-en-Provence

Sleepy Provence sums up the essence of *la douce vie* (the gentle life). Cloaked in lavender and spotted with hilltop villages, it's a region that sums up everything that's good about France.

Cruising the back roads and browsing the markets are the best ways to get acquainted. **Carpentras** and **Vaison-la-Romaine** are particularly detour-worthy, while artistic **Aix-en-Provence** encapsulates the classic Provençal vibe, with its pastel buildings and Cézanne connections.

✕ 🛏 p45

The Drive ❯❯ The gorges are 230km northeast of Aix-en-Provence, via the A51 and D952.

TRIP HIGHLIGHT

⓭ Gorges du Verdon

Complete your cross-France adventure with an unforgettable expedition to the **Gorges du Verdon** – sometimes known as the Grand Canyon of Europe. This deep ravine slashes 25km through the plateaus of Haute-Provence; in places, its walls rise to a dizzying 700m, twice the height of the Eiffel Tower (321m).

The two main jumping-off points are the villages of **Moustiers Ste-Marie**, in the west, and **Castellane**, in the east. Drivers and bikers can take in the canyon panorama from two vertigo-inducing cliffside roads, but the base of the gorge is only accessible on foot or by raft.

Eating & Sleeping

Paris ❶

✗ Holybelly   International €

(www.holybel.ly; 19 rue Lucien Sampaix, 10e; breakfast €5-11.50, lunch mains €13.50-16.50; ⏱9am-6pm Thu, Fri, Mon, from 10am Sat & Sun; Ⓜ Jacques Bonsergent) This outstanding barista-run coffee shop and kitchen is always rammed with a buoyant crowd, who never tire of Holybelly's exceptional service, Belleville-roasted coffee and cuisine. Sarah's breakfast pancakes served with egg, bacon, homemade bourbon butter and maple syrup are legendary, while her lunch menu features everything from traditional braised veal shank to squid *à la plancha*.

🛏 Hôtel Amour   Boutique Hotel €€

(☎01 48 78 31 80; www.hotelamourparis.fr; 8 rue Navarin, 9e; d €170-230; 📶; Ⓜ St-Georges, Pigalle) Craving romance in Paris? The inimitable black-clad Amour ('Love') features original design and nude artwork in each of the rooms, some more explicit than others. The icing on the cake is the hip ground-floor bistro with summer patio garden, a tasty spot for breakfast, lunch or dinner and everything in between. Rooms don't have a TV, but who cares when you're in love?

Chartres ❸

✗ Le Tripot   Bistro €€

(☎02 37 36 60 11; www.letripot.wixsite.com/chartres; 11 place Jean Moulin; 2-/3-course lunch menus €15/18, 3-course dinner menus €29.50-45, mains €13.50-22; ⏱noon-1.45pm & 7.30-9.15pm Tue & Thu-Sat, noon-1.45pm Sun) Tucked off the tourist trail and easy to miss, even if you do chance down its narrow street, this atmospheric space with low beamed ceilings is a treat for authentic and adventurous French fare like saddle of rabbit stuffed with snails, and grilled turbot in truffled hollandaise sauce. Locals are onto it, so booking ahead is advised.

🛏 Le Grand Monarque   Hotel €€€

(☎02 37 18 15 15; www.bw-grand-monarque.com; 22 place des Épars; d €145-215, f €275; ❄@📶) With its teal-blue shutters gracing its 1779 façade, lovely stained-glass ceiling, and treasure trove of period furnishings, old B&W photos and knick-knacks, the refurbished Grand Monarque (with air-con in some rooms) is a historical gem and very central. A host of hydrotherapy treatments are available at its spa. Its elegant restaurant, **Georges** (☎02 37 18 15 15; www.bw-grand-monarque.com; 22 place des Épars; 4-course menu from €75, 8-course tasting menu €95, mains €38-41; ⏱noon-2pm & 7.30-10pm Tue-Sat), has a Michelin star. Staff are charming.

Mont St-Michel ❺

🛏 Vent des Grèves   B&B €

(☎Estelle 02 33 48 28 89; www.ventdesgreves.com; 7-9 chemin des Dits, Ardevon; s/d/tr/q incl breakfast €42/52/62/72) This friendly, family-run B&B has five modern rooms, furnished simply, with magical views of the Mont. Outstanding value. Situated an easily walkable 1km east of the shuttle stop in La Caserne.

Bordeaux ❼

✗ Le Petit Commerce   Seafood €€

(05 56 79 76 58; 22 rue Parlement St-Pierre; 2-course lunch menu €14, mains €15-25; ⏱noon-midnight) This iconic bistro, with dining rooms both sides of a narrow pedestrian street and former Michelin-starred chef Stéphane Carrade in the kitchen, is the star turn of the trendy St-Pierre quarter. It's best known for its excellent seafood menu that embraces everything from Arcachon sole and oysters to eels, lobsters and *chipirons* (baby squid) fresh from St-Jean de Luz.

🛏 Mama Shelter — Design Hotel €€

(📞05 57 30 45 45; www.mamashelter.com/en/bordeaux; 19 rue Poquelin Molière; d/tr from €79/129) With personalised iMacs, video booths and free movies in every room, Mama Shelter leads the way in cutting-edge sleep. Crisp white rooms come in small, medium or large, with family-friendly XL doubles touting a sofa bed. The ground-floor restaurant (mains €13 to €29) sports the same signature rubber rings strung above the bar as other Philippe Starck–designed hotels, and weekends usher concerts, gigs and other cultural happenings onto the small stage.

Lyon ⑨

🍴 Le Poêlon d'Or — Bouchon €€

(📞04 78 37 65 60; www.lepoelondor-restaurant.fr; 29 rue des Remparts d'Ainay, 2e; lunch menus €17-20, menus €27-32; ⏲noon-2pm & 7.30-10pm Mon-Fri; Ⓜ Ampère-Victor Hugo) This upmarket *bouchon*, around the corner from the Musée des Tissus, is well known among local foodies who recommend its superb *andouillette* (chitterlings) and pike dumplings. Save room for the delicious chocolate mousse or the vanilla crème brûlée. Yummy. Well worth the detour.

🛏 Cour des Loges — Hotel €€€

(📞04 72 77 44 44; www.courdesloges.com; 2-8 rue du Bœuf, 5e; d €200-350, ste €250-600; ❄ @ 🛜 🐾; Ⓜ Vieux Lyon) Four 14th to 17th-century houses wrapped around a *traboule* (secret passage) with preserved features such as Italianate loggias make this an exquisite place to stay. Individually decorated rooms woo with designer bathroom fittings and bountiful antiques, while decadent facilities include a spa, a Michelin-starred restaurant (menus €95 to €115), a swish cafe and a cross-vaulted bar.

Aix-en-Provence ⑫

🍴 Le Petit Verdot — French €€

(📞04 42 27 30 12; www.lepetitverdot.fr; 7 rue d'Entrecasteaux; mains €19-25; ⏲7pm-midnight Mon-Sat) Great Provençal food and great Provençal wines — really, what more do you want from a meal in this part of France? It's all about hearty, honest dining here, with table tops made out of old wine crates, and a lively chef-patron who runs the place with huge enthusiasm. Expect slow-braised meats, seasonal veg, sinful desserts and some super wines to go with.

🛏 Villa Gallici — Historic Hotel €€€

(📞04 42 23 29 23; www.villagallici.com; 18 av de la Violette; r from €350; 🅿 ❄ 🛜 🐾) Baroque and beautiful, this fabulous villa was built as a private residence in the 18th century, and it still feels marvellously opulent. Rooms are more like museum pieces, stuffed with gilded mirrors, toile-de-Jouy wallpaper and filigreed furniture. There's a lovely lavender-filled garden for breakfast, plus a super pool for lazy evening swims. It even has its own wine cellar.

Paris & Northeastern France

FROM THE BOULEVARDS OF PARIS TO THE LOFTY CHALK CLIFFS OF THE CÔTE D'OPALE, northeastern France is primed with possibilities – whether that means touring Champagne's vineyards, sampling Alsatian cuisine, admiring art in Metz or simply moseying around Strasbourg's attractive city centre. And with its abundance of coast and countryside, it's a pleasure to drive, too.

It's a region whose long (and turbulent) history is plain to see. Two thousand years of royalty, renaissance and revolution have left their mark on the streets of Paris, while the scars of war can still be traced on the fields of Flanders. Elsewhere, cathedrals and châteaux hint at the splendour of a bygone age, and experimental art museums point to an equally flashy future.

Côte d'Opale Cliff-side beach at Cap Blanc-Nez
SAMERE FAHIM PHOTOGRAPHY / GETTY IMAGES ©

Paris & Northeastern France

Dover

Calais
Wissant
Ambleteuse
Boulogne-sur-Mer
Parc Naturel Régional des Caps et Marais d'Opale
Le Touquet-Paris-Plage
Fromelles

BELGIUM
BRUSSELS
Lille
Mons
Charleroi
Lens
Douai
Arras

3

St-Valery-sur-Somme

English Channel (La Manche)

Dieppe

Thiepval
4   **2**
Péronne
Amiens
St-Quentin

A26

Étretat

Neufchâtel-en-Bray

A29

Le Havre
Rouen
Forêt de Lyons

Caen

N158

Louviers
Vernon
Evreux

2

Reims

A4
Verzenay
Épernay   **5**
Le Mesnil-sur-Oger
Châlons-sur-Marne

Falaise

PARIS

Parc Naturel Régional Normandie-Maine

D939

Chartres

Troyes

Alençon
Forêt de Bellême

A11

0   100 km
0   50 miles

DON'T MISS

Centre Pompidou-Metz

It's hard to know here which is more avant-garde – the architecture or the art. Take in this groundbreaking gallery on Trip 2

Vimy Ridge

Walk through one of the only surviving trench systems from WWI on Trip 4

Musée Bartholdi

Visit the Colmar home of the man who made Lady Liberty – and see a life-sized model of the statue's ear – on Trip 6

Amiens

Marvel at one of France's most spectacular cathedrals in this charming (and largely underrated) city on Trip 4

Dunes de la Slack

Wander amid undulating, wind-sculpted sand dunes on Trip 3

Alsace Pathway on the Route des Vins

A Toast to Art

2

One for culture-vultures: an artistic tour across northeastern France, taking in art nouveau in Nancy, glorious glass in Baccarat and avant-garde experimentation in Metz and Strasbourg.

TRIP HIGHLIGHTS

35 km

Lens
Investigate northern France's exciting offshoot of Paris' Louvre Museum

405 km

Metz
Visit the sister institution of Paris' Centre Pompidou

START
● Lille
2
● Arras
● St-Quentin

Pont-à-Mousson
4
5
7 FINISH

Nancy
Explore the home of art nouveau
460 km

Strasbourg
Get lost among the canals and *winstubs* of Strasbourg's Petite France
650 km

7 DAYS
650KM /
404 MILES

GREAT FOR...

BEST TIME TO GO
April to July (avoid the school-holiday crowds).

ESSENTIAL PHOTO
Snap yourself sipping a coffee on Nancy's grand central square, place Stanislas.

BEST FOR SHOPPING
Strasbourg's old quarters for chocolate, glassware and other souvenirs.

Art nouveau architectural detail

51

A Toast to Art

France's northeast is one of the country's most artistic corners, thanks to the arrival of high-profile addresses like the Louvre-Lens and Metz's Centre Pompidou. But these glitzy contemporary museums are simply the continuation of a long artistic legacy. This high-culture tour takes in Gothic cathedrals, neoclassical squares, chic crystalware and art-nouveau mansions – not to mention some of Europe's most experimental art.

❶ Lille

Lille (Rijsel in Flemish) may be France's most underrated major city. In recent decades this once-grimy industrial metropolis has morphed into a glittering and self-confident cultural and commercial hub – and a key shopping, art and culture stop with an attractive old town and a trio of renowned art museums.

Classic works find a home at the **Palais des Beaux Arts** (Fine Arts Museum; ☎03 20 06 78

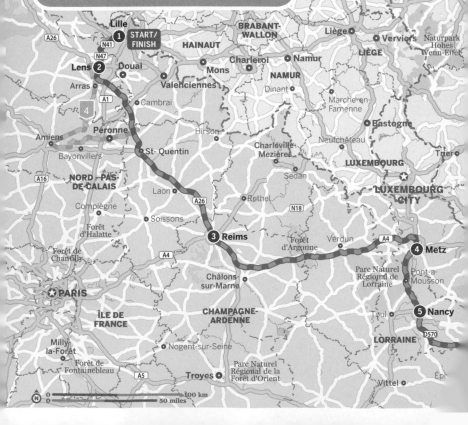

00; www.pba-lille.fr; place de la République; adult/child €7/4; ⏱2-5.50pm Mon, 10am-5.50pm Wed-Sun; 🚾; Ⓜ République Beaux-Arts), an illustrious fine-arts museum with a first-rate collection of 15th- to 20th-century paintings, including works by Rubens, Van Dyck and Manet.

Contrast these with the playful – and sometimes just plain weird – works on show at the **Musée d'Art Moderne** (📞03 20 19 68 88; www.musee-lam.fr; 1 allée du Musée, Villeneuve-d'Ascq; adult/child €7/5; ⏱10am-6pm Tue-Sun).

Big names including Braque, Calder, Léger, Miró, Modigliani and Picasso are the main draws. It's in Villeneuve-d'Ascq, 9km east of Gare Lille-Europe.

A few miles north at **La Piscine Musée d'Art et d'Industrie** (📞03 20 69 23 60; www.roubaix-lapiscine. com; 23 rue de l'Espérance, Roubaix; adult/child €5.50/ free; ⏱11am-6pm Tue-Thu, 11am-8pm Fri, 1-6pm Sat & Sun; Ⓜ Gare Jean Lebas), the building is almost as intriguing as the art: a glorious art-deco swimming pool has been beautifully converted into a cutting-edge gallery, showing contemporary paintings and sculptures.

 p73

The Drive » The quickest route to Lens is via the A1, but a less hectic route takes the N41 and N47. It's a 37km drive from the outskirts of Lille.

TRIP HIGHLIGHT

❷ Lens

A coal-mining town 37km south of Lille

might not seem like the most obvious place to continue investigation of French art, but *au contraire*. The jewel in the crown of industrial Lens is the **Louvre-Lens** (📞03 21 18 62 62; www.louvrelens. fr; 99 rue Paul Bert; multimedia guide €3; ⏱10am-6pm Wed-Mon). An offshoot of the Paris original, this innovative gallery showcases hundreds of treasures from Paris' venerable Musée du Louvre in state-of-the-art exhibition spaces. The centrepiece, the 120m-long Galerie du Temps, displays a semi-permanent collection of judiciously chosen objects – some of them true masterpieces – from the dawn of civilisation to the mid-1800s.

The Drive » Follow the N17 south of town and join the A26 toll road for 178km to Reims, about a two- to 2½-hour drive away.

❸ Reims

Along with its towering Gothic cathedral and Champagne connections,

LINK YOUR TRIP

4 **In Flanders Fields**
WWI French battlefields are covered in this emotional tour; loop back at the end to Lille, and it makes an ideal combo with this trip.

6 **Alsace Accents**
To extend your journey, pick up the Route des Vins d'Alsace after ending this trip in Strasbourg.

...eims is also worth visiting for its splendid **Musée des Beaux-Arts** (8 rue Chanzy; adult/child €4/ free; ⊙10am-noon & 2-6pm Wed-Mon), located inside an 18th-century abbey. Highlights include 27 works by Camille Corot (only the Louvre has more), 13 portraits by German Renaissance painters Cranach the Elder and the Younger, lots of Barbizon School landscapes, and two works each by Monet, Gauguin and Pissarro. But its most celebrated possession is probably Jacques-Louis David's world-famous *The Death of Marat,* depicting the Revolutionary leader's bloody, just-murdered corpse in the bathtub. It's one of only four known versions of the painting in the world, and is worth the admission fee on its own.

 p57, p83

The Drive » Metz is 192km east of Reims via the A4 toll road, another two-hour drive.

TRIP HIGHLIGHT

❹ Metz

Opened in 2010 to much fanfare, the swoopy, spaceship facade of the **Centre Pompidou-Metz** (www.centrepompidou-metz. fr; 1 parvis des Droits de l'Homme; adult/child €7/free; ⊙10am-6pm Mon & Wed-Thu, to 7pm Fri-Sun) fronts one of France's boldest galleries. Drawing on the Pompidou's fantastic modern art collection, it's gained a reputation for ambitious exhibitions, such as the recent one spotlighting the graphic works of American conceptual artist Sol LeWitt.

While you're in town, don't miss Metz's amazing **Cathédrale St-Étienne** (www.cathedrale-metz. fr; place St-Étienne; audioguide €7, combined ticket treasury & crypt adult/child €4/2; ⊙8am-6pm, treasury & crypt 9am-12.30pm & 1.30-6pm Mon-Sat, 1-6pm Sun), a lacy wonder lit by kaleidoscopic curtains of stained glass. It's known as

BRUCE YUANYUE BI / GETTY IMAGES ©

'God's lantern' for good reason – look out for the technicolour windows created by the visionary artist Marc Chagall.

 p57

The Drive » The most scenic option to Nancy is the D657, which tracks the banks of the Moselle River. Head southwest on the A31 toll road, then take exit 30a (signed to Jouy les Arches). Follow the road through rolling Alsatian countryside as far as Pont-à-Mousson, then continue through town on the D657 all the way to Nancy. It's a point-to-point drive of about 65km.

✓ TOP TIP: STRASBOURG CENT SAVERS

The Strasbourg Pass Musées (www.musees. strasbourg.eu; one/three-day pass €12/18) covers admission to all of Strasbourg's museums; buy it at museums. Alternatively, the three-day Strasbourg Pass (adult/child €18.90/9.45) includes one museum, a trip up to the 66m-high viewing platform at the city's cathedral platform, half-day bicycle rental and a boat tour.

Baccarat Crystal display

⑤ Nancy

Home of the art-nouveau movement, Nancy has an air of grace and refinement that's all its own. Start your art appreciation at the **Musée de l'École de Nancy** (School of Nancy Museum; www. ecole-de-nancy.com; 36-38 rue du Sergent Blandan; adult/child €6/4; ⊙10am-6pm Wed-Sun), an art-nouveau showpiece of dreamy interiors and curvy glass, housed in a 19th-century villa 2km southwest of the centre.

Next, head into the city's heart, magnificent **place Stanislas**, a vast neoclassical square that's now a Unesco World Heritage site. Designed by Emmanuel Héré in the 1750s, it's encircled by glorious buildings, including the **hôtel de ville** and the **Opéra National de Lorraine**, and contains a treasure trove of statues, rococo fountains and wrought-iron gateways.

On one side of the square is the city's **Musée des Beaux-Arts** (http://mban.nancy.fr; 3 place Stanislas; adult/child €6/4, audioguide €3; ⊙10am-6pm Wed-Mon), where Caravaggio, Rubens, Picasso and Monet hang alongside works by Lorraine-born artists, including the dreamlike landscapes of Claude Lorrain and the pared-down designs of Nancy-born architect Jean Prouvé (1901–84).

On nearby Grand Rue, the regal Renaissance Palais Ducal was once home to the Dukes of Lorraine. It's now the **Musée Lorrain** (www.musee-lorrain. nancy.fr; 64 & 66 Grande Rue; adult/child €6/4; ⊙10am-12.30pm & 2-6pm Tue-Sun), with a rich fine-art and history collection, including medieval statuary and faience (glazed pottery).

✗ p57

DETOUR: MUSÉE LALIQUE

Start: **7** Strasbourg

René Lalique was one of the great figures of the art-nouveau movement, and the **Musée Lalique** (www.musee-lalique.com; rue du Hochberg, Wingen-sur-Moder; adult/child €6/3; ⏰10am-7pm daily, closed Mon Oct-Mar) provides a fitting tribute to his talents.

At home on the site of the old Hochberg glassworks, this museum investigates Lalique's fascination with naturalistic forms (especially flowers, insects and foliage) and the curves of the female body. The collection illustrates his astonishing breadth of work, from gem-encrusted jewellery to perfume bottles and sculpture.

The museum is 60km north of Strasbourg in Wingen-sur-Moder.

The Drive » Head south from Nancy on the main A330 toll road. Take exit 7, signed to Flavigny-sur-Moselle, which will take you onto the rural riverside D570. Stay on this road all the way to Bayon, then cross the river through town, following the D22 east through quiet countryside to Baccarat. It's a drive of 78km.

- - - - - - - - - - -

6 Baccarat

The glitzy glassware of Baccarat was considered the height of sophistication in 18th-century France, and its exquisite crystal could be found gracing mansions and châteaux all over Europe.

The **Musée Baccarat** (www.baccarat.fr; 2 rue des Cristalleries; adult/child €5/free; ⏰9am-noon & 2-6pm Tue-Sun) displays 1100 pieces, and the boutique out front is almost as dazzling as the museum. Nearby crystal shops sell lesser, and less expensive, brands.

Glass aficionados will also want to stroll across the River Meurthe to the 1950s-built **Église St-Rémy** (1 av de Lachapelle; ⏰8am-5pm), whose austere facade conceals a blindingly bright interior containing 20,000 Baccarat panels.

The Drive » Take the D590 southeast to Raon-l'Étape, then turn northeast on the D392A, a lovely back road that winds up through woodland and mountains, offering great views of the Vosges en route. Eventually you'll link up with the D1420, which will take you on to Strasbourg. It's a good two-hour drive of about 100km.

- - - - - - - - - - -

TRIP HIGHLIGHT

7 Strasbourg

Finish with a couple of days exploring the architectural splendour of Strasbourg and visiting the **Musée d'Art Moderne et Contemporain** (MAMCS; www.musees.strasbourg.eu; 1 place Hans Jean Arp; adult/child €7/free; ⏰10am-6pm Tue-Sun; 🚇Musée d'Art Moderne), a striking glass-and-steel cube showcasing fine art, graphics and photography. The art's defiantly modern: Kandinsky, Picasso, Magritte and Monet canvases can all be found here, alongside curvaceous works by Strasbourg-born abstract artist Jean Arp.

Afterwards, have a good wander around **Grande Île**, Strasbourg's historic and Unesco-listed old quarter, as well as **Petite France**, the canal district.

✕ p57

Eating & Sleeping

Reims ❸

✕ Brasserie
Le Boulingrin   Brasserie €€

(📞03 26 40 96 22; www.boulingrin.fr; 29-31 rue de Mars; menus €20-29; ⏰noon-2.30pm & 7-10.30pm Mon-Sat) A genuine, old-time brasserie – the decor and zinc bar date back to 1925 – whose ambience and cuisine make it an enduring favourite. From September to June, the culinary focus is on *fruits de mer* (seafood) such as Breton oysters. There's always a €9.50 lunch special.

⟟ Les Telliers   B&B €€

(📞09 53 79 80 74; http://telliers.fr; 18 rue des Telliers; s €67-84, d €79-120, tr €116-141, q €132-162; 🅿🛜) Enticingly positioned down a quiet alley near the cathedral, this bijou B&B extends one of Reims' warmest *bienvenues*. The high-ceilinged rooms are big on art-deco character, and handsomely decorated with ornamental fireplaces, polished oak floors and the odd antique. Breakfast costs an extra €9 and is a generous spread of pastries, fruit, fresh-pressed juice and coffee.

Metz ❹

✕ L'Imaginarium   French €€

(📞03 87 30 14 40; http://imaginarium-restaurant.com; 2 rue de Paris; mains €20-23; ⏰noon-2pm & 7-10pm Wed-Sat, noon-2pm Sun & Tue) Decorated with one-of-a-kind artworks, this sleek, monochrome bistro by the river is one of Metz's top foodie addresses. The season-driven menu emphasises clean, bright flavours in dishes such as house-smoked salmon with beetroot-and-raspberry gazpacho, and duck breast in a peanut crust with artichoke.

⟟ Hôtel de
la Cathédrale   Historic Hotel €€

(📞03 87 75 00 02; www.hotelcathedrale-metz. fr; 25 place de Chambre; d €75-120; 🛜) You can expect a friendly welcome at this classy little

hotel, occupying a 17th-century town house in a prime spot right opposite the cathedral. Climb the wrought-iron staircase to your classically elegant room, with high ceilings, hardwood floors and antique trappings. Book well ahead for a cathedral view.

Nancy ❺

✕ À la Table du
Bon Roi Stanislas   French €€

(At the Table of Good King Stanislas; 📞03 83 35 36 52; http://tablestan.free.fr; 7 rue Gustave Simon; menus €19-43; ⏰7.15-9.30pm Mon & Wed, 12.15-1.30pm & 7.15-9.30pm Tue & Thu-Sat, 12.15-1.30pm Sun) À la Table du Bon Roi Stanislas dishes up good old-fashioned French food with lashings of bonhomie. Menu classics feature escargots with dill and duck cooked in red wine with fig confit. There's terrace seating in summer.

Strasbourg ❼

✕ Winstub S'Kaechele   French €€

(📞03 88 22 62 36; www.skaechele.fr; 8 rue de l'Argile; mains €12-18.50; 🚇Grand'Rue) Traditional French and Alsatian grub doesn't come more authentic than at this snug, amiable *winstub* (wine tavern), run with love by couple Karine and Daniel. Cue wonderfully cosy evenings spent in stone-walled, lamplit, wood-beamed surrounds, huddled over dishes such as escargots oozing Roquefort, fat pork knuckles braised in pinot noir, and *choucroute garnie* (sauerkraut garnished with meats).

⟟ Cour du Corbeau   Boutique Hotel €€

(📞03 90 00 26 26; www.cour-corbeau.com; 6-8 rue des Couples; r €145-175, ste €220-260; ✳🛜; 🚇Porte de l'Hôpital) A 16th-century inn lovingly converted into a boutique hotel, Cour du Corbeau wins you over with its half-timbered charm and its location, just steps from the river. Gathered around a courtyard, rooms blend original touches like oak parquet and Louis XV furnishings with mod cons like flat-screen TVs.

Northern Coast

3

Stretching for 140km along the English Channel, the sublime Côte d'Opale enchants with its lofty chalk cliffs, rolling hills, sandy beaches, scrub-dotted sand dunes and charming seaside villages.

TRIP HIGHLIGHTS

11 km

Cap Blanc-Nez
Breathtaking views across the English Channel

● Calais
START

2

4

Boulogne-sur-Mer ●

Cap Gris-Nez
Just 28km from the White Cliffs of Dover

29km

Le Touquet-Paris-Plage ●

148 km

St-Valery-sur-Somme
A charming old port with a pint-sized walled city

122 km
Parc du Marquenterre Bird Sanctuary
Home to an astonishing 300 species of bird

10

St-Valery-sur-Somme ● Le Crotoy

12

FINISH

2–4 DAYS
148KM / 92 MILES

GREAT FOR...

BEST TIME TO GO
May to August for long days and warm weather.

ESSENTIAL PHOTO
The Channel panorama from atop Cap Blanc-Nez.

BEST FOR HISTORY
A colossal German bunker, part of Nazi Germany's Atlantic Wall, houses Musée du Mur de l'Atlantique.

Côte d'Opale Cliffs at Cap Blanc-Nez

3 Northern Coast

Named for the ever-changing interplay of greys and blues in the sea and sky, the Côte d'Opale (Opal Coast) is on spectacular display between Calais and Boulogne-sur-Mer. Further south, the relatively flat coastline is broken by the estuaries, wetlands and tidal marshes created by the Rivers Canche, Authie and Somme. The area has several attractive beach resorts and excellent spots for bird-watching and seal spotting.

1 Calais

France's premier trans-Channel port is a short hop from England by car ferry, Eurotunnel rail shuttle or super-fast Eurostar train. Begin the itinerary at Rodin's famous sculpture **The Burghers of Calais** (place du Soldat Inconnu) (Les Bourgeois de Calais; 1895), in front of Calais' Flemish- and Renaissance-style **Hôtel de Ville** (city hall). Then head to the city's sandy, cabin-lined **beach**, whose singularly riveting attraction is watching huge car ferries as they sail majestically to and from Dover. The sand continues westward along 8km-long, dune-lined **Blériot Plage**, broad and gently sloping. It's named for the pioneer aviator Louis Blériot, who began the first ever trans-Channel flight from here – it lasted 27 minutes – in 1909.

✗ 🛏 p65

The Drive ⟫ Take the D940 west, past Blériot Plage in the commune of Sangatte, and a further 5km southwest to reach Cap Blanc-Nez.

TRIP HIGHLIGHT

2 Cap Blanc-Nez

Just past Sangatte, the coastal dunes give way to cliffs that culminate in windswept, 134m-high **Cap Blanc-Nez**, which affords breathtaking views of the Bay of Wissant, the port of Calais,

the Flemish countryside (pock-marked by Allied bomb craters, eg on the slopes of Mont d'Hubert) and the distant chalk cliffs of Kent. A grey stone obelisk honours the WWI Dover Patrol. Paths lead to a number of massive WWII German bunkers.

The Drive » It's an 8km descent on the D940 from Cap Blanc-Nez to Wissant.

❸ Wissant

The attractive seaside village of **Wissant** (www. terredes2capstourisme.fr) – population 1030 – long home to both fishers and farmers, is centered around a 15th-century church. It's a good base for exploring the area between Cap Blanc-Nez and Cap Gris-Nez, including a wide-at-low-tide beach that's long, flat and clean – perfect for young children and kitesurfers.

LINK YOUR TRIP

4 **In Flanders Fields**
From Calais, drive 110km to the southeast, on the A16 and A25, to start this trip in Lille.

7 **Monet's Normandy**
From St-Valery-sur-Somme, it's a 164km drive south to Giverny.

The Drive » From Wissant, take the D940 southwestward for 6km. About 700m past the centre of Audinghen, turn right onto the D191 and continue northwest for 3.5km.

- - - - - - - - - - - -

TRIP HIGHLIGHT

4 Cap Gris-Nez

Topped by a lighthouse and a radar station that keeps track of the more than 500 ships that pass by here each day, the 45m-high cliffs of **Cap Gris-Nez** are only 28km from the white cliffs of the English coast. The name, which means 'grey nose' in French, is a corruption of the archaic English 'craig ness', meaning 'rocky promontory'. The area is a stopping-off point for millions of migrating birds. The parking lot is a good starting point for hikes, such as along the **GR120 du Littoral** coastal trail (marked with red and white blazes).

The Drive » From Cap Gris-Nez, take the D191 3.5km southeast back to the D940 and turn right. After about 100m, at the Maison du Site des Deux Caps tourist office, turn right again and continue for 400m for the Musée du Mur de l'Atlantique.

- - - - - - - - - - - -

5 Musée du Mur de l'Atlantique

Oodles of WWII hardware, including a massive, rail-borne 283mm German artillery piece with a range of 86km (more than enough to hit the English coast), are on display at the well-organised **Musée du Mur de l'Atlantique** (Atlantic Wall Museum; ☑03 21 32 97 33; www.batterietodt.com; rte du Musée, Hameau de Haringzelle, Audinghen; adult/child €8.50/5; ☺10am-5.30pm daily, to 7pm Jul & Aug, closed mid-Nov–early Feb). It is housed in Batterie Todt, a colossal, round German pillbox.

The Drive » From Audinghen it's just under 5km south along the D940 to Ambleteuse. On the way you'll pass the colourful village of Audresselles, still active as a fishing port. It's a great place to dine on super-fresh seafood.

- - - - - - - - - - - -

6 Ambleteuse

The seaside village of Ambleteuse (population 1880) is home to Fort Mahon (Fort d'Ambleteuse), a small fortress built by Louis XIV in the 1680s, and a pebbly beach. At the **Musée 39-45** (☑03 21 87 33 01; www.musee3945. com; 2 rue des Garennes; adult/child €8.50/5.50; ☺10am-6pm, weekends only Mar & Nov, closed Dec-Feb), popular period songs accompany visitors as they stroll past dozens of life-size tableaux of WWII military and civilian life. The museum also screens archival films. The dashing but wildly impractical French officers' dress uniforms of 1931 hint at possible reasons why France fared so poorly on the battlefields of 1940.

The Drive » From Ambleteuse drive 1.5km southeast along the D940 to reach the Dunes de la Slack.

- - - - - - - - - - - -

7 Dunes de la Slack

Just south of Ambleteuse along the estuary of the tiny River Slack, wind-sculpted sand dunes are covered with – and stabilised by – clumps of

---

BRASSERIE ARTISANALE DES 2 CAPS

Historic farm buildings deep in the countryside house the **Brasserie Artisanale des 2 Caps** (☑03 21 10 56 53; www.2caps.fr; ferme de Belle Dalle, Tardinghen; tours €4.50; ☺10am-7pm Tue-Sat & 3-7pm Sun Jul & Aug, 10am-noon & 2-5pm Tue-Sat Sep-Jun), one of northern France's best microbreweries. Sample and buy here, or look for 2 Caps, Blanche de Wissant and Noire de Slack in area pubs. Brewmaster Christophe Noyon offers occasional 90-minute tours. Situated 1.5km along the D249 from the church in the village of Tardinghen, which is midway between Wissant and Audinghen.

Ambleteuse Village and Fort Mahon

marram grass and brambles such as privet and wild rose. The best way to appreciate the undulating landscape of **Dunes de la Slack** is to follow the marked walking paths that criss-cross the area.

The Drive » From the Dunes de la Slack head south on the D940 for 10km to reach Boulogne-sur-Mer.

❽ Boulogne-sur-Mer

France's most important fishing port, Boulogne-sur-Mer (population 42,780) is home to **Nausicaã** (☎03 21 30 99 99; www.nausicaa. co.uk; bd Ste-Beuve; adult/child €19/12.50; ⏰9.30am-6.30pm Sep-Jun, to 7.30pm Jul & Aug, closed 3 weeks Jan), one of Europe's premier aquariums. Boulogne-sur-Mer's **Basse-Ville** (Lower City) is a bustling but uninspiring assemblage of postwar structures, but

the attractive **Haute-Ville** (Upper City), perched high above the rest of town and girded by a 13th-century wall, is an island of centuries-old buildings and cobblestone streets. You can walk all the way around this 'Fortified City' atop the ancient stone walls – look for signs for the **Promenade des Remparts**.

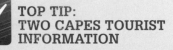 p65

The Drive » From Boulogne-sur-Mer, take the D940 south for 28km. At Les Étaples, take a right onto the D939 and continue for 4km.

❾ Le Touquet-Paris-Plage

This leafy beach resort was hugely fashionable in the interwar period, when the British upper crust found it positively smashing. The town

---

✓ **TOP TIP: TWO CAPES TOURIST INFORMATION**

The **Maison du Site des Deux Caps** (☎03 21 21 62 22; www.lesdeuxcaps.fr; cnr D940 & D191, Hameau de Haringzelle, Audinghen; ⏰10am-12.30pm & 2-5.30pm Apr-Sep, closed Mon Oct-Dec, Feb & Mar, closed Jan) serves as a visitors information centre for the 'two capes', ie the area around and between Cap Blanc-Nez and Cap Gris-Nez. Staff have English brochures, rent out bicycles – both regular (per half-/whole day €7/10) and electric (€10/15) – and sell hiking maps.

✓ TOP TIP: NATURE WALKS

Nonprofit **Eden 62** (📞03 21 32 13 74; www.eden62. fr; ⏱mid-Feb–Oct) organises two-hour nature walks several times a week. They're in French but tourists, including families, are welcome. No need to reserve – just show up at the meeting point.

was a favourite of Noël Coward, and in 1940 a politically oblivious PG Wodehouse was taken prisoner here by the Germans. These days it remains no less posh and no less British, though it also attracts plenty of chic Parisians.

🛏 p65

The Drive » From Les Étaples, take the D940 south for 34km. Just past the village of Rue, turn right onto the D4, continuing westward on the D204, for a total of 6km.

- - - - - - - - - - - -

TRIP HIGHLIGHT

❿ Parc du Marquenterre Bird Sanctuary

An astonishing 300 species of bird have been sighted at the 2-sq-km **Parc du Marquenterre** (📞03 22 25 68 99; www. parcdumarquenterre.fr; 25bis chemin des Garennes, St-Quentin-en-Tourmont; adult/ child €10.50/7.90, binoculars €4/2; ⏱10am-5pm mid-Feb– mid-Nov, Sat & Sun only mid-Nov–mid-Feb), **an important migratory stopover between the UK, Iceland,**

Scandinavia and Siberia and the warmer climes of West Africa. Three marked **walking circuits** (2km to 6km) take you to marshes, dunes, meadows, freshwater ponds, a brackish lagoon and 13 observation posts. Year round, the park's friendly **guides** – they're the ones carrying around telescopes on tripods – are happy to help visitors, especially kids, spot and identify birds.

The Drive » From the Parc du Marquenterre, take the D204 east for 4km to the D4 and turn right. After 4.5km continue onto the D104 for the 2km to Le Crotoy.

- - - - - - - - - - - -

⓫ Le Crotoy

Occupying a wonderfully picturesque spot on the northern bank of the Baie de Somme (Somme estuary), laid-back Le Crotoy is a lovely place to relax. Attractions include **guided walks** (📞03 22 27 47 36, 06 28 05 13 02; www. promenade-en-baie.com; 5 allée des Soupirs; adult/child 2hr walk €12/6, 3hr walk €15/7, 5hr walk €18/7; ⏱9am–

12.30pm & 2-5pm, closed afternoons Dec & Jan) of the Somme estuary – vast expanses are exposed at low tide – and the only sandy beach in northern France that faces south; restaurants and cafes can be found nearby. Jules Verne wrote *Twenty Thousand Leagues Under the Sea* (1870) while living here.

The Drive » St-Valery-sur-Somme is 16km around the Somme estuary from Le Crotoy. Take the D104 to the D940, follow it for 11km and then turn right onto the D3.

- - - - - - - - - - - -

TRIP HIGHLIGHT

⓬ St-Valery-sur-Somme

This old port town (population 2700) has a charming maritime quarter, a pocket-sized walled city and an attractive seaside promenade. The colours of St-Valery-sur-Somme are the colours of maritime Picardy: the deep brick reds of the houses and the sea hues that range from a sparkling blue to overcast grey are accented by dashes of red, white and blue from flapping French flags, just like in an Impressionist seascape. Grey and harbour seals can often be spotted off **Pointe du Hourdel**, 8km northwest of town.

✕ 🛏 p65

Eating & Sleeping

Calais ❶

✗ Histoire Ancienne   Bistro €€

(☎03 21 34 11 20; www.histoire-ancienne.com; 20 rue Royale; menus €17.90-32; ☺noon-2pm Mon, noon-2pm & 6-9.30pm Tue-Sat; ☜🖉) Bistro-style French dishes, made with fresh ingredients, are served in a classic dining room that feels like 1930s Paris. Our favourites include mushroom cream soup and peppersteak flambé with brandy. Service is prompt and friendly.

🛏 Le Cercle de Malines   B&B €€

(☎03 21 96 80 65; www.lecercledemalines.fr; 12 rue de Malines; d incl breakfast €85-125, q €150; ☜) Built in 1884, this stately town house has been elegantly furnished in a modern spirit, with generous public areas and a lovely back garden. Our choice among the five spacious rooms is 'La Leavers', with its claw-footed Victorian bathtub. Situated 1.2km south of the tourist office on a quiet street behind the main post office.

Boulogne-sur-Mer ❽

✗ Le Châtillon   Seafood €

(☎03 21 31 43 95; www.le-chatillon.com; 6 rue Charles Tellier; breakfast €6.80-12, lunch mains €12-24, menus €22; ☺5am-4.30pm Mon-Fri, 4am-1.30pm Sat; ☜) With its red banquettes and brass maritime lanterns, not to mention its early breakfasts, this restaurant has long been a favourite of fishers hungry after spending the night at sea. Lunch specialities include fish, oysters and squid; sandwiches are available all day. Book ahead for lunch. Situated past the old car-ferry terminal in an industrial area dominated by fish warehouses.

🛏 Les Terrasses de l'Enclos   B&B €€

(☎03 91 90 05 90; www.enclosdeleveche.com; L'enclos de l'Évêché, 6 rue de Pressy; d incl breakfast €75-120; ☜) An imposing 19th-century mansion next to the basilica has been turned into Boulogne's most elegant accommodation. The five rooms are spacious, comfortable and full of old-time character.

Le Touquet-Paris-Plage ❾

🛏 Hôtel Bristol   Hotel €€

(☎03 21 05 49 95; www.hotelbristol.fr; 17 rue Jean Monnet; d €95-190; @☜) Opened in 1927, this 47-room hotel is just 200m from the beachfront promenade. Public areas retain something of a prewar vibe, but the bar is pure 1970s.

St-Valery-sur-Somme ⓬

✗ Le Bistrot des Pilotes   Neobistro €€

(☎03 22 60 80 39; www.lespilotes.fr; 37 quai Blavet; lunch/dinner menus from €19/25; ☺noon-2.30pm & 7-9.30pm Wed-Sat, noon-2.30pm Sun Feb-Jun & Sep-Dec, daily Jul & Aug) Market-fresh cuisine with a twist, outdoor tables on the waterfront, a good selection of seafood dishes and Picard classics, and great *mousse au chocolat* make this place a perennial favourite.

🛏 Au Vélocipède   B&B €€

(☎03 22 60 57 42; www.auvelocipede.fr; 1 rue du Puits Salé; d/tr incl breakfast €99/140; ☜) Two town houses facing the church are now a swish B&B. The eight supremely comfortable rooms are huge, with naked wooden floors, hip furnishings and modern slate-and-cream bathrooms. Those up in the attic (Vélo 3 and Vélo 4) are especially romantic. Cash only.

In Flanders Fields

4

WWI history comes to life on this tour of Western Front battle-fields where Allied and German troops endured four years of trench warfare. Lille, Arras and Amiens offer urban counterpoints.

TRIP HIGHLIGHTS

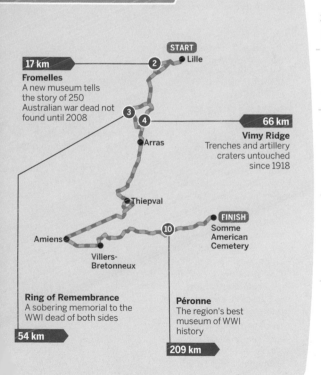

17 km

Fromelles
A new museum tells the story of 250 Australian war dead not found until 2008

START Lille

Arras

66 km
Vimy Ridge
Trenches and artillery craters untouched since 1918

Thiepval

FINISH
Somme American Cemetery

Amiens

Villers-Bretonneux

Ring of Remembrance
A sobering memorial to the WWI dead of both sides

54 km

Péronne
The region's best museum of WWI history

209 km

3 DAYS
235KM / 146 MILES

GREAT FOR...

BEST TIME TO GO
March to November; a few sites close in December and January.

ESSENTIAL PHOTO
The staggering list of missing soldiers' names at Thiepval.

BEST FOR HISTORY
Historial de la Grande Guerre, Péronne's first-rate WWI museum.

Fields of red poppies

4 In Flanders Fields

Shortly after WWI broke out in 1914, Allied troops established a line of resistance against further German advances in the northern French countryside near Arras, initiating one of the longest and bloodiest standoffs in military history. This tour of Flanders and Picardy takes in some of France's most important WWI battle sites and memorials, along with the charming cities of Lille, Arras and Amiens.

1 Lille

A convenient gateway to northern France's WWI battlefields, cosmopolitan Lille offers an engaging mix of grand architecture and Flemish culture. Stop in for dinner at an *estaminet* (traditional Flemish restaurant) and stroll around the bustling pedestrianised centre, whose highlights include the **Vieille Bourse**, a 17th-century Flemish Renaissance extravaganza decorated with caryatids and cornucopia, and the neighbourhood of **Vieux Lille** (Old Lille), where restored 17th- and 18th-century brick houses are home to chic boutiques.

✕ 🛏 p73

The Drive ≫ Take the westbound A25, the southbound N41, the D207 and finally the D141B to Fromelles, a distance of 17km.

TRIP HIGHLIGHT

2 Fromelles

The death toll was horrific – 1917 Australians and 519 Britons killed in just one day of fighting – yet the 1916 Battle of Fromelles was largely forgotten until 2008, when the remains of 250 of the fallen were discovered. They are now buried in the **Fromelles (Pheasant Wood) Cemetery**; 141 have been identified thanks to DNA testing. Next door, the excellent **Musée de la Bataille de Fromelles** (📞 03 59 61 15 14;

www.musee-bataille-fromelles. fr; rue de la Basse Ville; museum adult/child €6.50/4; ⊘ cemetery 24hr, museum 9.30am-5.30pm Wed-Mon), opened in 2014, evokes life in the trenches with reconstructed bunkers, photographs and biographies.

The Drive » Take the D22 4km south to the N41, turn southwest and after 3km turn south onto the N47; continue for 12km before turning west onto the A21. Get off at the D937, drive southeast for 5km and then follow the signs to Notre-Dame de Lorette. Total distance: 37km.

TRIP HIGHLIGHT

❸ Ring of Remembrance

It's hard not to be overwhelmed by the folly and waste of the Western Front at the **Ring of Remembrance** (Anneau de la Mémoire; Ablain-St-Nazaire; ⊘9am-4.15pm, to 5.30pm or 6.30pm Apr-Sep) as you

LINK YOUR TRIP

2 **A Toast to Art**
From Vimy, detour 9km to Lens for this tour of northern France's arts scene.

3 **Northern Coast**
From Bony, head northwest to Calais (200km) to begin this spectacular drive along the Channel coast.

walk past panel after panel engraved with 580,000 names: WWI dead from both sides who are listed in strict alphabetical order, without reference to nationality, rank or religion.

The Drive ›› Return to the D937 and drive south for 6km. Then take the D49 east for 3km, the D917 north for 1km and finally the D55E2 northwest. Total distance: 12.5km

TRIP HIGHLIGHT

④ Vimy Ridge

Right after the war, the French attempted to erase all signs of battle and return northern France to agriculture and normalcy. The Canadians took a different approach, deciding that the most evocative way to remember their fallen was to preserve part of the crater-pocked battlefield exactly the way it looked when the guns fell silent. As a result, the best place to get some sense of the hell known as the Western Front is the chilling, eerie moonscape of **Vimy Ridge** (☎03 21 50 68 68; www.veterans.gc.ca; Vimy; ⊙visitor centre 11am-5pm Mon, 9am-5pm Tue-Sun). A new **Visitor Educational Centre**, set to open in April 2017, will be staffed by bilingual Canadian students who'll run free guided tours.

The Drive ›› Follow the D55E2, N17 and D917 12km into Arras.

⑤ Arras

Contemplating the picture-perfect Flemish-style façades of Arras' two gorgeous market squares, the **Grand' Place** and the **Petite Place** (Place des Héros), it's hard to believe that almost the entire city centre was reduced to rubble during WWI (it was reconstructed in the 1920s). To get a sense of life in wartime Arras, head 1.5km south to **Carrière Wellington** (Wellington Quarry; ☎03 21 51 26 95; www.explorearras.com; rue Arthur Delétoille; adult/child €6.90/3.20; ⊙10am-12.30pm & 1.30-6pm, closed Jan), a subterranean quarry that served as a staging area for the Allies' 1917 spring offensive. Prior to the attack, 500 New Zealand soldiers worked round the clock for five months expanding Arras' medieval quarries to accommodate kitchens, a hospital and several thousand Commonwealth troops. Reminders of these events are everywhere, from Maori-language graffiti to candle burn marks from the Easter Mass celebrated underground the day before the troops stormed German front lines.

✗ ⊨ p73

The Drive ›› Take the D919, D174 and D73 31km southwest to the Newfoundland Memorial, detouring briefly at KM 15 to the Ayette Indian and Chinese Cemetery, a Commonwealth cemetery where Hindi, Arabic and Chinese inscriptions mark the graves of Indian soldiers and Chinese labourers recruited by the British government.

⑥ Newfoundland Memorial

On 1 July 1916 the volunteer Royal Newfoundland Regiment stormed entrenched German positions and was nearly wiped out. The evocative **Beaumont-Hamel Newfoundland Memorial** (☎03 22 76 70 86; www.veterans.gc.ca; Beaumont-Hamel; ⊙Welcome Centre 11am-5pm Mon, 9am-5pm Tue-Sun) preserves the battlefield much as it was at fighting's end. Climb to the bronze caribou statue, on a hillside surrounded by native Newfoundland plants, for views of the shell craters, barbed-wire barriers and zigzag trenches that still fill with mud in winter. The on-site welcome centre offers guided tours.

The Drive ›› Head 5km east-southeast on the D73 through tiny Beaumont-Hamel, across a pretty valley, past the 36th (Ulster) Division Memorial (site of a Northern Irish war monument and a homey tearoom) and on to the arches of the Thiepval Memorial.

⑦ Thiepval

On a lonely, windswept hilltop, the towering **Thiepval Memorial** (☎03 22 74 60 47; www.cwgc.org; Thiepval; ⊙museum 9.30am-

PARIS & NORTHEASTERN FRANCE 4 IN FLANDERS FIELDS

70

5pm, closed mid-Dec–mid-Jan) to 'the Missing of the Somme' marks the site of a German stronghold that was stormed on 1 July 1916 with unimaginable casualties. Thiepval catches visitors off guard, both with its monumentality and its staggering simplicity: inscribed below the enormous arch, which is visible from miles around, are the names of more than 72,000 British and South African soldiers whose remains were never recovered or identified. The **Museum at Thiepval**, run by Péronne's outstanding Historial de la Grande Guerre (p72), opened in 2016.

Thievpal Memorial to 'the Missing of the Somme'

The Drive » A 44km ride on the D73 and the D929 brings you to Amiens.

---

❽ Amiens

Amiens' attractive pedestrianised city centre offers a relaxing break from the battlefields. Climb the north tower of breathtaking 13th-century **Cathédrale Notre Dame** (place Notre Dame; north tower adult/child €5.50/free, audioguide €4; ☺ cathedral 8.30am-5.15pm daily, north tower to mid-afternoon Wed-Mon), a Unesco World Heritage Site, for stupendous views of the town; a free, 45-minute **light show** bathes the cathedral's façade in vivid medieval colours nightly in summer.

Across the Somme River, gondola-like boats offer tours of the **Hortillonnages** (☏03 22 92 12 18; apsseh@wanadoo.fr; 54 bd Beauvillé; adult/child €6/4; ☺1.30-5pm Apr-Oct), vast market gardens that have supplied the city with vegetables and flowers since the Middle Ages.

Literature buffs will love the **Maison de Jules Verne** (☏03 22 45 45 75; www.amiens.fr/maison-jules-verne; 2 rue Charles Dubois; adult/child €7.50/4, English audioguide €2; ☺10am-12.30pm & 2-6pm Mon & Wed-Fri, 2-6pm Sat & Sun year-round, 2-6.30pm Tue & from 11am Sat & Sun mid-Apr–mid-Oct), the turreted home where Jules Verne wrote some of his best-known works of science fiction.

✗ 🛏 p73

The Drive » Take the D1029 19km east to Villers-Bretonneux.

---

❾ Villers-Bretonneux

During WWI, 46,000 of Australia's 313,000 volunteer soldiers met their deaths on the Western Front (14,000 others perished elsewhere). In the village of Villers-Bretonneux, the **Musée Franco-Australien** (☏03 22 96 80 79; www.musee australien.com; 9 rue Victoria, Villers-Bretonneux; adult/child €5/3; ☺9.30am-5.30pm Mon-Sat, to 4.30pm Nov-Feb), scheduled to reopen in late 2016 after comprehensive renovations, displays a collection of highly personal WWI Australiana, including letters and photographs that evoke life on the front. The names of 10,982 Australian soldiers whose remains were never found are engraved on the base of the 32m-high

DETOUR:
CLAIRIÈRE DE L'ARMISTICE

Start: ⑪ Somme American Cemetery

On the 11th hour of the 11th day of the 11th month of 1918, WWI officially ended at **Clairière de l'Armistice** (Armistice Clearing), 7km northeast of the city of Compiègne, with the signing of an armistice inside the railway carriage of Allied supreme commander Maréchal Ferdinand Foch. In the same forest clearing, in an almost identical railroad car, the **Musée de l'Armistice** (📞03 44 85 14 18; www. musee-armistice-14-18.fr; adult/child €5/3; ⏱10am-5.30pm Apr-Sep, closed Tue Oct-Dec, Feb & Mar, closed Jan) commemorates these events with memorabilia, newspaper clippings and stereoscopic photos that capture – in 3D – all the mud, muck and misery of WWI; some of the furnishings, hidden away during WWII, were the ones actually used in 1918.

From the Somme American Cemetery, take the D1044, D1 and D1032 94km southwest towards Compiègne, then follow signs 8km east along the N1031 and D546 to Clairière de l'Armistice.

Australian National War Memorial (📞03 21 21 77 00; www.ww1westernfront.gov.au), 2km north of town.

The Drive » From the Australian National War Memorial, take the D23 briefly north, then meander east through pretty rolling country, roughly paralleling the Somme River, along the D71, D1 and D1017 into Péronne.

TRIP HIGHLIGHT

⑩ Péronne

Housed in a fortified medieval château, Péronne's award-winning museum, **Historial de la Grande Guerre** (📞03 22 83 14 18; www.historial.org; Château de Péronne; adult/child incl audioguide €9/4.50; ⏱9.30am-5pm, closed Wed Oct-Mar, closed mid-Dec–mid-Feb), provides a superb overview of WWI's historical and cultural context, telling the story

of the war chronologically, with equal space given to the French, British and German perspectives. Visually engaging exhibits, including period films and bone-chilling engravings by Otto Dix, capture the aesthetic sensibilities, enthusiasm, naive patriotism and unimaginable violence of the time.

For excellent English-language brochures about the battlefields, visit Péronne's **tourist office** (📞03 22 84 42 38; www. hautesomme-tourisme.com; 16 place André Audinot; ⏱10am-noon & 2-5pm or 6pm Mon-Sat Sep-Jun, plus 9am-12.30pm & 1.30-6.30pm Sun Jul & Aug), opposite the museum.

🛏 p73

The Drive » The American cemetery is 24km east-northeast of Péronne via the D6, D406 and D57.

⑪ Somme American Cemetery

In late September 1918, just six weeks before the end of WWI, American units – flanked by their Commonwealth allies – launched an assault on the Germans' heavily fortified Hindenburg Line. Some of the fiercest fighting took place near the village of Bony, on the sloping site now occupied by the 1844 Latin crosses and Stars of David of the serene **Somme American Cemetery** (www.abmc. gov; Bony; ⏱9am-5pm); the names of 333 other men whose remains were never recovered are inscribed on the walls of the **Memorial Chapel**.

Eating & Sleeping

Lille ❶

✗ Au Vieux de la Vieille　　Flemish €

(✆03 20 13 81 64; www.estaminetlille.fr; 2-4 rue des Vieux Murs; mains €12-15; ☺noon-2pm & 7-10pm daily, to 10.30pm Fri & Sat; 🛜) Hops hang from the rafters at this *estaminet* (Flemish-style eatery), where specialities include *carbonade flamande* (braised beef slow-cooked with beer, onions, brown sugar and ginger bread) and *Welsh au Maroilles* (toast and ham smothered with Maroilles cheese melted in beer). From about March to October there's outdoor seating on picturesque place aux Oignons.

🛏 Grand Hôtel Bellevue　　Historic Hotel €€

(✆03 20 57 45 64; www.grandhotelbellevue. com; 5 rue Jean Roisin; d €100-200; ❉ @ 🛜; Ⓜ Rihour) Opened in 1913, this grand establishment has 60 spacious rooms with high ceilings, all-marble bathrooms, gilded picture frames and a mix of inlaid-wood antiques and ultra-modern furnishings. For an extra €20 you can have fine views of place du Général de Gaulle – a bargain! Doubles as the honorary consulate of Brazil.

Arras ❺

✗ Café Georget　　Bistro €

(✆03 21 71 13 07; 42 place des Héros; plat du jour €9.50, sandwiches from €3.50; ☺café 8am-9pm daily, lunch noon-2pm Mon-Sat; 🛜) Madame Delforge has been presiding over this unpretentious old-time café – and preparing dishes *comme à la maison* (as she would at home) – since 1985. Drop by for a quick trip back to the France of François Mitterrand.

🛏 La Corne d'Or　　B&B €€

(✆03 21 58 85 94; www.lamaisondhotes.com; 1 place Guy Mollet; d incl breakfast €125-155;

🛜) Occupying a magnificent *hôtel particulier* (private mansion) built in 1748, this very romantic B&B is filled with antiques, art and books on WWI. Some of the five imaginatively designed rooms and suites still have their original woodwork and marble fireplaces. Australian host Rodney, formerly of Australia's Department of Veterans' Affairs, is a great resource.

Amiens ❽

✗ Le T'chiot Zinc　　Bistro €

(✆03 22 91 43 79; 18 rue de Noyon; menus €15.90-29.90; ☺noon-2.30pm Mon-Sat & 7-10.30pm Tue-Sat; 🛜🍴) Inviting, bistro-style decor reminiscent of the belle époque provides a fine backdrop for tasty, homestyle French and Picard cuisine, including fish dishes and *caqhuse* (pork in a cream, wine vinegar and onion sauce).

🛏 Hôtel Marotte　　Boutique Hotel €€€

(✆03 60 12 50 00; www.hotel-marotte.com; 3 rue Marotte; d €165-300, q €365-435; ❉ @ 🛜) Modern French luxury at its most elegant and romantic. All 12 light-drenched rooms are huge (at least 35 sq metres), but the two sauna suites (100 sq metres), sporting one-piece stone bathtubs weighing 1½ tonnes, are really luxury apartments. Perfect for a honeymoon.

Péronne ❿

🛏 Hôtel Le Saint-Claude　　Hotel €€

(✆03 22 79 49 49; www.hotelsaintclaude. com; 42 place du Commandant Louis Daudré; d €86-112; 🛜) Originally a *relais de poste* (coaching inn), the Saint-Claude is in the centre of Péronne just 200m from the Historial. The 40 contemporary rooms are decorated in adventurous colours and have ultra-modern bathrooms.

Classic Trip

Champagne Taster

5

From musty cellars to vine-striped hillsides, this Champagne adventure whisks you through the heart of the region to explore the world's favourite celebratory tipple. It's time to quaff!

TRIP HIGHLIGHTS

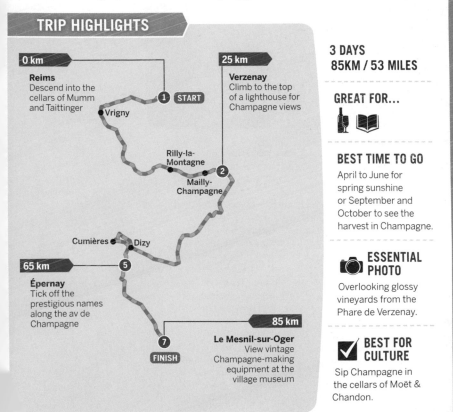

0 km

Reims
Descend into the cellars of Mumm and Taittinger

● Vrigny

1 START

25 km

Verzenay
Climb to the top of a lighthouse for Champagne views

Rilly-la-Montagne

Mailly-Champagne

2

Cumières ● ● Dizy

65 km

5

Épernay
Tick off the prestigious names along the av de Champagne

7

FINISH

85 km

Le Mesnil-sur-Oger
View vintage Champagne-making equipment at the village museum

3 DAYS
85KM / 53 MILES

GREAT FOR...

BEST TIME TO GO

April to June for spring sunshine or September and October to see the harvest in Champagne.

ESSENTIAL PHOTO

Overlooking glossy vineyards from the Phare de Verzenay.

BEST FOR CULTURE

Sip Champagne in the cellars of Moët & Chandon.

** agne** Vineyards along the Marne River

Classic Trip

5 Champagne Taster

'My only regret in life is that I didn't drink enough Champagne,' wrote the economist John Maynard Keynes, but by the end of this tour, you'll have drunk enough bubbly to last several lifetimes. Starting and ending at the prestigious Champagne centres of Reims and Épernay, this fizz-fuelled trip includes stops at some of the world's most famous producers – with ample time for tasting en route.

125 km to [1]

TRIP HIGHLIGHT

❶ Reims

There's nowhere better to start your Champagne tour than the regal city of **Reims**. Several big names have their *caves* (wine cellars) nearby. **Mumm** (✆03 26 49 59 70; www.mumm.com; 34 rue du Champ de Mars; tours incl tasting €20-45; ☺tours 9.30am-1pm & 2-6pm daily, shorter hours & closed Sun Oct-Mar), pronounced 'moom', is the only *maison* in central Reims. Founded in 1827, it's the world's third-largest Champagne

producer. One-hour tours explore its enormous cellars, filled with 25 million bottles of bubbly, and include tastings of several vintages.

North of town, **Taittinger** (✆03 26 85 45 35; www.taittinger.com; 9 place St-Niçaise; tours €17-45; ☺9.30am-5.30pm, shorter hours & closed weekends Oct-Mar) provides an informative overview of how Champagne is actually made – you'll leave with a good understanding of the production process, from grape to bottle. Parts of the cellars

occupy Roman stone quarries dug in the 4th century.

Before you leave town, don't forget to drop by **Waïda** (5 place Drouet d'Erlon; ⏰7.30am-7.30pm Tue-Fri, 7.30am-8pm Sat, 8am-2pm & 3.30-7.30pm Sun), an old-fashioned confectioner which sells Reims' famous *biscuits roses* (pink biscuits), a sweet treat traditionally nibbled with a glass of Champagne.

✕ 🛏 p83

The Drive ❯❯ The countryside between Reims and Épernay is carpeted with vineyards, fields and back roads that are a dream to drive through. From Reims, head south along the D951 for 13km. Near Mont Chenot, turn onto the D26, signposted to Rilly and the 'Route Touristique du Champagne'. The next 12km takes you through the pretty villages of Rilly-la-Montagne and Mailly-Champagne en route to Verzenay.

LINK YOUR TRIP

1 **Essential France**
Lying 150km west of Épernay, Paris marks the beginning of our epic journey around France's most essential sights.

2 **A Toast to Art**
Pick up our art-themed tour in Reims, where it takes in the city's renowned Musée des Beaux-Arts.

demonstrates the four authorised techniques for tying grapevines to guide wires.

The Drive » Continue south along the D26 for 3km.

❸ Verzy

This village is home to several small vineyards that provide an interesting contrast to the big producers. **Étienne and Anne-Laure Lefevre** (☏03 26 97 96 99; www.champagne-etienne-lefevre.com; 30 rue de Villers; ⏰9-11.30am & 1.30-5.30pm Mon-Sat) run group tours of their family-owned vineyards and cellars – if you're on your own, ring ahead to see if you can join a pre-arranged tour. There are no flashy videos or multimedia shows – the emphasis is firmly on the nitty-gritty of Champagne production.

For a glass of fizz high above the treetops, seek out the sleek **Perching Bar** (www.perchingbar. eu; Forêt de Brise-Charrette; ⏰noon-2pm & 4-8pm Wed-Sun mid-Apr–mid-Dec) deep in the forest.

The Drive » Stay on the D26 south of Verzy, and enjoy wide-open countryside views as you spin south to Ambonnay. Detour west onto the D19, signed to Bouzy, and bear right onto the D1 along the northern bank of the Marne River. When you reach the village of Dizy, follow signs onto the D386 to Hautvillers. It's a total drive of 32km or 45 minutes.

❹ Hautvillers

Next stop is the hilltop village of Hautvillers, a hallowed name among Champagne aficionados: it's where a Benedictine monk by the name of Dom Pierre Pérignon is popularly believed to have created Champagne in the late 16th century. The great man's tomb lies in front of the altar of the **Église Abbatiale**.

The village itself is well worth a stroll, with a jumble of lanes, timbered houses and stone-walled vineyards. On place de la République, the **tourist office** (☏03 26 57 06 35; www.tourisme-hautvillers. com; place de la République; ⏰9.30am-1pm & 1.30-5.30pm Mon-Sat, 10am-4pm Sun, shorter hours winter) hands out free maps detailing local vineyard walks; one-hour guided tours cost €3 (€5 with a tasting).

Steps away is **Au 36** (www.au36.net; 36 rue Dom Pérignon; ⏰10.30am-6pm Tue-Sun, closed Christmas–early Mar), a wine boutique with a 'wall' of Champagne quirkily arranged by aroma. There's a tasting room upstairs; a two-/three-glass session costs €12/16.

The Drive » From the centre of the village, take the rte de Cumières for grand views across the vine-cloaked slopes. Follow the road all the way to the D1, turn left and follow signs to Épernay's *centre-ville*, 6km to the south.

TRIP HIGHLIGHT

❷ Verzenay

Reims marks the start of the 70km **Montagne de Reims Champagne Route**, the prettiest (and most prestigious) of the three signposted road routes that wind their way through the Champagne vineyards. Of the 17 *grand cru* villages in Champagne, nine lie on and around the Montagne, a hilly area whose sheltered slopes and chalky soils provide the perfect environment for viticulture (grape growing).

Most of the area's vineyards are devoted to the pinot noir grape. You'll pass plenty of producers offering *dégustation* (tasting) en route. It's up to you how many you choose to visit – but whatever you do, don't miss the panorama of vines seen from the top of the **Phare de Verzenay** (Verzenay Lighthouse; www. lepharedeverzenay.com; D26; lighthouse adult/child €3/2, museum €8/4, combined ticket €9/5; ⏰10am-5pm Tue-Fri, to 5.30pm Sat & Sun, closed Jan), a lighthouse constructed as a publicity gimmick in 1909. Nearby, the **Jardin Panoramique**

⑤ Épernay

The prosperous town of **Épernay** is the self-proclaimed *capitale du champagne* and is home to many of the most illustrious Champagne houses. Beneath the streets are an astonishing 110km of subterranean cellars, containing an estimated 200 million bottles of vintage bubbly.

Most of the big names are arranged along the grand av de Champagne. **Moët & Chandon** (☑03 26 51 20 20; www.moet.com; 20 av de Champagne; adult incl 1/2 glasses €23/28, 10-18yr €10; ⊙tours 9.30-11.30am & 2-4.30pm Apr–mid-Nov, 9.30-11.30am & 2-4.30pm Mon-Fri mid-Nov–Mar) **offers** frequent and fascinating one-hour tours of its prestigious cellars, while at nearby **Mercier** (☑03 26 51 22 22; www.champagnemercier.fr; 68-70 av de Champagne; adult incl 1/2/3 glasses €14/19/22 Mon-Fri, €16/21/25 Sat & Sun, 12-17yr €8; ⊙tours 9.30-11.30am & 2-4.30pm,

CHAMPAGNE KNOW-HOW

Types of Champagne

» **Blanc de Blancs** Champagne made using only chardonnay grapes. Fresh and elegant, with very small bubbles and a bouquet reminiscent of 'yellow fruits' such as pear and plum.

» **Blanc de Noirs** A full-bodied, deep golden Champagne made solely with black grapes (despite the colour). Often rich and refined, with great complexity and a long finish.

» **Rosé** Pink Champagne (mostly served as an aperitif) with a fresh character and summer-fruit flavours. Made by adding a small percentage of red pinot noir to white Champagne.

» **Prestige Cuvée** The crème de la crème of Champagne. Usually made with grapes from Grand Cru vineyards and priced and bottled accordingly.

» **Millésimé Vintage** Champagne produced from a single crop during an exceptional year. Most Champagne is nonvintage.

Sweetness

» **Brut** Dry; most common style; pairs well with food.

» **Extra Sec** Fairly dry but sweeter than Brut; nice as an aperitif.

» **Demi Sec** Medium sweet; goes well with fruit and dessert.

» **Doux** Very sweet; a dessert Champagne.

Serving & Tasting

» **Chilling** Chill Champagne in a bucket of ice for 30 minutes before serving. The ideal serving temperature is 7°C to 9°C.

» **Opening** Grip the bottle securely and tilt it at a 45-degree angle facing away from you. Rotate the bottle slowly to ease out the cork – it should sigh, not pop.

» **Pouring** Hold the flute by the stem at an angle and let the Champagne trickle gently into the glass – less foam, more bubbles.

» **Tasting** Admire the colour and bubbles. Swirl your glass to release the aroma and inhale slowly before tasting the Champagne.

ALEXEY FEDORENKO / GETTY IMAGES ©

ONZEG / GETTY IMAGES ©

WHY THIS IS A CLASSIC TRIP
KERRY CHRISTIANI, WRITER

You can sip Champagne anywhere, but a road trip really slips under the skin of these Unesco-listed vineyards. Begin with an eye-opening, palate-awakening tour and tasting at *grande maison* cellars in Épernay and Reims. I love the far-reaching view from Phare de Verzenay and touring the back roads in search of small producers, especially when the aroma of new wine hangs in the air and the vines are golden in autumn.

Top: Fortress, Champagne
Left: Glasses of Champagne
Right: Marne River with Épernay in background

YVES TALENSAC / GETTY IMAGES ©

closed mid-Dec–mid-Feb)
tours take place aboard
a laser-guided under-
ground train.

Serious quaffers might
prefer the intimate tours
at **Champagne Georges
Cartier** (☏03 26 32 06 22;
www.georgescartier.com; 9
rue Jean Chandon Moët; adult
incl 1/2 glasses €12/16, 2-glass
Grand Cru €22, 3-glass vintage
€35; ⊗tours 10.30am, noon,
2.30pm, 4pm Tue-Sun), whose
warren of cellars and passageways, hewn out of the
chalk in the 18th century,
is incredibly atmospheric.
Look out for the fasci-
nating WWII graffiti.
Tours are followed by a
tasting of the *maison*'s
Champagnes.

Finish with a climb up
the 237-step tower at **De
Castellane** (☏03 26 51 19
11; www.castellane.com; 57
rue de Verdun; adult incl 1 glass
€14, under 12yr free; ⊗tours
10am-11pm & 2-5pm, closed
Christmas–mid-Mar), which
offers knockout views
over the town's rooftops
and vine-clad hills.

✕ ⨭ p83

The Drive » Head south of
town along av Maréchal Foch
or av du 8 Mai 1945, following
'Autres Directions' signs across
the roundabouts until you see
signs for Cramant. The village is
10km southeast of Épernay via
the D10.

- - - - - - - - - - - -

❻ **Cramant**
You'll find it hard to miss
this quaint village, as
the northern entrance is

THE SCIENCE OF CHAMPAGNE

Champagne is made from the red pinot noir (38%), the black pinot meunier (35%) or the white chardonnay (27%) grape. Each vine is vigorously pruned and trained to produce a small quantity of high-quality grapes. Indeed, to maintain exclusivity (and price), the designated areas where grapes used for Champagne can be grown and the amount of wine produced each year are limited.

Making Champagne according to the *méthode champenoise* (traditional method) is a complex procedure. There are two fermentation processes, the first in casks and the second after the wine has been bottled and had sugar and yeast added. Bottles are then aged in cellars for two to five years, depending on the *cuvée* (vintage).

For two months in early spring the bottles are aged in cellars kept at 12°C and the wine turns effervescent. The sediment that forms in the bottle is removed by *remuage*, a painstakingly slow process in which each bottle, stored horizontally, is rotated slightly every day for weeks until the sludge works its way to the cork. Next comes *dégorgement:* the neck of the bottle is frozen, creating a blob of solidified Champagne and sediment, which is then removed.

heralded by a two-storey-high Champagne bottle. From the ridge above the village, views stretch out in all directions across the Champagne countryside, taking in a patchwork of fields, farmhouses and rows upon rows of endless vines. Pack a picnic and your own bottle of bubbly for the perfect Champagne country lunch.

The Drive » Continue southeast along the D10 for 7km, and follow signs to Le-Mesnil-sur-Oger.

TRIP HIGHLIGHT

❼ Le Mesnil-sur-Oger

Finish with a visit to the excellent **Musée de la Vigne et du Vin** (☏03 26 57 50 15; www.champagne-launois.fr; 2 av Eugène Guillaume, cnr D10; adult incl 3 flutes €12; ☺tours 10am Mon-Fri, 10.30am Sat & Sun), where a local wine-growing family has assembled a collection of century-old Champagne-making equipment. Among the highlights is a massive 16-tonne oak-beam grape press dating to 1630. Reservations can be made by phone or online; ask about the availability of English tours when you book.

Round off your trip with lunch at **La Gare** (☏03 26 51 59 55; www.lagarelemesnil.com; 3 place de la Gare; menus €18-26; ☺noon-1.30pm Mon-Wed, noon-1.30pm & 7-9pm Thu-Sat; 🖌), which prides itself on serving bistro-style grub prepared with seasonal produce, simple as pork tenderloin with cider and potatoes. There's a €9 menu for *les petits.*

Eating & Sleeping

Reims ❶

🍴 Brasserie
Le Boulingrin Brasserie €€

(☎03 26 40 96 22; www.boulingrin.fr; 29-31 rue de Mars; menus €20-29; ⊗ noon-2.30pm & 7-10.30pm Mon-Sat) A genuine, old-time brasserie – the decor and zinc bar date back to 1925 – whose ambience and cuisine make it an enduring favourite. From September to June, the culinary focus is on *fruits de mer* (seafood) such as Breton oysters. There's always a €9.50 lunch special.

🍴 l'Assiette
Champenoise Gastronomy €€€

(☎03 26 84 64 64; www.assiettechampenoise. com; 40 av Paul-Vaillant-Couturier, Tinqueux; menus €95-255; ⊗ noon-2pm & 7.30-10pm Thu-Mon, 7.30-10pm Wed) Heralded far and wide as one of Champagne's finest tables and crowned with the holy grail of three Michelin stars, L'Assiette Champenoise is headed up by chef Arnaud Lallemen. Listed by ingredients, his intricate, creative dishes rely on outstanding produce and play up integral flavours – be it Breton lobster, or milk-fed lamb with preserved vegetables. One for special occasions.

🛏 Les Telliers B&B €€

(☎09 53 79 80 74; http://telliers.fr; 18 rue des Telliers; s €67-84, d €79-120, tr €116-141, q €132-162; ℙ ⊚) Enticingly positioned down a quiet alley near the cathedral, this bijou B&B extends one of Reims' warmest *bienvenues*. The high-ceilinged rooms are big on art-deco character, and handsomely decorated with ornamental fireplaces, polished oak floors and the odd antique. Breakfast costs an extra €9 and is a generous spread of pastries, fruit, fresh-pressed juice and coffee.

Épernay ❺

🍴 La Cave à
Champagne Regional Cuisine €€

(☎03 26 55 50 70; www.la-cave-a-champagne. com; 16 rue Gambetta; menus €20-38; ⊗ noon-2pm & 7-10pm Thu-Mon; 🍴) 'The Champagne Cellar' is well regarded by locals for its *champenoise* cuisine (snail-and-pig's-trotter casserole, fillet of beef in pinot noir), served in a warm, traditional, bourgeois atmosphere. You can sample four different Champagnes for €28.

🍴 La Grillade
Gourmande French €€

(☎03 26 55 44 22; www.lagrilladegourmande. com; 16 rue de Reims; menus €19-59; ⊗ noon-2pm & 7.30-10pm Tue-Sat) This chic, red-walled bistro is an inviting spot to try chargrilled meats and dishes rich in texture and flavour, such as crayfish pan-fried in Champagne and lamb cooked in rosemary and honey until meltingly tender. Diners spill out onto the covered terrace in the warm months.

🛏 La Villa
Eugène Boutique Hotel €€€

(☎03 26 32 44 76; www.villa-eugene.com; 84 av de Champagne; s €160-177, d €216-343, ste €380-398; ℙ ❄ ⊚ ☀) Sitting handsomely astride the av de Champagne in its own grounds with an outdoor pool, La Villa Eugène is a class act. It's lodged in a beautiful 19th-century town mansion that once belonged to the Mercier family. The roomy doubles exude understated elegance, with soft, muted hues and the odd antique. Splash out more for a private terrace or four-poster bed.

Alsace Accents

6

French and German cultures come together in Alsace, renowned for its cosy winstubs and centuries-old wine culture. Enjoy castles, vineyards, pastel-shaded towns and the canals of Colmar.

TRIP HIGHLIGHTS

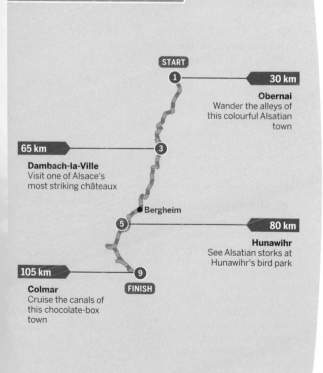

START

1 — **30 km**

Obernai
Wander the alleys of this colourful Alsatian town

65 km — **3**

Dambach-la-Ville
Visit one of Alsace's most striking châteaux

● Bergheim

5 — **80 km**

Hunawihr
See Alsatian storks at Hunawihr's bird park

105 km — **9**

FINISH

Colmar
Cruise the canals of this chocolate-box town

3 DAYS
105KM / 66 MILES

GREAT FOR...

BEST TIME TO GO
May to October for the best chance of sunshine.

ESSENTIAL PHOTO
While punting along the flower-decked canals of Colmar in a romantic rowboat.

BEST FOR FAMILIES
Watching the storks at the Centre de Réintroduction Cigognes & Loutres.

6 Alsace Accents

Gloriously green and reassuringly rustic, the Route des Vins d'Alsace is one of France's most evocative drives. Vines march up the hillsides to castle-topped crags and the mist-shrouded Vosges, and every mile or so a roadside cellar or half-timbered village invites you to stop and raise a toast. The official route runs between Marlenheim and Thann, but we've factored in a stop at Colmar, too.

TRIP HIGHLIGHT

1 Obernai

Sitting 31km south of Strasbourg (take the A35 and turn off at exit 11) is the typically Alsatian village of **Obernai**. Life still revolves around the **Place du Marché**, the market square where you'll find the 16th-century town hall, the Renaissance **Puits aux Six Seaux** (Six Bucket Well) and the bell-topped **Halle aux Blés** (Corn Exchange). Visit on Thursday mornings for the weekly market.

There are lots of flower-decked alleyways to explore – don't miss **ruelle des Juifs** – and you can access the town's 13th-century **ramparts** in front of the **Église St-Pierre et St-Paul**.

✗ 🛏 p91

The Drive ›› Follow the D422 and D1422 for 9km south of Obernai, then turn off onto the D62. Mittelbergheim is another 1.5km west, among dreamy vine-covered countryside.

2 Mittelbergheim

Serene and untouristy, hillside Mittelbergheim sits amid a sea of grapevines and wild tulips, its streets lined with red-roofed houses.

Like most Alsatian towns, it's home to numerous wineries, each marked by a wrought-iron sign. **Domaine Gilg** (www.domaine-gilg.com; 2

rue Rotland; ⏰8am-noon
& 1.30-6pm Mon-Fri, to 5pm
Sat, 9.30-11.30am Sun) is a
family-run winery that's
won many awards for
its Grand Cru sylvaners,
pinots and rieslings.

From the car park
on the D362 next to the
cemetery, a vineyard
trail, the **Sentier Viticole**,
winds towards the
twin-towered **Château
du Haut Andlau** and the
forested Vosges.

The Drive » Follow rue
Principale onto the D425,
signed to Eichhoffen. The road
winds through lush Alsatian
countryside and becomes the
D35 as it travels to Dambach-la-
Ville, 12km south.

TRIP HIGHLIGHT

❸ Dambach-la-Ville

Dambach is another
chocolate-box village,
with lots of pre-1500
houses painted in ice-
cream shades of pistachio,

 **LINK
YOUR
TRIP**

2 **A Toast to Art**
Our art tour ends in
Strasbourg, so it's a natural
addition to this trip along
the Route des Vins d'Alsace.

16 **The Jura**
Travel 170km
southwest to Besançon to
take a jaunt through the
mountains and plateaus of
the Jura.

…amel and raspberry. ʉo the southwest is the **Château du Haut Kœnigsbourg** (www.haut-koenigs bourg.fr; Orschwiller; adult/child €9/5; ⊘9.15am-6pm, shorter hours winter), a turreted castle hovering above vineyards and hills. The castle dates back nine centuries, but it was rebuilt (with typical grandiosity) by Kaiser Wilhelm II in 1908. The wraparound panorama from its pink-granite ramparts alone is worth the admission fee.

The Drive ≫ Stay on the D35, which becomes the D1B as it nears Ribeauvillé, 22km south. It's a truly lovely drive, travelling through carpets of vines and quiet villages. You'll see the turn-off to the château about halfway to Ribeauvillé.

- - - - - - - - - - -

④ Ribeauvillé

Nestled snugly in a valley and presided over by a castle, medieval Ribeauvillé is a Route des Vins must – so you'll definitely share it with crowds during the busy season. Along the main street, keep an eye out for the 17th-century **Pfifferhüs** (Fifers' House; 14 Grand'Rue), which once housed the town's fife-playing minstrels; the **Hôtel de Ville** and its Renaissance fountain; and the nearby clock-topped **Tour des Bouchers** (Butchers' Bell Tower).

It's also worth stopping in at the **Cave de Ribeauvillé** (☏03 89 73 20 35; www.vins-ribeauville.com; 2 rte de Colmar; ⊘8am-noon & 2-6pm Mon-Fri, 10am-noon & 2-6pm Sat & Sun), France's oldest winegrowers' cooperative, founded in 1895. It has an interesting viniculture museum and offers free tastings of its excellent wines. It's two roundabouts north from the tourist office.

✕ 🛏 p91

The Drive ≫ Hunawihr is located 2.5km south of Ribeauvillé.

TRIP HIGHLIGHT

⑤ Hunawihr

Cigognes (white storks) are Alsace's most emblematic birds. They feature in many folk tales and are believed to bring good luck (as well as newborn babies). They've been roosting on rooftops here for centuries, but their numbers fell dramatically during the 20th century as a result of environmental damage and habitat loss.

Thankfully, conservation programs have helped revive the birds' fortunes. The **Centre de**

DRIVING THE ROUTE DES VINS

The Route des Vins is signposted, but a copy of Blay's colour-coded map Alsace Touristique (€5.95) comes in handy.

Tourist offices supply free English-language maps – *The Alsace Wine Route* and *Alsace Grand Cru Wines* – detailing Alsace's prestigious AOC regions, and there's info online at www.alsace-route-des-vins.com.

Parking can be a nightmare in the high season, especially in Ribeauvillé and Riquewihr; your best bet is to park outside the town centre and walk for a few minutes.

Riquewihr Vineyards surrounding the village

Réintroduction Cigognes & Loutres (Stork & Otter Reintroduction Centre; www.cigogne-loutre.com; rte des Vins; adult/child €9.50/8.50; ⏰10am-6.30pm, closed Nov-Mar) houses more than 200 storks, plus cormorants, penguins, otters and sea lions.

The Drive » Backtrack to the D1B and travel 4km south, following signs to Riquewihr. Distant hills unfold to the south as you drive.

❻ Riquewihr

Competition is stiff, but Riquewihr just may be *the* most enchanting town on the Route des Vins. Medieval ramparts enclose a maze of twisting lanes and half-timbered houses, each brighter and lovelier than the next.

On rue du Général de Gaulle, the **Maison de Hansi** (16 rue du Général de Gaulle; adult/child €3/2; ⏰9.30am-12.30pm & 1.30-6.30pm, shorter hours winter) offers a glimpse into the imagination of Colmar-born illustrator Jean-Jacques Waltz (1873-1951), aka Hansi, whose idealised images of Alsace are known around the world.

Meanwhile, the **Tour des Voleurs** (Thieves' Tower; €4, incl Dolder €6; ⏰10.30am-1pm & 2-6pm Easter-Oct) houses a gruesome torture chamber that's guaranteed to enthral the kids.

The late 13th-century, half-timbered **Dolder** (www.musee-riquewihr.fr; €4, incl Tour des Voleurs €6; ⏰2-6pm Sat & Sun Apr-Nov, daily Jul–mid-Aug), topped by a 25m bell tower, is worth a look for its panoramic views and small local-history museum.

The Drive » A scenic minor road winds 7km south from av Méquillet in Kaysersberg to Kientzheim, then joins the D28 for another 1km to Kaysersberg.

7 Kaysersberg

Just 10km northwest of Colmar, Kaysersberg is another instant heart-stealer with its backdrop of vines, castle and 16th-century bridge. An old-town saunter through the **Vieille Ville** brings you to the Renaissance **hôtel de ville** and the red-sand-stone **Église Ste-Croix** (⊙9am-4pm), whose altar has 18 painted panels of the Passion and the Resurrection.

Kaysersberg was also the birthplace of Albert Schweitzer (1875–1965), a musicologist, doctor and winner of the Nobel Peace Prize. His house is now a **museum** (126 rue du Général de Gaulle; adult/child €2/1; ⊙9am-noon & 2-6pm Easter–early Nov).

The Drive » Take the N415 southeast of Kaysersberg for 7km, passing through Ammerschwihr and then following signs to Katzenthal.

8 Katzenthal

A mere 5km south of Kaysersberg, Katzenthal is great for tiptoeing off the tourist trail. *Grand cru* vines ensnare the hillside, topped by the medieval ruins of Châteu du Wineck, where walks through forest and vineyard begin.

It's also a great place for some wine tasting thanks to **Vignoble Klur** (⌨03 89 80 94 29; www.klur.net; 105 rue des Trois Epis; 2-bed apt €82-96, 4-bed apt €105-120), an organic, family-run winery that also offers cookery classes, vineyard walks and back-to-nature holidays.

The Drive » Rejoin the D415. Colmar is another 8km south and is clearly signed.

TRIP HIGHLIGHT

9 Colmar

At times the Route des Vins d'Alsace fools you into thinking it's 1454, but in Colmar the illusion is complete.

Mosey around the canal quarter of **Petite Venise** (Little Venice) then head along **rue des Tanneurs**, with its rooftop verandahs for drying hides, and **quai de la Poissonnerie**, the former fishermen's quarter. Afterwards, hire a **rowboat** (per 30 minutes €6) beside the rue de Turenne bridge for that Venetian vibe.

The town also has some intriguing museums. The star attraction at the **Musée d'Unterlinden** (www.musee-unterlinden.com; 1 rue d'Unterlinden; adult/child €13/8; ⊙10am-6pm Mon, Wed & Fri-Sun, to 8pm Thu) is the Rétable d'Issenheim (Issenheim Altarpiece), a medieval masterpiece that depicts scenes from the New Testament.

Meanwhile, the **Musée Bartholdi** (www.musee-bartholdi.fr; 30 rue des Marchands; adult/child €5/free; ⊙10am-noon & 2-6pm Wed-Mon Mar-Dec) is the birthplace of sculptor Frédéric Auguste Bartholdi, architect of the Statue of Liberty. Highlights include a full-sized model of Lady Liberty's left ear (the lobe is watermelon-sized!) and the family's sparklingly bourgeois apartment.

Look out for the miniature version of the statue on the rte du Strasbourg (N83), erected to mark the centenary of Bartholdi's death.

✗ ⊨ p91

Eating & Sleeping

Obernai ❶

✗ La Fourchette
des Ducs   Gastronomy €€€
(📞03 88 48 33 38; www.lafourchettedesducs.
com; 6 rue de la Gare; menus €120-155; ⊘7-
9.30pm Tue-Sat, noon-1.30pm Sun) A great
believer in fastidious sourcing, chef Nicolas
Stamm serves regional cuisine with gourmet
panache and a signature use of herbs to a
food-literate crowd at this two-Michelin-starred
restaurant. The tasting *menus* go with the
seasons, featuring specialities like Alsatian
pigeon with *baerewecke* (spiced fruit cake) and
veal with truffles and Menton lemon *jus* – simple
but sublime.

🛏 Le Gouverneur   Historic Hotel €
(📞03 88 95 63 72; www.hotellegouverneur.
com; 13 rue de Sélestat; s €55-80, d €65-95,
tr €75-120, q €85-130; 🅿🛜) Overlooking a
courtyard, this old-town hotel strikes perfect
balance between half-timbered rusticity and
contemporary comfort. Its petite rooms have a
boutiquey feel, with bursts of vivid colour and
art-slung walls. The family-friendly team can
provide cots and high chairs free of charge.

Ribeauvillé ❹

✗ Wistub Zum Pfifferhüs   French €€
(📞03 89 73 62 28; 14 Grand'Rue; menus €26-
54; ⊘noon-1.30pm & 6.30-8.30pm Fri-Tue) If
it's good old-fashioned Alsatian grub you're
after, look no further than this snug wine tavern,
which positively radiates rustic warmth with
its beams, dark wood and checked tablecloths.
Snag a table for copious dishes like *choucroute
garnie* (sauerkraut with smoked meats), pork
knuckles and *coq au riesling* (chicken braised in
riesling and herbs).

🛏 Le Clos
Saint Vincent   Boutique Hotel €€€
(📞03 89 73 67 65; www.leclossaintvincent.
com; Osterbergweg; s €150-270, d €170-300,
tr €280-320; 🅿🛜🏊) Gasp you might as you
crest the hill and gaze out across the vines
and the wooded peaks of the Vosges from this
elegant guesthouse. The sound is silence and
the smart, light-drenched rooms capitalise on
those incredible views, as does the restaurant,
serving French cuisine inspired by the seasons.
An indoor pool and a little spa area invite
relaxation.

Colmar ❾

✗ L'Atelier
du Peintre   Gastronomy €€€
(📞03 89 29 51 57; www.atelier-peintre.fr; 1 rue
Schongauer; lunch menus €25-30, dinner menu
€45; ⊘noon-1.30pm & 7-9.30pm Wed-Sat,
7-9.30pm Tue) With its art-slung walls and
carefully composed cuisine, this Michelin-
starred bistro lives up to its 'painter's studio'
name. Seasonal masterpieces like roast quail-
breast fillets with hazelnut cream, fricassee of
wild mushrooms and quince, salsify and oregano
jus are cooked with verve and served with
panache. The two-course lunch is a snip at €25.

🛏 Hôtel les Têtes   Historic Hotel €€
(📞03 89 24 43 43; www.maisondestetes.com;
19 rue des Têtes; r €160-305; ❄🛜) Luxurious
but never precious, this hotel occupies the
magnificent Maison des Têtes. Each of its 21
rooms has rich wooden panelling, an elegant
sitting area, a marble bathroom and romantic
views. The plushest rooms have their own
Jacuzzis. With its wrought ironwork and stained
glass, the restaurant provides a sumptuously
historic backdrop for French-Alsatian
specialities (menus €45 to €95).

STRETCH YOUR LEGS PARIS

Start Place de la Concorde

Finish Panthéon

Distance 4.5km

Duration 3 hours

Paris is one of the world's most strollable cities, whether that means window-shopping on the boulevards or getting lost among the lanes of Montmartre. This walk starts by the Seine, crosses to the Île de la Cité and finishes in the Latin Quarter, with monuments and museums aplenty en route.

Take this walk on Trip

1

Place de la Concorde

If it's Parisian vistas you're after, the place de la Concorde makes a fine start. From here you can see the Arc de Triomphe, the Assemblée Nationale (the lower house of parliament), the Jardin des Tuileries and the Seine. Laid out in 1755, the square was where many aristocrats lost their heads during the Revolution, including Louis XVI and Marie Antoinette. The obelisk in the centre originally stood in the Temple of Ramses at Thebes (now Luxor).

The Walk >> Walk east through Jardin des Tuileries.

Jardin des Tuileries

This 28-hectare landscaped **garden** (⊙7am-11pm Jun-Aug, shorter hours Sep-May; 🚻; MᵀTuileries, Concorde) was laid out in 1664 by André Le Nôtre, who also created Versailles' gardens. Filled with fountains, ponds and sculptures, the gardens are now part of the Banks of the Seine World Heritage Site, created by Unesco in 1991.

The Walk >> Walk across place du Carrousel onto the Cour Napoléon.

Musée du Louvre

Overlooking the Cour Napoléon is the mighty Louvre, with its controversial 21m-high glass **Grande Pyramide**, designed by IM Pei in 1989. Nearby is the **Pyramide Inversée** (Upside-Down Pyramid), which acts as a skylight for the underground Carrousel du Louvre shopping centre.

The Walk >> Continue southeast along riverside Quai du Louvre to the Pont Neuf metro station.

Pont Neuf

As you cross the Seine, you'll walk over Paris' oldest bridge – ironically known as the 'New Bridge', or Pont Neuf. Henri IV inaugurated the bridge in 1607 by crossing it on a white stallion.

The Walk >> Cross the Pont Neuf onto the Île de la Cité. Walk southeast along Quai des Horloges, and then turn right onto bd du Palais.

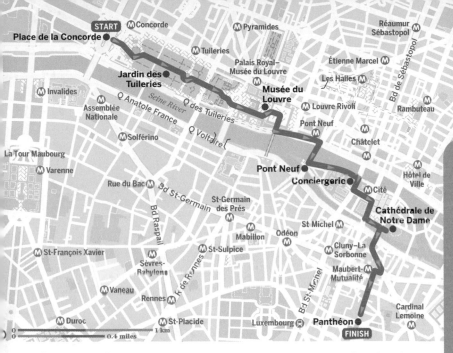

Conciergerie

On bd du Palais, elegant **Conciergerie** (www.monuments-nationaux.fr; 2 bd du Palais, 1er; adult/child €8.50/free, joint ticket with Sainte-Chapelle €15; ◎9.30am-6pm; Ⓜ Cité) is a royal palace that became a prison and torture chamber for enemies of the Revolution. The 14th-century Salle des Gens d'Armes (Cavalrymen's Hall) is Europe's largest surviving medieval hall. The nearby church of **Sainte-Chapelle** (joint ticket with Conciergerie €15) has stunning stained glass.

The Walk » Continue east along rue de Lutèce, then cross place du Parvis Notre Dame and walk towards the cathedral.

Cathédrale de Notre Dame

At the eastern end of Île de la Cité, showstopper **Notre Dame** (www.cathedraledeparis.com; 6 place du Parvis Notre Dame, 4e; cathedral free, towers adult/child €8.50/free; ◎ cathedral 8am-6.45pm Mon-Fri, to 7.15pm Sat & Sun; Ⓜ Cité) is the heart of Paris – it's from here that all distances in France are measured.

Built in stages between the 11th and 15th centuries, it's on a gargantuan scale; the interior is 130m long, 48m wide and 35m high. Don't miss the three rose windows, the 7800-pipe organ and a walk up the gargoyle-covered Gothic towers.

The Walk » Cross the river on Pont au Double and follow rue Lagrange to bd St-Germain. Then take rue des Carmes and rue Valette south to the place du Panthéon.

Panthéon

Once you reach the left bank you're in the Latin Quarter, the centre of Parisian higher education since the Middle Ages, and home to the city's top university, the Sorbonne. Here you'll find the **Panthéon** (www.monum.fr; place du Panthéon, 5e; adult/child €8.50/free; ◎10am-6.30pm; Ⓜ Maubert-Mutualité or RER Luxembourg), the neoclassical mausoleum where some of France's greatest thinkers are entombed, including Voltaire, Rousseau and Marie Curie.

The Walk » Walk east to place Monge, take line 7 to Palais Royal Musée du Louvre, then line 1 west to Concorde.

Normandy & Brittany

NORMANDY OFFERS SOME OF FRANCE'S MOST ICONIC SIGHTS, including the poignant memorials along the D-Day beaches. This beautiful region also enjoys a variety of dramatic coastal landscapes, quiet pastoral villages and architectural gems ranging from Rouen's medieval old city to the maritime charms of Honfleur and the striking postwar modernism of Le Havre.

Further west, beyond its world-famous sights such as stunning St-Malo, charming Dinan and delightful Pont-Aven, Brittany has a wonderfully undiscovered feel. Unexpected gems include the little-known towns of Quimper and Vannes, the megaliths of Carnac and the Presqu'Île de Crozon.

Étretat White cliffs overlook the ocean
FABIO NODARI / GETTY IMAGES ©

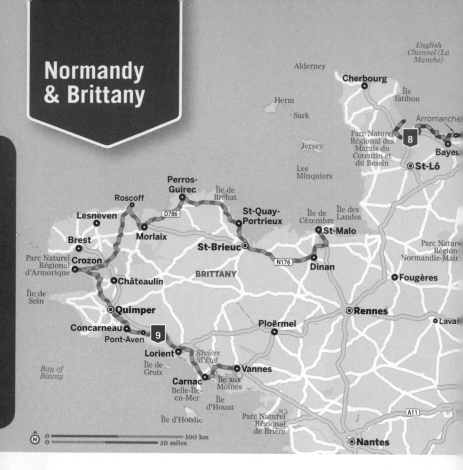

Normandy & Brittany

7 Monet's Normandy 4 Days
Investigate the origins of impressionism, from Étretat's cliffs to Monet's waterlily garden. (p99)

Classic Trip
8 D-Day's Beaches 3 Days
Follow the course of the WWII invasion on Normandy's beaches. (p107)

9 Breton Coast 8 Days
Brittany's coastline is all about big beaches and wild views. (p117)

10 Tour des Fromages 5 Days
Fatten yourself up on this tour of Normandy's creamy cheeses. (p125)

✓ DON'T MISS

Distillerie Christian Drouin

Taste Normandy's top tipples – *calvados* and cider – at this traditional distillery. Refresh yourself on Trip **10**

Musée d'Art Moderne André Malraux

This museum in Le Havre contains the best impressionist collection outside Paris. Soak it all in on Trip **7**

Dinan

Explore this beautiful medieval town replete with narrow cobblestone streets and squares lined with half-timbered houses. Discover it on Trip **9**

Longues-sur-Mer

See where parts of the famous D-Day film, *The Longest Day* (1962), was filmed – on Trip **8**

Île de Batz

Find brilliant sand beaches on this tiny speck of paradise. Get away from it all on Trip **9**

Dinan Old town on the Rance River

Monet's Normandy

7

This eclectic trip takes art-lovers on a fascinating spin around eastern Normandy. En route you'll hit the key landscapes and cities that inspired Monet, the father of impressionism.

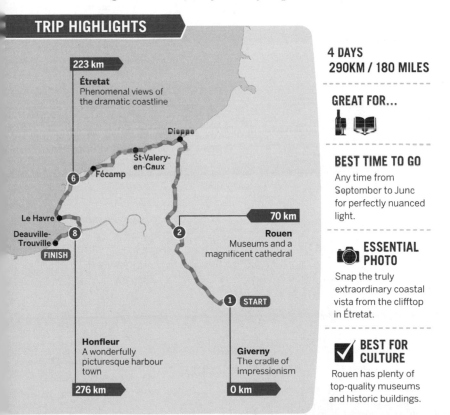

223 km

Étretat
Phenomenal views of the dramatic coastline

Dieppe

St-Valery-en-Caux

Fécamp

6

Le Havre

Deauville-Trouville

8

FINISH

70 km

2

Rouen
Museums and a magnificent cathedral

1 START

Honfleur
A wonderfully picturesque harbour town

276 km

Giverny
The cradle of impressionism

0 km

4 DAYS
290KM / 180 MILES

GREAT FOR...

BEST TIME TO GO
Any time from September to June for perfectly nuanced light.

ESSENTIAL PHOTO
Snap the truly extraordinary coastal vista from the clifftop in Étretat.

BEST FOR CULTURE
Rouen has plenty of top-quality museums and historic buildings.

7

Monet's Normandy

Be prepared for a visual feast on this three-day trip around the eastern part of Normandy – the cradle of impressionism. Starting from the village of Giverny, location of the most celebrated garden in France, you'll follow in the footsteps of Monet and other impressionist megastars, taking in medieval Rouen, the dramatic Côte d'Albâtre, Le Havre, Honfleur and Trouville. This is your chance to see first-hand why so many painters have been attracted to this place.

TRIP HIGHLIGHT

❶ Giverny

The tiny country village of Giverny is a place of pilgrimage for devotees of impressionism. Monet lived here from 1883 until his death in 1926, in a rambling house – surrounded by flower-filled gardens – that's now the immensely popular **Maison et Jardins de Claude Monet** (📞 02 32 51 28 21; www.fondation-monet. com; 84 rue Claude Monet; adult/child €9.50/5.50, incl Musée des Impressionnismes Giverny €16.50/8.50;

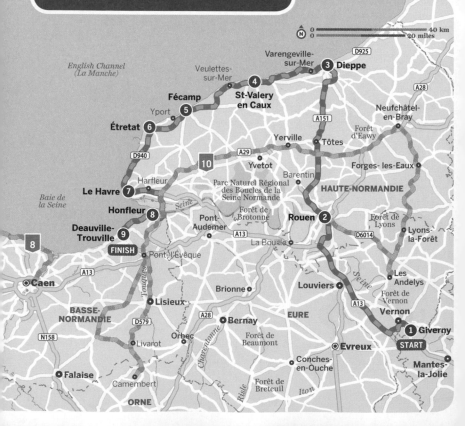

⏱9.30am-6pm Easter-Oct). His pastel-pink house and Water Lily studio stand on the periphery of the garden (called 'Clos Normand'), with its symmetrically laid-out gardens bursting with flowers.

The Drive » It's a 70km trip (one hour) to Rouen. Head to Vernon and follow signs to Rouen along the A13. A more scenic (but longer) route is via Les Andelys, along the east bank of the Seine.

- - - - - - - - - -

TRIP HIGHLIGHT

② Rouen

With its elegant spires and atmospheric medieval quarter complete with narrow lanes and wonky half-timbered houses, it's no wonder that Rouen has inspired numerous painters, including Monet. Some

LINK YOUR TRIP

10 Tour des Fromages

From Honfleur or Rouen you can embark on a gastronomic drive, and taste and learn about some of the best cheese in France at various cheese museums.

8 D-Day's Beaches

From Trouville, it's an easy 50km drive west to Caen, the obvious starting point for the D-Day beaches.

of his works, including one of his studies of the stunning **Gothic cathedral** (www.cathedrale-rouen. net; place de la Cathédrale; ⏱2-7pm Mon, 9am-7pm Tue-Sat, 8am-6pm Sun Apr-Oct, shorter hours Nov-Mar), are displayed at the splendid **Musée des Beaux-Arts** (☎02 35 71 28 40; www. mbarouen.fr; esplanade Marcel Duchamp; ⏱10am-6pm Wed-Mon). Feeling inspired? Sign up for an art class with the **tourist office** (☎02 32 08 32 40; www. rouentourisme.com; 25 place de la Cathédrale; ⏱9am-7pm Mon-Sat, 9.30am-12.30pm & 2-6pm Sun May-Sep, 9.30am-12.30pm & 1.30-6pm Mon-Sat Oct-Apr) and create your own Rouen Cathedral canvas from the very room in which Monet painted his series of that building.

If you're at all interested in architectural glories, the 14th-century **Abbatiale St-Ouen** (place du Général de Gaulle; ⏱10am-noon & 2-6pm Tue-Thu, Sat & Sun), which is a marvellous example of the Rayonnant Gothic style, is a must-see abbey. There's also much Joan of Arc lore in Rouen (she was executed here in 1431). For the story of her life don't miss the spectacular audio-visual displays in the **Historial Jeanne d'Arc** (☎02 35 52 48 00; www.historialjeannedarc.fr; 7 rue St-Romain; adult/child €10/7; ⏱10am-6pm Tue-Sun).

🍴 🛏 p105, p131

The Drive » Follow signs to Dieppe. Count on 45 minutes for the 65km trip.

- - - - - - - - - -

③ Dieppe

Sandwiched between limestone cliffs, Dieppe is a small-scale fishing port with a pleasant seafront promenade. Still used by fishing vessels but dominated by pleasure craft, the **port** makes for a bracing sea-air stroll. High above the city on the western cliff, the 15th-century **Château-musée** (☎02 35 06 61 99; www.dieppe.fr; rue de Chastes; adult/child €4.50/ free; ⏱10am-noon & 2-5pm Wed-Mon Oct-May, 10am-6pm Jun-Sep) is the town's most imposing landmark. Monet immortalised **Pourville**, a seaside village on the western outskirts of Dieppe.

The Drive » Take the scenic coastal roads (D75 and D68), rather than the inland D925, via the resort towns of Pourville, Varengeville-sur-Mer, Quiberville, St-Aubin-sur-Mer, Sotteville-sur-Mer and Veules-les-Roses (35km, 45 minutes).

- - - - - - - - - -

④ St-Valery en Caux

You're now in the heart of the scenic Côte d'Albâtre (Alabaster Coast), which stretches from Dieppe southwest to Étretat. With its lofty bone-white cliffs, this wedge of coast is a geological wonder world that charmed a generation of impressionists, including Monet.

Once you get a glimpse of sweet little St-Valery en Caux, with its delightful port, lovely stretch of stony beach and majestic cliffs, you'll see why.

The Drive » Take the coastal road (D79) via Veulettes-sur-Mer. Count on an hour for the 36km trip.

- - - - - - - - - - - -

❺ Fécamp

After all that driving along the Côte d'Albâtre, it's time to stop for a glass of Bénédictine at the **Palais de la Bénédictine** (☎02 35 10 26 10; www. benedictinedom.com; 110 rue Alexandre Le Grand; adult/child €8.50/3.50; ☺tickets sales 10.30-11.30am & 2.30-4.30pm mid-Dec–mid-Apr, longer hours mid-Apr–mid-Dec, closed early Jan–mid-Feb). Opened in 1900, this unusually ornate factory is where all the Bénédictine liqueur in the world is made.

Be sure to drive up north to **Cap Fagnet** (110m), which offers gobsmacking views of the town and the coastline.

The Drive » Follow signs to Étretat (17km, along the D940). You could also start on the D940 and turn off onto the more scenic D11 (via Yport).

- - - - - - - - - - - -

TRIP HIGHLIGHT

❻ Étretat

Is Étretat the most enticing town in Normandy? It's picture postcard everywhere you look. The dramatic white cliffs that bookend the town,

DADO DANIELA / GETTY IMAGES ©

the **Falaise d'Aval** to the southwest and the **Falaise d'Amont** to the northeast, will stick in your memory. Once at the top, you'll pinch yourself to see if it's real – the views are sensational. Such irresistible scenery made Étretat a favourite of painters, especially Monet, who produced more than 80 canvases of the scenery here.

The Drive » Follow signs to Le Havre (28km, along the D940 and the D147). Count on about half an hour for the journey.

- - - - - - - - - - - -

❼ Le Havre

It was in Le Havre that Monet painted the defining impressionist view. His 1873 canvas of the harbour at dawn was entitled *Impression: Sunrise*. Monet wouldn't

Honfleur Boats on the Old Harbour

recognise present-day Le Havre: all but obliterated in September 1944 by Allied bombing raids, the city centre was totally redesigned after the war by Belgian architect Auguste Perret. Make sure you visit the **Musée d'Art Moderne André Malraux** (MuMa; ☎02 35 19 62 72; 2 bd Clemenceau, adult/child incl audioguide €5/free; ☺11am-6pm Mon & Wed-Fri, to 7pm Sat & Sun), which houses a truly fabulous collection of impressionist works, with canvases by Monet, Eugène Boudin, Camille Corot and many more. Then take in the **Église St-Joseph** (bd François 1er; ☺10am-6pm), a modern church whose interior is a luminous work of art – thanks to 13,000 panels of coloured glass on its walls and tower.

✗ ⊨ p105

The Drive » Follow signs to Pont de Normandie, which links Le Havre to Honfleur (toll €5.40).

✗ ⊨ p105

TRIP HIGHLIGHT

8 Honfleur

Honfleur is exquisite to look at. (No, you're not dreaming!) Its heart is the amazingly pictur-esque **Vieux Bassin** (Old

103

CLAUDE MONET

The undisputed leader of the impressionists, Claude Monet was born in Paris in 1840 and grew up in Le Havre, where he found an early affinity with the outdoors.

From 1867 Monet's distinctive style began to emerge, focusing on the effects of light and colour and using the quick, undisguised broken brushstrokes that would characterise the impressionist period. His contemporaries were Pissarro, Renoir, Sisley, Cézanne and Degas. The young painters left the studio to work outdoors, experimenting with the shades and hues of nature, and arguing and sharing ideas. Their work was far from welcomed by critics; one of them condemned it as 'impressionism', in reference to Monet's *Impression: Sunrise* when exhibited in 1874.

From the late 1870s Monet concentrated on painting in series, seeking to recreate a landscape by showing its transformation under different conditions of light and atmosphere. In 1883 Monet moved to Giverny, planting his property with a variety of flowers around an artificial pond, the Jardin d'Eau, in order to paint the subtle effects of sunlight on natural forms. It was here that he painted the *Nymphéas* (Water Lilies) series.

For more info on Monet and his work, visit www.giverny.org.

Harbour), from where explorers once set sail for the New World. Marvel at the extraordinary 15th-century wooden **Église Ste-Catherine** (place Ste-Catherine; ⊙9am-5.15pm or later), complete with a roof that from the inside resembles an upturned boat, then wander the warren of flower-filled cobbled streets lined with wooden and stone buildings.

Honfleur's graceful beauty has inspired numerous painters, including Eugène Boudin, an early impressionist painter born here in 1824, and Monet. Their works are displayed at the **Musée Eugène Boudin** (☎02 31 89 54 00; www.musees-honfleur.fr; 50 rue de l'Homme de Bois; adult/child Jun-Oct €7.50/free, Nov-May €5.80/4.30; ⊙10am-1pm & 2-6pm Wed-Mon Jun-Oct, 2.30-

5.30pm Wed-Mon & 10am-noon Sat & Sun Nov-May). Honfleur was also the birthplace of composer Erik Satie. The fascinating **Les Maisons Satie** (☎02 31 89 11 11; www.musees-honfleur.fr; 67 bd Charles V & 90 rue Haute; adult/child €6.20/free; ⊙10am-7pm Wed-Mon May-Sep, to 6pm Oct-Apr) is packed with surrealist surprises, all set to his ethereal compositions.

✕ ⌸ p105, p131

The Drive » From Honfleur it's a 14km trip to Trouville along the D513 (about 20 minutes).

- - - - - - - - - - - - -

❾ Deauville-Trouville

Finish your impressionist road trip in style by heading southwest to the twin seaside resorts of Deauville and Trouville,

which are only separated by a bridge but maintain distinctly different personalities. Exclusive, expensive and brash, Deauville is packed with designer boutiques, deluxe hotels and public gardens of impossible neatness, and is home to two racetracks and a high-profile American film festival.

Trouville, another veteran beach resort, is more down to earth. During the 19th century the town was frequented by writers and painters, including Monet, who spent his honeymoon here in 1870. No doubt he was lured by the picturesque port, the 2km-long sandy beach lined with opulent villas, and the laid-back seaside ambience.

Eating & Sleeping

Rouen ②

✖ Bar à Huitres — Seafood €

(place du Vieux Marché; mains €10-16, oysters per half-dozen/dozen from €10/17; ⊘10am-2pm Tue-Sat) For remarkably fresh seafood, grab a seat at the horseshoe-shaped bar at this casual but polished eatery inside Rouen's covered market. Specials change daily based on what's fresh, from giant shrimp to dorado and fillet of sole, all cooked up to perfection. Don't neglect the restaurant's namesake – the satisfying *huîtres* (oysters) with several different varieties on offer.

🛏 La Boulangerie — B&B €

(☎06 12 94 53 15; www.laboulangerie.fr; 59 rue St-Nicaise; s from €67, d €77-92, q €154 incl breakfast; P ✿) Tucked into a quiet side street 1.2km northeast of the cathedral, this adorable B&B, above an historic bakery, has three bright, pleasingly decorated rooms, adorned with artwork and attractive details (such as exposed beam ceilings). Your charming host Aminata is a gold mine of local information. Parking available for €5.

Le Havre ⑦

✖ La Taverne Paillette — Brasserie €€

(☎02 35 41 31 50; www.taverne-paillette. com; 22 rue Georges Braque; lunch menu €15, mains €16-26; ⊘noon-midnight daily) Solid brasserie food is the order of the day at this Le Havre institution – think big bowls of mussels, generous salads, gargantuan seafood platters and, in the Alsatian tradition, eight types of *choucroute* (sauerkraut). Situated five blocks north of Église St-Joseph, at the northeast corner of a park called Le Square St-Roch.

🛏 Hôtel Vent d'Ouest — Boutique Hotel €€

(☎02 35 42 50 69; www.ventdouest.fr; 4 rue de Caligny; d €100-150, ste €170, q €215, apt €185; ✿) Decorated with maritime flair, this stylish establishment has nautical memorabilia downstairs, and cheerfully painted rooms upstairs with sisal flooring and attractive furnishings; ask for one with a balcony. There are lovely common areas where you can while away the hours when the weather inevitably sours, including an enticing café-bar with leather armchairs. There's a restaurant and a spa on-site.

Honfleur ⑧

✖ La Fleur de Sel — Gastronomy €€€

(☎02 31 89 01 92; www.lafleurdesel-honfleur.com; 17 rue Haute; menus €32-62; ⊘noon-1.30pm & 7.15-9pm & Wed-Sun) Honfleur-raised Vincent Guyon cooked in some of Paris' top kitchens before returning to his hometown to make good and open his own (now celebrated) restaurant. Guyon uses the highest quality locally sourced ingredients and plenty of invention (with roast meats and wild-caught seafood featuring ginger and kaffir-lime vinaigrettes, Camembert foams and hazelnut tempura) in his beautifully crafted dishes. Reserve ahead.

🛏 La Maison de Lucie — Boutique Hotel €€€

(☎02 31 14 40 40; www.lamaisondelucie.com; 44 rue des Capucins; d €170-200, ste €250-330; P ✿) This marvellous little hideaway has just nine rooms and three suites, which ensures intimacy. Some of the bedrooms, panelled in oak, have Moroccan-tile bathrooms and boast fantastic views across the harbour to the Pont de Normandie. The shady terrace is a glorious place for a summer breakfast. There's a chic jacuzzi in the old brick-vaulted cellar. No lift.

Classic Trip

D-Day's Beaches

8

Explore the events of D-Day, when Allied troops stormed ashore to liberate Europe from Nazi occupation. From war museums to landing beaches, it's a fascinating and sobering experience.

TRIP HIGHLIGHTS

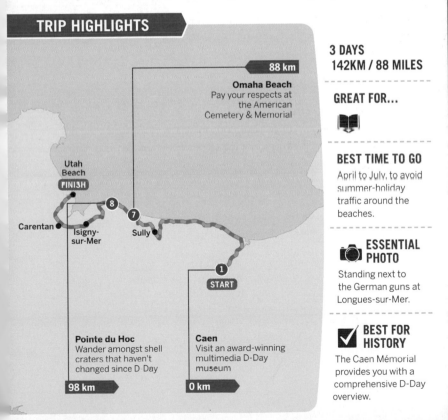

88 km

Omaha Beach
Pay your respects at the American Cemetery & Memorial

Utah Beach
FINISH

8
7

Carentan
Isigny-sur-Mer
Sully

1
START

Pointe du Hoc
Wander amongst shell craters that haven't changed since D Day

98 km

Caen
Visit an award-winning multimedia D-Day museum

0 km

3 DAYS
142KM / 88 MILES

GREAT FOR...

BEST TIME TO GO
April to July, to avoid summer-holiday traffic around the beaches.

ESSENTIAL PHOTO
Standing next to the German guns at Longues-sur-Mer.

BEST FOR HISTORY
The Caen Mémorial provides you with a comprehensive D-Day overview.

8 D-Day's Beaches

The beaches and bluffs are quiet today, but on 6 June 1944 the Normandy shoreline witnessed the arrival of the largest armada the world has ever seen. This patch of the French coast will forever be synonymous with D-Day (known to the French as Jour-J), and the coastline is strewn with memorials, museums and cemeteries — reminders that though victory was won on the Longest Day, it came at a terrible price.

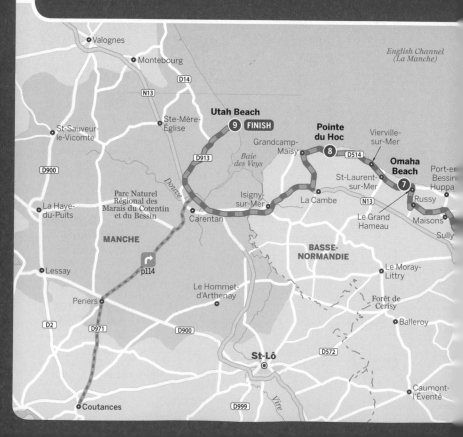

TRIP HIGHLIGHT

❶ Caen

Situated 3km northwest of Caen, the award-winning **Mémorial – Un Musée pour la Paix** (Memorial – A Museum for Peace; ☎02 31 06 06 44; www.memorial-caen.fr; esplanade Général Eisenhower; adult/child €20/17; ⏰9am-7pm daily early Feb-early Nov, 9.30am-6.30pm Tue-Sun early Nov-early Feb, closed 3 weeks in Jan) is a brilliant place to begin with some background on the historic events of D-Day, and the wider context of WWII. Housed in a purpose-designed building covering 14,000 sq metres, the memorial offers an immersive experience, using sound, lighting, film, animation and audio testimony to evoke the grim realities of war, the trials of occupation and the joy of liberation.

The visit begins with a whistle-stop overview of Europe's descent into total war, tracing events from the end of WWI through to the rise of fascism in Europe, the German occupation of France and the Battle of Normandy. A second section focuses on the Cold War. There's also the well-preserved original bunker used by German command in 1944.

On your way around, look out for an original Typhoon fighter plane and a full-size Sherman tank.

✗ 🛏 p115

The Drive » From the museum, head northeast along Esplanade Brillaud de Laujardière, and follow signs to Ouistreham. You'll join the E46 ring road; follow it to exit 3a (Porte d'Angleterre), and merge onto the D515 and D84 to Ouistreham. Park on the seafront on bd Aristide Briand. In all it's a trip of 18km.

❷ Ouistreham

On D-Day, the sandy seafront around Ouistreham was code named **Sword Beach** and was the focus

---

[Map]

20 km
10 miles

Baie de la Seine

Longues-sur-Mer ❺ — ❹ (D514) — ❸ Courseulles-sur-Mer
Juno & Gold Beaches
Arromanches
Crepon
Douvres
Rade de Caen
❻ Bayeux
Beny-sur-Mer (D79)
Ouistreham ❷
(D514)
❶
Ranville
(N13) **START** ❶ **Caen** p132 (A13)
(D6)
Fortenay-le-Pesnel
30 km to ❼
(A84)
CALVADOS
(N158)
Villers-Bocage
Amayé-sur-Orne
Orne

LINK YOUR TRIP

❶ Essential France
The island abbey of Mont St-Michel is about 140km from the Normandy coastline, about two hours' drive via the A84 motorway.

❼ Monet's Normandy
From the end of our Monet-themed trip at Fécamp, drive southwest on the A29 and A13 to Caen, a journey of just under 130km.

of attack for the British 3rd Infantry Division.

There are precious few reminders of the battle today, but on D-Day the scene was very different: most of the surrounding buildings had been levelled by artillery fire, and German bunkers and artillery positions were strung out along the seafront. Sword Beach was the site of some of the most famous images of D-Day – including the infamous ones of British troops landing with bicycles, and bagpiper Bill Millin piping troops ashore while under heavy fire.

The Drive » Follow the seafront west onto rue de Lion, following signs for 'Overlord – L'Assaut' onto the D514 towards Courseulles-sur-Mer, 18km west. Drive through town onto rue de Ver, and follow signs to 'Centre Juno Beach'.

- - - - - - - - - - - -

❸ Juno & Gold Beaches

On D-Day, Courseulles-sur-Mer was known as **Juno Beach**, and was stormed mainly by Canadian troops. It was here that the exiled French General Charles de Gaulle came ashore after the landings – the first 'official' French soldier to set foot in mainland Europe since 1940. He was followed by Winston Churchill on 12 June and King George VI on 16 June. A Cross of Lorraine marks the historic spot.

The area's only Canadian museum, the **Juno Beach Centre** (☎02 31 37 32 17; www.junobeach. org; voie des Français Libres, Courseulles-sur-Mer; adult/child €7/5.50, incl guided tour of Juno Beach €11/9; ☉9.30am-7pm Apr-Sep, 10am-5pm Oct-Mar, closed Jan) has exhibits on Canada's role in the war effort and the landings, and offers guided tours of Juno Beach (€5.50) from April to October.

A short way west is **Gold Beach**, attacked by the British 50th Infantry on D-Day.

The Drive » Drive west along the D514 for 14km to Arromanches. You'll pass a carpark and viewpoint marked with a statue of the Virgin Mary, which overlooks Port Winston and Gold Beach. Follow the road into town and signs to Musée du Débarquement.

- - - - - - - - - - - -

❹ Arromanches

This seaside town was the site of one of the great logistical achievements of D-Day. In order to unload the vast quantities of cargo needed by the invasion forces without capturing one of the heavily defended Channel ports, the Allies set up prefabricated

---

D-DAY IN FIGURES

Code named 'Operation Overlord', the D-Day landings were the largest military operation in history. On the morning of 6 June 1944, swarms of landing craft – part of an armada of more than 6000 ships and 13,000 aeroplanes – hit the northern Normandy beaches, and tens of thousands of soldiers from the USA, the UK, Canada and elsewhere began pouring onto French soil. The initial landing force involved some 45,000 troops; 15 more divisions were to follow once successful beachheads had been established.

The majority of the 135,000 Allied troops stormed ashore along 80km of beaches north of Bayeux that were codenamed (from west to east) Utah, Omaha, Gold, Juno and Sword. The landings were followed by the 76-day Battle of Normandy, during which the Allies suffered 210,000 casualties, including 37,000 troops killed. German casualties are believed to have been around 200,000; another 200,000 German soldiers were taken prisoner. About 14,000 French civilians also died.

For more background and statistics, see www. normandiememoire.com and www.6juin1944.com.

marinas off two landing beaches, code named **Mulberry Harbour**. These consisted of 146 massive cement caissons towed over from England and sunk to form a semicircular breakwater in which floating bridge spans were moored. In the three months after D-Day, the Mulberries facilitated the unloading of a mind-boggling 2.5 million men, four million tonnes of equipment and 500,000 vehicles.

At low tide, the stanchions of one of these artificial quays, **Port Winston** (named after Winston Churchill), can still be seen on the sands at Arromanches.

Beside the beach, the **Musée du Débarquement** (Landing Museum; ☎02 31 22 34 31; www.musee-arroman ches.fr; place du 6 Juin; adult/child €7.90/5.80; ◷9am-12.30pm & 1.30-6pm Apr-Sep, 10am-12.30pm & 1.30-5pm Oct-Mar, closed Jan) explains the logistics and importance of Port Winston.

The Drive ›› Continue west along the D514 for 6km to the village of Longues-sur-Mer. You'll see the sign for the Batterie de Longues on your right.

- - - - - - - - - - - - -

❺ Longues-sur-Mer

At Longues-sur-Mer you can get a glimpse of the awesome firepower available to the German defenders in the shape of two 150mm artillery guns, still housed in their

D-DAY DRIVING ROUTES

There are several signposted driving routes around the main battle sites – look for signs for 'D-Day-Le Choc' in the American sectors and 'Overlord – L'Assaut' in the British and Canadian sectors. A free booklet called *The D-Day Landings and the Battle of Normandy*, available from tourist offices, has details on the eight main routes.

Maps of the D-Day beaches are available at *tabacs* (tobacconists), newsagents and bookshops in Bayeux and elsewhere.

concrete casements. On D-Day they were capable of hitting targets more than 20km away – including Gold Beach (to the east) and Omaha Beach (to the west).

Parts of the classic D-Day film, *The Longest Day* (1962), were filmed here.

The Drive ›› Backtrack to the crossroads and head straight over onto the D104, signed to Vaux-sur-Aure/Bayeux for 8km. When you reach town, turn right onto the D613, and follow signs to the 'Musée de la Bataille de Normandie'.

- - - - - - - - - - - - -

❻ Bayeux

Though best known for its medieval tapestry, Bayeux has another claim to fame: it was the first town to be liberated after D-Day (on the morning of 7 June 1944).

It's also home to the largest of Normandy's 18 Commonwealth military cemeteries – the **Bayeux War Cemetery**, situated on bd Fabien Ware. It contains 4848 graves of

soldiers from the UK and 10 other countries – including Germany. Across the road is a memorial for 1807 Commonwealth soldiers whose remains were never found. The Latin inscription reads: 'We, whom William once conquered, have now set free the conqueror's native land'.

Nearby, the **Musée Mémorial de la Bataille de Normandie** (Battle of Normandy Memorial Museum; ☎02 31 51 46 90; www.bayeux museum.com; bd Fabien Ware; adult/child €7/4; ◷9.30am-6.30pm May-Sep, 10am-12.30pm & 2-6pm Oct-Apr, closed Jan-mid-Feb) explores the battle through photos, personal accounts, dioramas and film.

✕ ⌷ p115

The Drive ›› After overnighting in Bayeux, head northwest out of town on the D6 towards Port-en-Bessin-Huppain. You'll reach a Super-U supermarket after about 10km. Go round the roundabout and turn onto the D514 for another 8km. You'll see signs to the 'Cimetière Americain' near the

WHY THIS IS A CLASSIC TRIP
OLIVER BERRY, WRITER

You'll have heard the D-Day story many times before, but there's nothing quite like standing on the beaches where this epic struggle played out. D-Day marked the turning point of WWII and heralded the end for Nazism in Europe. Paying your respects to the soldiers who laid down their lives in the name of freedom is an experience that will stay with you forever.

Top: Arromanches and Gold Beach
Left & Right: Normandy American Cemetery & Memorial

hamlet of Le Bray. Omaha Beach is another 4km further on, near Vierville-sur-Mer.

- - - - - - - - - - - -

TRIP HIGHLIGHT

❼ Omaha Beach

If anywhere symbolises the courage and sacrifice of D-Day, it's Omaha – still known as 'Bloody Omaha' to US veterans. It was here, on the 7km stretch of coastline between Vierville-sur-Mer, St-Laurent-sur-Mer and Colleville-sur-Mer, that the most brutal fighting on D-Day took place. US troops had to fight their way across the beach towards the heavily defended cliffs, exposed to underwater obstacles, hidden minefields and withering crossfire. The toll was heavy: of the 2500 casualties at Omaha on D-Day, more than 1000 were killed, most within the first hour of the landings.

High on the bluffs above Omaha, the **Normandy American Cemetery & Memorial** (☎02 31 51 62 00; www.abmc. gov; Colleville-sur-Mer; ⊗9am–6pm mid-Apr–mid-Sep, to 5pm mid-Sep–mid-Apr) provides a sobering reminder of the human cost of the battle. Featured in the opening scenes of *Saving Private Ryan*, this is the largest American cemetery in Europe, containing the graves of 9387 American soldiers, and a memorial to 1557 comrades 'known only unto God'.

Start off in the very thoughtfully designed visitor centre, which has moving portrayals of some of the soldiers buried here. Afterwards, take in the expanse of white marble crosses and Stars of David that stretch off in seemingly endless rows, surrounded by an immaculately tended expanse of lawn.

The Drive » From the Vierville-sur-Mer seafront, follow the rural D514 through quiet countryside towards Grandcamp-Maisy. After about 10km you'll see signs to 'Pointe du Hoc'.

TRIP HIGHLIGHT

❽ Pointe du Hoc

West of Omaha, this craggy promontory was the site of D-Day's most audacious military exploit. At 7.10am, 225 US Army Rangers commanded by Lt Col James Earl Rudder scaled the sheer 30m cliffs, where the Germans had stationed a battery of artillery guns trained onto the beaches of Utah and Omaha. Unfortunately, the guns had already been moved inland, and Rudder and his men spent the next two days repelling counter-

DETOUR: COUTANCES

Start: ❾ Utah Beach

The lovely old Norman town of **Coutances** makes a good detour when travelling between the D-Day beaches and Mont St-Michel. At the town's heart is its Gothic **Cathédrale de Coutances** (http://cathedralecoutances.free.fr; parvis Notre-Dame; ⏰8.30am-noon & 2-5.30pm). Interior highlights include several 13th-century windows, a 14th-century fresco of St Michael skewering the dragon, and an organ and high altar from the mid-1700s. You can climb the lantern tower on a tour (adult/child €7/4).

Coutances is about 50km south of Utah Beach by the most direct route.

attacks. By the time they were finally relieved on 8 June, 81 of the rangers had been killed and 58 more had been wounded.

Today the **site** (☎02 31 51 90 70; www.abmc.gov; ⏰9am-6pm mid-Apr–mid-Sep, to 5pm rest of year), which France turned over to the US government in 1979, looks much as it did on D-Day, complete with shell craters and crumbling gun emplacements.

The Drive » Stay on the D514 to Grandcamp-Maisy, then continue south onto the D13 dual carriageway. Keep going till you reach the turn-off for the D913, signed to St-Marie-du-Mont/Utah Beach. It's a 44km drive.

❾ Utah Beach

The D-Day tour ends at St-Marie-du-Mont, also known as **Utah Beach**, which was assaulted by soldiers of the US 4th and 8th Infantry Divisions. The beach was relatively lightly defended, and by midday the landing force had linked with paratroopers from the 101st Airborne. By nightfall, some 20,000 men and 1700 vehicles had arrived on French soil, and the road to European liberation had begun.

Today the Utah Beach site is marked by military memorials and the **Musée du Débarquement** (Utah Beach Landing Museum; ☎02 33 71 53 35; www.utah-beach.com; Ste-Marie du Mont; adult/child €8/4; ⏰9.30am-7pm Jun-Sep, 10am-6pm Oct-May, closed Jan) inside the former German command post.

Eating & Sleeping

Caen ❶

✗ À Contre
Sens   Modern French €€

(📱02 31 97 44 48; www.acontresenscaen.fr; 8 rue Croisiers; mains €30-35, menus €25-54; 🕙 noon-1.15pm Wed-Sat & 7.30-9.15pm Tue-Sat) A Contre Sens's stylish interior and serene atmosphere belie the hotbed of seething creativity happening in the kitchen. Under the helm of chef Anthony Caillot, meals are thoughtfully crafted and superbly presented. Recent selections included pollack cooked in seawater with risotto of oysters, cabbage and coconut, and a juicy thick-cut pork chop with carmelised onions.

✗ Café Mancel   Norman €€

(📱02 31 86 63 64; www.cafemancel.com; Château de Caen; menus €18-36; 🕙 noon-10pm Tue-Sat, to 2pm Sun) In the same building as the Musée des Beaux-Arts, stylish Café Mancel serves up delicious, traditional French cuisine – everything from pan-fried Norman-style beefsteak to hearty Caen-style *tripes*. Has a lovely sun terrace, which also makes a fine spot for a drink outside of busy meal times.

🛏 Hôtel des Quatrans   Hotel €€

(📱02 31 86 25 57; www.hotel-des-quatrans.com; 17 rue Gémare; d from €100; 🖥) This typically modern hotel has 47 comfy, unfussy rooms in white and chocolate. Promotional deals are often available online.

Bayeux ❻

✗ Alchimie   Modern French €€

(lunch menu €12) On a street lined with restaurants, Alchimie has a simple but elegant design that takes nothing from the beautifully presented dishes. Choose from the day's specials listed on a chalkboard menu, which might include hits like *brandade de morue* (baked codfish pie). It's a local favourite, so call ahead.

✗ Au Ptit
Bistrot   Modern French €€

(📱02 31 92 30 08; 31 rue Larcher; lunch menu €17-20, dinner menu €27-33, mains €16-19; 🕙 noon-2pm & 7-9pm Tue-Sat) Near the cathedral, this friendly, welcoming eatery whips up creative, beautifully prepared dishes that highlight the Norman bounty without a lick of pretension. Recent hits include chestnut soup, duck breast and bulgur with seasonal fruits and roasted pineapple, and black cod with spinach and spicy guacamole. Reservations are essential.

🛏 Les Logis
du Rempart   B&B €

(📱02 31 92 50 40; www.lecornu.fr; 4 rue Bourbesneur; d €60-105, tr €110-130; 🖥) The three rooms of this delightful *maison de famille* ooze old-fashioned cosiness. Our favourite, the Bajocasse, has parquet flooring, a canopy bed and Toile de Jouy wallpaper. The shop downstairs is the perfect place to stock up on top quality, homemade cider and *calvados* (apple brandy). Two-night minimum stay.

🛏 Villa Lara   Boutique Hotel €€€

(📱02 31 92 00 55; www.hotel-villalara.com; 6 place de Québec; d €190-360, ste €390-520; 🅿 ❄🖥) Newly constructed in the past decade, this 28-room hotel, Bayeux's most luxurious, sports minimalist colour schemes, top-quality fabrics and decor that juxtaposes 18th- and 21st-century tastes. Amenities include a bar and a gym. Most rooms have cathedral views.

Breton Coast

9

On this maritime-flavoured drive you'll experience serene seaside towns, sparkling beaches, dramatic storm-lashed headlands and the world's greatest concentration of megalithic sites.

TRIP HIGHLIGHTS

290 km

Presqu'île de Crozon
Watch giant waves batter the cliffs of this stunning peninsula

0 km

St-Malo
Stroll along the ramparts for panoramic views over this walled city

Roscoff

1 START

4

Quimper

FINISH

8   **9**

Carnac
Travel through time in the region's fields of prehistoric megaliths

542 km

Vannes
Admire the arty and alternative streets of bustling Vannes

642 km

8 DAYS
642KM / 399 MILES

GREAT FOR...

BEST TIME TO GO
April and May can see fine sunny weather and no crowds.

ESSENTIAL PHOTO
Standing on the precipice of the cliffs of Pointe du Raz.

BEST FOR FAMILIES
Splashing about on the beaches of Concarneau or Carnac.

9 Breton Coast

This is a trip for explorers who want to experience a very different slice of French life. Instead of the Eiffel Tower, fine wine and sun-soaked beaches, you'll take in a drama-filled coastline, excellent seafood, medieval towns, prehistoric mysticism and a proud Celtic streak.

1 St-Malo

Once renowned for being a haven for pirates and adventurers, the enthralling walled town of St-Malo is today a genteel mast-filled port hemmed by pretty beaches and guarded by an array of offshore islands. The walled quarter of **Intra-Muros** is arguably the most interesting urban centre in Brittany, but it's not as old as it appears. Most of the town was flattened in WWII and has been lovingly rebuilt.

Beyond the walls of Intra-Muros is the **Fort de la Cité**, which was used as a German base during WWII. One of the bunkers now houses the **Mémorial 39-45** (☏02 99 82 41 74; www.ville-saint-malo.fr; Fort de la Cité d'Alet, St-Servan; adult/child €6/3; ☺ guided visits 10.15am, 11am, 2pm, 3pm, 4pm & 5pm Jul-Aug, 2.30pm, 3.15pm & 4.30pm Tue-Sun Apr-Jun & Sep, shorter hrs Oct), which depicts St-Malo's violent WWII history.

✖ ⌂ p123

The Drive » The 33km, half-hour drive along the D137 between St-Malo and Dinan is through a largely built-up area of interest. Be warned that this road, like most others around St-Malo, can be subject to heavy traffic and delays.

2 Dinan

Set high above the fast-flowing Rance River, Dinan's old town is like something straight out of the Middle Ages, with narrow cobblestoned streets and squares that are lined with crooked half-timbered houses. The appeal isn't lost on summer visitors, but by around 6pm it's as though someone has waved a magic wand: most of the crowds dis-

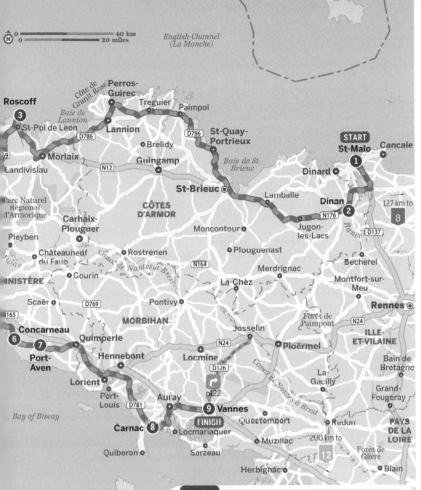

English Channel
(La Manche)

0 —— 40 km
0 —— 20 miles

Roscoff
③

Côte de Granit Rose

Perros-Guirec
②

Treguier
Paimpol

St-Pol de Leon
Baie de Lannion

Lannion
D786

Brelidy

St-Quay-Portrieux

D786

Cancale

START
St-Malo
①

Dinard ○

Morlaix
②

Landivisiau

Guingamp
N12

Baie de St Brieuc

Dinan
②
N176

127 km to
⑧

St-Brieuc ○

Lamballe

D137

Parc Naturel Regional d'Armorique

Carhaix-Plouguer

CÔTES D'ARMOR

Moncontour ○

Jugon-les-Lacs

Rance

Becherel

Pleyben

Châteauneuf du Faou

Rostrenen

Plouguenast

Merdrignac

Montfort-sur-Meu

INISTÈRE

Gourin

Crarx de Nantes à Brest

N164

La-Chèz ○

Forêt de Paimpont

N24

Rennes ◎

Scaër ○
D769

Pontivy ○

MORBIHAN

Josselin

ILLE-ET-VILAINE

Concarneau
⑥ ⑦

Quimperle

Hennebont

Locmine
N24

Ploërmel ○

Bain de Bretagne

Port-Aven

Lorient

D126

La-Gacilly

Grand-Fougeray

Port-Louis
D781

Auray

p122

FINISH
Vannes
⑨

Canal de Nantes à Brest

Carnac
⑧

Locmariaquer

Qu-stembert

Redon

Muzillac

200 km to
⑫

PAYS DE LA LOIRE

Bay of Biscay

Quiberon ○

Sarzeau

Herbignac ○

Forêt de Gâvre

Blain ○

perse and a sense of calm falls over the town.

The Drive » Take the wiggly and very slow (count on a 3½-hour drive) coastal D786 between Dinan and Roscoff. Highlights include the pretty port of Paimpol and the breathtaking Côte de Granit Rose, which extends west of the town of Perros-Guirec. This leg is 220km.

LINK YOUR TRIP

⑧ D-Day's Beaches
Combining a drive around the Breton coast with the war memorials of Normandy is easy. Caen is 170km along the A84 from St-Malo.

⑫ Caves & Cellars of the Loire
From Vannes it's 268km to Montsoreau, where you can pick up our tour of the Western Loire's cave dwellings and wine cellars.

MIGHTY MEGALITHS

Two perplexing questions arise from the region's Neolithic menhirs, dolmens, cromlechs, tumuli and cairns. Just *how* did the original constructors hew, then haul these blocks (the heaviest weighs 300 tonnes), millennia before the wheel and the mechanical engine reached Brittany? And *why?*

Theories and hypotheses abound, but common consensus is that they served some kind of sacred purpose – a spiritual impulse like that behind so many monuments built by humankind.

Just north of Carnac (p122) there is a vast array of monoliths set up in several distinct alignments, all visible from the road, though fenced for controlled admission. The main information point for the Carnac alignments is the **Maison des Mégalithes** (🎧02 97 52 29 81; www.menhirs-carnac.fr; rte des Alignements, D196; tour adult/child €6/free; ☉9.30am-8pm Jul & Aug, 10am-5pm Sep-Apr, 9am-6pm May & Jun), which explores the history of the site and has a rooftop viewpoint overlooking the alignments. Sign up for a one-hour guided visit; times vary considerably depending on the time of year but they run several times a day (in French) during the summer. English tours are available once a week in July and August – call to confirm times.

Opposite the Maison des Mégalithes – with the largest menhir field – with 1099 stones – is the **Alignements du Ménec**, 1km north of Carnac-Ville. From here, the D196 heads northeast for about 1.5km to the equally impressive **Alignements de Kermario** (parts of which are open year-round). Climb the stone **observation tower** midway along the site to see the alignment from above.

The **Tumulus de Kercado** lies just east of Kermario and 500m to the south of the D196. It's the massive burial mound of a neolithic chieftain dating from 3800 BC. Deposit your fee (€1) in an honour box at the entry gate. The easternmost of the major groups is the **Alignements de Kerlescan**.

Be sure to visit the **Musée de Préhistoire** (🎧02 97 52 22 04; www.museedecarnac. fr; 10 place de la Chapelle, Carnac-Ville; adult/child €6/2.50; ☉10am-6.30pm Jul & Aug, 10am-12.30pm & 2-6pm Wed-Mon Apr-Jun & Sep, shorter hours Oct-Mar) in Carnac-Ville to see incredible neolithic artefacts found throughout the region.

---

❸ Roscoff

Set around an arcing harbour studded with granite cottages and seafront villas, Roscoff is one of the more captivating cross-channel ferry ports.

After you've explored the town, set sail for the peaceful **Île de Batz**, which sits a short way offshore. The mild island climate supports the luxuriant **Jardins Georges Delaselle** (🎧02 98 61 75 65; www.jardin-georgesdelaselle.fr; adult/child €5/2.50; ☉11am-pm Apr-Oct), with more than 1500 plants from all five continents.

Ferries (adult/child return €9/4, bikes €8, 15 minutes each way) between Roscoff and Île de Batz run every 30 minutes in July and August; less frequently the rest of the year.

🍴🛏 p123

The Drive » Taking the D69, D18 and D791, drive the 86km between Roscoff and Crozon, the main town on the Presqu'île de Crozon. You'll follow the western edge of the Parc Naturel Régional d'Armorique, a beautiful region of rocky uplands that joins the Crozon peninsula. Stop at famous Breton parish closes (enclosed churches with special architecture) at St-Thégonnec, Guimiliau or Sizun.

TRIP HIGHLIGHT

❹ Presqu'île de Crozon

With long sweeps of golden sand, silent loch-

Quimper Place Terre au Duc

like estuaries bordered by dense forest, pretty rocky coves lapped by azure waters, and huge cliffs hammered by slate-grey Atlantic swells, the anchor-shaped Crozon Peninsula is without doubt one of the most scenic spots in Brittany.

At the western extremity of the peninsula, **Camaret-sur-Mer** is a classic fishing village that lures artists. Three kilometres south of the village is the spectacular **Pointe de Pen-Hir** headland.

Nearby **Morgat** is one of the prettier resorts in this part of Brittany, with colourful houses clustered at one end of a long sandy beach.

🛏 p123

The Drive » Using the D63 it's just 55km from Crozon, the main town on the peninsula, to Quimper. But if you turn off onto the D7 at Plonévez-Porzay and travel 102km, you'll reach wonderful Pointe du Raz, one of Brittany's most spectacular rocky points. Then you can swing back east on the D784 via Audierne for the 60km to Quimper.

- - - - - - - - - - - -

⑤ Quimper

Small enough to feel like a village, with its slanted half-timbered houses and narrow cobbled streets, and large enough to buzz as the troubadour of Breton culture and arts, Quimper is the Finistère region's thriving capital.

At the centre of the city is the **Cathédrale St-Corentin** (place St-Corentin; ⊘8.30am-noon & 1.30-6.30pm Mon-Sat, 8.30am-noon & 2-6.30pm Sun), with its distinctive dip, said to symbolise Christ's inclined head as he was dying on the cross. Beside the cathedral, the superb

Musée Départemental Breton (☎02 98 95 21 60; www.museedepartemental breton.fr; 1 rue du Roi Gradlon; adult/child €5/free; ⊘9am-12.30pm & 1.30-5pm Tue-Sat, 2-5pm Sun Sep-Jun, 9am-6pm daily Jul & Aug) showcases Breton history, furniture, costumes, crafts and archaeology.

The Drive » Rather than taking the faster N165 between Quimper and Concarneau, meander along the more scenic D783. Even on this slower road you only need 30 minutes to travel the 22km.

- - - - - - - - - - - -

⑥ Concarneau

The sheltered harbour of Concarneau is one of the busiest fishing ports in Brittany and is a hugely popular summer holiday destination. In the middle of the harbour is the old quarter of the **Ville Close**, encircled by medieval walls and crammed

DETOUR: JOSSELIN

Start: 9 Vannes

In the shadow of an enormous, cone-turreted 14th-century castle, the story-book village of Josselin lies on the banks of the Oust River, 43km northeast of Vannes. Place Notre Dame, a beautiful square of 16th-century half-timbered houses, is the little town's heart, but it's for the magnificent **Château de Josselin** (☑02 97 22 36 45; www.chateaujosselin.com; place de la Congrégation; adult/child €9/5.50; ☺11am-6pm mid-Jul–Aug, 2-6pm Apr–mid-Jul & Sep, 2-5.30pm Sat & Sun Oct) that you'd really make this detour. The treasure-filled château can only be visited by guided tour.

From Vannes it's an easy one-hour drive along the D126 through an increasingly green and rural landscape of cows and forests.

with enchanting old stone houses.

Surrounding the town are numerous attractive **beaches** and coves, which are sheltered from the anger of the Atlantic and are ideal for families.

The Drive ❯❯ Cross the picturesque Moros River on the D783 and trundle on for 16km (30 minutes) through rural scenery to Pont-Aven.

7 Pont-Aven

The tiny village of Pont-Aven, nestled in the 'valley of willows', is a delightful place to break your journey eastward. Long ago discovered by artists like Paul Gauguin (1848–1903), it's brimming with galleries. For an insight into the town's place in art history, stop by the excellent **Musée**

des Beaux-Arts de Pont-Aven (☑02 98 06 14 43; www.museepontaven.fr; place de l'Hôtel de Ville; adult/child €7/free; ☺10am-7pm Jul & Aug, 10am-6pm Tue-Sun Apr-Jun, Sep & Oct, 2pm-5.30pm Tue-Sun Mar, Nov & Dec, closed Jan). The town also has excellent eateries, so it's perfect for a pit-stop.

The Drive ❯❯ From Port-Aven to Carnac it's a fast but dull one-hour (81km) drive down the N165 dual carriageway past the large industrial city of Lorient.

TRIP HIGHLIGHT

8 Carnac

With enticing beaches and a pretty town centre, Carnac would be a popular tourist town even without its collection of magnificent megalithic sites (p120), which predate Stonehenge by

around 100 years. The area surrounding the town has 3000 of these upright stones – the world's largest concentration – erected between 5000 and 3500 BC.

The Drive ❯❯ Rather than taking the N165 to Vannes, opt for the beautiful coastal route. From Carnac head south to Carnac Plage and wind east to attractive La Trinité-sur-Mer. Join the D781 and then the D28 inland to Auray (well worth a poke around). From here join the D101, which swings into Vannes. This 40km route takes just over an hour.

TRIP HIGHLIGHT

9 Vannes

Street art, sculptures and intriguing galleries pop up unexpectedly through the half-timbered, lively cobbled city of Vannes, which has a quirky, creative bent. Surrounding the pretty walled old town is a broad moat. Along its eastern edge, a flower-filled garden gives superb views of the ramparts. Inside, explore the web of narrow alleys ranged around the 13th-century Gothic **Cathédrale St-Pierre**.

The nearby Golfe du Morbihan is one of France's most attractive stretches of coastline. From April to September, **Navix** (☑08 25 13 21 00; www.navix.fr; ☺Apr-Sep) and other companies run a range of cruises.

🛏 p123

Eating & Sleeping

❶ St-Malo

✖ Breizh Café   Crêperie €

(☎ 02 99 56 96 08; www.breizhcafe.com; 6
rue de l'Orme; crêpes €9-13; ☻ noon-2pm &
7-10pm Wed-Sun) This will be one of your most
memorable meals in Brittany. The creative
chef combines traditional Breton ingredients
and *galette* and crêpe styles with Japanese
flavours and brilliant textures and presentation.
Seaweed and delightful seasonal pickles meets
local ham, organic eggs and roast duck. Save
room for dessert, such as the transcendent
Amuoo Crêpe, a crêpe roll (like a sushi roll) of
melted Valrhona chocolate and ginger-caramel
made with *beurre salé* (salted butter).

🛏 La Maison des Armateurs   Hotel €€

(☎ 02 99 40 87 70; www.maisondesarmateurs.
com; 6 Grand Rue; d €110-210, f/ste from
€190/230; ☻ closed Dec; ❄ 🛜) No language
barrier here – La Maison des Armateurs is run
by a helpful French American couple. Despite
the austere granite-fronted setting, the inside
of this sassy four-star hotel is all sexy, modern
minimalism: modern furniture throughout,
gleaming bathrooms with power showers and
cool chocolate, pale orange and neutral grey
tones. Families can plump for the super-sized
suites. Check the website for deals.

Roscoff ❸

✖ Le Surcouf   Brasserie €€

(☎ 02 98 69 71 89; www.surcoufroscoff.fr; 14 rue
Amiral Réveillère; menus lunch €13, dinner €19-
80; ☻ 11.30am-1.30pm & 6.30-9.30pm) Bang
in the heart of Roscoff, this brasserie serves
excellent seafood. You can choose your own

crab and lobster from the window tank, tuck into
the classic fish soup or opt for a heaping platter
of fresh shellfish. Plate-glass windows keep
things light and bright, and the dining room has
a steady chatter.

🛏 Hôtel aux Tamaris   Hotel €€

(☎ 02 98 61 22 99; www.hotel-aux-tamaris.com;
49 rue Édouard Corbière; d €85-120; ☻ mid-
Jan–Dec; 🛜) This smart, family-run place in an
old granite building overlooking the water at the
western end of town is an excellent choice, with
well-equipped, light, seabreeze-filled rooms, all
with a pleasant maritime aura and yacht sails
for ceilings. Rooms with sea views cost more.
Expect locally sourced goodies at breakfast (€7
to €11). Bikes for hire.

Presqu'île de Crozon ❹

🛏 Hôtel de la Baie   Hotel €

(☎ 02 98 27 07 51; www.hoteldelabaie-crozon-
morgat.com; 46 bd de la Plage, Morgat; d €49-88,
studio €97; 🛜) One of the *very* few places to
remain open year-round, this friendly, family-
run spot on Morgat's promenade has renovated
rooms, some with views over the ocean, and is
one of the best deals around.

Vannes ❾

🛏 La Villa Garennes   B&B €€

(☎ 06 76 01 80 83; www.hotel-lebretagne-
vannes.com; 3 rue Monseigneur Tréhiou; d incl
breakfast €75-105; 🛜) A stone's throw from the
ramparts, this very attractive option has five
charmingly and uniquely decorated rooms in a
handsome stone building. They're light, airy and
furnished with great taste, and breakfasts come
in for warm praise.

Tour des Fromages

10

On this gastronomic drive you'll devour some of the best cheese in France and see where the seaside inspired artists, where Joan of Arc was executed and where Richard the Lionheart prowled.

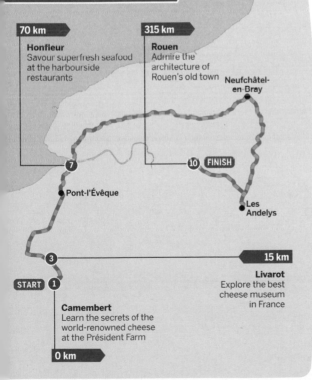

70 km

Honfleur
Savour superfresh seafood at the harbourside restaurants

315 km

Rouen
Admire the architecture of Rouen's old town

Neufchâtel-en-Bray

7

Pont-l'Évêque

10 FINISH

Les Andelys

3

15 km

Livarot
Explore the best cheese museum in France

START **1**

Camembert
Learn the secrets of the world-renowned cheese at the Président Farm

0 km

5 DAYS
315KM / 196 MILES

GREAT FOR...

BEST TIME TO GO
In May Pont L'Évêque celebrates all that is cheese during the Fête du Fromage.

ESSENTIAL PHOTO
Snap a shot of the Seine from the platform near the Château Gaillard.

BEST FOR HISTORY
Pay your respects to the memory of Joan of Arc in Rouen.

10 Tour des Fromages

More cheese, please! It's said that in France there is a different variety of cheese for every day of the year. On this driving culinary extravaganza, you'll taste – and learn about – some of the very finest of French cheeses. Cheese cravings sated, explore the backstreets of Rouen, build castles made of sand on the seashore and clamber up to castles made of stone in the interior.

TRIP HIGHLIGHT

❶ Camembert

Thanks to a delicious soft cheese, the name Camembert is known the world over. Therefore, it can come as a surprise to learn that Camembert is merely a small, but very picturesque, classic Norman village of half-timbered buildings. The big attraction here is, of course, the aforementioned cheese, and you can learn all about it during a guided tour of the **Président Farm** (📞02 33 12 10 37; www.maisonducamem

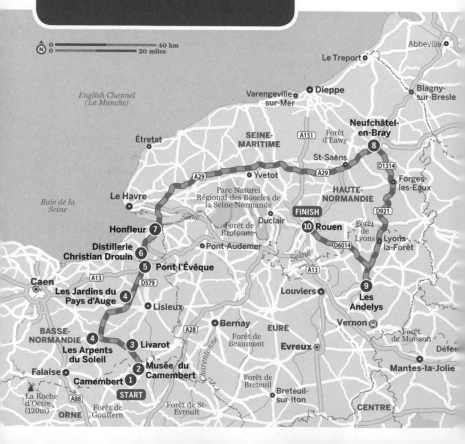

bert.com; adult/child €3.50/1.50; ⏰10am-noon & 2-5pm daily May-Sep, Wed-Sun Apr & Oct, closed Nov–late Mar), an early 19th-century farm restored by Président, one of the region's largest Camembert producers.

The Drive » It's a 5km, 10-minute drive along the D246 and then the D16 from Camembert village to the Musée du Camembert in Vimoutiers.

- - - - - - - - - - - -

② Musée du Camembert

Recently reopened after two years of extensive

renovations, the small **Musée du Camembert** (📞02 33 39 30 29; www.musee ducamembert.fr; 10 Av du Général de Gaulle; adult/child €3/2; ⏰2-6pm Apr-Oct), in the village of Vimoutiers, gives you the lowdown on the history and culture of the smelly stuff. It's a privately run affair; you might have to call for them to open up.

The Drive » It's another 10-minute drive north to stop 3, Livarot, along the D579.

- - - - - - - - - - - -

TRIP HIGHLIGHT

③ Livarot

Although not as famous internationally as Camembert, Livarot is a big deal in France. The town where the cheese of the same name originated is home to probably the best cheese tour in Normandy.

Le Village Fromager (L'Atelier Fromager; 📞02 31 48 20 10; www.graindorge. fr; 42 rue du Général Leclerc; ⏰9.30am-5pm Mon-Sat & 10.30am-5.30pm Sun Jul & Aug, 9.30am-1pm & 2-5.30pm Mon-Sat Apr-Jun & Sep-Oct, shorter

hours rest of year) offers a free tour and tasting at the Graindorge factory. A self-guided tour accompanied by multimedia displays leads through a series of whiffy viewing rooms where you can watch Livarot, Camembert and Pont l'Évêque being made.

After you've expanded your waistline on the cheese tour, work it all off again with a walk around the town. Its wobbly-wiggly half-timbered buildings make it a real charmer.

The Drive » Head west along the D4 from Livarot to the village of St-Pierre-sur-Dives. The D271 leads to Les Arpents du Soleil winery a little south of the village en route to Grisy. Retrace your route to St-Pierre-sur-Dives, then head north on the D16 all the way to Crèvecoeur-en-Auge, and follow the road onto the D101 to Les Jardins du Pays d'Auge.

- - - - - - - - - - - -

④ St-Pierre-sur-Dives

From Livarot, we're detouring a little further west. Just outside the

SOMME

D929

Amiens

Longueau

A16

NORD - PAS-DE-CALAIS

Beauvais

OISE

Forêt d'Halatte

Bray

A16

Forêt d'Ermenonville

Forêt de Chantilly

110km to

PARIS

ÎLE DE FRANCE

Versailles

§ **LINK YOUR TRIP**

④ **In Flanders Fields** The war memorials of northern France are a powerful symbol of the wastefulness of war. Amiens, the start of our Flanders Fields drive, is 120km from Rouen.

⑤ **Champagne Taster** From Rouen it's 284km to Reims and the start of another culinary adventure – this one fuelled by the bubbly stuff.

village of Saint-Pierre-sur-Dives is something of a surprise for Normandy – not a cider farm, but a renowned vineyard, **Les Arpents du Soleil** (☎02 31 40 71 82; www.arpents-du-soleil.com; Chemin des Vignes, Grisy; guided tour adult €6.70; ⊙shop 2-6.30pm Mon-Fri, 10am-5pm Sat), a winemaker since medieval times. The current crop includes three dry whites and a fruity, oaky pinot noir. The shop is open year-round, and offers the chance to try the estate's wines, but guided tours only run on certain days, so phone ahead.

A bit further north towards Cambremer are **Les Jardins du Pays d'Auge** (☎06 84 43 59 29; www.lesjardinsdupaysdauge.com; Rte des 3 Rois, Cambremer; adult/child €7.90/5; ⊙10am-6.30pm May-Sep), a bucolic 4-hectare garden surrounded by typical Norman half-timbered buildings, as well as a museum of old tools. There's also a sweet country cafe where you can try no fewer than 80 crêpes and galettes.

The Drive » A gentle countryside cruise of just over half an hour (22km) up the D101 will see you easing into Pont l'Évêque.

ATLANTIDE PHOTOTRAVEL / GETTY IMAGES ©

- - - - - - - - - - - - -

⑤ Pont l'Évêque

Since the 13th century this unpretentious little town with rivers meandering through its centre has been known for its eponymous cheese. Although two-thirds of the town was destroyed in WWII, careful reconstruction has brought much of it back to life. Half-timbered buildings line the main street, and 1960s stained glass bathes the 15th-century Église St-Michel in coloured light.

There is no shortage of **cheese shops** in town.

If you're passing through over the second weekend in May, don't miss the **Fête du Fromage**, when the townsfolk throw a little party for cheese – only in France!

The Drive » To get to the Distillerie Christian Drouin, your next stop, head out of Pont l'Évêque in a northeasterly direction on the D675. At the

Honfleur Boats on the Old Harbour

roundabout on the edge of the town, take the third exit (rue Saint-Mélaine/D677) and continue for about 2.5km until you see the farm on your left.

⑥ Distillerie Christian Drouin

In case you were starting to wonder if Normandy was merely a one-cheese pony, pay a visit to the **Distillerie Christian**

Drouin (📞02 31 64 30 05; www.calvados-drouin.com; rte de Trouville, Coudray-Rabut; 🕑9am-noon & 2-6pm Mon-Sat), which will let you in on the delights of Norman cider and *calvados* (that other classic Norman tipple). Entrance is free.

The Drive ≫ It's a simple enough 17km drive along the D579 to Honfleur and your first sea views (yes, the sun will be out by the time you get there...).

TRIP HIGHLIGHT

⑦ Honfleur

Long a favourite with painters, Honfleur is arguably Normandy's most charming seaside town.

On the west side of the **Vieux Bassin** (Old Harbour), with its many pleasure boats, **quai Ste-Catherine** is lined with tall, taper-thin houses –

many protected from the elements by slate tiles – dating from the 16th to the 18th centuries. The **Lieutenance**, at the mouth of the old harbour, was once the residence of the town's royal governor.

Initially intended as a temporary structure, the **Église Ste-Catherine** (place Ste-Catherine; ☺9am-5.15pm or later) has been standing in the square for more than 500 years. The church is particularly notable for its double-vaulted roof and twin naves, which from the inside resemble a couple of overturned ships' hulls.

✕ 🛏 p105, p131

The Drive ≫ You've had nice, mellow country lanes so far. Time to speed things up for the 111km race (not too fast, please!) down the A29 to Neufchâtel-en-Bray.

- - - - - - - - - - - - -

⑧ Neufchâtel-en-Bray

The small market town of Neufchâtel-en-Bray is renowned for its heart-shaped cheese called, imaginatively, Neufchâtel. To buy it in the most authentic way, try to time your arrival to coincide with the Saturday-morning **market**.

Appetite satisfied, it's now time for some

culture. Check out the **Musée Mathon-Durand** (☎02 35 93 06 55; Grande Rue Saint-Pierre; adult/child €2.35/ free; ☺3-6pm Tue-Sun), inside a gorgeous medieval building that once belonged to a knight. He's long since gone off to fight dragons in the sky, and today the house contains a small museum of local culture.

The Drive ≫ The most obvious route between Neufchâtel-en-Bray and stop 9, Les Andelys, is along the A28, but that means skirting around Rouen – time it badly and you'll be sitting in traffic breathing in carbon monoxide. Instead, take the more serene D921 back road. Going this way should take you about 80 minutes to cover the 75km.

- - - - - - - - - - - - -

⑨ Les Andelys

On a hairpin curve in the Seine lies Les Andelys (the 's' is silent), the old part of which is crowned by the ruins of Château Gaillard, the 12th-century hilltop fastness of Richard the Lionheart.

Built from 1196 to 1197, **Château Gaillard** (☎02 32 54 41 93; adult/child €3.20/2.70; ☺10am-1pm & 2-6pm Mon & Wed-Sun, 2-6pm Tue late Mar-Oct) secured the western border of English territory along the Seine until Henry IV ordered its destruction in 1603. Fantastic views of the Seine's white cliffs

can be enjoyed from the platform a few hundred metres up the one-lane road from the castle.

🛏 p131

The Drive ≫ It's a 45km, 50-minute scamper (well, as long as you don't hit rush-hour traffic) down the D6014 to your final stop, Rouen.

- - - - - - - - - - - - -

TRIP HIGHLIGHT

⑩ Rouen

With its elegant spires, beautifully restored medieval quarter and soaring Gothic cathedral, the ancient city of Rouen is one of Normandy's highlights. It was here that the young French heroine Joan of Arc (Jeanne d'Arc) was tried for heresy.

Rouen's stunning **Cathédrale Notre Dame** (www.cathedrale-rouen.net; place de la Cathédrale; ☺2-7pm Mon, 9am-7pm Tue-Sat, 8am-6pm Sun Apr-Oct, shorter hrs Nov-Mar) is the famous subject of a series of paintings by Monet.

Rue du Gros Horloge runs from the cathedral west to **place du Vieux Marché**, where you'll find the thrillingly bizarre **Église Jeanne d'Arc**, with its fish-scale exterior. It sits on the spot where the 19-year-old Joan was burned at the stake.

✕ 🛏 p105, p131

Eating & Sleeping

Honfleur ⑦

✕ La Fleur de Sel   Gastronomy €€€

(📞02 31 89 01 92; www.lafleurdesel-honfleur.
com; 17 rue Haute; menus €32-62; 🕙noon-
1.30pm & 7.15-9pm & Wed-Sun) Honfleur-raised
Vincent Guyon cooked in some of Paris' top
kitchens before returning to his hometown to
make good and open his own (now celebrated)
restaurant. Guyon uses the highest quality
locally sourced ingredients and plenty of
invention (with roast meats and wild-caught
seafood featuring ginger and kaffir-lime
vinaigrettes, Camembert foams and hazelnut
tempura) in his beautifully crafted dishes.
Reserve ahead.

🛏 La Petite Folie   B&B €€

(📞06 74 39 46 46; www.lapetitefolie-honfleur.
com; 44 rue Haute; d incl breakfast €145-195,
apt €195-275; 🛜) Penny Vincent, an American
who moved to France from San Francisco, and
her French husband Thierry are the gracious
hosts at this elegant home, built in 1830 and
still adorned by the original stained glass and
tile floors. Each room has a different design,
with original artwork, and the best are filled
with vintage furnishings and overlook the pretty
garden. The lovely common areas make a fine
spot for an evening glass of wine. La Petite Folie
also rents nicely designed apartments on the
same street.

Les Andelys ⑨

🛏 Hôtel de la
Chaîne d'Or   Hotel €€

(📞02 32 54 00 31; www.hotel-lachainedor.com;
27 rue Grande, Petit Andely; s €79, d €95-150, f
€160; 🅿🛜) Packed with character, this little
hideaway is rustically stylish without being

twee. The 12 rooms are spacious, tasteful and
romantic, with antique wood furnishings and
plush rugs; some are so close to the Seine you
could almost fish out the window.

Rouen ⑩

✕ La Rose des Vents   Modern French €

(📞02 35 70 29 78; 37 rue St-Nicolas; mains €16;
🕙noon-3pm Tue-Sat) Tucked away inside a
secondhand shop, this stylish establishment
is hugely popular with foodies and hipsters.
Patrons rave about the two lunch mains, which
change weekly according to what's available in
the market. They can usually whip up something
for vegetarians as well. Reservations are
recommended.

🛏 La Boulangerie   B&B €

(📞06 12 94 53 15; www.laboulangerie.fr; 59
rue St-Nicaise; s from €67, d €77-92, q €154 incl
breakfast; 🅿🛜) Tucked into a quiet side street
1.2km northeast of the cathedral, this adorable
B&B, above an historic bakery, has three bright,
pleasingly decorated rooms, adorned with
artwork and attractive details (such as exposed
beam ceilings). Your charming host Aminata is a
gold mine of local information. Parking available
for €5.

🛏 Hôtel de
Bourgtheroulde   Luxury Hotel €€€

(📞02 35 14 50 50; www.hotelsparouen.com;
15 place de la Pucelle; r €195-254; 🅿❄🛜🏊)
Rouen's finest hostelry (now owned by the
Marriott) serves up a sumptuous mix of early
16th-century architecture – Flamboyant Gothic,
to be precise – and sleek, modern luxury. The 78
rooms are spacious and gorgeously appointed.
Amenities include a pool (19m), sauna and spa
in the basement, and a lobby bar with live piano
music on Saturday evening.

STRETCH YOUR LEGS
CAEN

Start/Finish Château de Caen

Distance 4.5km

Duration 3 hours

Soaring Romanesque churches, picturesque medieval plazas and a mighty castle are all features of this stroll around Caen's historic centre. Although much of Caen was destroyed during WWII, there are still some extraordinary remnants from the past – along with vibrant streets sprinkled with outdoor cafes, colourful shops and new-wave Norman eateries.

Take this walk on Trip

8

Château de Caen

Caen's mighty **castle** (http://musee-de-nor mandie.caen.fr; ⊗8am-10pm; **P**) looms above the centre; its massive battlements must have inspired fear in William the Conqueror's enemies when he established the fortress in 1060. Inside the castle walls, tiny 12th-century Église St-Georges has fine stained-glass windows, and the Échiquier is the oldest building in Normandy and the site of William's first Ducal palace. Don't miss the views from the ramparts behind the building.

The Walk » Exiting the castle grounds, turn right on rue de Geôle and then left onto rue Calibourg. Follow this as it turns into rue Croisiers and rue St-Sauveur. You'll pass Église St-Sauveur (on your right) just before reaching the plaza.

Place St-Sauveur

This lovely plaza is the oldest in the historic centre, and survived the devastating bombing raids of WWII relatively unscathed. Lined with some of elegant 18th-century mansions, the plaza was once home to a medieval market (come on a Friday to browse today's market vendors), and served as a site of public execution for a time. Cafes with outdoor tables facing the plaza make fine vantage points for contemplating the past.

The Walk » Continue southwest along rue St-Sauveur. Turn left at the roundabout. After 50m you'll see Hôtel de Ville (City Hall) on your right, and the church towers of the abbey on the far right.

Abbaye-aux-Hommes

Known as the 'men's abbey', this former Benedictine **monastery** (Abbaye-St-Étienne; ☎02 31 30 42 81; rue Guillaume le Conquérant; church free, cloisters €2; ⊗ church 9.30am-1pm & 2-7pm Mon-Sat, 2-6.30pm Sun, cloisters 8.30am-5pm Mon-Fri, 9.30am-1pm & 2pm-5.30pm Sat & Sun) is the most impressive Romanesque building in Normandy. Soaring spires seem to pierce the sky. Approaching the building, head right to visit the imposing church, where you can see William the Conqueror's tomb (rebuilt, as it was destroyed and rebuilt several times over the centuries). To view the medieval cloister head straight

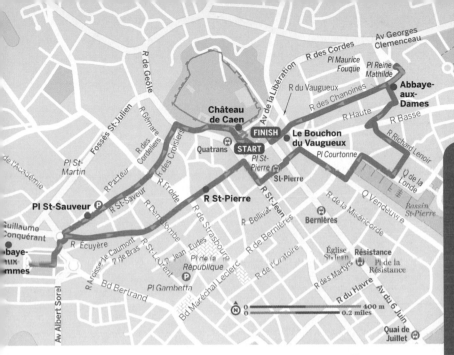

into Hôtel de Ville, which occupies much of the former monastery.

The Walk » Leaving the Abbaye-aux-Hommes, walk back to the roundabout, and take the first right along rue Écuyère, which turns into rue St-Pierre after a few blocks

Rue St-Pierre

One of Caen's most elegant streets, this narrow, cobblestone lane is lined with boutiques and cafes. Medieval **Église St-Pierre** (place St-Pierre; ☺8.30am-6pm Mon-Sat, from 9.30am Sun) anchors its eastern end, and at the other end rue St-Pierre intersects rue Écuyère, a bar-lined street that a draws festive crowd by night.

The Walk » Take a right on busy av de la Libération and follow this past the pleasure boats docked on Bassin St-Pierre. Turn left on rue Michel Cabieu, left again on rue Richard Lenoir and right on rue Manissier.

Abbaye-aux-Dames

The 'women's abbey' is another 11th-century stunner once used as a Benedictine nunnery. William the Conqueror and his wife Matilda founded this **church**

complex (Abbaye-de-la-Trinité; ☑02 31 06 98 98; place Reine Mathilde), which has a magnificent interior. Don't miss the columns topped with 900-year-old carvings near the choir.

The Walk » It's an easy downhill walk along rue des Chanoines heading west. After taking a very slight left onto rue Montoir Poissonnerie, look for the restaurant on your left.

Le Bouchon du Vaugueux

End the day's wanders with a meal of creative Norman cooking. The giant wine cork marks the spot at this tiny **bistrot gourmand** (☑02 31 44 26 26; www.bouchonduvaugueux.com; 12 rue Graindorge; lunch menu €16-24, dinner menu €22-34; ☺noon-2pm & 7-10pm Tue-Sat), which matches imaginative contemporary cuisine with a first-rate wine selection, sourced from small producers all over France. Staff are happy to translate the chalk-board menu. Reservations recommended.

The Walk » From the restaurant it's a two-minute saunter back to the castle, completing the day's loop.

Loire Valley & Central France

WORLD-RENOWNED CHÂTEAUX AND FINE WINES may be the two most obvious reasons to visit central France, but they're only the tip of the iceberg. This region was also once the site of Europe's grandest volcanoes, its largest concentration of cave dwellings and some of its finest medieval architecture. When you've had your fill of château gawking and vineyard hopping, make some time for roads less travelled: wind through the Auvergne's magnificent landscape of green pastures and vestigial cinder cones; go underground to discover the Loire's ancient troglodyte culture; or spend a week exploring Burgundy's medieval churches, abbeys and walled towns.

Central France is also prime walking and cycling country; look for paths wherever you go.

Loire Valley Village and vineyards

Loire Valley & Central France

Classic Trip

11 **Châteaux of the Loire 5 Days**
Tour France's greatest châteaux, from austere medieval towers to exuberant royal palaces. (p139)

12 **Caves & Cellars of the Loire 3 Days**
Discover the Loire's subterranean world: wine cellars, cave dwellings and mushroom farms. (p149)

13 **Volcanoes of the Auvergne 4 Days**
Green pastures, volcanic scenery, fabulous hiking and some of France's finest cheeses. (p159)

14 **Medieval Burgundy 6 Days**
Search for medieval treasures in Burgundy's churches, monasteries and fortified villages. (p167)

15 **Route des Grands Crus 2 Days**
Sample France's most venerable vintages on this wine-lover's tour of Burgundy. (p175)

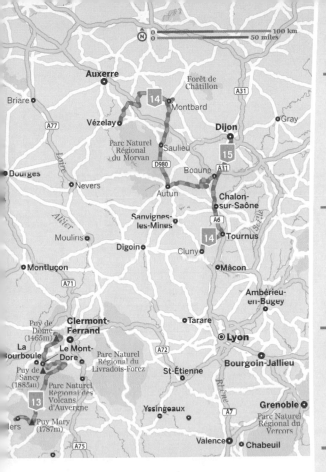

uy de Dôme Volcanic cone among verdant pastures

✔️ DON'T MISS

Château de Chambord

The Loire's star expression of Renaissance architecture, capped by its world-famous double-helix staircase. Discover it on Trip 11

Ancient Green Volcanoes, Auvergne

The Auvergne's three dormant volcanoes are a hiker's paradise. Climb them on Trip 13

Temptation of Eve, Musée Rolin, Autun

This startlingly sensual image is the work of 12th-century stone carver Gislebertus. See it on Trip 14

Caveau de Puligny-Montrachet

Sample some of Burgundy's extraordinary white wines without breaking the bank. Enjoy them on Trip 15

Château de La Rochepot

Enjoy superb views of France's countryside from this medieval castle. Visit it on Trip 15

137

Classic Trip

Châteaux of the Loire

11

For centuries, France's longest river has been a backdrop for royal intrigue and extravagant castles. This trip weaves nine of the Loire Valley's most spectacular and sublimely beautiful châteaux.

TRIP HIGHLIGHTS

5 DAYS
189KM / 118 MILES

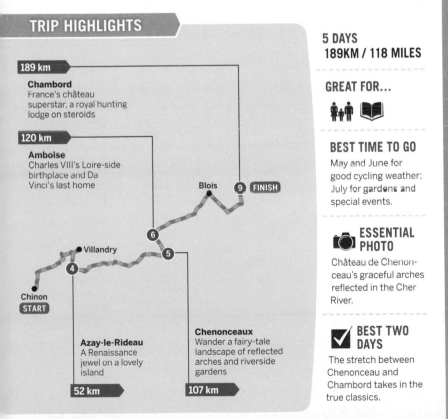

189 km

Chambord
France's château superstar, a royal hunting lodge on steroids

120 km

Amboise
Charles VIII's Loire-side birthplace and Da Vinci's last home

Blois **9** FINISH

6

Villandry

5

4

Chinon
START

Azay-le-Rideau
A Renaissance jewel on a lovely island

52 km

Chenonceaux
Wander a fairy-tale landscape of reflected arches and riverside gardens

107 km

GREAT FOR...

BEST TIME TO GO
May and June for good cycling weather; July for gardens and special events.

ESSENTIAL PHOTO
Château de Chenonceau's graceful arches reflected in the Cher River.

BEST TWO DAYS
The stretch between Chenonceau and Chambord takes in the true classics.

Classic Trip

11 Châteaux of the Loire

From warring medieval warlords to the kings and queens of Renaissance France, a parade of powerful men and women have left their mark on the Loire Valley. The result is France's most magnificent collection of castles. This itinerary visits nine of the Loire's most iconic châteaux, ranging from austere medieval fortresses to ostentatious royal pleasure palaces. Midway through, a side trip leads off the beaten track to four lesser-known châteaux.

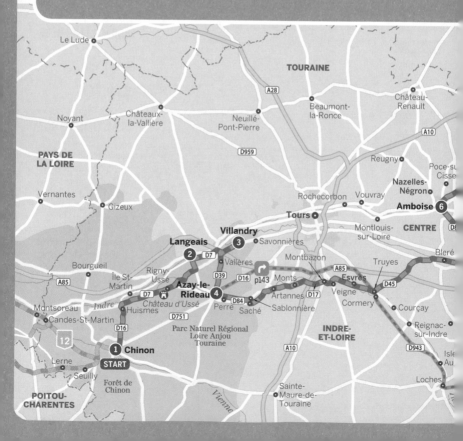

❶ Chinon

Tucked between the medieval **Forteresse Royale de Chinon** (☏02 47 93 13 45; www.forteressechinon. fr; adult/child €8.50/6.50; ⊙9.30am-7pm May-Aug, to 5pm or 6pm Sep-Apr) – a magnificent hilltop castle – and the Vienne River, Chinon is forever etched in France's collective memory as the venue of Joan of Arc's first meeting with Charles VII, future king of France, in 1429. Highlights include superb panoramas from the castle's ramparts and,

down in the medieval part of town (along rue Voltaire), several fine buildings dating from the 15th to 17th centuries.

✗ ⌂ p147, p157

The Drive » Follow the D16 north of Chinon for 10km, then head 15km east on the D7 past the fairy-tale Château d'Ussé (the inspiration for the fairy tale *Sleeping Beauty*) to Lignières, where you catch the D57 3km north into Langeais.

❷ Langeais

The most medieval of the Loire châteaux, the **Château de Langeais** (☏02

47 96 72 60; www.chateau-de-langeais.com; adult/child €9/5; ⊙9.30am-6.30pm Apr–mid-Nov, 10am-5pm mid-Nov–Mar) – built in the 1460s – is superbly preserved inside and out, looking much as it did at the tail end of the Middle Ages, with crenellated ramparts and massive towers dominating the surrounding village. Original 15th-century furniture and Flemish tapestries fill its flagstoned chambers. In one room, a life-size wax-figure tableau portrays the marriage of Charles VIII and Anne of Brittany, held here on 6 December 1491, which brought about the historic union of France and Brittany.

Langeais presents two faces to the world. From the town you see a fortified castle, nearly windowless, with machicolated walls rising forbiddingly from the drawbridge. But the sections facing

LINK YOUR TRIP

12 Caves & Cellars of the Loire

Tour wineries and centuries-old cave dwellings between Chinon and Saumur.

14 Medieval Burgundy

Three hours east of Blois, steep yourself in the world of Burgundy's medieval churches and abbeys.

Classic Trip

the courtyard have large windows, ornate dormers and decorative stonework designed for more refined living.

Behind the château is a ruined stone **keep** constructed in 994 by warlord Foulques Nerra, France's first great château builder. It is the oldest such structure in France.

🍴 p147

The Drive 》 Backtrack south across the Loire River on the D57, then follow the riverbank east 10km on the D16 to Villandry.

③ Villandry

The six glorious landscaped gardens at the **Château de Villandry** (☎02 47 50 02 09; www.chateauvillandry.com; 3 rue Principale; chateau & gardens adult/child €10.50/6.50, gardens only €6.50/4.50, audio-guides €4; ☺9am-btwn 5pm & 7pm year-round, château interior closed mid-Nov–mid-Dec & early Jan-early Feb) are among the finest in France, with over 6 hectares of cascading flowers, ornamental vines, manicured lime trees, razor-sharp box hedges and tinkling fountains. Try to visit when the gardens are blooming, between April and October; midsummer is most spectacular.

Wandering the pebbled walkways, you'll see the classical **Jardin d'Eau** (Water Garden), the **Labyrinthe** (Maze) and the **Jardin d'Ornement** (Ornamental Garden), which depicts various kinds of love (fickle, passionate, tender and tragic). But the highlight is the 16th-century-style **Jardin des Simples** (Kitchen Garden), where cabbages, leeks and carrots are laid out to create nine geometrical, colour-coordinated squares.

For bird's-eye views across the gardens and the nearby Loire and Cher Rivers, climb to the top of the **donjon** (keep), the only medieval remnant in this otherwise Renaissance-style château.

The Drive 》 Go southwest 4km on the D7, then turn south 7km on the D39 into Azay-le-Rideau.

TRIP HIGHLIGHT

④ Azay-le-Rideau

Romantic, moat-ringed **Azay-le-Rideau** (☎02 47 45 42 04; www.azay-le-rideau.fr; adult/child €8.50/free, audioguide €4.50; ☺9.30am-6pm Apr-Sep, to 7pm Jul & Aug, 10am-5.15pm Oct-Mar) is one of France's absolute gems, wonderfully adorned with elegant turrets, delicate stonework and steep slate roofs, and surrounded by a shady, landscaped park. Built in the 1500s, the château's most famous feature is its Italian-style **loggia staircase** overlooking the central courtyard, decorated with the royal salamanders and ermines of François I and Queen Claude. The interior decor is mostly 19th century; the **Salon de Biencourt** was given historically coherent furnishings and comprehensively restored in 2016. The lovely English-style gardens were restored and partly replanted in 2015.

The Drive 》 Follow the D84 east 6km through the tranquil Indre valley, then cross the river south into Saché, home to an attractive château and Balzac museum. From Saché continue 26km east on the D17, 11km northeast on the D45 and 9km east on the D976. Cross north over the Cher River and follow the D40 east 1.5km to Chenonceaux village and the Château de Chenonceau.

TRIP HIGHLIGHT

⑤ Chenonceaux

Spanning the languid Cher River atop a supremely graceful arched bridge, the **Château de Chenonceau** (☎02 47 23 90 07; www.chenonceau.com; adult/child €13/10, with audio-guide €17.50/14; ☺9am-7pm or later Apr-Sep, to 5pm or 6pm Oct-Mar) is one of France's most elegant châteaux. It's hard not to be moved and exhilarated by the glorious setting, the formal gardens, the magic of the architecture and the château's fascinating history. The interior is decorated with rare furnishings and a fabulous art collection.

This extraordinary complex is largely the work of several remarkable women (hence its nickname, Le Château des Dames). The distinctive arches and the eastern formal garden were added by Diane de Poitiers, mistress of King Henri II. Following Henri's death, Catherine de Médicis, the king's scheming widow, forced Diane (her second cousin) to exchange Chenonceau for the rather less grand Château de Chaumont. Catherine completed the château's construction and added the yew-tree maze and the western rose garden. Chenonceau had an 18th-century heyday under the aristocratic Madame Dupin, who made it a centre of fashionable society; guests included Voltaire and Rousseau.

The château's pièce de résistance is the 60m-long, chequerboard-floored **Grande Gallerie** over the Cher. From 1940 to 1942 it served as an escape route for refugees fleeing from German-occupied France (north of the Cher) to the Vichy-controlled south.

The Drive » Follow the D81 north 13km into Amboise; 2km south of town, you'll pass the **Mini-Châteaux** theme park, whose intricate scale models of 44 Loire Valley châteaux are great fun for kids!

DETOUR:
SOUTH OF THE LOIRE RIVER

Start: ❹ Azay-le-Rideau

Escape the crowds by detouring to four less-visited châteaux between Azay-le-Rideau and Chenonceaux.

First stop: **Loches**, where Joan of Arc, fresh from her victory at Orléans in 1429, famously persuaded Charles VII to march to Reims and claim the French crown. The undisputed highlight here is the **Cité Royale** (☏02 47 59 01 32; www.chateau-loches. fr; ⊙24hr), a vast citadel that spans 500 years of French château architecture in a single site, from Foulques Nerra's austere 10th-century **keep** to the Flamboyant Gothic and Renaissance styles of the **Logis Royal**. To get here from Azay-le-Rideau, head 55km east and then southeast along the D751, A85 and D943.

Next comes the quirky **Château de Montrésor** (☏02 47 92 60 04; www. chateaudemontresor.fr; Montrésor; adult/child €8/4; ⊙10am-7pm Apr–mid-Nov, 10am-6pm Sat & Sun mid-Nov–Mar), 19km east of Loches on the D760, still furnished much as it was over a century ago, when it belonged to Polish-born count, financier and railroad magnate Xavier Branicki. The eclectic decor includes a Cuban mahogany spiral staircase, a piano once played by Chopin and a treasury room filled with Turkish hookahs, plus other spoils from the 17th-century Battle of Vienna.

Next, head 20km north on the D10 and D764 to the **Château de Montpoupon** (☏02 47 94 21 15; www.chateau-loire-montpoupon.com; adult/child €9/5; ⊙10am-7pm Apr-Sep, shorter hours winter), idyllically situated in rolling countryside. Opposite the castle, grab lunch at the wonderful **Auberge de Montpoupon** (☏02 47 59 01 18; www.chateau-loire-montpoupon.com; Céré-la-Ronde; mains €11.50-18.50; ⊙lunch Tue-Sun, dinner Tue-Sat Apr-Oct).

Continue 12km north on the D764 to **Château de Montrichard**, another ruined 11th-century fortress constructed by Foulques Nerra. After visiting the château, picnic in the park by the Cher River or taste sparkling wines at **Caves Monmousseau** (☏02 54 32 35 15; www.monmousseau.com; 71 route de Vierzon, Montrichard; ⊙10am-12.30pm & 1.30-6pm Apr-Oct, 10am-noon & 2-5pm Mon-Sat Nov-Mar).

From Montrichard, head 10km west on the D176 and D40 to rejoin the main route at Chenonceaux.

Classic Trip

WHY THIS IS A CLASSIC TRIP
DANIEL ROBINSON, WRITER

Travel doesn't get more quintessentially French – or splendidly pampering – than this tour of the most famous Loire Valley châteaux, which brings together so many of the things I love most about France: supremely refined architecture, richly dramatic history, superb cuisine and delectable wines. My family especially enjoys the forbidding medieval fortresses of Langeais and Loches, which conjure up a long-lost world of knights, counts and court intrigue.

Top: Le Close Lucé
Left: Chapelle St-Hubert
Right: Château Royal d'Amboise

6 Amboise

Perched on a rocky escarpment above town, the **Château Royal d'Amboise** (02 47 57 00 98; www.chateau-amboise.com; place Michel Debré; adult/child €11.20/7.50, incl audioguide €15.20/10.50; 9am-6pm or 7.30pm Mar–mid-Nov, 9am-12.30pm & 2-5.15pm mid-Nov–Feb) was a favoured retreat for all of France's Valois and Bourbon kings. The ramparts afford thrilling views of the town and river, and you can visit the furnished **Logis** (Lodge) and the Flamboyant Gothic **Chapelle St-Hubert** (1493), where Leonardo da Vinci's presumed remains have been buried since 1863.

Amboise's other main sight is **Le Clos Lucé** (02 47 57 00 73; www.vinci-closluce.com; 2 rue du Clos Lucé; adult/child €15/10.50; 9am-7pm or 8pm Feb-Oct, 9am or 10am-5pm or 6pm Nov-Jan,), the grand manor house where Leonardo da Vinci (1452–1519) took up residence in 1516 and spent the final years of his life at the invitation of François I. Already 64 by the time he arrived, Da Vinci spent his time sketching, tinkering and dreaming up ingenious contraptions. Fascinating models of his many inventions are on display inside the home and around its lovely 7 hectare gardens.

✕ ⊨ p147

hind a tapestry while the deed was done). Dramatic and graphic oil paintings illustrate these events next door in the Council Room.

✗ p147

The Drive » Cross the Loire and head 16km southeast into Cheverny via the D765 and D102.

- - - - - - - - - - - -

⑧ Cheverny

Perhaps the Loire's most elegantly proportioned château, **Cheverny** (www.chateau-cheverny.fr; av du Château; château & gardens adult/child €10.50/7.50; ◷9.15am-7pm Apr-Sep, 10am-5.30pm Oct-Mar) represents the zenith of French classical architecture: the perfect blend of symmetry, geometry and aesthetic order. Inside are some of the most sumptuous and elegantly furnished rooms anywhere in the Loire Valley. Highlights include the formal **Dining Room**, with panels depicting the story of Don Quixote; the **King's Bedchamber**, with ceiling murals and tapestries illustrating stories from Greek mythology; and a children's **playroom** complete with toys from the time of Napoléon III.

Cheverny's **kennels** house pedigreed hunting dogs; feeding time, known as **Soupe des Chiens**, takes place most days at 11.30am. Behind the château, the 18th-century **Orangerie**, which sheltered priceless artworks, including the *Mona Lisa*, during WWII, is now a warm-season tearoom.

Tintin fans may recognise the château's façade as the model for Captain Haddock's ancestral home, Marlinspike Hall.

🛏 p147

The Drive » Take the D102 10km northeast into Bracieux, then turn north on the D112 for the final 8km run through forested Domaine National de Chambord, the largest walled park in Europe. Catch your first dramatic glimpse of France's most famous château on the right as you arrive in Chambord.

- - - - - - - - - - - -

TRIP HIGHLIGHT

⑨ Chambord

A crowning achievement of French Renaissance architecture, **Château de Chambord** (www.chambord.org; adult/child €11/9, parking €4-6; ◷9am-5pm or 6pm; ♿) – with 440 rooms, 365 fireplaces and 84 staircases – is by far the largest, grandest and most visited château in the Loire Valley. Begun in 1519 by François I (r 1515–47) as a weekend hunting lodge, it quickly grew into one of the most ambitious and expensive architectural projects ever attempted by a French monarch.

Rising through the centre of the structure, the world-famous **double-helix staircase** – reputedly designed by Leonardo da Vinci – ascends to the great **lantern tower** and rooftop, where you can marvel at a skyline of cupolas, domes, turrets, chimneys and lightning rods and gaze out across the vast grounds.

The Drive » Follow D952 northeast along the Loire's northern bank, enjoying 35km of beautiful river views en route to Blois. The town of Chaumont-sur-Loire makes a pleasant stop for its imposing château and gardens.

- - - - - - - - - - - -

⑦ Blois

Seven French kings lived in **Château Royal de Blois** (www.chateaudeblois.fr; place du Château; adult/child €10/5, audioguide €4/3; ◷9am-6pm or 7pm Apr-Oct, 9am-noon & 1.30-5.30pm Nov-Mar), whose four grand wings were built during four distinct periods in French architecture: Gothic (13th century), Flamboyant Gothic (1498–1501), early Renaissance (1515–20) and classical (1630s). You can easily spend half a day immersing yourself in the château's dramatic and bloody history and extraordinary architecture.

In the Renaissance wing, the most remarkable feature is the spiral **loggia staircase**, decorated with fierce salamanders and curly Fs, heraldic symbols of François I. The **King's Bedchamber** was the setting for one of the bloodiest episodes in the château's history. In 1588 Henri III had his arch-rival, Duke Henri I de Guise, murdered by royal bodyguards (the king is said to have hidden be-

Eating & Sleeping

Chinon ❶

🛏 Hôtel de France   Hotel €€

(📞02 47 93 33 91; www.bestwestern-hoteldefrance-chinon.com; 47 place du Général de Gaulle, aka place de la Fontaine; d €99-139, apt €175; ❄ 🛜) Run impeccably by the same couple since 1979, this Best Western–affiliated hotel, right in the centre of town, has 30 rooms arrayed around an inner courtyard. Tastefully decorated in a contemporary style, many have views of the château – as does the magnificent, flowery terrace on the roof. Offers enclosed bicycle parking. No lift.

Langeais ❷

🍴 Au Coin des Halles   Bistro €€

(📞02 47 96 37 25; www.aucoindeshalles.com; 9 rue Gambetta; lunch menus €16.50, other menus €26-55; ⏱12.15-2pm & 7.15-9pm Fri-Tue) Half a block from the entrance to the château, this elegant eatery is mi-bistrot, mi-gastro (half-bistro, half-gastronomic restaurant), serving delicious cuisine du marché (cuisine based on what's available fresh in the markets) grown and raised by local producers.

Amboise ❻

🍴 La Fourchette   French €€

(📞06 11 78 16 98; 9 rue Malebranche; lunch/dinner menus €17/30; ⏱noon-1.30pm Tue-Sat, 7-8.30pm Fri & Sat, plus Tue & Wed evenings summer) Hidden away in a back alley off rue Nationale, this is Amboise's favourite address for family-style French cooking – chef Christine will make you feel as though you've been invited to her house for lunch. The menu has just two

entrées, two mains and two desserts. It's small, so reserve ahead.

🛏 Le Vieux Manoir   B&B €€

(📞02 47 30 41 27; www.le-vieux-manoir.com; 13 rue Rabelais; d incl breakfast €150-220, f €330, cottages €260-310; ⏱late Mar-1 Nov; 🅿 ❄ 🛜) Set in a lovely walled garden, this restored mansion has oodles of old-time charm. The six rooms and two cottages, decorated with antiques, get lots of natural light, and owners Gloria and Bob (expat Americans who once ran an award-winning Boston B&B) are generous with their knowledge of the area.

Blois ❼

🍴 L'Orangerie du Château   Gastronomy €€€

(📞02 54 78 05 36; www.orangerie-du-chateau.fr; 1 av Dr Jean Laigret; menus €38-84; ⏱noon-1.45pm & 7-9.15pm Tue-Sat; 🅿) This Michelin-starred restaurant serves cuisine gastronomique inventive inspired by both French tradition and culinary ideas from far away lands. The wine list comes on a tablet computer. For dessert try the speciality, soufflé.

Cheverny ❽

🛏 La Levraudière   B&B €

(📞02 54 79 81 99; www.lalevraudiere.fr; 1 chemin de la Levraudière; d incl breakfast €80, 5-person ste €150; 🛜) In a peaceful farmhouse from 1892, amid 3.5 hectares of grassland, La Levraudière's four rooms are comfortable and homey and come with king-size beds. Sonia Maurice, the friendly owner, speaks English and is happy to supply local cycling maps. Situated 2.5km south of the Château de Cheverny.

Caves & Cellars of the Loire

12

This tour of caves, wine cellars and châteaux explores the best of the western Loire Valley, home to habitations troglodytiques (cave dwellings) and some of France's finest food and wine.

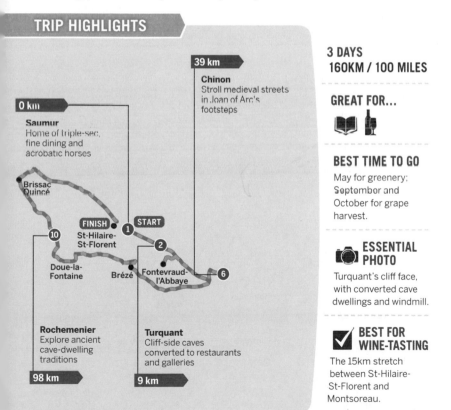

TRIP HIGHLIGHTS

39 km

Chinon
Stroll medieval streets in Joan of Arc's footsteps

0 km

Saumur
Home of triple-sec, fine dining and acrobatic horses

Brissac Quincé

FINISH — **St-Hilaire-St-Florent** — **1** — **START**

10

2

Doue-la-Fontaine — **Brézé** — **Fontevraud-l'Abbaye** — **6**

Rochemenier
Explore ancient cave-dwelling traditions

98 km

Turquant
Cliff-side caves converted to restaurants and galleries

9 km

3 DAYS
160KM / 100 MILES

GREAT FOR...

BEST TIME TO GO
May for greenery; September and October for grape harvest.

ESSENTIAL PHOTO
Turquant's cliff face, with converted cave dwellings and windmill.

BEST FOR WINE-TASTING
The 15km stretch between St-Hilaire-St-Florent and Montsoreau.

12 Caves & Cellars of the Loire

The Loire Valley's easily excavated *tuffeau* (soft limestone) has been central to the area's culture for millennia. From Merovingian quarries that did a booming trade in Christian sarcophagi, to medieval and Renaissance châteaux, to modern restaurants, mushroom farms and wine cellars ensconced in one-time cave dwellings, this tour offers an intro to local troglodyte culture and opportunities to savour the region's renowned gastronomy and wines.

TRIP HIGHLIGHT

① Saumur

Start your tour in sophisticated Saumur, one of the Loire Valley's great gastronomic and viticultural centres.

For an overview of the region's wines and wine producers, along with free tastings, head to the riverside **Maison des Vins** (☏02 41 38 45 83; 7 quai Carnot; ☻10am-1pm & 3-7pm Mon-Sat & 10am-1pm Sun Jun-Aug, 10am-12.30pm & 2.30-6pm Tue-Sat early Apr-May, Sep & Oct). Next, explore Saumur's other claim

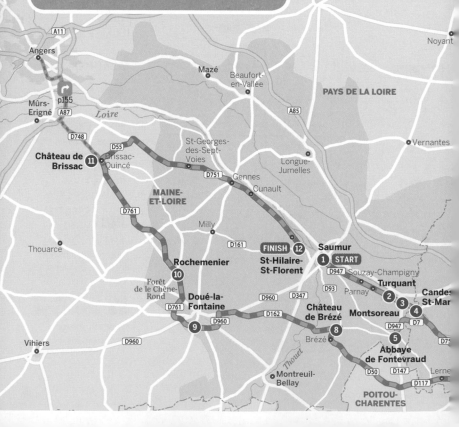

to fermented fame at **Distillerie Combier** (☎02 41 40 23 02; www.combier. fr; 48 rue Beaurepaire; tours adult/child €4/free; ⏱tours 10.30am, 2.30pm & 4.30pm Tue-Sun Apr-Oct, plus Mon Jun-Sep, shop 10am-12.30pm & 2-6pm or 7pm Tue-Sat, plus Sun Apr-Oct & Dec, plus Mon Jun-Sep & Dec), where triple sec liqueur was invented in 1834; tours of the still-functioning distillery offer an engaging, behind-the-scenes look at vintage architecture by Eiffel, gleaming century-old copper stills and fragrant vats full of Haitian bitter

oranges. Around town, make sure to try Saumur's iconic aperitif, *soupe saumuroise* – made with triple sec, lemon juice and sparkling wine.

Other Saumur highlights include the fairy-tale, 13th-century **Château de Saumur** (☎02 41 40 24 40; www.chateau saumur.com; adult/child €7/5; ⏱10am-1pm & 2-5.30pm Tue-Sun Apr-Oct, longer hours mid Jun–mid-Sep, closed Nov-Mar) and the **École Nationale d'Équitation** (☎02 41 53 50 60; www.cadrenoir.fr; av de l'École Nationale d'Équitation St-Hilaire-St-Florent; tours adult/child €8/6; ⏱tours Mon-Sat early Feb-early Nov), a renowned equestrian academy that has long trained France's Olympic teams and the Cadre Noir, an elite group of riding instructors. Take a one-hour guided visit or book ahead for one of the not-to-be-missed **Cadre Noir performances** (☎02 41 53 50 80; www.cadrenoir. fr; présentation adult/child €19/13, gala €30 65), 'horse ballets' (held in April, May, July, September and October) that show off

the equines' astonishing acrobatic capabilities and discipline.

🍴 🛏 p156

The Drive » Southeast of Saumur, the D947 meanders for 10km through the villages of Souzay-Champigny and Parnay, home to several tasting rooms, including **Château Villeneuve**, **Clos des Cordeliers**, **Château de Parnay** and **Château de Targé**. Troglodyte dwellings pockmark the cliff face to your right as a hilltop windmill signals your arrival in Turquant.

- - - - - - - - - -

TRIP HIGHLIGHT

❷ Turquant

Backed by chalk-coloured, cave-riddled cliffs, picturesque Turquant is a showcase for the creative adaptation of historic troglodyte dwellings. The town's 'main street' runs parallel to the D947, past a handful of art galleries, restaurants and other enterprises featuring designer windows and colourful doors wedged into the cliff face.

Turn right off the main road to **Le Troglo des Pommes Tapées** (☎02 41

LINK YOUR TRIP

1 Essential France
Head east to Chambord to join this country-wide circuit of iconic French sights.

11 Châteaux of the Loire
In Chinon, connect to this classic tour of the Loire Valley's most famous châteaux.

51 48 30; www.letroglodes
pommestapees.fr; 11 rue des
Ducs d'Anjou; adult/child
€6.50/4; ⊙10am-12.30pm &
2-6.30pm Apr-late Sep, 2-6pm
Sat & Sun Oct–mid-Nov), a
cave house whose owners
have revived the tradi-
tional art of oven-drying
and hand-flattening
apples into the artisa-
nal delicacy known as
pommes tapées. Guided
tours are followed by
tastings of dried apples.

Turquant's *tuffeau*
cliffs have also been
adapted for use as wine
cellars by producers such
as **La Grande Vignolle**
(📞02 41 38 16 44; www.
filliatreau.com; ⊙10am-6pm
Apr-Oct, 2-6pm Thu & Fri,
10am-6pm Sat & Sun Feb, Mar,
Nov & Dec) and **Domaine
des Amandiers** (www.
domaine-des-amandiers.com).

✗ 🏠 p156

The Drive » It's just a
3km hop, skip and jump to
Montsoreau along the D947 and
D751. Alternatively, follow the
narrow Route des Vins (parallel
and slightly south of the D947)
to the 16th-century windmill
Moulin de la Herpinière, then
continue into Montsoreau via
tiny Chemin de la Herpinière.

- - - - - - - - - - - - - - -

❸ Montsoreau

Beautifully perched on
the edge of the Loire, the
Château de Montsoreau
(📞02 41 67 12 60; www.
chateau-montsoreau.com;
passage du Marquis de Geoffre;
adult/child €9.20/5.50, adult
incl Fontevraud €15; ⊙10am-
7pm early Apr–mid-Nov, to

5pm mid-Dec–early Jan; 🅿)
was built in 1455 by one
of Charles VII's advisers
and later became famous
thanks to an Alexandre
Dumas novel *La Dame de
Monsoreau.* The crown-
ing attraction here is the
dazzling view from the
rooftop, extending from
the Loire's confluence
with the Vienne to the
domes and turrets of
Saumur. In the warm
season, enjoy free wine-
tasting in the castle's
cellars.

Nearby, the **Maison du
Parc** (📞02 41 38 38 88; www.
parc-loire-anjou-touraine.fr; 15
av de la Loire; ⊙9.30am-1pm
& 2-6pm or 7pm daily Apr-Sep,
Tue-Sun Oct, Sat & Sun Mar)
offers information on the
**Parc Naturel Régional
Loire-Anjou-Touraine**,
which protects 2530 sq
km of the surrounding
landscape.

The Drive » Follow the D751
1km southeast into Candes-
St-Martin, enjoying pretty river
views on your left.

- - - - - - - - - - - - - - -

❹ Candes-St-Martin

Recognised as one of
France's prettiest vil-
lages, Candes-St-Martin
occupies an idyllic spot
at the confluence of the
Vienne and Loire Rivers.
A long-time pilgrimage
site, the town's 12th- to
13th-century **church**
venerates the spot where
St Martin died in 397.
Wander down to the
benches overlooking the
waterfront along rue du

YURI TURKOV / SHUTTERSTOCK ©

Confluent (a pleasant
spot for a picnic), or follow the brown 'Panorama
Piétons' signs uphill from
the church for higher-
altitude perspectives.

The Drive » Snake 6km
south along the D751, D7
and D947, following signs for
Fontevraud-l'Abbaye. From the
D7/D947 junction, a worthwhile
800m detour leads northwest
to the artisanal soap factory
Savonnerie Martin de Candre.

- - - - - - - - - - - - - - -

❺ Abbaye Royale de
Fontevraud

The highlight of this
12th-century **abbey** (📞02
41 51 73 52; www.abbayede-
fontevraud.com; adult/child

Abbaye Royale de Fontevraud Twelfth-century abbey complex

€11/7.50, 1½hr audioguide €4.50; ⊙9.30am-6pm Apr-Oct, 10am-5pm Nov, Dec, Feb & Mar) complex is the vast but movingly simple **church**, notable for its soaring pillars, Romanesque domes and the polychrome stone tombs of four illustrious Plantagenets: Henry II, King of England (r 1154–89); his wife, Eleanor of Aquitaine (who retired to Fontevraud following Henry's death); their son Richard the Lionheart; and the wife of his brother King John, Isabelle of Angoulême. The **cloister** is surrounded by one-time dormito-ries, workrooms, prayer halls and a wonderful Gothic-vaulted refectory, while outside there are medieval-style gardens and a multi-chimneyed kitchen.

The Drive ›› Backtrack 5km to the D751 and follow it 13km southeast and then north toward Chinon. Immediately after crossing the Vienne River, take the D749 and head east 3km, paralleling the riverfront into town.

TRIP HIGHLIGHT

⑥ Chinon

Renowned for its towering hilltop château, site of Joan of Arc's fateful first encounter with Charles VII (1429), and charming medieval quarter, the riverside village of Chinon is home to several fine restaurants, making it a prime candidate for an overnight stay. For customised half-day tours of adjacent AOC wine-growing areas, including Chinon, Cravant, Saumur-Champigny, St-Nicolas-de-Bourgeuil and Touraine, contact bilingual Chinon native **Alain Caillemer** (☏02 47 95 87 59; www.loirewinery tours.com; half-day tours per couple €85).

✗ ⮞ p147, p157

The Drive » Zigzag 8km southwest of Chinon through lovely rolling farmland along the D749A, D751E, D759, D24 and D117, following signs for La Devinière.

❼ Musée Rabelais

Set among fields and vineyards with rural sweeping views, **La Devinière** farmstead is the birthplace of François Rabelais – doctor, Franciscan friar, theoretician, author and all-around Renaissance man – and was the inspiration for his five satirical Gargantua and Pantagruel novels. The farmstead's rambling buildings hold the **Musée Rabelais** (La Devinière; ☎02 47 95 91 18; www.musee-rabelais.fr; 4 rue de la Devinière, Seuilly; adult/child €5.50/4.50; ☺10am-7pm Jul & Aug, 10am-12.30pm & 2-6pm Apr-Sep, to 5pm Oct-Mar, closed Tue Oct-Mar), featuring early editions of Rabelais's work and a charcoal portrait of the author by Matisse.

The Drive » Follow the D117 west through the gorgeous village of Seuilly, home to an 11th-century abbey. After 8km, cross the D147 and continue another 13km west-northwest along the D48, D50, D310, D110 and D93 into Brézé.

❽ Château de Brézé

Off-the-beaten-track **Château de Brézé** (☎02 41 51 60 15; www.chateaudebreze.com; 2 rue du Château, Brézé; adult/child €11.50/9.50, incl

tour €14.50/12.50; ☺10am-6pm or 7pm Feb-Dec) sits on top of a network of subterranean rooms and passages; a self-guided tour takes you to kitchens, wine cellars, defensive bastions and a troglodyte dwelling from the time of the Norman invasions (11th century). Above ground, much of the U-shaped château dates from the 19th century, as do the many intricately painted neo-Gothic and neo-Renaissance interiors. Don't miss the top floor of the West Tower, used in the 1800s as quarters for lower-ranking servants

The Drive » Chart a meandering 22km course through relatively flat farm country into Doué-la-Fontaine via the D93, D162, D163 and D960.

❾ Doué-la-Fontaine

At the southeastern edge of this small industrial town, stop to visit the fascinating **Troglodytes et Sarcophages** (☎06 77 77 06 94; www.troglo-sarcophages.fr; 1 rue de la Croix Mordret; adult/child €4.90/3.30; ☺2.30-7pm daily Jun-Aug, Sat & Sun May, tours 3pm daily Feb, Easter, All Saints Day & Christmas school holidays), a Merovingian quarry where sarcophagi were produced from the 6th to the 9th centuries and exported via the Loire as far as England and Belgium. Reserve ahead for a 90-minute lantern-lit tour.

Nearby, **Les Perrières** (☎02 41 59 71 29; www.les-perrieres.com; 545 rue des Perrières; adult/child €7/4.50; ☺10am-12.30pm & 2-6pm Tue-Sun Mar-Oct) is a vast network of 18th- and 19th-century stone quarries sometimes called the 'cathedral caves' because of their soaring sloping walls, said to resemble Gothic arches.

The Drive » Skirt the southern edge of Doué-la-Fontaine via the D960 for 4km, then continue 5km north on the D761 to the Rochemenier exit. Follow signs the remaining 1.5km into Rochemenier.

TRIP HIGHLIGHT

❿ Rochemenier

Surrounded by peaceful countryside, the museum-village of **Rochemenier** (☎02 41 59 18 15; www.troglodyte.fr; 14 rue du Musée; adult/child €6.10/3.70; ☺9.30am-7pm Apr-Sep, 10am-6pm Tue-Sun Oct-Nov & Feb-Mar) preserves the remains of two troglodyte farmsteads that were inhabited until the 1930s, complete with houses, stables and an underground chapel. Throughout the complex, farm tools and photos of former residents evoke the hard-working spirit and simple pleasures that defined life underground for many generations. Displays in the last room focus on international cave-dwelling cultures, including places as far afield as China and Turkey.

🛏 p157

DETOUR: ANGERS

Start: ⑪ Château de Brissac

Looming above the river, Angers's forbidding medieval castle – historic seat of the once-mighty counts and dukes of Anjou – is ringed by moats, 2.5m-thick walls made of dark schist, and 17 massive round towers. Inside is one of Europe's great medieval masterpieces, the stunning **Tenture de l'Apocalypse** (Apocalypse tapestry), a 104m-long series of tapestries commissioned in 1375 to illustrate the story of the final battle between good and evil, as prophesied in the Bible's Book of Revelations.

Just outside the château, taste and learn about the region's AOC wines at the **Maison des Vin d'Angers**. Afterwards stroll through Angers' pedestrianised centre, where you'll find cafes, restaurants, excellent art museums and the whimsical **Maison d'Adam** (place Ste-Croix), a remarkably well-preserved medieval house decorated with bawdy carved figurines.

To get here, head 28km northwest from Brissac on the D748, A87 and N260, following signs for Angers-Centre.

The Drive » Return to the D761, then follow it 15km northwest to Brissac-Quincé, where signs direct you 1.5km further to the château.

- - - - - - - - - - - - - -

⑪ Château de Brissac

This imposing, seven-storey **château** (📞02 41 91 22 21; www.chateau-brissac.fr; Brissac-Quincé; adult/child incl tour €10/4.50, gardens only €5/free; ⊙tours 10am-noon & 2-5.30pm Wed-Mon Apr-Oct, 10am-5.30pm daily Jul & Aug, plus 2pm & 4pm Wed-Mon Feb & Christmas school holidays) – France's tallest castle – has 204 rooms, many of them sumptuously furnished with antique furniture, Flemish tapestries and twinkling chandeliers. The serene 70-hectare gardens have 19th-century stables, and vineyards boasting three AOC vintages.

The Drive » Follow the D55 6km northeast, then wind 15km east-southeast on the D751 through forests and sunflower fields to rejoin the Loire at Gennes. From here, a particularly scenic stretch of the D751 follows the Loire's sandy banks 12km to St-Hilaire-St-Florent. Along the way, the villages of St-Georges-des-Sept-Voies (p157) and Chênehutte-Trèves-Cunault offer enticing eating and sleeping options.

- - - - - - - - - - - - - -

⑫ St-Hilaire-St-Florent

This western suburb of Saumur is home to a number of wineries and cave-based attractions. At the **Musée du Champignon** (📞02 41 50 31 55; www.musee-du-champignon.com; rte de Gennes; adult/child €8.40/6; ⊙10am-6pm early Feb–mid-Nov), learn oodles of mushroom facts and trivia as you wander deep into a cave where countless varieties of fungi are cultivated. Almost next door, **Pierre et Lumière** (📞02 41 50 70 04; www.pierre-et-lumiere.com; rte de Gennes; adult/child €8.40/6; ⊙10am-6pm or 7pm Feb-Nov) displays intricate limestone sculptures of famous Loire Valley monuments.

East towards Saumur, tasting rooms invite you to sample local AOC vintages, including Crémant de Loire and Saumur Brut; well-established wineries along this route include **Ackerman** (www.ackerman.fr), **Gratien et Meyer** (www.gratienmeyer.com), **Langlois-Château** (📞02 41 40 21 40; www.langlois-chateau.fr; 3 rue Léopold Palustre; tours adult/child €5/free; ⊙shop 10am-12.30pm & 2-6.30pm Apr–mid-Oct) and **Veuve Amiot** (www.veuveamiot.fr).

Eating & Sleeping

Saumur ❶

✖ Le Pot de Lapin   Modern French €€

(☎02 41 67 12 86; 35 rue Rabelais; mains €12-22; ◷noon-2pm & 7-9.30pm Tue-Sat) Jazz wafts from the cheery dining room, decorated with tools of the winemaker's art, through the wine bar and onto the street-side terrace as Chef Olivier works the tables, proposing perfect wine pairings. Start with a local bubbly, then move on to foie gras with onion-and-fruit chutney or monkfish with cream. Situated 1km southeast along the river from the centre.

✖ L'Escargot   Traditional French €€

(☎02 41 51 20 88; 30 rue du Maréchal Leclerc; lunch/dinner menus from €20/30; ◷noon-1.30pm Thu, Fri, Sun & Mon, 7.30-9.30pm Thu-Mon; 🛜) A Saumur fixture for over half a century, this place is all about traditional recipes done really well, like *escargots* with 'three butters' (flavored with herbs, walnuts and Roquefort) or *carré d'agneau rôti à l'ail et au thym* (loin of lamb roasted with garlic and thyme).

✖ Le Gambetta   Gastronomy €€€

(☎02 41 67 66 66; www.restaurantlegambetta. com; 12 rue Gambetta; lunch menus €28, other menus €35-109; ◷noon-1.30pm Tue & Thu-Sun, 7.15-9pm Tue & Thu-Sat) This is one to write home about: a truly outstanding restaurant combining refined elegance and knock-your-socks-off creative French cuisine. Some menus include wine pairings perfectly chosen to complement the parade of gorgeously presented dishes, punctuated by surprise treats from the kitchen.

🛏 Hôtel de Londres   Hotel €

(☎02 41 51 23 98; www.lelondres.com; 48 rue d'Orléans; d €74-114, q €125, apt €140; P ❄ @ 🛜) Built as an *hôtel de grand standing* (luxury hotel) and named in honour of the British capital in 1837, this family-run hotel – entirely renovated in 2016 – has 27 spacious rooms decorated in jolly colours and two family-friendly apartments, all with big windows and gleaming bathrooms. Lobby perks include afternoon tea (€2.50) and a well-stocked BD (comics) library. No lift (yet).

🛏 Château de Beaulieu   B&B €€

(☎02 41 50 83 52; www.chateaudebeaulieu. fr; 98 rte de Montsoreau; d incl breakfast €100-130, d/q €150/180; ◷mid-Mar–mid-Nov; P 🛜 🐾) Irish expats Mary and Conor welcome you to their 1727 château with a glass of *crémant de Saumur* (sparkling wine). Rooms are imaginatively and comfortably done up and the mood among gregarious guests is one of extended family. Sun yourself by the pool (next to the vineyard) or play billiards in the grand salon. Situated 2.5km southeast of Saumur.

🛏 Château de Verrières   Heritage Hotel €€€

(☎02 41 38 05 15; www.chateau-verrieres. com; 53 rue d'Alsace; r €180-240, ste €295-345; ◷closed mid-Jan–mid-Feb; P @ 🛜 🐾) This splendid 1890 château, surrounded by a 1.6-hectare English park, is sumptuous throughout, with wood-panelled salons, marble fireplaces, original artwork, antique writing desks and cast-iron bathtubs. Some of the 10 bedrooms, each different, offer views of the sun rising over Saumur's château.

Turquant ❷

✖ L'Hélianthe   Modern French €€

(☎02 44 10 12 39; www.restaurant-helianthe.fr; ruelle Antoine Cristal; mains €16; ◷noon-2pm & 7-8.45pm Thu-Tue Apr–mid-Nov, Sat & Sun winter) Tucked into a cliff behind Turquant's *mairie* (town hall), this atmospheric restaurant has a hearty menu firmly based on local products and classic French flavours.

🛏 Demeure de la Vignole   Design Hotel €€

(☎02 41 53 67 00; www.demeure-vignole. com; 3 impasse Marguerite d'Anjou; d €130-165, 4-person ste €270-290; ◷closed mid-Nov–mid-Mar; 🛜 🐾) This swish hotel has 12 richly decorated rooms, five of them in caves. The 15m swimming pool is carved into the rock face, too. Very homey, and not just for hobbits. A wonderful change from the ordinary.

Chinon ⑥

✖ Au Chapeau
Rouge   Gastronomy €€

(✆02 47 98 08 08; www.auchapeaurouge.fr;
49 place du Général de Gaulle, aka place de la
Fontaine; lunch menus €22.50, dinner menus
€29-58; ⊙noon-1pm Wed-Sun, 7.30-8.45pm
Tue-Sat; 🛜) Secluded behind a red-and-gold
awning, this sparkling and very elegant eatery
makes top-quality French dishes using local
products – look for Loire fish, lamb, asparagus
and saffron, Touraine truffles, and Ste-Maure-
de-Touraine, a delicious chèvre. In winter
specialities include melt-in-your-mouth hare
and foie-gras terrine. Has vegetarian options
from June to August.

✖ Les Années 30   French €€

(✆02 47 93 37 18; www.lesannees30.com;
78 rue Haute St-Maurice; lunch/dinner menus
from €18/27; ⊙12.15-1.45pm & 7.30-9.30pm
Thu-Mon) Expect the kind of meal you came
to France to eat, with exquisite attention to
flavours and detail, served in relaxed intimacy.
The menu ranges from traditional duck fillet to
unusual choices such as pan-fried venison fillet
with redcurrant sauce. The interior dining room
is golden-lit downstairs and cool blue upstairs;
in summer dine outside under the pergola.

🛏 Hôtel de France   Hotel €€

(✆02 47 93 33 91; www.bestwestern-
hoteldefrance-chinon.com; 47 place du Général
de Gaulle, aka place de la Fontaine; d €99-139,
apt €175; ❈🛜) Run impeccably by the same
couple since 1979, this Best Western–affiliated
hotel, right in the centre of town, has 30 rooms
arrayed around an inner courtyard. Tastefully
decorated in a contemporary style, many have
views of the château – as does the magnificent,
flowery terrace on the roof. Offers enclosed
bicycle parking. No lift.

Rochemenier ⑩

🛏 Les Délices
de la Roche   B&B €

(✆02 41 50 15 26; www.delicesdelaroche.com;
16 rue du Musée, Rochemenier; d €60; 🛜)
Friendly young hosts Henri and Sabrina rent
out five simple, spacious rooms in the peaceful
countryside near Rochemenier's troglodyte
village. You can dine at the restaurant (menus
from €22.90) or at their table d'hôte (adults €22,
children €1 per year of their age; reserve ahead).

St-Georges-des-Sept-Voies ⑪

✖ Auberge la
Sansonnière   French €€

(✆02 41 57 57 70; www.auberge-sansonniere.
com; St-Georges-des-Sept-Voies; menus €25-58;
⊙12.15-1.30pm Tue-Sun, 7.30-9pm Tue-Sat)
Surrounded by sunflower fields, this stone-built
country inn, with a wood-beamed dining room,
serves exquisite traditional French menus that
evolve with the seasons and focus on fresh local
products, including fish and vegetables.

Volcanoes of the Auvergne

13

Green pastures and volcanic scenery feature on this tour of the Parc Naturel Régional des Volcans d'Auvergne. Get ready for great hiking, hearty mountain meals and acclaimed cheeses.

TRIP HIGHLIGHTS

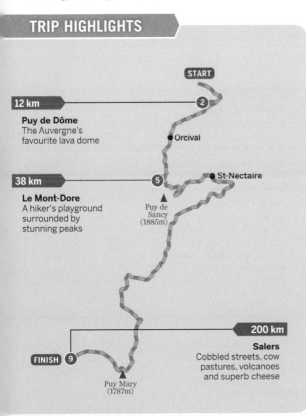

START

12 km

Puy de Dôme
The Auvergne's favourite lava dome

● Orcival

● St-Nectaire

38 km

Le Mont-Dore
A hiker's playground surrounded by stunning peaks

▲ Puy de Sancy (1885m)

200 km

Salers
Cobbled streets, cow pastures, volcanoes and superb cheese

FINISH ⑨

▲ Puy Mary (1787m)

**4 DAYS
200KM / 125 MILES**

GREAT FOR...

BEST TIME TO GO
May to September for warm weather and snow-free trails.

ESSENTIAL PHOTO
The symmetrical crags of Roches Tuilière and Sanadoire framing the lush greenery below Col de Guéry.

BEST FOR FAMILIES
The volcanic theme park Vulcania.

13 Volcanoes of the Auvergne

Aeons ago, Europe's biggest volcanoes shaped the landscape of south-central France, blowing their tops with awe-inspiring force. On this trip you'll experience the wild beauty of the Auvergne's vestigial volcanoes — Puy de Dôme, Puy de Sancy and Puy Mary — but you'll also discover a tamer Auvergne whose picturesque patchwork of eroded cinder cones and verdant pastures is home to family-friendly hiking trails, symphonies of cowbells and some of France's finest cheese.

① Vulcania

For a dramatic introduction to volcano-land, start at this educational, highly entertaining **theme park** 15km west of Clermont-Ferrand. The brainchild of two French geologists, it has such highlights as the dynamic 3D film **Awakening of the Auvergne Giants**, depicting volcanic eruptions complete with air blasts and water spray, and the **Cité des Enfants** (Kids' City), with activities specially geared towards three- to seven-year-olds.

The Drive » Head southeast 7km along the D941 to the D942, where full-on views of Puy de Dôme beckon you 2km southwest to the junction with the D68 at the mountain's base.

TRIP HIGHLIGHT

② Puy de Dôme

Towering above the surrounding landscape, the symmetrical volcanic cone of **Puy de Dôme** (1464m) was already an iconic Auvergnat landmark long before the Romans built a temple to Mercury on its summit in the 1st century. Hop aboard spiffy cog railway the **Panoramique des Dômes** (www.panoramiquedesdomes.fr; adult/child one-way €9.80/4.90, return €12.30/6.20; ◷10am-7pm Apr-Jun & Sep, 9am-9pm Jul & Aug, 10am-5pm Wed-Sun Oct-Mar) to reach the top; or if you're feeling fit, walk up the steep 45-minute **Chemin des Muletiers** footpath. Either way, you'll

be rewarded with stunning views of the **Chaîne des Puys**, a 40km expanse of extinct cinder cones stretching to the horizon. The summit is also prime hang-gliding territory; operators such as **Aero Parapente** (☎06 61 24 11 45; www.aeroparapente.fr; €150; ◷Feb-Oct) will take you soaring over the surrounding countryside for €80.

The Drive » The 20km drive to Orcival skirts Puy de Dôme's southern flanks on the D942, then continues southwest on the D216 and D27, passing through increasingly hilly and pastoral countryside dotted with lovely stone and slate barns.

---

3 Orcival

Backed by a leafy green hillside and bisected by a rushing stream, photogenic Orcival clusters around a gorgeous Romanesque church that houses one of the

LINK YOUR TRIP

35 Cave Art of the Vézère Valley

Detour three hours west of Le Mont-Dore to discover France's oldest cave art.

36 Dordogne's Fortified Villages

Explore centuries-old castles and fortified villages along the Dordogne River, three hours downstream from Le Mont-Dore.

Auvergne's most famous *Vierges noires* (black Madonnas, icons typical of the region). An object of veneration throughout the year, she's paraded through the streets with special fanfare on Assumption Day (15 August). The town also springs to life on Saturday mornings in summer, when a colourful market fills the main square. In summertime, head 2km north of town to visit the elegant grounds of **Château de Cordès** (☏04 73 21 15 89; www.chateau-cordes-orcival.com; garden & chateau/ garden only €8/4, child free; ☺10am-noon & 2-6pm daily Jul-Aug, plus Sun afternoons Jun), laid out by Versailles garden designer Le Nôtre.

🛏 p165

The Drive » The D27 climbs 8km through verdant hills and evergreen forest to a spectacular viewpoint just before **Col de Guéry** (1268m), where the dramatic volcanic crags **Roche Tuilière** (1288m) and **Roche Sanadoire** (1286m) rise in symmetry from the land below.

4 Col de Guéry

This mountain pass, flanked by the Auvergne's highest lake, offers varied opportunities for outdoor recreation; check in with the **Centre Montagnard Cap Guéry** (☏04 73 65 20 09; www.capguery.com; ☺Dec-Mar) for maps of the wild hiking terrain. Chilly **Lac de Guéry** (1268m) offers excellent fishing for trout and perch. Purchase fishing licences (€25) at the Auberge du Lac de Guéry on the lakeshore.

🛏 p165

The Drive » Spellbinding mountain views unfold as you approach the Massif du Sancy, a wall of peaks that's often snowcapped late into the spring. A sinuous 9km drive along the D983 and D996 drops you straight into downtown Le Mont-Dore.

GUY CHRISTIAN / HEMIS.FR / GETTY IMAGES ©

TRIP HIGHLIGHT

5 Le Mont-Dore

Ringed by rugged peaks at the heart of the Parc Naturel Régional des Volcans d'Auvergne, this historic spa town makes a great base for exploring the surrounding high country. A **téléphérique** (one way/return adult €7.30/9.70, child €5.50/7.30; ☺9am-12.10pm & 1.30-5pm mid-Nov–Sep, 9am-6pm Jul & Aug) whisks hikers through a landscape of precipitous crags to the foot of **Puy de Sancy** (1885m), the tallest peak in the Massif Central mountain range; across town, a tortoise-slow but creakily atmospheric 1890s-vintage **funiculaire** (rue René Cassin; one way/return adult €4.50/5.90, child €3.70/4.50; ☺10am-12.10pm & 2-5.40pm Wed-Sun May-early Oct, to 6.40pm daily Jul & Aug) lumbers up to Les Capucins, an upland plateau (1245m) where well-marked trails fan out in all directions. Several fine hikes and mountain-biking routes also start in downtown Le Mont-Dore, including the **Chemin de la Grande Cascade**, which leads to a 32m-high waterfall.

For route guides and high-resolution topo maps, visit Le Mont-Dore's tourist office, in a riverside park downtown. Nearby streets are filled with outdoors-oriented shops and purveyors of local charcuterie and cheeses such as **La Petite Boutique du Bougnat** (1 & 4 rue Montlosier; ☺9am-12.30pm & 2.30-7pm mid-Dec–Oct).

✖ 🛏 p165

Parc Natural Régional des Volcans d'Auvergne Hiking in the mountains

The Drive » Begin with a spectacular traverse of 1451m **Col de la Croix St-Robert**, passing through 17km of wide-open high country along the D36. Next trundle along the D996 for 12km, enjoying pretty views of **Lac de Chambon**, popular with boaters, hikers and campers, and Murol's hilltop castle, before reaching St-Nectaire.

- - - - - - - - - - - - -

6 St-Nectaire

Tiny St-Nectaire is famous for its 12th-century Romanesque church, stunningly set against a mountain backdrop, and its herds of happy bovines, who make this one of the Auvergne's dairy capitals. From the upper town (St-Nectaire-le-Haut), climb 3km on the D150 to **La Ferme Bellonte** (www.st-nectaire. com; rue du 10 août 1944, Farges; ☺ milking 6-7am & 3.15-4.15pm, cheese-making 7-8am & 5-6pm; 👪), a working farm that offers free milking and cheese-making demonstrations twice daily, plus guided tours of the caves across the street where the cheese is aged.

🛏 p165

The Drive » Follow the D996 7km downstream to tiny Rivallet, then head southwest 15km on the D978 into Besse, watching on the left for the medieval cliff dwellings Les Grottes de Jonas, which include a chapel, spiral staircases and a manor house carved directly into the rock.

- - - - - - - - - - - - -

7 Besse-et-Ste-Anataise

Basalt-brick cottages, cobbled lanes and a lovely old belfry are reason enough to visit this pretty mountain village, but hikers and mountain bikers will also appreciate the fine network of trails surrounding **Lac Pavin**, a crater lake 6km west of town. For a taste of mountain culture, visit during the **Transhumance de la Vierge**

CHEESE COUNTRY

The Auvergne produces some of France's finest cheeses, including five Appellation d'Origine Protégée (AOP) varieties: the semihard, cheddar-like Cantal and nutty Salers, both made from the milk of high-pasture cows; St-Nectaire, rich, flat and semisoft; Fourme d'Ambert, a mild, smooth blue cheese; and Bleu d'Auvergne, a powerful, creamy blue cheese with a Roquefort-like flavour.

To taste them on their home turf, follow stretches of the signposted **Route des Fromages** (www.fromages-aop-auvergne.com), which links local farms and producers. A downloadable map is available on the website.

Local cheeses figure strongly in many traditional Auvergnat dishes, including *aligot* (puréed potato with garlic and Tomme or Cantal cheese) and *truffade* (sliced, diced or mashed potatoes with Cantal cheese), usually served with a huge helping of *jambon d'Auvergne* (local ham).

Noire, when local cows are herded to rich upland pastures on 21 July and back downhill in late September, accompanied by street fairs and fireworks.

The Drive » Leave the Massif du Sancy behind and head south 82km towards the wilder, less populated Monts du Cantal. A curvy course through farmland and river valleys along the D978 and D678 leads to a supremely scenic, sustained climb along the D62 and D680, bringing you face to face with Puy Mary, the southernmost of the Auvergne's three classic peaks.

❽ Puy Mary

Barely wide enough to accommodate parked cars, the vertiginous mountain pass of Pas de Peyrol (1589m) hugs the base of pyramid-shaped Puy Mary (1787m), the Cantal's most charismatic peak.

A trail, complete with staircases for the steeper sections, leads to the summit (about one hour round-trip). Find walking routes for all abilities on www.puymary.fr.

The Drive » The 20km descent along the D680 switchbacks steeply through a wonderland of high-country scenery before plunging into fragrant evergreen forest and following a long ridgeline into Salers.

TRIP HIGHLIGHT

❾ Salers

Pretty Salers perches on a hilltop surrounded by fields full of long-horned brown cattle that produce the region's eponymous AOP cheese. With a compact core of 16th-century stone buildings and long views up towards **Puy Mary**, it's a relaxing

place to linger. From central place Tyssandier d'Escous, you can walk up to the **belvédère** for panoramic views, or descend into the town's cobbled streets filled with shops selling cheese and locally made knives. Spare some time to peer within a former Knights Templar house, now the **Musée de Salers** (☏04 71 40 75 97; rue des Templiers; adult/child €5/free; ☺10am-12.30 & 2-5.30pm Mon-Thu & Sun, 2-5.30pm Sat mid-Apr–mid-Oct), for local history in an enigmatic setting. Day hikes range from an easy 75-minute circuit of the stone-walled pastures surrounding town to high-mountain rambles through wide-open country around the base of 1592m-high **Puy Violent**.

 p165

Eating & Sleeping

Orcival ❸

🛏 Hôtel Notre Dame　　　Hotel €

(📞04 73 65 82 02; www.hotelnotredame-orcival.
com; s/d/f €48/59/63; ⊘Feb-Dec; 🛜) Expect
an effusive welcome at this delightful family-run
hotel, right in front of Orcival's mighty basilica.
Five of its seven clean, comfortable rooms have
glorious views overlooking the basilica. Family
rooms are vast, and each has a kettle, TV and
wi-fi. Generous breakfasts (€9.50) consist
of local cheeses, homemade jams, plus fresh
bread and cakes.

Col de Guéry ❹

🛏 Auberge du Lac de Guéry　　Hotel €

(📞04 73 65 02 76; www.auberge-lac-guery.
fr; d €64; ⊘Feb–mid-Oct; 🅿🛜) In a scenic
position right on the lakeshore, this comfortable
inn has small, simple rooms and unbeatable
access to hiking and fishing. Spare time for
the fine country restaurant (menus €23-45,
summer only). The kindly owner can help
arrange fishing permits.

Le Mont-Dore ❺

🍴 La Golmotte　　Auvergnat Cuisine €€

(📞04 73 65 05 77; www.aubergelagolmotte.
com; rte D996; menus €18-39; ⊘noon-2pm
Wed-Sun, 7-9pm Wed-Sat) The excellent regional
cuisine at this mountainside inn is worth the
3km trek up the main road towards Orcival and
Murol. Tuck into mouthwatering country pâté
sweetened with onion relish, bream lavished
in tarragon butter, and Auvergnat classics like
truffade and *pounti* (a prune-studded savoury
cake). La Golmotte has four simple but snug
chambres d'hôte (doubles from €58).

🛏 Grand Hôtel　　　Hotel €

(📞04 73 65 02 64; www.hotel-mont-dore.com;
2 rue Meynadier; s €53-63, d €63-73, q €93-103;

⊘mid-Dec–mid-Nov; 🅿🛜) The romantic
ambiance of this turreted 1850 hotel is amply
delivered within its rooms, which have a sharp
modern design and comfortable wrought-iron
beds. The best have balconies looking towards
the mountains. Meanwhile time spent in the spa
(€5) is the perfect balm for calf muscles that
sting from exertion up in the mountains.

St-Nectaire ❻

🛏 Villa du Pont Romain　　B&B €

(📞04 73 88 41 62; http://lavilladupontromain.
free.fr; 6 av Alphonse Cellier, St-Nectaire; s/d/q
€40/55/85 incl breakfast; 🅿🛜) This three-
room B&B is an excellent bargain, both for the
quality of its spacious lodgings and the effusive
welcome from its owners. There is a chalet
vibe to the nostalgic pictures and antique skis
bedecking the lounge room, which has a pool
table and mini-library, while the rooms are
wooden floored and wonderfully cosy, with the
largest sleeping four people.

Salers ❾

🍴 La Diligence　　Auvergnat €

(📞04 71 40 75 39, www.ladiligence-salers.com;
rue de Beffroi; mains €15; ⊘noon-3.30pm &
7-10.30pm Tue-Sat late-Mar–Oct) Wear your
loose pants for filling regional cuisine like
boudin noir (blood sausage), *pounti* (a prune-
studded savoury cake) and expertly cooked
omelettes at this welcoming restaurant in the
centre of Salers.

🛏 Hôtel Saluces　　　Hotel €€

(📞04 71 40 70 82; www.hotel-salers.fr; rue de la
Martille; d/tr/q from €78-95/125/150; ⊘mid-
Dec–mid-Nov; @🛜) Half a block below the
square, the delightful Hôtel Saluces offers nine
spacious and individually decorated rooms with
modern amenities, in an ancient stone building
with a sunny interior courtyard. There's an
adjoining creperie and *salon de thé* to unwind in.

Medieval Burgundy

14

Fortified hill towns, medieval monasteries, exquisite Romanesque capitals and multicoloured tiled roofs share the stage with rolling vineyards and verdant hiking trails on this idyllic meander.

TRIP HIGHLIGHTS

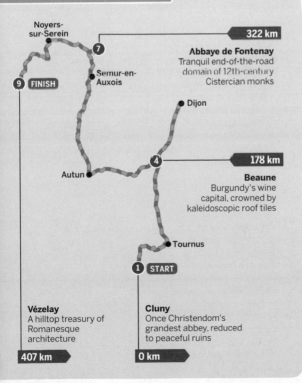

Noyers-sur-Serein

7

322 km

Abbaye de Fontenay
Tranquil end-of-the-road domain of 12th-century Cistercian monks

Semur-en-Auxois

9 **FINISH**

Dijon

4

178 km

Beaune
Burgundy's wine capital, crowned by kaleidoscopic roof tiles

Autun

Tournus

1 **START**

Vézelay
A hilltop treasury of Romanesque architecture

407 km

Cluny
Once Christendom's grandest abbey, reduced to peaceful ruins

0 km

6 DAYS
407KM / 252 MILES

GREAT FOR...

BEST TIME TO GO
From May wildflower season through to the October wine harvest.

ESSENTIAL PHOTO
Vézelay's sinuous sweep of stone houses crowned by a hilltop basilica.

BEST FOR OUTDOORS
The riverside walking trails around Noyers-sur-Serein.

emur-en-Auxois Medieval town on the Armançon River

14 Medieval Burgundy

Between the Middle Ages and the 15th century, Burgundy saw a tremendous flowering of ecclesiastical architecture, from Cistercian and Benedictine monasteries to Romanesque basilicas, coupled with active patronage of the arts by the powerful dukes of Burgundy. This medieval meander shows you all the highlights, while mixing in opportunities for wine tasting and for walking in the gorgeous rolling countryside that makes Burgundy one of France's most appealing regions.

TRIP HIGHLIGHT

1 Cluny

Built between 1088 and 1130, the monumental Benedictine **Église Abbatiale** (Abbey Church; ☏03 85 59 15 93; www.cluny-abbaye.fr; place du 11 Août 1944; combined ticket with Musée d'Art et d'Archéologie adult/child €9.50/free; ⊗9.30am-7pm Jul & Aug, to 6pm Apr-Jun & Sep, to 5pm Oct-Mar) – Christendom's largest church until the construction of St Peter's in Rome – once held sway over 1100 monasteries stretching from Poland to Portugal. Today you'll need a good imagination to conjure up the abbey's 12th-century glory, but its fragmentary remains, bordered by the giant shade trees of the grassy **Parc Abbatial**, are a delightful place to wander.

Get oriented at the **Musée d'Art et d'Archéologie** (rue de l'Abbatiale; combined ticket with Église Abbatiale adult/child €9.50/free; ⊗9.30am-7pm Jul & Aug, to 6pm Apr-Jun & Sep, to 5pm Oct-Mar), with its scale model of the Cluny complex and 3D 'virtual tour' of the abbey's original medieval layout, then climb the **Tour des Fromages** (rue Mercière; €2, combined ticket with Église Abbatiale & Musée d'Art et d'Archéologie adult/child €11/1; ⊗9.30am-6.30pm May-Sep, shorter hours Oct-Apr) for a bird's-eye view of the abbey's remains,

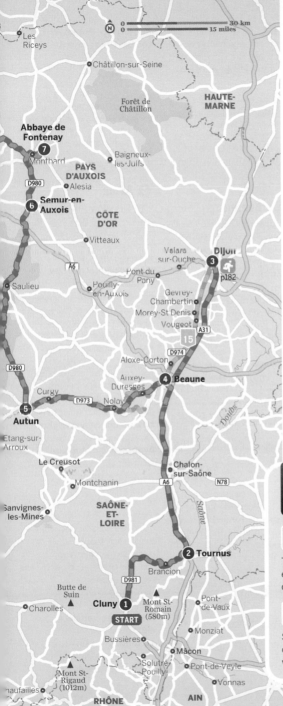

including the striking octagonal Clocher de l'Eau Bénite (Tower of the Holy Water) and the Farinier (Granary), where eight splendid capitals from the original church are displayed.

✕ ⨼ p173

The Drive » Head 13km north along the D981 to Cormatin, with its Renaissance-style château, then squiggle 25km east along the D14 past Chapaize's 11th-century Église St-Martin, Ozenay's château and the medieval hill town of Brancion before descending into Tournus.

- - - - - - - - - - - - - - - - -

② Tournus

Tournus' superb 10th- to 12th-century Benedictine abbey, **Abbatiale St-Philibert** (www.tournus.fr/le-site-abbatial-de-saint-philibert; ⊘8am-6pm), makes a striking first impression, with its austere Roman-esque façade peeking out through a medieval stone gate flanked by

LINK YOUR TRIP

11 Châteaux of the Loire

Three hours west of Vézelay, explore the Loire Valley's classic châteaux.

15 Route des Grands Crus

Switch gears in Beaune to discover Burgundy's best wines.

LOIRE VALLEY & CENTRAL FRANCE **14** MEDIEVAL BURGUNDY

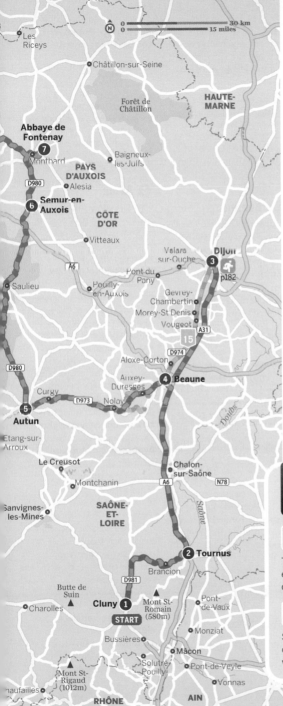

169

twin rounded towers; its apse holds an extremely rare 12th-century **floor mosaic** of the calendar and the zodiac, discovered by chance in 2002. The medieval centre also boasts fine restaurants – good for a lunch stop.

The Drive » From Tournus, zip 96km straight up the A6 and A31 to Dijon.

- - - - - - - - - - - - - -

❸ Dijon

Long-time capital of medieval Burgundy, Dijon was the seat of power for a series of enlightened dukes who presided over the region's 14th- and 15th-century golden age, filling the city with fine art and architecture, and a wonderful medieval centre, best explored on foot (p182).

Topping the list of must-see attractions are the 13th-century **Église Notre Dame** (place Notre-Dame; ☺8am-7pm) with its remarkable facade of pencil-thin columns and leering gargoyles; the **Palais des Ducs et des États de Bourgogne** (Palace of the Dukes & States of Burgundy; place de la Libéra-tion), the Burgundy dukes' monumental palace, which also houses Dijon's superb art museum, the **Musée des Beaux-Arts** (☎03 80 74 52 09; http://mba.dijon.fr; 1 rue Rameau; audio-guide €4, tours €6; ☺9.30am-6pm May-Oct, 10am-5pm Nov-Apr, closed Tue year-round); and the **historic mansions**

that line surrounding streets, especially rue des Forges, rue Verrerie, rue Vannerie and rue de la Chouette.

The Drive » Zip 44km south on the A31 to Beaune, or take the slower but much more scenic Route des Grands Crus (p175) through the Côte de Nuits vineyards.

- - - - - - - - - - - - - -

TRIP HIGHLIGHT

❹ Beaune

Burgundy's prosperous and supremely appealing viticultural capital, Beaune, is surrounded by vineyards producing an impressive array of appellations including Côte de Nuits and Côte de Beaune. Sipping local vintages at sunset on a cafe terrace here is one of France's great pleasures.

The architectural jewel of Beaune's historic centre is the **Hôtel-Dieu des Hospices de Beaune** (☎03 80 24 45 00; www.hospices-de-beaune.com; rue de l'Hôtel-Dieu; adult/child €7.50/3; ☺9am-6.30pm mid-Mar–mid-Nov, 9-11.30am & 2-5.30pm mid-Nov–mid-Mar), a 15th-century charity hospital topped by stunning turrets and pitched rooftops covered in multi-coloured tiles. Interior highlights include the barrel-vaulted **Grande Salle** with its dragon-embellished beams; an 18th-century **pharmacy** lined with ancient flasks; and the multipanelled 15th-century Flemish

masterpiece **Polyptych of the Last Judgement**.

✗ 🛏 p173, p181

The Drive » A super-scenic 49km drive along the D973 weaves southwest through gorgeous vineyard country, climbing past La Rochepot's striking 13th-century castle before turning west to Autun.

- - - - - - - - - - - - - -

❺ Autun

Two millennia ago, Autun (Augustodunum) was one of Roman Gaul's most important cities. Its next heyday came 1100 years later, when **Cathédrale St-Lazare** (place du Terreau; ☺cathedral 8am-7pm Sep-Jun, plus 9-11pm Jul & Aug, chapter room summer only) was built to house St Lazarus' sacred relics. Climb through the old city's narrow cobblestone streets to see the cathedral's fantastical Romanesque capitals and famous 12th-century **tympanum** depicting the Last Judgement, carved by Burgundy's master sculptor Gislebertus. Across the street, the **Musée Rolin** (☎03 85 52 09 76; 3 rue des Bancs; adult/child €6/free; ☺9.30am-noon & 1.30-6pm Wed-Mon Apr-Sep, shorter hours Mar, Oct & Nov, closed Dec-Feb) houses Gislebertus' precociously sensual masterpiece, the *Temptation of Eve,* alongside Gallo-Roman artefacts and modern paintings.

Roman treasures around town include the town gates **Porte**

Semur-en-Auxois Old town houses and towers

d'Arroux and **Porte St-André**, the 16,000-seat **Théâtre Romain**, the **Temple de Janus** and the **Pierre de Couhard**, a 27m-high remnant of a Gallo-Roman pyramid.

Autun is an excellent base for exploring nearby **Parc Naturel Régional du Morvan** (www.parcdumorvan .org). the park's website offers downloadable hiking, biking and equestrian itineraries.

The Drive » The D980 runs 70km north from Autun to Semur-en-Auxois; halfway along, there's a fine collection of Romanesque capitals at Saulieu's 12th-century Basilique de St-Andoche.

6 Semur-en-Auxois

Perched on a granite spur, surrounded by a hairpin turn in the Armançon River and guarded by four massive pink-granite bastions, Semur-en-Auxois was once an important religious centre boasting no fewer than six monasteries.

Pass through the two concentric medieval gates, **Porte Sauvigne** and **Porte Guillier**, onto pedestrianised **rue Buffon**; then meander west through the old town to **Promenade du Rempart** for panoramic views from atop Semur's medieval battlements. Be sure to stop in at historic **Pâtisserie Alexandre** (📞03 80 97 08 94; rue de la Liberté; ⏰7.30am-7pm Tue-Fri, 7am-1pm & 2-7pm Sat, to 1pm Sun) for some *granit rose de l'auxois* (a local pink confection laden with sugar, orange-infused chocolate, cherries, almonds and hazelnuts).

Semur is especially atmospheric at night, when the ramparts are illuminated, and around Pentecost, when the **Fêtes Médiévales du Roi Chaussé** fill the streets with medieval-themed parades and markets.

The Drive » Follow the D980 20km north into Montbard, then hop 2km east on the D905 before joining the sleepy northbound D32 for the idyllic 3km home stretch into Fontenay.

TRIP HIGHLIGHT

❼ Abbaye de Fontenay

Founded in 1118 and restored to its medieval glory a century ago, the Unesco-listed **Abbaye de Fontenay** (Fontenay Abbey; ☎03 80 92 15 00; www.abbaye defontenay.com; adult/child self-guided tour €10/7, guided tour €12.50/7.90; ☉10am-6pm Easter–mid-Nov, 10am-noon & 2-5pm mid-Nov–Easter) offers a glimpse of the austere, serene surroundings in which Cistercian monks lived lives of contemplation, prayer and manual labour. Set in a bucolic wooded valley, the abbey includes an unadorned Romanesque church, a barrel-vaulted monks' dormitory, landscaped gardens and Europe's first metallurgical factory, with a remarkable water-driven forge from 1220.

From the parking lot, the **GR213 trail** forms part of two verdant walking circuits: one to Montbard (13km return), the other (11.5km) through Touillon and Le Petit Jailly. Maps and botanical field guides are available in the abbey shop.

The Drive » Backtrack to the D905, follow it 14km west-northwest to Rougemont, then take the westbound D956 21km into Noyers.

TRIP HIGHLIGHT

❽ Noyers-sur-Serein

Tucked into a sharp bend in the Serein River, picturesque medieval Noyers is surrounded by pastureland and wooded hills. The town's cobbled streets, accessed via two imposing **stone gateways**, lead past 15th- and 16th-century gabled houses, wood and stone archways and several art galleries.

Noyers is a superb base for **walking**. Just outside the clock-topped southern gate, **Chemin des Fossés** threads its way between the Serein and the village's 13th-century fortifications, 19 of whose original 23 towers still remain. Continue along the Serein's right bank, joining **Balade du Château** and climbing past Noyer's utterly ruined château to a series of belvederes with dreamy views over the town and the surrounding countryside.

In summer, the **Rencontres Musicales de Noyers** (www.musicalesde noyers.com) brings classical concerts and jazz sessions to town.

The Drive » Snake 14km southward through the peaceful Serein valley via the D86, then head 11km west on the D11 from Dissangis to Joux-la-Ville before charting a southwest course down the D32, D9, D606 and D951 for the final 24km run into Vézelay.

TRIP HIGHLIGHT

❾ Vézelay

Rising from lush rolling countryside and crowned by a venerable medieval basilica, Vézelay is one of France's loveliest hilltop villages. Founded in the 9th century on a former Roman and then Carolingian site, the magnificent **Basilique Ste-Madeleine** (www.basiliquedevezelay.org; ☉7am-8pm) gained early fame as a starting point for the Santiago de Compostela pilgrimage route. Among its treasures are a 12th-century **tympanum**, with a carving of an enthroned Jesus radiating his holy spirit to the Apostles; several beautifully carved Romanesque **capitals**, including the Mystical Mill, which depicts Moses grinding grain into a flour sack held by St Paul; and a mid-12th-century **crypt** reputed to house one of Mary Magdalene's bones. Concerts of sacred music are held here June to September.

The **park** behind the basilica affords wonderful views and walking access to the verdant Vallée de Cure. From **Porte Neuve**, Vézelay's old town gate, a footpath descends via the 12th-century chapel of **La Cordelle** to the village of **Asquins**. Another nice walk is the **Promenade des Fossés**, which circumnavigates Vézelay's medieval ramparts.

✕ 🛏 p173

Eating & Sleeping

Cluny ❶

🍴 La Table d'Héloïse · Burgundian €€

(☎03 85 59 05 65; www.hostelleriedheloise.
com/restaurant-cluny; 7 rue de Mâcon; lunch
menu €20, dinner menus €27-52; ☺12.15-
1.45pm Fri-Tue, 7.30pm-8.45pm Mon, Tue
& Thu-Sat) South of town, this family-run
restaurant with a charmingly cosy, newly
remodeled interior is a terrific place to sample
firmly traditional Burgundian specialities,
from the dexterously prepared *fricassée
d'escargots* (snail stew) to the tender Charolais
rumpsteak to the ripe Époisses cheese and the
devastatingly delicious homemade desserts.
Book ahead for a table in the light-filled
verandah overlooking the Grosne river.

🛏 Le Clos de l'Abbaye · B&B €

(☎03 85 59 22 06; www.closdelabbaye.fr; 6
place du Marché; s/d €65/70, q €105-120; 📶)
At this handsome old house directly adjoining
the abbey, the three spacious, comfortable and
stylishly decorated bedrooms and two family-
friendly suites are flanked by a lovely garden
with facilities for kids. Friendly, energetic
owners Claire and Pascal are excellent tour
advisers who direct guests to little-known
treasures. There's a wonderful Saturday
morning market just outside the front door.

Beaune ❹

🍴 Caves Madeleine · French €€

(☎03 80 22 93 30; 8 rue du Faubourg Madeleine;
mains €19-27; ☺noon-1.30pm & 7.15-9.45pm
Mon, Tue & Thu-Sat) Focusing on fresh-from-
the-farm meat and vegetables produced within
a 100km radius of Beaune, this cosy little
restaurant changes its menu daily. Reserve
ahead for a private table, or enjoy a more

convivial experience at the long shared table
backed by well-stocked wine racks.

🛏 Abbaye de Maizières · Historic Hotel €€€

(☎03 80 24 74 64; www.
hotelabbayedemaizieres.com; 19 rue Maizières;
d €180-245, ste €290-410, ❄ @ 🛜) This
character-laden four-star establishment inside
a 12th-century abbey oozes history, yet all 12
rooms have been luxuriously modernised. Some
rooms boast Cistercian stained-glass windows
and exposed beams; those on the top floor offer
views over Beaune's famed multicolour tile
roofs. There's no lift, but the friendly staff will
help haul your luggage upstairs.

Vézelay ❽

🍴 À la Fortune du Pot · Burgundian €

(☎03 86 33 32 56; www.fortunedupot.com;
6 place du Champ du Foire; menus €18.50-24;
☺noon-2pm & 7-9pm) Well-placed in the
square at the foot of Vézelay's main street, this
French-Colombian-run restaurant with English
iPad menus is at its best in sunny weather,
when tables spill out onto the terrace. Build
your own two- to three-course menu featuring
Burgundian classics such as *escargots*, *tarte
à l'Époisses* (Époisses cheese tart) and *bœuf
bourguignon*.

🛏 Cabalus · Guesthouse €

(☎03 86 33 20 66; www.cabalus.com; rue St-
Pierre; r €42-62, breakfast €10) An atmospheric
place to stay, Cabalus has four spacious rooms
in a 12th-century building right next to the
cathedral. They're sparsely decorated but come
with sturdy beams, ancient tiles and stone
walls. Note that the cheaper rooms have shared
toilets. Organic breakfasts (€9) are served at
the cafe downstairs.

Route des Grands Crus

15

The picture-book Route des Grands Crus laces together Burgundy's most reputed vineyards. And, yes, opportunities abound for pleasurable wine tasting in historic surrounds.

TRIP HIGHLIGHTS

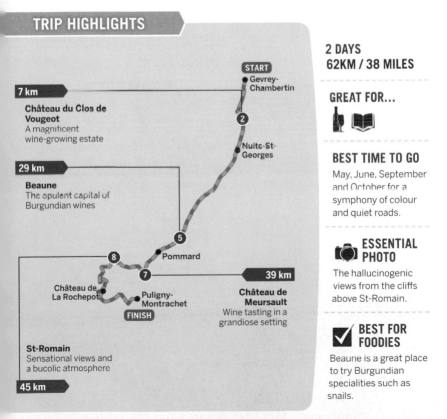

START
Gevrey-Chambertin

7 km

Château du Clos de Vougeot
A magnificent wine-growing estate

2

Nuits-St-Georges

29 km

Beaune
The opulent capital of Burgundian wines

5

Pommard

8

7

39 km

Château de Meursault
Wine tasting in a grandiose setting

Château de La Rochepot

Puligny-Montrachet

FINISH

St-Romain
Sensational views and a bucolic atmosphere

45 km

2 DAYS
62KM / 38 MILES

GREAT FOR...

BEST TIME TO GO
May, June, September and October for a symphony of colour and quiet roads.

ESSENTIAL PHOTO
The hallucinogenic views from the cliffs above St-Romain.

BEST FOR FOODIES
Beaune is a great place to try Burgundian specialities such as snails.

15 Route des Grands Crus

Swinging from Gevrey-Chambertin to Puligny-Montrachet, this route is like a 'greatest hits' of Burgundy, with its bucolic views, patchwork of immaculate hand-groomed vines, atmospheric wine cellars and attractive stone villages. If you're looking for an upscale wine château experience, you've come to the right place. Now is your chance to sample some of the most prestigious reds and whites in the world.

❶ Gevrey-Chambertin

Kick-start your epicurean adventure by visiting this picturesque village, which enjoys a world-class reputation among wine enthusiasts – it produces nine out of the 32 Grands Crus wines from Burgundy. All are reds made from pinot noir.

The Drive » From Gevrey-Chambertin it's a relaxed drive along the D122 to Château du Clos de Vougeot, 7km south via Morey-St-Denis and Chambolle-Musigny.

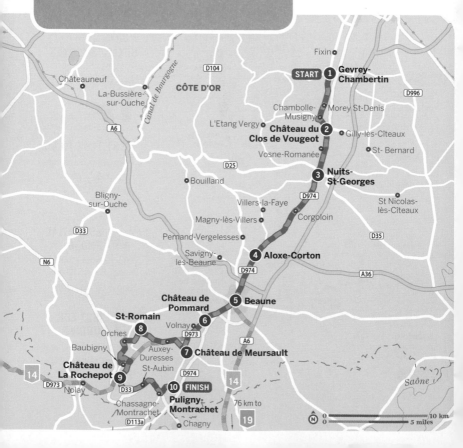

② Château du Clos de Vougeot

An essential stop on the Route des Grands Crus, the magnificent wine-producing **Château du Clos de Vougeot** (☏ 03 80 62 86 09; www.closde vougeot.fr; Vougeot; adult/child €7.50/2.50; ⊙ 9am-6.30pm Sun-Fri & to 5pm Sat Apr-Oct, 10am-5pm Nov-Mar) is re-garded as the birthplace of Burgundian wines. Originally the property of the Abbaye de Cîteaux, 12km southeast from here, the 16th-century country castle served as a getaway for the monks, who stored equipment and produced wines here for several centuries. Tours uncover the work-

LINK YOUR TRIP

14 Medieval Burgundy

It's easy to combine this trip with our itinerary focusing on medieval Burgundy, either from Beaune or La Rochepot.

19 Beaujolais Villages

In the mood for more full-bodied wines? Motor 1¼ hours south to Villefranche-sur-Saône and make your way up to Roche de Solutré.

ings of enormous wine presses and casks.

The Drive » Pick up the D974 to Nuits-St-Georges, 4.5km south via Vosne-Romanée.

③ Nuits-St-Georges

It's worth spending a little time in attractive Nuits-St-Georges. Splashed around town are a dozen domaines selling superb reds and whites, but an essential port of call on any wine-tasting itinerary is **L'Imaginarium** (☏ 03 80 62 61 40; www.imaginarium-bour gogne.com; av du Jura; adult incl basic/grand cru tasting €9/17, child €6; ⊙ 2-7pm Mon, 10am-7pm Tue-Sun). This gleaming modern museum is a great place to learn about Burgundy wines and winemaking techniques. It's fun and entertaining, with movies, exhibits and interactive displays.

Architecture buffs should take a look at the appealing 17th-century **belfry** of the former town hall and the Romanesque **Église St-Symphorien**, slightly away from the town centre.

The Drive » Continue along the D974 towards Beaune. After passing through the village of Ladoix-Serrigny, look out for the sign to Château Corton-André on the right. It's a 10-minute drive from Nuits-St-Georges (11.5km) to Aloxe-Corton.

④ Aloxe-Corton

Surrounded by manicured vineyards, tiny Aloxe-

Corton is a real charmer. It's great for wine-lovers, with producers hand-ily scattered around the village. A good start-ing point is **Domaines d'Aloxe-Corton** (☏ 03 80 26 49 85; place du Chapitre; ⊙ 10am-1pm & 3-7pm Thu-Mon Apr–mid-Nov), a polished wine shop representing several makers of the terrific Aloxe-Corton *appellation* (delectable reds and whites).

No visit to Aloxe-Corton would be complete without visiting the high-flying **Château Corton-André** (☏ 03 80 26 28 79; www.pierre-andre.com; rue Cortons; ⊙ 10am-1pm & 2.30-6pm). With its splendid cellars and tiled roofs, it's a wonderful place for a tasting session in atmospheric surrounds.

🛏 p181

The Drive » Pick up the buoy N74 to Beaune, 5.5km due south.

⑤ Beaune

Beaune's *raison d'être* and the source of its *joie de vivre* is wine: making it, tasting it, selling it, but most of all, drinking it. Consequently Beaune is one of the best places in France for wine-tasting.

The amoeba-shaped old city is enclosed by thick stone **ramparts**, which are lined with overgrown gardens and ringed by a pathway that makes for a lovely stroll. The most striking attraction of

Beaune's old city is the magnificent **Hôtel-Dieu des Hospices de Beaune**.

Underneath Beaune's buildings, streets and ramparts, millions of dusty bottles of wine are being aged to perfection in cool, dark cellars. Stop in at **Patriarche Père et Fils** (☏03 80 24 53 01; www.patriarche.com; 7 rue du Collège; audioguide tour €17; ⏱9.30-11.30am & 2-5.30pm), Burgundy's largest cellars, where 5km of corridors are lined with about five million bottles, the oldest a Beaune Villages AOC from 1904! Sample 13 wines along the way and take home the *tastevin*

(small silver tasting cup). Another venerable winery is **Bouchard Père & Fils** (☏03 80 24 80 45; www. bouchard-pereetfils.com; 15 rue du Château; tours €25; ⏱10am-12.30pm & 2.30-6.30pm Tue-Sat year-round, plus 10am-12.30pm Sun Apr-Dec), housed in a medieval fortress.

🍴🛏 p173, p181

The Drive » Take the D974 (direction Autun), then the D973 to Pommard (5.5km).

- - - - - - - - - - - - -

⑥ Château de Pommard

For many red-wine-lovers, a visit to the superb **Château de Pommard** (☏03

80 22 12 59; www.chateaude pommard.com; 15 rue Marey Monge, Pommard; guided tours incl 4-wine tasting adult/child €25/free; ⏱9.30am-6.30pm Mar-Nov, to 5.30pm Dec-Feb) is the ultimate Burgundian pilgrimage. The impressive cellars contain many vintage bottles.

The Drive » Follow signs to Meursault (5km), via Volnay. Château de Meursault is signposted in the centre of the village.

- - - - - - - - - - - - -

TRIP HIGHLIGHT

⑦ Château de Meursault

One of the most elegant of the Route des Grands

St-Romain Oak wine barrels being made for Burgundy vineyards

Crus châteaux, **Château de Meursault** (📞03 80 26 22 75, www.chateau-meursault. com; 5 rue du Moulin Foulot, Meursault; admission incl 7-wine tasting €21; ⏱10am-noon & 2-6pm Oct-Apr, 10am-6.30pm May-Sep) has beautiful grounds and produces prestigious white wines. Guided tours visit the estate's labyrinth of underground *caves* (cellars), the oldest dating to the 12th century.

The Drive ≫ From the centre of Meursault, follow signs to Auxey-Duresses and Nolay (D23), then signs to Auxey-Duresses and St-Romain (D17E). Then take the D973 (direction

Auxey-Duresses). Leaving Auxey-Duresses, take the D17E to Auxey-le-Potit and St Romain (6.5km from Meursault).

TRIP HIGHLIGHT

8 St-Romain

Off-the-beaten-path St-Romain is a bucolic village situated right where vineyards meet pastureland, forests and cliffs. For drop-dead views over the village and the valley, drive up to the panoramic viewpoint (it's signposted), which is perched atop a cliff near the ruins of a castle.

🍴 🛏 p181

The Drive ≫ Pass through St-Romain and follow the D17 towards Ivry en Montagne, then turn left onto the D17 (direction Orches, Baubigny, Falaises). It's a lovely drive with scenic vistas until you reach Baubigny. In Baubigny take the D111D to La Rochepot. It's an 8km drive from St-Romain.

9 Château de La Rochepot

With its conical towers and multicoloured tile roofs rising from thick woods above the ancient village of La Rochepot, the **Château de La Rochepot** (📞03 80 20 04 00; www. larochepot.com; La Rochepot;

BURGUNDY WINE BASICS

Burgundy's epic vineyards extend approximately 258km from Chablis in the north to the Rhône's Beaujolais in the south and comprise 100 Appellations d'Origine Contrôlée (AOC). Each region has its own appellations and traits, embodied by a concept called *terroir* – the earth itself imbuing its produce, such as grapes, with unique qualities.

Here's an ever-so-brief survey of some of Burgundy's major growing regions:

Côte d'Or vineyards The northern section, the Côte de Nuits, stretches from Marsannay-la-Côte (near Dijon) south to Corgoloin and produces reds known for their robust, full-bodied character. The southern section, the Côte de Beaune, lies between Ladoix-Serrigny and Santenay and produces great reds and great whites. Appellations from the area's hilltops are the Hautes-Côtes de Nuits and Hautes-Côtes de Beaune.

Chablis & Grand Auxerrois Four renowned chardonnay white-wine appellations from 20 villages around Chablis. Part of the Auxerrois vineyards, Irancy produces excellent pinot-noir reds.

Châtillonnais Approximately 20 villages around Châtillon-sur-Seine producing red and white wines.

Côte Chalonnaise The southernmost continuation of the Côte de Beaune's slopes is noted for its excellent reds and whites.

Mâconnais Known for rich or fruity white wines, such as the Pouilly-Fuissé chardonnay.

Want to know more? Take a class!

École des Vins de Bourgogne (☑03 80 26 35 10; www.ecoledesvins-bourgogne.com; 6 rue du 16e Chasseurs) Offers a variety of courses.

Sensation Vin (☑03 80 22 17 57; www.sensation-vin.com; 1 rue d'Enfer; ☺10am-7pm) Offers introductory tasting sessions (no appointment needed) as well as tailor-made courses.

---

adult/child €8/6; ☺10am-5.30pm Wed-Mon Easter-Nov) is a dream come true for photographers and history buffs. This marvellous medieval fortress offers fab views of surrounding countryside.

The Drive 》 Follow the D973 (direction Nolay); after 200m turn hard left onto the D33 that plunges down to St-Aubin. In St-Aubin turn left onto the D906 (direction Chagny), and eventually left again onto the D113A to Puligny-Montrachet. It's a 10km trip from La Rochepot.

🔟 Puligny-Montrachet

Puligny-Montrachet makes a grand finale to your trip. Beloved of white-wine aficionados (no reds in sight), this bijou appellation is revered thanks to five extraordinary Grands Crus. At the **Caveau de Puligny-Montrachet** (☑03 80 21 96 78; www.caveau-puligny.com; 1 rue de Poiseul; ☺9.30am-7pm Easter-Oct, 10am-noon & 3-6pm Tue-Sun rest of year) you can sample various local wines in a comfortable and relaxed setting. This wine-bar–cellar is run by the knowledgeable Julien Wallerand and Emilien Masuyer, who provide excellent advice (in decent English).

✕ 🛏 p181

Eating & Sleeping

Aloxe-Corton ❹

🛏 Villa Louise
Hôtel   Hotel €€

(📞03 80 26 46 70; www.hotel-villa-louise.
fr; 9 rue Franche; d €98-225, breakfast €16;
🅿 @ 🛜 ♨) In the pretty village of Aloxe-
Corton, this tranquil mansion houses elegant,
modern rooms, each of them dreamily different.
The expansive garden stretches straight to the
edge of the vineyard and a separate gazebo
shelters the sauna and pool. Genteel Louise
Perrin presides, and has a private *cave*, perfect
for wine tastings.

Beaune ❺

🍴 Loiseau
des Vignes   Gastronomy €€€

(📞03 80 24 12 06; www.bernard-loiseau.com;
31 rue Maufoux; lunch menus €23-29, dinner
menus €59-99; 🕐 noon-2pm & 7-10pm Tue-Sat)
For an upscale meal with your significant other,
this Michelin-starred culinary shrine is the place
to go. Expect exquisite concoctions ranging
from caramelised pigeon to *quenelles de sandre*
(pike-fish dumplings). At lunchtime even the
most budget-conscious can indulge thanks to
bargain-priced midday *menus*. In summer, the
verdant garden is a plus.

🛏 Abbaye
de Maizières   Historic Hotel €€€

(📞03 80 24 74 64; www.hotelabbayede
maizieres.com; 19 rue Maizières; d €180-245,
ste €290-410; ❄ @ 🛜) This character-laden
four-star establishment inside a 12th-century
abbey oozes history, yet all 12 rooms have been
luxuriously modernised. Some rooms boast
Cistercian stained-glass windows and exposed
beams; those on the top floor offer views over
Beaune's famed multicolour tile roofs. There's
no lift, but the friendly staff will help haul your
luggage upstairs.

St-Romain ❽

🍴 Les Roches   Burgundian €€

(📞03 80 21 21 63; www.les-roches.fr; Bas
Village; menus €29; 🕐 noon-1.30pm & 7-8.30pm
Thu-Mon) In the heart of the village, this sweet
little spot with a pleasant outdoor setting
serves farm-fresh fare and well-executed
Burgundian specialities, including snails and
bœuf bourguignon.

🛏 Domaine Corgette   Rental House €€

(📞03 80 21 68 08; www.domainecorgette.com;
14 rue de la Perrière; d or q €150, 🅿 🛜) Tucked
in the centre of the quiet village of St-Romain,
this renovated winery has five light and airy
rooms with crisp linen and classic touches like
ornamental fireplaces and wood floors. Guests
share access to a kitchen, a comfortable sitting
area and a sun-drenched terrace. The rate is
identical for two to four people, and there's a
three-night minimum stay.

Puligny-Montrachet ❿

🍴 La Table
d'Olivier Leflaive   Bistro €€€

(📞03 80 21 37 65; www.olivier-leflaive.com; 10
place du Monument; mains €24-26, dégustation
menus €60-75; 🕐 12.30-2pm & 7.30-9pm Mon-Sat
early Feb-mid-Dec) This is the address in Puligny-
Montrachet. The trademark four-course 'Repas
Dégustation' (tasting menu) combines seasonal
French classics with global flavours, and comes
paired with six to nine wines served in 6cl glasses.

🛏 La Maison
d'Olivier Leflaive   Boutique Hotel €€€

(📞03 80 21 37 65; www.olivier-leflaive.com; place
du Monument; d €175-245; 🕐 closed Christmas-
early Feb; 🅿 ❄ @ 🛜) Occupying a tastefully
renovated 17th-century village house in the heart
of Puligny-Montrachet, this 13-room venture
delivers top service and classy comfort. Best of
all, it offers personalised wine tours and tastings,
and an acclaimed restaurant right downstairs.

STRETCH YOUR LEGS
DIJON

Start/Finish Place de la Libération

Distance 1.5km

Duration 3 hours

Discover the legacy of the Dukes of Burgundy on this easy stroll through Dijon's historic centre, taking in the city's grand old ducal palace, half-timbered houses and bustling market, with an optional midday break at one of Dijon's finest restaurants.

Take this walk on Trip

14

Place de la Libération

Dijon's magnificent central square, dating from 1686, serves up picture-postcard views of the **Palais des Ducs et des États de Bourgogne** (place de la Libération) – the monumental palace that served as home to Burgundy's powerful dukes during Dijon's 14th- and 15th-century heyday as a European artistic and cultural capital.

The Walk » Head briefly west on rue Rameau, then turn right under the arches of the ducal palace to reach the tourist office, starting point for climbing Tour Philippe Le Bon.

Tour Philippe Le Bon

For dizzying perspectives over the old city's narrow streets and gracious squares, climb the winding steps up this 46m-high mid-15th-century **tower** (place de la Libération; adult/child €3/free; ☉tours every 45min 10.30am-noon & 1.45-5.30pm daily Apr–mid-Nov, hourly 2-4pm Tue, 11am-4pm Sat & Sun mid-Nov–Mar). On clear days, views from the terrace up top extend all the way to Mont Blanc. Reserve tours at the **tourist office** (www.visitdijon.com; 11 rue des Forges; ☉9.30am-6.30pm Mon-Sat, 10am-6pm Sun Apr-Sep, 9.30am-1pm & 2-6pm Mon-Sat, 10am-4pm Sun Oct-Mar).

The Walk » Go west along rue des Forges, admiring the attractive old *hôtels particuliers* (private mansions) at No 34, 38 and 40. Turn two blocks north on rue Odebert to place des Halles.

Les Halles

Dijon's **covered market** (rue Quentin; ☉8am-1pm Tue & Thu-Sat) buzzes with life when vendors hawk fruit, veggies, fish, meat, Dijon mustard and fine Burgundian cheeses such as Époisses and Chaource. Surrounding the square are restaurants, bars and cafes, perfect for a people-watching break.

The Walk » Duck into teeny impasse Quentin opposite the market's southeastern corner and follow its rightward bend towards rue Musette. A left turn here brings you face to face with the gargoyles of Église Notre Dame.

Église Notre Dame

Built between 1220 and 1240, Dijon's most extraordinary **church** (place Notre-

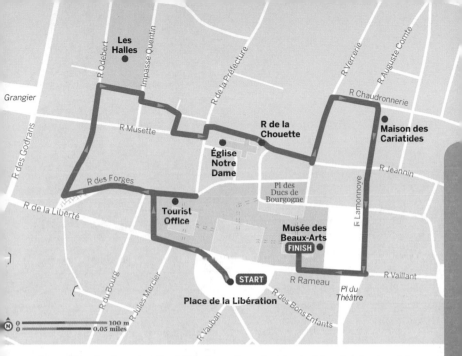

Dame; ⏱8am-7pm) sports a three-tiered facade lined with leering gargoyles separated by two rows of pencil-thin columns. Atop the church, the 14th-century **Horloge à Jacquemart**, transported from Flanders in 1383 by Philip the Bold, chimes every quarter-hour.

The Walk » Exiting the church, turn right and immediately right again onto rue de la Chouette.

Rue de la Chouette

This street is named after the small stone *chouette* (owl) carved into the exterior corner of the chapel diagonally across from No 24. Said to grant happiness and wisdom to those who stroke it, it has been worn smooth by generations of fortune-seekers; try it for yourself!

The Walk » One block beyond the back of the church, turn left onto rue Verrerie, passing a picturesque series of half-timbered medieval houses before turning right on rue Chaudronnerie.

Maison des Cariatides

Its facade a riot of stone caryatids, soldiers and vines, this early-17th-century mansion houses a delightful Michelin-starred **restaurant** (www.lamaisondescariatides.fr; 28 rue Chaudronnerie; lunch menu €21-27; ⏱noon-2pm & 7-10pm Tue-Sat), with exposed beams and stone walls forming an impressive backdrop for delicious French and regional cuisine. It's best at midday, thanks to bargain-priced lunch *menus* and pleasant terrace seating out back.

The Walk » Loop back towards Place de la Libération, following rue Lamonnoye and rue Rameau to the courtyard of the Palais des Ducs, entry point to Dijon's art museum.

Musée des Beaux-Arts

These sprawling **galleries** (http://mba.dijon.fr; 1 rue Rameau; tours €6; ⏱9.30am-6pm Wed-Mon May-Oct, 10am-5pm Wed-Mon Nov-Apr) constitute one of France's most outstanding museums. Don't miss wood-panelled Salle des Gardes, housing ornate, carved late-medieval sepulchres of dukes John the Fearless and Philip the Bold. Other sections focus on Egyptian art and six centuries of European painting.

The Walk » Loop back to Place de la Libération along rue Rameau.

Alps, Jura & Rhône Valley

FROM THE RHÔNE RIVER TO EUROPE'S HIGHEST MOUNTAIN, eastern France is a crazy quilt of inspirational landscapes, atmospheric cities and bucolic villages.

Our itineraries head in all directions from Lyon. To the northwest, narrow roads snake through the vine-covered Beaujolais, one of France's most underrated wine-growing areas; to the south, the Rhône flows through increasingly sunny country past Gallo-Roman ruins, medieval hilltop fortresses and precipitous gorges. East lie the mountains: the Jura, land of Comté and *vin jaune;* the Vercors' poppy-strewn plateaux and limestone peaks; Haute-Provence's lavender fields and multihued canyons; and, towering high above, the spellbinding Alps and hulking Mont Blanc.

Gorges de l'Ardèche Limestone gorges along the Ardèche River

✓ DON'T MISS

Château-Chalon
This is the perfect spot to sample the Jura's distinctive 'yellow' wine. Stay in a turreted B&B on Trip **16**

Bonneval-sur-Arc
Hidden on Europe's highest mountain pass, this village in Vanoise National Park is a nature-lover's hideaway Escape here on Trip **17**

Gîte d'Alpage de la Molière
Homemade raspberry pie and spectacular mountain views welcome hikers at this eatery. Rest your feet here on Trip **18**

Domaine des Vignes du Paradis – Pascal Durand
This family-run domaine welcomes visitors. Stop in to sip award-winning St-Amour red on Trip **19**

Sentier Aval des Gorges
Driving the Gorges de l'Ardèche scenic route is spectacular. Discover this easy-to-miss trail on Trip **20**

The Jura 16

On this trip through mountains and vineyards, you'll clamber over magnificent citadels, explore deep forests of beech, oak and fir, taste the region's famous yellow wine and relax into its unhurried culture.

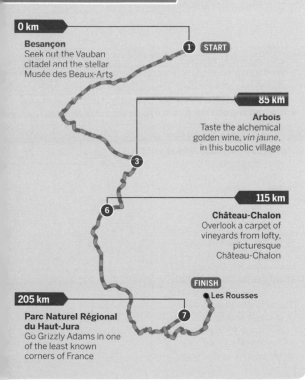

0 km

Besançon
Seek out the Vauban citadel and the stellar Musée des Beaux-Arts

1 START

85 km

Arbois
Taste the alchemical golden wine, *vin jaune*, in this bucolic village

3

115 km

6

Château-Chalon
Overlook a carpet of vineyards from lofty, picturesque Château-Chalon

FINISH
● Les Rousses

205 km

Parc Naturel Régional du Haut-Jura
Go Grizzly Adams in one of the least known corners of France

7

5 DAYS
227KM / 141 MILES

GREAT FOR...

BEST TIME TO GO
Come between June and September, when the sun shines; winter is best left to cross-country skiers.

 ESSENTIAL PHOTO
Snap the hawks' view from the top of the Telesiège Val Mijoux.

☑ **BEST FOR FAMILIES**
Camping and tramping in the Parc Naturel Régional du Haut-Jura.

16 The Jura

Subalpine, but still formidable, the high Jura mountains contrast starkly with the rolling, bucolic lowlands, famed for Comté cheese and golden wine. In fact, this trip is full of contrasts: one day you might check out Egyptian mummies, the next you'll be eating with vignerons at a cheery *bistrot*, and beyond that dangling above limestone escarpments in a chairlift. Despite such abundance, the Jura remains one of France's least visited territories.

TRIP HIGHLIGHT

❶ Besançon

Home to a monumental Vauban citadel and France's first public museum, birthplace of Victor Hugo and the Lumière brothers, Besançon has an extraordinary background. Somehow, despite its graceful 18th-century old town and first-rate restaurants, it remains something of a secret.

The Unesco-listed **Citadelle de Besançon** (www.citadelle.com; 99 rue des Fusillés de la Résistance; adult/child €10.60/8.50; ⏰10am-5pm Jan-Mar & Oct-Dec, 9am-6pm Apr-Jun & Sep, 9am-7pm Jul & Aug, closed early Jan) is a formidable feat of engineering, designed by the prolific Marquis de Vauban for Louis XIV in the late 17th century. Inside (and included in the ticket price) are a number of **museums**.

Founded in 1694, the **Musée des Beaux-Arts et d'Archéologie** (☎03 81 87 80 67; www.mbaa.besancon.fr; 1 place de la Révolution; adult/child €5/free; ⏰9.30am-noon & 2-6pm Mon & Wed-Fri, 9.30am-6pm Sat & Sun) is France's oldest museum. The stellar collection includes such archaeological exhibits as Egyptian mummies, neolithic tools and Gallo-Roman mosaics, and boasts a cavernous drawing cabinet with 5500 works including Dürer, Delacroix, Rubens,

Goya, Matisse and Rodin masterpieces.

🍴 🛏 p195

The Drive » From Besançon you can opt for the fast A36 (51km, 45 minutes) or the marginally slower but more enjoyable D673 (46km, 55 minutes) to Dole.

❷ Dole

Almost every town in France has at least one street, square or garden named after Louis Pasteur, the great 19th-century chemist who invented pasteurisation and developed the first rabies vaccine. The Jura takes this veneration further: the illustrious man was a local lad, born in 1822 in the well-preserved medieval town of Dole.

🔗 LINK YOUR TRIP

15 Route des Grands Crus

Need a drink before starting our Jura tour? Combine it with our Route des Grands Crus drive; its starting point of Gevrey-Chambertin is 62km from Dole along the A39.

17 Alpine Adventure

If the heights of the Jura appeal then you'll love our Alpine Adventure, which begins in Lyon, a 135km drive from Mijoux down the A42.

A scenic stroll along the Canal des Tanneurs in Dole's historic tanner's quarter brings you to Pasteur's childhood home, **La Maison Natale de Pasteur** (La Maison de Natale Pasteur; ☑03 84 72 20 61; www.musee-pasteur.com; 43 rue Pasteur, Dole; adult/child €5/free; ☺2-6pm Feb-Apr, Oct & Nov, 9.30am-12.30pm & 2-6pm May-Sep), now an atmospheric museum housing exhibits including his cot, first drawings and university cap and gown.

The Drive » It's a 45-minute, 36km doddle down the D905 and D469 to Arbois.

- - - - - - - - - - - -

❸ Arbois

The charming village of Arbois is well worth a visit. In 1827 the Pasteur family settled here, and Louis' laboratory and workshops are on display at **La Maison de Louis Pasteur** (☑03 84 66 11 72; www.terredelouispasteur.fr; 83 rue de Courcelles, Arbois; adult/child €6.50/4; ☺2-6pm Feb-Apr, Oct & Nov, 9.30am-12.30pm & 2-6pm May-Sep).

If science is a bit too dusty for you then may we tempt you with a glass of wine? Arbois sits at the heart of the Jura wine region, renowned for its *vin jaune*. The history of this nutty 'yellow wine' is told in the **Musée de la Vigne et du Vin du Jura** (☑03 84 66 40 45; www.arbois.fr; adult/child €3.50/free; ☺10am-noon & 2-6pm Wed-Mon Mar-Oct, 2-6pm Wed-Mon Nov-Feb), housed in the whimsical, turreted Château Pécauld. Afterwards clear your head by walking the 2.5km-long **Chemin des Vignes** trail, which wends its way through the vines, starting from the steps next to the Château Pécauld.

✕ ⊨ p195

The Drive » Clamber steeply uphill for five minutes (3km) along the D246 to reach the spectacularly situated village of Pupillin.

- - - - - - - - - - - -

❹ Pupillin

High above Arbois is tiny Pupillin, a cute yellow-brick village famous for its wine production. Some 10 *caves* (wine cellars) are open to visitors.

The Drive » Head southwest out of Pupillin on the N83 and in 9km (15 minutes) you'll have dropped to the town of Poligny.

LIQUID GOLD

Legend has it that *vin jaune* (yellow wine) was invented when a winemaker found a forgotten barrel, six years and three months after he'd initially filled it, and discovered its contents miraculously transformed into a gold-coloured wine.

A long, undisrupted fermentation process gives Jura's signature wine its unique characteristics. Savagnin grapes are harvested late and their sugar-saturated juices left to ferment for a minimum of six years and three months in oak barrels. A thin layer of yeast forms over the wine, which prevents it from oxidising, and there are no top-ups to compensate for evaporation (called *la part des anges* – 'the angels' share'). In the end, 100L of grape juice ferments down to 62L of *vin jaune* (lucky angels), which is then bottled in special 0.62L bottles called *clavelin*. *Vin jaune* is renowned for its ageing qualities, with prime vintages easily keeping for more than a century. A 1774 vintage, a cool 220 years old at the time, was sipped by an awestruck committee of experts in 1994.

La Percée du Vin Jaune (www.percee-du-vin-jaune.com; entry & 14 tasting tickets €14; ☺Feb) festival takes place annually in early February to celebrate the first tasting of the vintage produced six years and three months earlier. Villages take it in turn to hold the two-day celebrations, at which the new vintage is blessed and rated, and street tastings, cooking competitions, cellar visits and auctions keep *vin jaune* aficionados fulfilled.

Arbois Vineyard outside the village

5 Poligny

So, you need a little cheese to accompany all that wine? Comté is the pre-eminent AOC cheese of the Jura, and the small town of Poligny is the 'capital' of an industry that produces 40 million tonnes of its sweet, nutty goodness a year. Learn how 450L of milk is transformed into a 40kg wheel, smell some of its 83 aromas, and have a nibble at the **Maison du Comté** (☎03 84 37 78 40; www.maison-du-comte.com; av de la Résistance; adult/child €5/3; ☺2-5pm Tue-Sun Apr-

Jun, Sep & Oct, 10am-noon & 2-5.30pm Jul & Aug). Dozens of *fruitières* (cheese cooperatives) are open to the public. Poligny's **tourist office** (☎03 84 37 24 21; www.poligny-tourisme.com; 20 place des Déportés; ☺10am-12.30pm & 1.30-5.30pm Mon-Fri, 10am-12.30pm & 2-5pm Sat) stocks an abundance of info on cheesemakers and wineries in the region.

🛏 p195

The Drive » Take the D68 out of town, and after about 4km veer right onto the D96. After a further 4km, make a sharp right onto the D5 and cruise through pretty countryside into Château-Chalon. It's 15km in total.

TRIP HIGHLIGHT

6 Château-Chalon

Despite a name that conjures up images of grand castles, Château-Chalon is actually a pocket-sized medieval village of honey-coloured stone perched on a hilltop and surrounded by vineyards known for their legendary *vin jaune*.

🛏 p195

The Drive » Leave Château-Chalon in a northeasterly direction on the D5 and then double back to the D70 and the town of Lons-le-Saunier. From here the D52, D470 and D436 will be your route into the high-mountain bliss of the Parc

SPECIALITY FOOD & DRINK

It's hot, it's soft and it's packed in a box. Vacherin Mont d'Or is the only French cheese to be eaten with a spoon – hot. Made between 15 August and 15 March with *lait cru* (unpasteurised milk), it derives its unique nutty taste from the spruce bark in which it's wrapped. Connoisseurs top the soft-crusted cheese with chopped onions, garlic and white wine, wrap it in aluminium foil and bake it for 45 minutes to create a *boîte chaude* (hot box). Only 11 factories in the Jura are licensed to produce Vacherin Mont d'Or.

Mouthe, 15km south of Métabief Mont d'Or, is the mother of *liqueur de sapin* (fir-tree liqueur). *Glace de sapin* (fir-tree ice cream) also comes from Mont d'Or, known as the North Pole of France due to its seasonal subzero temperatures (record low: -38°C). Sampling either is rather like ingesting a Christmas tree. Then there's *Jésu* – a small, fat version of *saucisse de Morteau* (Morteau sausage), easily identified by the wooden peg on its end, attached after the sausage is smoked with pinewood sawdust in a traditional *tuyé* (mountain hut).

Naturel Régional du Haut-Jura and the village of Lajoux. In total it's 90km and 1½ hours.

TRIP HIGHLIGHT

⑦ Parc Naturel Régional du Haut-Jura

Experience the Jura at its rawest in the Haut-Jura Regional Park, an area of 757 sq km stretching from Chapelle-des-Bois in the north almost to the western tip of Lake Geneva.

A great place to start is the **Maison du Parc** (☎03 84 34 12 30; www.parc-haut-jura.fr; 9 Qua le Village, Lajoux; adult/child €5/3; ☺9am-12.30pm & 1.30-6pm Tue-Sun Jun & school holidays, Tue-Fri other times), a visitor centre with an interactive sensorial museum that explores the region and its history through sound, touch and smell. The Maison du Parc is in the village of Lajoux, 19km east of St-Claude

and 5km west of Mijoux on the Swiss border.

🛏 p195

The Drive ⟩⟩ From the Maison du Parc the D436 will have you switchbacking 5km down the valley into the village of Mijoux.

⑧ Mijoux

Close to the small ski resort of Mijoux there are some fabulous panoramas of Lake Geneva, framed by the French Alps and Mont Blanc. For the best views, ride the **Telesiège Val Mijoux** (adult/child one way €7/4.50; ☺8.45am-4.45pm daily late Dec–late Mar, Sat & Sun early Jul–late Aug) from Mijoux or drive to the **Col de la Faucille** (7km along the D936), high above the village.

The Drive ⟩⟩ It's a 20-minute, 20km drive along the D936 and D1005 to Les Rousses through forest and pastureland.

⑨ Les Rousses

The driving tour comes to a close in the resort of Les Rousses, on the northeastern edge of the park and hard up against the Swiss border. This is the Haut-Jura's prime sports hub for winter (skiing) and summer (walking and mountain biking) alike. The resort comprises four small, predominantly cross-country ski areas: Prémanon, Lamoura, Bois d'Amont and the village Les Rousses. Find out more at the Maison du Tourisme, home to the **tourist office** (Station des Rousses; ☎03 84 60 02 55; www.lesrousses.com; 495 rue Pasteur, Les Rousses; ☺hours vary, see website for details) and the **ESF** (☎03 84 60 01 61; www.esf-lesrousses.com; 495 rue Pasteur, Maison du Tourisme, Les Rousses) ski school.

Eating & Sleeping

Besançon ①

✗ Le Saint-Pierre   Modern French €€€

(☎03 81 81 20 99; www.restaurant-saintpierre.com; 104 rue Battant; menus €40-75; ☺noon-1.30pm Mon-Fri, 7.30-9pm Mon-Sat) Crisp white tablecloths, exposed stone and subtle lighting are the backdrop for intense flavours, such as lobster lasagne with spinach and lobster bouillon, which are expertly paired with regional wines. At €40 the three-course *menu du marché*, which includes wine and coffee, is excellent value.

⨌ Residence Charles Quint   Apartment €

(☎03 81 82 00 21; www.residence-charlesquint.com; 3 rue du Chapitre; d/apt €80/110; 🛜) Slumbering behind the cathedral, in the shade of the citadel, this discreetly grand 18th-century town house is now a sublime 'residence' featuring period furniture, sumptuous fabrics, a peaceful private garden and a wood-panelled dining room. Parking (€5 per night) is available and a buffet breakfast (€13.50) can be taken at the nearby Hotel Sauvage. Minimum three-night stay.

Arbois ③

✗ Bistrot des Claquets   French €

(☎03 84 66 04 19; www.bistrot-des-claquets.com; 33 rue de Faramand; 2-/3-course menus €13/16; ☺7.30am-9pm Tue-Sat; 🍴) Loved by *vignerons* (wine growers) and other locals, this unpretentious, convivial little *bistrot* serves fantastic French country fare, but only at lunchtime! If you miss the *petit salé* (lentils with salt pork), *blanquettes de veau* (poached veal in white sauce) or whatever else is cooking that day, it's still worth popping in to sample the *vin jaune* and happy chatter.

⨌ Closerie les Capucines   B&B €€

(☎03 84 66 17 38; www.closerielescapucines.com; 7 rue de Bourgogne; d/q incl breakfast from €125/250; ☺Feb-Dec; @🛜🖳) A 17th-century

stone convent has been lovingly transformed into this boutique B&B, with five rooms remarkable for their pared-down elegance, a tree-shaded garden by the river and a plunge pool.

Poligny ⑤

⨌ Hôtel de la Vallée Heureuse   Hotel €€

(☎03 84 37 12 13; www.hotelvalleeheureuse.com; rte de Genève; s/d/q €99/133/185; lunch menus €29, dinner menus €42-70; 🖳) In a beautifully converted 18th-century mill by a rushing stream, this serene country retreat has 11 large, tastefully decorated rooms and a restaurant specialising in traditional French cuisine. Run by the welcoming Isabelle and Patrice, it's on the road from the centre of town towards Champagnole and Geneva (N5), 400m past the sign indicating that you're leaving Poligny.

Château-Chalon ⑥

⨌ Le Relais des Abbesses   B&B €

(☎03 84 44 98 56; www.relais-des-abbesses.fr; 36 rue de la Roche; s incl breakfast €75-100, d incl breakfast €80-105; ☺Mar–mid-Nov; 🛜) Agnès and Gérard have attractively decorated their five spacious, en-suite rooms – all with either hardwood or old tile floors – with Chinese lacquer furnishings.

Parc Naturel Régional du Haut-Jura ⑦

⨌ Le Clos d'Estelle   B&B €

(☎03 84 42 01 29; www.leclosdestelle.com; 1 La Marcantine, Charchilla; d/q with breakfast €85/140; @) Surrounded by fields and sheep, Christine and Jean-Pierre warmly welcome guests to four very spacious, wood-built *chambres d'hôte* (B&B) in their mid-19th-century farmhouse. Situated in Charchilla (pronounced 'shar-*shiy*-a'), 200m down the hill behind the church.

Alpine Adventure

17

With their combination of retina-burning splendour and the sturdy charms of time-worn mountain culture, France's Alps provide an incomparable setting for a summer road trip.

TRIP HIGHLIGHTS

START **1**

95 km

Chamonix
Experience Mont Blanc's magnetic allure in Europe's mountaineering capital

3

Val d'Isère

Col de l'Iseran

6

0 km

Annecy
Wander flowery canal banks and swim a pure Alpine lake

215 km

Bonneval-sur-Arc
The quintessential Alpine village, tucked beyond Europe's highest paved pass

Col du Galibier

Briançon

St-Véran
FINISH

6 DAYS
363KM / 225 MILES

GREAT FOR...

BEST TIME TO GO
Mid-June to mid-September, when mountain passes are snow free.

ESSENTIAL PHOTO
Alpine crags and colourful boats reflected in the lake at Annecy.

BEST TWO DAYS
The section between Annecy and Chamonix, for classic French Alpine scenery.

Classic Trip

17 Alpine Adventure

A study in superlatives, this outdoorsy ramble through the heart of the French Alps runs from Annecy (perhaps France's prettiest lake-city) to Mont Blanc (Western Europe's highest peak) to Col de l'Iseran (its highest mountain pass) to Bonneval-sur-Arc (an Alpine village of incomparable charm) to St-Véran (France's most elevated village). Along the way you'll have ample opportunity for high-adrenaline mountain adventures: hiking, mountain biking, white-water rafting, riding knee-trembling cable cars and crossing the French Alps' most spectacular passes.

TRIP HIGHLIGHT

① Annecy

There's no dreamier introduction to the French Alps than Annecy. The mountains rise steep, wooded and snow-capped above startlingly turquoise Lac d'Annecy, providing a sublime setting for the medieval town's photogenic jumble of geranium-strewn houses, romantic canals and turreted rooftops.

Summer is the prime time to visit, when everyone is outdoors, socialis-ing at pavement cafes, swimming in the lake (among Europe's purest) and boating, walking or cycling around it. Evening street performers feature during July's **Les Noctibules** festival, and there are lakeside fireworks during August's **Fête du Lac**.

Wander through the narrow medieval streets of the **Vieille Ville** (Old Town) to find the whimsical 12th-century **Palais de l'Isle** (☎04 56 49 40 37; www.musees.agglo-annecy. fr; 3 passage de l'Île; adult/ child €3.80/2; ☻10am-noon

& 2-5pm Wed-Mon Oct-May,
10am-5pm Wed-Mon Jun-Sep)
on a triangular islet in
the Canal du Thiou. Next
stroll the tree-fringed
lakefront through the
flowery **Jardins de
l'Europe**, linked to the
popular picnic spot
Champ de Mars by
the graceful **Pont des
Amours** (Lovers' Bridge)
and presided over by
the dour, commanding
Château d'Annecy (www.
musees.agglo-annecy.fr,
rampe du Château; adult/child
€5.20/2.60; ⊙10am-noon
& 2-5pm Wed-Mon Oct-May,
10.30am-6pm daily Jun-Sep).

Cycling paths encircle
the lake, passing by several
pretty **beaches** en route.
Boats (per hour from
€15 to €50) can be hired
along the canal-side quays,
and several companies
offer **adventure sports**.
For details, visit Annecy's
tourist office (☑04 50 45 00
33; www.lac-annecy.com; 1 rue

**LINK
YOUR
TRIP**

16 **The Jura**
Discover the gentler
pleasures of eastern
France's 'other' mountains,
three hours north of Annecy.

18 **Foothills of the
Alps**
Join this nature-lover's
jaunt through high-country
plateaux and dramatic
canyons, two hours west of
Briançon.

Jean Jaurès, courtyard of Centre Bonlieu; ⊙9am-12.30pm & 1.45-6pm Mon-Sat year-round, plus 9am-12.30pm & 1.45-6pm Sun mid-May–mid-Sep, 9am-12.30pm Sun Apr–early Oct & Dec).

✕ 🛏 p205

The Drive » This 70km drive starts with a pretty southeastwards run along Annecy's lakefront, passing through the wildlife-rich wetlands of Bout du Lac on the lake's southern tip before continuing east on the D1508, then northeast on the D1212 and D909 into St-Gervais.

- - - - - - - - - - - -

❷ St-Gervais-les-Bains

Basking in the shadow of Mont Blanc, St-Gervais-les-Bains is a peaceful Savoyard village, centred on a Baroque church and old-fashioned carousel.

Panoramic **hiking trails** in the Bettex, Mont d'Arbois and Mont Joly areas head off from town. Some of the best mountain-biking terrain is marked between Val d'Arly, Mont Blanc and Beaufortain.

For spirit-soaring mountain views with zero effort, board the **Tramway du Mont Blanc** (☎04 50 53 22 75; www.compagniedumontblanc.co.uk; rue de la Gare; return to Bellevue/Nid d'Aigle €31/36; ⊙5 departures daily mid-Dec–early Apr, 8 daily early-Jun to early Jul & late Aug to mid-Sep), France's highest train. Since 1913 it has been labouring up to Bellevue (1800m) in winter and Mont Lachat (2113m) in summer.

Train buffs will also love the narrow-gauge **Mont Blanc Express** (www.mont-blanc-express.com), which trundles along a century-old rail line from St-Gervais-Le-Fayet station to Martigny in Switzerland.

🛏 p205

The Drive » The 24km route to Chamonix follows the D902, N205 and D243 into the heart of the Alps.

- - - - - - - - - - - -

TRIP HIGHLIGHT

❸ Chamonix

An outdoors playground of epic proportions, Chamonix sits directly at the foot of Western Europe's highest peak, the bone-white dome of Mont Blanc (4810m).

Climbers with the necessary skill, experience and stamina flock here for the incomparable **Mont Blanc ascent**. If you're not quite ready to scale 'the big one', consider circumnavigating it on the classic six- to 10-day **Tour du Mont Blanc**, which takes in majestic glaciers and peaks in France, Italy and Switzerland; local outfitters organise excursions including half-board in *refuges* (mountain huts), lift tickets and luggage transport. Other peak experiences include Chamonix' dozens of **day hikes**, the unforgettable cable-car ascent to **Aiguille du Midi** and the **train ride** (www.compagniedumontblanc.fr; 35 place de la Mer de Glace; adult/child return €31/26.40; ⊙10am-4.30pm) to France's largest glacier, the glistening 200m-deep **Mer de Glace** (Sea of Ice).

Chamonix has an unparalleled menu of adrenaline sports including **rafting**, **canyoning**, **mountain biking** and **paragliding** down from the heights of Planpraz (2000m) or Aiguille du Midi (3842m). For details, visit the **tourist office** (☎04 50 53 00 24; www.chamonix.com; 85 place du Triangle de l'Amitié; ⊙8.30am-7pm winter & summer, 9am-12.30pm & 2-6pm low season).

✕ 🛏 p205

✓ TOP TIP: WINTER DRIVING

Parts of this route (notably the northern stretches around Annecy and Chamonix) are accessible to drivers in winter, but the high mountain passes further south are strictly off-limits outside summer.

HIKING CHAMONIX

Chamonix boasts 350km of spectacular high-altitude trails, many reached by cable car. In June and July there's enough light to walk until at least 9pm. Here are a few recommended walks to get you started.

» **Lac Blanc** From the top of **Les Praz l'Index Téléphérique** (www.compagniedumontblanc.co.uk; adult/child one-way from Les Praz €23/19.60; ⊗Dec-Apr & Jun-Sep) or at **La Flégère** (☎04 50 53 22 75; www.compagniedumontblanc.co.uk; 35 rte des Tines; adult/child from Les Praz €13/11.70; ⊗8.45am-4pm Dec-Apr & Jun-Sep), the line's midway point, gentle 1¼- to two-hour trails lead to 2352m Lac Blanc, a turquoise-coloured lake ensnared by mountains. Stargazers can overnight at the **Refuge du Lac Blanc** (☎04 50 53 49 14; refugedulacblanc@gmail.com; dm incl half board €55; ⊗mid-Jun–Sep), a wooden chalet favoured by photographers for its top-of-Europe Mont Blanc views.

» **Grand Balcon Sud** This easygoing trail skirts the western side of the valley, stays at around 2000m and commands a terrific view of Mont Blanc. Reach it on foot from behind Le Brévent's *télécabine* station.

» **Grand Balcon Nord** Routes starting from the Plan de l'Aiguille include the challenging Grand Balcon Nord, which takes you to the dazzling Mer de Glace, from where you can walk or take the Montenvers (p200) train down to Chamonix.

The Drive » From Chamonix, take the E25/N205 southeast 17km through the Mont Blanc Tunnel into Italy. From the Aosta/Courmayeur exit, continue 31km southwest back towards France along the SS26. Once across the border, follow the D1090 and D84 southwest, then the D902 southeast for a total of 40km into Val d'Isère.

- - - - - - - - - -

❹ Val d'Isère

This world-renowned, end-of-the-valley resort is home to the gargantuan **Espace Killy** (www.espacekilly.com) skiing area, named after French triple Olympic gold medallist Jean-Claude Killy. Even in July, you can ski the **Pisaillas Glacier** above town, though many summer visitors also come to hike, mountain bike and enjoy off-season hotel discounts.

The trails weaving into the nearby valleys of **Parc National de la Vanoise** are a hiker's dream. For more of a challenge, play among the peaks at neighbouring La Daille's two **via ferrata** (fixed-rope routes).

Mountain biking (VTT) is big in Val, especially since the resort hosted stages of the UCI World Cup in 2012. Five lifts offer cyclists access to 16 downhill routes, seven endurance runs and two cross-country circuits. Bike rental is available at local sport shops. **Bureau des Guides** (☎03 77 08 09 76; www.guides-montagne-valdisere.com) arranges guided hiking, mountain biking, canyoning and rock-climbing excursions.

Visit the **tourist office** (☎04 79 06 06 60; www.valdisere.com; place Jacques Mouflier, Centre Village; ⊗8.30am-7.30pm daily Dec-Apr & Jun-Aug, 9am-noon & 2-6pm Mon-Fri low season) for details on family-friendly activities, from donkey trekking to farm visits.

The Drive » Prepare for a dizzying climb as you leave Val d'Isère, steeply switchbacking 17km up the D902 to Col de l'Iseran.

- - - - - - - - - -

❺ Col de l'Iseran

No doubt about it, you're really far above sea level here! Indeed, the D902 over Col de l'Iseran (2770m) is the highest paved through road in Europe. Meteorological conditions at the summit are notoriously fickle – witness the Tour de France stage that was supposed to pass through here on 8 July 1996 but had to be

Classic Trip

WHY THIS IS A CLASSIC TRIP
HUGH MCNAUGHTAN, WRITER

The Alps rival any region of France for drama, beauty and excitement. You'll be hard-pressed to stay on schedule when passing through such an intensely photogenic part of the world: every valley and hamlet seems to demand you pull over and give it the attention its splendour demands. But stay on track and you'll leave with memories of historic fortified towns, glittering Alpine lakes and towering peaks that will never fade.

Above: Canal du Thiou and château, Annecy
Left: Val d'Isère ski resort

AIGUILLE DU MIDI

A great broken tooth of rock rearing above glaciers, snowfields and rocky crags, 8km from the hump of Mont Blanc, the Aiguille du Midi (3842m) is one of Chamonix' most distinctive landmarks. If you can handle the height, don't miss taking a trip up here; the 360-degree views of the French, Swiss and Italian Alps are breathtaking.

All year round the vertiginous **Téléphérique de l'Aiguille du Midi** (www.compagniedumontblanc.co.uk; place de l'Aiguille du Midi; adult/child return to Aiguille du Midi €58.50/49.70, to Plan de l'Aiguille summer €31/26.40, winter €17/14.50; ⊘1st ascent btwn 7.10am & 8.30am, last btwn 3.30pm & 5pm), one of the world's highest cable cars, climbs to the summit. Halfway up, Plan de l'Aiguille (2317m) is a terrific place to start hikes or paraglide. In summer you'll need to obtain a boarding card (marked with the number of your departing *and* returning cable car) in addition to a ticket. Bring warm clothes; even in summer the temperature rarely rises above -10°C up top!

From the Aiguille du Midi, between late June and early September you can continue for a further 30 minutes of mind-blowing scenery – think suspended glaciers, spurs, séracs and shimmering ice fields – in the smaller bubbles of the **Télécabine Panoramique Mont Blanc** (☑04 50 53 22 75; Aiguille du Midi; adult/child return from Chamonix €80/68; ⊘last departure from Aiguille du Midi 2.30pm) to Pointe Helbronner (3466m) on the France–Italy border. From there, the **SkyWay Monte Bianco** (www.montebianco.com; Pointe Helbronner; one-way adult/child €36/25.20; ⊘8.30am-4.30pm, earlier starts in summer) can take you all the way to Courmayeur, in Italy's Val d'Aosta.

rerouted due to snow and -5°C temperatures!

The Drive ≫ Spellbinding views unfold as you navigate the D902's hairpin turns 14km downhill into Bonneval-sur-Arc.

TRIP HIGHLIGHT

❻ Bonneval-sur-Arc

Heralded as one of the *plus beaux villages de la France* (prettiest villages in France), this high mountain hamlet is filled with stone and slate cottages that wear their winter preparations proudly (notice all the woodpiles up on 2nd-floor porches).

Bonneval makes a tranquil base for exploring the 530-sq-km **Parc National de la Vanoise** (www.parcnational-vanoise.fr),

whose rugged snow-capped peaks, mirrorlike lakes and vast glaciers dominate the landscape between the Tarentaise and Maurienne Valleys. This incredible swath of wilderness was designated France's first national park in 1963, protecting habitat for marmots, chamois and France's largest colony of ibexes, along with 20 pairs of golden eagles and the odd bearded vulture.

The park is a hiker's heaven between June and September. The **Grand Tour de Haute Maurienne** (www.hautemaurienne.com), a seven-day hike around the upper reaches of the valley, takes in national-park highlights. For information on local day

hikes, visit Bonneval-sur-Arc's **tourist office** (☑04 79 05 95 95; www.bonneval-sur-arc.com; ⊘9am-noon & 2-6pm late-Dec–mid-Apr).

🛏 p205

The Drive ≫ Cruise 55km down the Arc River valley on the D902/D1006 through Lanslebourg and Modane to St-Michel de Maurienne, then climb 35km through the ski resort of Valloire to the ethereal heights of Col du Galibier.

----

❼ Col du Galibier

The signposts say you're simply crossing the departmental border from Savoie into the Hautes Alpes. The landscape says that you've entered another universe. Col du Galibier (2642m) is

a staggeringly beautiful Alpine pass, whose forbidding remoteness may make you feel like the last living person on earth. To the west lies the Parc National des Écrins, a 918-sq-km expanse of high mountain wilderness. Stop and savour the top-of-the-world feeling before returning to the squiggling ribbon of roadway below.

The Drive » Despite the distance on the signpost (35km), the incredibly twisty and scenic descent into Briançon on the D902 and D1091 feels longer; stupendous views will stop you in your tracks every couple of minutes. Enjoy every horn-tooting, head-spinning, glacier-gawping moment, with views of thundering falls, sheer cliffs and jagged peaks razoring above thick larch forests.

- - - - - - - - - - - - -

❽ Briançon

Perched astride a high rocky outcrop, the fairy-tale walled city of Briançon affords views of the snowcapped Écrins peaks from almost every corner. The centre's Italian ambience is no coincidence; Italy is just 20km away.

Briançon's old town is a late-medieval time capsule, its winding cobbled lanes punctuated by shuttered, candy-coloured town houses and shops selling whistling marmots. The steep main street, **Grande Gargouille**, links two town gates, **Porte de Pignerol** and **Porte d'Embrun**. Crowning the old city is the massive **Fort du Château**. Daily **guided walks** are run by **Service du Patrimoine** (✆04 92 20 29 49; www.ville-briancon.fr; Porte de Pignerol, Cité Vauban; tours adult/child €6.20/4.60; ◷10am-noon & 2-5.30pm Tue-Fri & Sun Sep-Jun, or Mon-Sat in Jul & Aug).

Briançon's biggest drawcard is its Unesco-listed ensemble of 17th- and early-18th-century structures designed by pioneering French military architect Vauban, including the old town's signature **star-shaped fortifications**, the coral-pink **Collégiale Notre Dame et St Nicolas**, several nearby **forts** and the **Pont d'Asfeld** bridge.

There are outstanding **hiking** opportunities to be found in the mountains of nearby **Parc National des Écrins** (www.ecrins-parcnational.fr).

Pick up maps and info at the **Maison du Parc** (✆04 92 21 42 15; www.ecrins-parcnational.fr; place du Médecin Général Blanchard; ◷10.30am-6.30pm Jul & Aug, 2-6pm Mon-Fri Sep-Jun). For guided treks, glacier traverses, mountain biking, rafting, kayaking, canyoning and *via ferrate,* check with **Bureau des Guides et Accompagnateurs** (✆04 92 20 15 73; www.guides-briancon.fr; 24 rue Centrale; ◷10am-noon & 3-7pm Mon-Fri, 3-7pm Sat & 10am-1pm Sun summer, 4-7pm rest of year).

The Drive » From Briançon resume your way southeast along the D902, then via the D947 and D5 to your final stop, St-Véran. Only 28km as the crow flies, this last section of tightly folded mountain road works out to 55km, and around 1¾ hours behind the wheel.

- - - - - - - - - - - - -

❾ St-Véran

What more fitting place to wind up a tour of the roof of Europe than France's highest village? Nestled a cool 2040m above sea level, in the midst of the Parc Naturel Régional du Queyras, St-Véran is listed as one of France's most beautiful villages and offers serene hiking in all directions.

Eating & Sleeping

Annecy ❶

✕ Le Denti — French €€

(☎04 50 64 21 17; 25bis av de Loverchy; lunch menus €22, other menus €32-42; ☺noon-1.15pm Thu-Mon, 7.30-9.15pm Mon & Thu-Sat) A few blocks off the beaten track but worth seeking out, this unassuming restaurant serves traditional French cuisine – their speciality is fish – prepared so the taste of the super-fresh ingredients shines through. The menu changes twice a month according to the seasonal produce available in the markets.

⊨ Hôtel Central — Boutique Hotel €

(☎04 50 45 05 37, www.hotelcentralannecy.com; 6bis rue Royale; d/tr €70/80; ℗☜) Forget the prosaic name – this splendid canal-side hotel, occupying a late 17th-century building in the pedestrianised heart of the city, provides comfortably the most eccentric and visually entertaining digs in Annecy. Choose the Chambre Couture (complete with dressmaker's doll and antique sewing machine), the psychedelic Chambre Coco, the Chambre Orientale or any of the other 11 rooms: they're all delightful.

St-Gervais-les-Bains ❷

⊨ Les Dômes de Miage — Campground €

(☎04 50 93 45 96; www.camping-mont-blanc.com; 197 rte des Contamines, St-Gervais; unpowered sites €21.20-26.60, powered sites €25.80-31.20; ☺mid-May–mid-Sep; ☜) Mont Blanc is your wake-up call at this well-equipped campground, beautifully set in wooded hills, 900m above sea level. The first-rate facilities include 150 pitches, a restaurant, volleyball courts, table tennis and other diversions.

Chamonix ❸

✕ Les Vieilles Luges — French €€

(☎06 84 42 37 00; www.lesvieillesluges.com; Les Houches; menus €20-35; ☺lunch daily winter, lunch & dinner by reservation summer, min 25 people) This impossibly atmospheric 250-year-old farmhouse can only be reached on skis or by a scenic 20-minute hike from the Maison Neuve chairlift. Hunker under low wood beams to savour dishes such as *grand-mère*'s *bœuf bourguignon* and creamy *farçon* (potato bake prepared with prunes, bacon and cream), washed down with *vin chaud* (mulled wine) warmed over a wood fire. Magic.

⊨ Auberge du Manoir — Hotel €€

(☎04 50 53 10 77; www.aubergedumanoir.com; 8 rte du Bouchet; s/d/q €133/154/225; ☺closed 2 weeks late Apr & 2 months autumn; ☜) This beautifully converted farmhouse, ablaze with geraniums in summer, offers 18 pine-panelled rooms that are quaint but never cloying, pristine mountain views, an outdoor hot tub, a sauna and a bar whose open fire keeps things cosy. It's family-owned, and prices fall during the week and in low season.

Bonneval-sur-Arc ❻

⊨ Auberge d'Oul — B&B €

(☎04 79 05 87 99; www.auberge-oul.com; 73480 Bonneval-sur-Arc; dm/d/q incl breakfast €26/58/108, incl half-board €37/80/148) Smack on the village square, this flowery-balconied, slate-walled *gîte* (self-catering cottage) has one seven-person dorm and three spotless, rustic rooms. The 2nd floor is a more private *chambre d'hôte* (B&B), and the entire *auberge* opens from mid-June to mid-September, and mid-December to the end of April. The half-board option offers great-value, home-cooked mountain meals.

Foothills of the Alps

18

This exhilarating outdoor adventure links two gorgeous, wild landscapes – the high green meadows and peaks of the Vercors, and the rugged canyon country of the Alpes de Haute-Provence.

TRIP HIGHLIGHTS

START ① | **0 km**

Lans-en-Vercors
Escape to green meadows, limestone peaks and breathtaking gorges

④
Die

110 km

Chichilianne
A hiker's favourite since 1492, below awe-inspiring Mont Aiguille

Sisteron

320 km

Moustiers-Ste-Marie
Lavender-scented gateway to Europe's Grand Canyon

⑦

Gorges du Verdon
FINISH

6 DAYS
475KM / 295 MILES

GREAT FOR...

BEST TIME TO GO
June and September, for good weather without peak summer crowds.

ESSENTIAL PHOTO
The dizzying view of the Gorges du Verdon from Belvédère de l'Escale.

BEST FAMILY HIKE
The high-country loop from La Molière, near Lans-en-Vercors.

Gorges du Verdon Paddlers on the Verdon River

18 Foothills of the Alps

In the transition zone between the Alps and Provence lie some of France's most magnificent and least explored landscapes. Extending from the Vercors plateau to the Verdon River, this trip starts in poppy-strewn pastures where cowbells jingle beneath limestone peaks and ends among the lavender fields and arid gorges of Haute-Provence. Along the way, there's plenty of outdoorsy excitement for the entire family.

TRIP HIGHLIGHT

❶ Lans-en-Vercors

Lans-en-Vercors (1020m) is idyllically set among the sloping pastures, plateaux and chiselled limestone peaks of the 1750-sq-km **Parc Naturel Régional du Vercors**, 28km southwest of Grenoble. With stunning vistas and wildlife including marmots, ibex and chamois, the park draws families seeking low-key outdoor adventure. Hikers of any age will enjoy the easy, supremely scenic 7km high-country loop from **La Molière** to **Pas de Bellecombe**, with its built-in lunch stop at Gîte d'Alpage de la Molière (p213). To reach the trailhead, go 20km north of Lans-en-Vercors via Autrans, following the D106 and a partly unpaved forest road. Alternatively, **Les Accompagnateurs Nature et Patrimoine** (☎04 76 95 08 38; www.accompagnateur-vercors.com;) offers **guided walks** (adult/child €27/20) throughout the Vercors.

🗙 🛏 p213

The Drive » Follow the D531 southwest from Lans-en-Vercors, descending to enter the magnificent Gorges de la Bourne after about 10km.

❷ Gorges de la Bourne

Cliff walls up to 600m high crowd around the road through these deep and dramatic gorges, cut

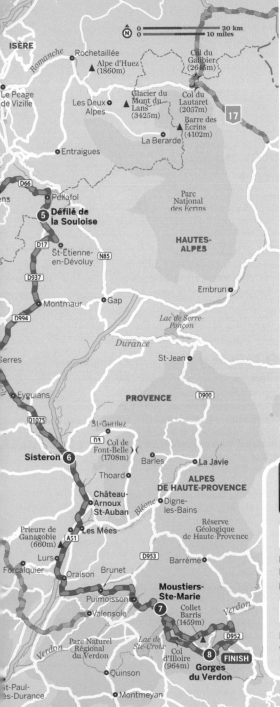

by the eponymous Bourne as it rushes off the Vercors plateau. Watch for narrow turnouts alongside the roadway where you can pull off and admire the views.

The Drive » Near the end of the gorges, bear left on the D103 and proceed 20km south through the pretty mountain villages of St-Julien-en-Vercors and St-Martin-en-Vercors. At St-Agnan-en-Vercors continue 5km south on the D518 to the Grotte de la Luire.

❸ Grottes de la Luire

The Vercors was a hotbed of the French Resistance in WWII. This **cave** (www.grottedelaluire.com; Le passage, 26420 Saint Agnan en Vercors; adult/child €8.50/6; 🕑17 Dec-13 Nov) outside the town of St-Agnan-en-Vercors served as a field hospital for Resistance fighters for five days in July 1944 before German troops raided it, killing

LINK YOUR TRIP

17 **Alpine Adventure**
Head northeast from Lans-en-Vercors to explore France's most awe-inspiring peaks.

22 **Lavender Route**
Wander the purple-fringed back roads of Provence, west of Moustiers-Ste-Marie.

many patients on-site and taking the rest to Grenoble to be shot or deported. Memorial plaques mark the site, and lantern-lit tours are offered in summer.

The Drive » The D518 travels 30km south to Die, culminating in a switchbacking descent from Col de Rousset. The D93 and D539 continue southeast 14km through sun-drenched farmland to Châtillon-en-Diois, a good lunch stop. The final 31km stretch along the D120 and D7 snakes over Col de Menée (1457m) to Chichilianne, affording spellbinding views of Mont Aiguille en route.

TRIP HIGHLIGHT

④ Chichilianne

Its lovely hayfields strewn with red poppies in late spring, Chichilianne has deep roots in mountaineering history, dating back to 1492 when Antoine Deville scaled massive cube-shaped Mont Aiguille by order of King Charles VIII (accompanied by stonemasons and master carpenters who helped build ladders and attach ropes!). Long nicknamed the 'inaccessible mountain', and celebrated by writers such as Rabelais, Mont Aiguille continues to capture the imagination of all who venture near.

Superb high-country hikes around Chichilianne include the **Sentier des Charenches** up Mont Aiguille's southern flanks, and the six-hour loop to the Vercors plateau via

Pas de l'Essaure and **Pas de l'Aiguille** (look for the monument to Resistance fighters who battled the Nazis at these high altitudes). Lower-elevation walks in surrounding valleys include the themed, family-oriented 5km walk, **Sentier des Artisans de la Terre**.

🛏 p213

The Drive » Follow the D7 and D526 east 17km to Mens, then cruise another 19km east on the D66 through hayfields backed by the Dévoluy massif's sawtooth ridgeline. Wind 8km south on the D66A and D537, descending to the Souloise River. Just before the bridge, turn left onto the D217, following signs for 'Sources des Gillardes' and parking at the trailhead.

⑤ Défilé de la Souloise

Forming the border between the *départements* of Isère and Hautes-Alpes, the sheer-faced **Souloise Gorge** is an idyllic spot to stretch your legs. From the parking area, an easy hike (200m each way) leads to the **Sources des Gillardes**, France's second-largest natural spring. Alternatively, continue downriver on the delightful **Canyon de l'Infernet** trail, through fragrant evergreen forest sandwiched between grey and orange rock walls. About 1km along, cross a bridge and loop back up the opposite bank to the parking area.

The Drive » Follow the D537 and D937 south through tiny St-Disdier, enjoying stunning views of the Massif de Dévoluy's austere rocky face, punctuated by the pencil-shaped spire of the 11th-century Mère Église. Zigzag south along the D117 (5km southeast), D17 (7km southwest) and D937 (16km south over Col de Festre). From here, follow the D994, D1075 and D4075 south 54km into Sisteron.

⑥ Sisteron

Perched on a promontory high above the Durance River, Sisteron's stunner is its **citadel** (www.citadelledesisteron.fr; €6.40; ◷9am-6pm Apr-Oct, to 7pm Jul & Aug). For centuries this imposing fortress guarded the strategic narrow passage between Dauphiné and Provence – though Napoléon did somehow sneak past here with 1200 soldiers after escaping Elba in 1815! Today it still commands bird's-eye perspectives of Sisteron's medieval streets, the eye-catching stratified rock face **Rocher de Baume** and the Durance Valley beyond. Architectural highlights include a 13th-century *chemin de ronde* (parapet walk) and a powder magazine designed by French military architect Vauban. On summer evenings the hilltop comes alive with open-air dance and classical-music concerts during the **Festival des Nuits de la Citadelle** (www.nuitsdelacitadelle.fr).

✕ p213

Chichilianne Mont Aiguille towers over the village

The Drive » Zip 39km along the A51 to Oraison. Take the D4 (5km), D907 (10km) and then the D108 (4km) southeast, climbing through Brunet to the Valensole plateau. Cruise 7km east through lavender fields on the D8, take the D953 (4km) into Puimoisson (passing roadside lavender stand Maison du Lavandin), and wind 14km into your next stop, Moustiers-Ste-Marie, along the D56 and the D952.

TRIP HIGHLIGHT

❼ Moustiers-Ste-Marie

Nicknamed Étoile de Provence (Star of Provence), enchanting Moustiers-Ste-Marie straddles the base of towering limestone cliffs – the beginning of the Alps and the end of Haute-Provence's rolling prairies. Winding streets climb among tile-roofed houses, connected by arched stone bridges spanning the picturesque creek (Le Riou) that courses through the village centre.

A 227m-long chain bearing a shining gold star stretches high above the village, legendarily placed there by the Knight of Blacas upon

211

DRIVING THE GORGES DU VERDON

This spine-tingling drive is one of France's classic road trips. A complete circuit of the Gorges from Moustiers-Ste-Marie involves 140km (about four hours without stops) of relentless hairpin turns on precarious rim-side roads, with spectacular scenery around every bend. The only village en route is La Palud-sur-Verdon (930m). Expect slow traffic and scant opportunities to overtake in summer.

From Moustiers, aim first for the **Route des Crêtes** (D952 & D23; ⊗closed 15 Nov-15 Mar), a 23km-long loop with 14 lookouts along the northern rim – ensure you drive the loop clockwise: there's a one-way portion midway. En route, the most thrilling view is from **Belvédère de l'Escale**, an excellent place to spot vultures. After rejoining the D952, the road corkscrews eastward, past **Point Sublime**, which overlooks serrated rock formations dropping to the river.

Return towards Moustiers via the **Corniche Sublime** (D955 to D90, D71 and D19), a heart-palpitating route along the southern rim, passing landmarks including the **Balcons de la Mescla** (Mescla Terraces) and **Pont de l'Artuby**, Europe's highest bridge.

---

his safe return from the Crusades. Below the star, the 14th-century **Chapelle Notre Dame de Beauvoir** (guided tours adult/child €3/free) clings to the cliff ledge like an eagle's nest. A steep trail climbs beside a waterfall to the chapel, passing 14 stations of the cross. On 8 September, a 5am Mass celebrates the Virgin Mary's nativity, followed by flutes, drums and breakfast on the square.

✕ ⊨ p213

The Drive ›› The trip to Gorges du Verdon is a classic. Follow the D952 19km southeast to La Palud-sur-Verdon, then the D23, winding from 9km above the western flank of the Verdon to your final destination.

❽ Gorges du Verdon

Dubbed the Grand Canyon of Europe, the breathtaking Gorges du Verdon slice 25km through Haute-Provence's limestone plateau. The narrow canyon bottom, carved by the Verdon's emerald-green waters, is only 8m to 90m wide; its steep, multi-hued walls, home to griffon vultures, rise as high as 700m – twice as tall as the Eiffel Tower! One of France's most scenic drives takes in staggering panoramas from the vertigo-inducing cliff-side roads on either side.

The canyon floors are accessible only by foot or raft. Dozens of blazed

trails traverse untamed countryside between Castellane and Moustiers, including the classic **Sentier Martel**, which uses occasional ladders and tunnels to navigate 14km of riverbanks and ledges. For details on 28 walks, pick up the excellent English-language *Canyon du Verdon* (€4.70) at Moustiers' **tourist office** (☎04 92 74 67 84; www.moustiers. eu; ⊗9.30am-7pm Mon-Fri, 9.30am-12.30pm & 2-7pm Sat & Sun Jul & Aug, 10am-noon & 2-6pm April-June & Sep, closes around 5pm rest of year; ☎). Rafting operators include **Guides pour l'Aventure** (www.guidesaventure.com) and **Aboard Rafting** (www. rafting-verdon.com).

Eating & Sleeping

Lans-en-Vercors ❶

✖ Gîte d'Alpage
de la Molière   French €

(☎06 09 38 42 42; gitedelamoliere.
aufilduvercors.org; 41 impasse des Frênes, Les
Epérouses, Autrans; menus €15-28; ☺lunch
daily Jun-Sep) High above Lans-en-Vercors, this
welcoming trail-side *refuge* with incomparable
views serves simple mountain fare (savoury
vegetable tarts, salad with smoked trout,
and raspberry, blueberry and walnut pies) on
umbrella-shaded picnic tables astride an Alpine
meadow. The picnic hampers, only €12 per
adult, are a great option for ramblers.

🛏 À la Crécia   B&B €

(☎04 76 95 46 98; www.gite-en-vercors.com;
436 Chemin des Cléments, Les Cléments; s/d/
tr/q incl breakfast €58/63/78/93) Renovated
by Véronique and Pascal, this eco-conscious
16th-century farm, home to goats, pigs and
poultry, has five large guest rooms panelled in
spruce and pine. Dinner is a feast of farm-fresh
produce, with wine included (*menus* €19). You'll
find it 1.8km south of Lans-en-Vercors' church,
on the far outskirts of the village.

Chichilianne ❹

🛏 Au Gai Soleil
de Mont-Aiguille   Hotel €

(☎04 76 34 41 71; www.hotelgaisoleil.com; d/
superior €48/73; 🛜🏊) At the foot of striking
Mont Aiguille, this simple inn has fabulous
views, superb access to local hiking routes,
a rustic country restaurant, a spa and two
massage rooms for treating weary muscles at
trail's end.

Sisteron ❻

✖ La Magnanerie   Gastronomic €€

(☎04 92 62 60 11; www.la-magnanerie.net; N85,
Aubignosc; menus lunch €22-29, dinner €32-55;
☺lunch 12.15-1.30pm, dinner 7.15-9.30pm
Tue-Sun; 🛜) A stylish, if starchy, restaurant and
hotel on the road 10km south of Sisteron. Chef
Stéphan Paroche is known for his colourful,
creative cooking – edible flowers and micro-
herbs adorn exquisite plates of fine French
food. Upstairs accommodation (€78 to €98) is
equally playful: some rooms have comic-book
murals, others are styled after classic cinematic
scenes. Reservations essential.

Moustiers-Ste-Marie ❼

✖ La Grignotière   Provencal €

(☎04 92 74 69 12; rte de Ste-Anne; mains €6-15;
☺11.30am-10pm May-Sep, to 6pm Feb–mid-May)
Hidden behind the pink facade of the Musée
de la Faïence is this utterly gorgeous, blissfully
peaceful garden restaurant. Tables sit between
olive trees and the colourful, eye-catching decor
– including the handmade glassware – is the
handiwork of talented, dynamic owner Sandrine.
Cuisine is 'picnic chic', meaning lots of creative
salads, tapenades, quiches and so on.

🛏 Ferme du Petit Ségriès   Farmstay €

(☎04 92 74 68 83; www.chambre-hote-verdon.
com; d incl breakfast €74-84; 🛜) Friendly
hosts Sylvie and Noël offer five colourful, airy
rooms in their rambling farmhouse, 5km west
of Moustiers on the D952 to Riez. Family-style
tables d'hôte (€30 with wine, served daily
except on Wednesday and Sunday) are served
at a massive chestnut table, or outside beneath
a foliage-covered pergola in summer. Bikes are
available for hire (from €15 per day).

Beaujolais Villages

19

With its lush green hills, cute villages and well-tended vineyards, Beaujolais is a landscape painting come to life. Explore its quaint localities, taste some excellent wines and enjoy the hush.

TRIP HIGHLIGHTS

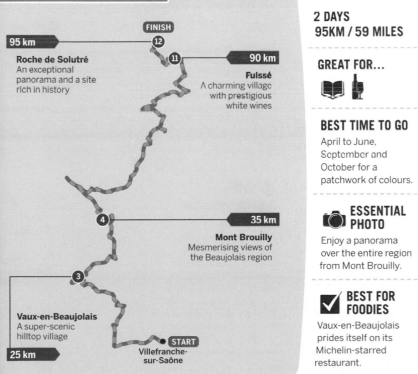

FINISH

12

95 km

Roche de Solutré
An exceptional panorama and a site rich in history

11

90 km

Fuissé
A charming village with prestigious white wines

4

35 km

Mont Brouilly
Mesmerising views of the Beaujolais region

3

Vaux-en-Beaujolais
A super-scenic hilltop village

25 km

START
Villefranche-sur-Saône

---

2 DAYS
95KM / 59 MILES

GREAT FOR...

BEST TIME TO GO
April to June, September and October for a patchwork of colours.

ESSENTIAL PHOTO
Enjoy a panorama over the entire region from Mont Brouilly.

BEST FOR FOODIES
Vaux-en-Beaujolais prides itself on its Michelin-starred restaurant.

19 Beaujolais Villages

Ah, Beaujolais, where the unhurried life is complemented by rolling vineyards, beguiling villages, old churches, splendid estates and country roads that twist into the hills. Once you've left Villefranche-sur-Saône, a rural paradise awaits and a sense of escapism becomes tangible. Be sure to factor in plenty of time for wine tasting.

5 Beaujeu

D337

Mont Brouilly

RHÔNE

Vaux-en-Beaujolais

D1

3

D35

Salles Arbuissonnas en Beaujolais

❶ Villefranche-sur-Saône

Your trip begins with a stroll along lively rue Nationale, where you'll find most of the shops and the Gothic **Collégiale Notre-Dame des Marais**, which boasts an elegant facade and a soaring spire. An excellent starting point for oenophiles, the **tourist office** (☏04 74 07 27 40; www.villefranche-beaujolais.fr; 96 rue de la Sous-Préfecture; ⊗9am-6pm Mon-Sat May-Sep, 10am-5pm Mon-Sat Oct-Apr) houses the **Espace des Vins du Beaujolais**, where you'll have the chance to learn about and sample the Beaujolais' 12 AOCs (Appellations d'Origine Contrôlée).

The Drive » At a roundabout about 800m south of the Collégiale, look out for the brown sign to 'Route des Vins du Beaujolais'. Pass through Gleizé, Lacenas, Denicé, St-Julien and Blacé before reaching Salles-Arbuissonas-en-Beaujolais. Count on a good half-hour to cover the 16km trip.

❷ Salles-Arbuissonnas-en-Beaujolais

As you pass through Salles-Arbuissonnas, keep an eye out for the superb 10th-century **priory** (☏04 74 07 31 94; rue du Chapitre; museum adult/child €4.50/free; ⊗museum 10am-12.30pm & 2-5pm Apr-Oct) and the adjoining Roman **cloister**.

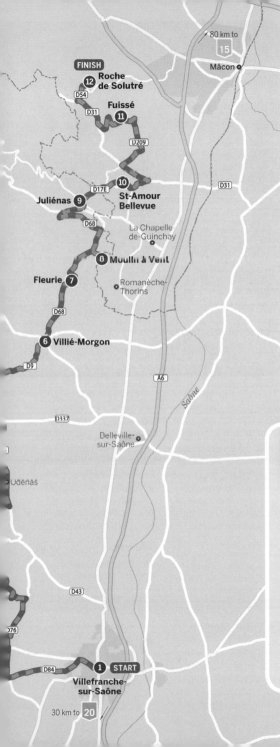

The Drive » Continue along the D35 to Vaux-en-Beaujolais (6.5km).

- - - - - - - - - - - - - - - -

TRIP HIGHLIGHT

❸ Vaux-en-Beaujolais

The village of Vaux-en-Beaujolais emerges like a hamlet in a fairy tale. You can't but be dazzled by the fabulous backdrop – it's perched on a rocky spur ensnared by a sea of vineyards. Don't leave Vaux without enjoying the fruity aroma of Beaujolais-Villages (the local appellation) at **La Cave de Clochemerle** (☎04 74 03 26 58; www.cavedeclochemerle. com; Place de la Mairie; ☺10am-12.30pm & 3-7pm), housed in atmospheric cellars.

🛏 p221

LINK YOUR TRIP

15 **Route des Grands Crus**

For more wine tasting and rolling vineyards, make a beeline for the Route des Grands Crus, which unfolds south of Dijon. Head to Mâcon and follow signs to Dijon.

20 **Rhône Valley**

For a change of scene, head to Lyon (via Mâcon) and discover the hidden gems of the Rhône Valley.

DAVID HUGHES / SHUTTERSTOCK ©

The Drive » Take the D133 to Le Perréon, then follow signs to St-Étienne-des-Oullières and Odenas. In Odenas, follow signs to Mont Brouilly (13km from Vaux-en-Beaujolais).

TRIP HIGHLIGHT

❹ Mont Brouilly

It would be a crime to explore the Beaujolais and not take the scenic road that leads to Mont Brouilly (485m), crowned with a small chapel. Hold on to your hat and lift your jaw off the floor as you approach the lookout at the summit – the view over the entire Beaujolais region and the Saône valley will be etched in your memory forever.

The Drive » Drive down to St-Lager, then take the D68 to Cercié and continue along the D337 to Beaujeu (9km from Mont Brouilly).

❺ Beaujeu

The historic Beaujolais wine capital, Beaujeu is an enchanting spot to while away a few hours. The **Caveau des Producteurs de Beaujolais-Villages** (☎04 74 04 81 18; Place de L'Hôtel de Ville; ⏰10.30am-1pm & 3.30-7pm late-Jan–Dec), located in the basement of the tourist office, is a great place to sip some excellent Beaujolais-Villages and Brouilly. It's also worth popping your head into the rewarding **La Maison du Terroir Beaujolais** (☎04 74 69 20 56; www.lamaisonduterroir

beaujolais.com; place de l'Hôtel de Ville; ⏰10am-12.30pm & 2-6pm Wed-Mon Mar-Dec), across the square from the tourist office. Housed in a wonderful Renaissance building, this produce shop has a wide array of Beaujolais wines, cheeses, jams and charcuterie.

The Drive » Head to Lantignié along the D78 and continue to Régnié-Durette, where you'll see signs to Villié-Morgon. The full drive covers a little over 9km.

❻ Villié-Morgon

Morgon wine, anybody? Expand your knowledge of the local *appellation* with a tasting session at

the vaulted **Caveau de Morgon** (☎04 74 04 20 99; www.morgon.fr; Château Font-crenne, Rue du Château Font-crenne; ⏰10am-noon & 2-6pm Feb-Dec), which occupies a grandiose 17th-century château in the heart of town – it doesn't get more atmospheric than this.

🛏 p221

The Drive » From Villié-Morgon, it's a relaxed 10km drive to Fleurie via Chiroubles. Follow the D18 and the D86 to Chiroubles, then signs to Fleurie.

❼ Fleurie

Beaujolais' rising star, Fleurie red wines are said to be sensuous, offering a

Beaujolais Vineyards line the valleys

combination of floral and fruity notes. A superb experience, **Château du Bourg** (☎06 08 86 49 02, 04 74 69 81 15; www.chateau-du-bourg.com; Le Bourg; ⊙by reservation), run by the Matray brothers (ask for Denis, who speaks some English), offers free tastings in a cool bistro-like setting and can arrange vineyard tours and cellar visits on request (€12). Tip: Grille-Midi, its signature vintage, is unforgettable.

✕ p221

The Drive » Take the D68 towards Chénas; after about 3km turn right onto the D68e

towards Romanèche-Thorins and you'll soon reach Moulin à Vent. It's a 4km drive from Fleurie.

- - - - - - - - - -

⑧ Moulin à Vent

Reason itself to visit this drowsy hamlet is the heritage-listed **Moulin à Vent** (Windmill). Dubbed the 'King of Beaujolais', the Moulin à Vent *appellation* is a particularly charming wine to sample in situ: its **Caveau du Moulin à Vent** (☎03 85 35 58 09; www.moulin-a-vent. net; 1673 route du Moulin à Vent; ⊙10am-12.30pm & 2.30-7pm daily Jul & Aug, 10am 12.30pm & 2.30-6pm Thu-Mon Sep–mid-Dec & Mar-Jun), across the

road from the windmill, provides a prime wine-tasting opportunity.

The Drive » From Moulin à Vent retrace your route back towards Chénas and take the D68 to Juliénas. It's an easy 6.6km drive.

- - - - - - - - - -

⑨ Juliénas

One of the best-kept secrets in Beaujolais is this delightful village famed for its eponymous vintage. A beauty of a castle, the 16th-century **Château de Juliénas** (☎04 74 04 49 98, 06 96 76 95 41; www.chateaudejulienas. com; Château de Juliénas; ⊙by reservation) occupies

WHEN BEAUJEU GOES WILD

A colourful time to motor in Beaujeu is around the third week in November. At the stroke of midnight on the third Thursday (ie Wednesday night), the *libération* (release) or *mise en perce* (tapping; opening) of the first bottles of cherry-bright Beaujolais Nouveau is celebrated around France and the world. In Beaujeu there's free Beaujolais Nouveau for all as part of the Sarmentelles de Beaujeu – a giant street party that kicks off on the Wednesday leading up to the Beaujolais Nouveau's release for five days of wine tasting, live music and dancing.

a delightful estate; tours can be arranged by phoning ahead. No doubt you'll be struck by the cellars, the longest in the region. Tours can be followed by an *aperi'vin* (tasting and snacks; €16). Another atmospheric venture set in a disused church, **Cellier de la Vieille Église** (🖉04 74 04 42 98; Le Bourg; 🕙10am-12.30pm & 3-6pm, closed Tue Oct-Apr) is a great place to sip wines of the Juliénas *appellation*.

🛏 p221

The Drive » Follow the road to St-Amour Bellevue along the D17e and the D486ter (3.5km from Juliénas).

⑩ St-Amour Bellevue

Not to be missed in St-Amour: the **Domaine des Vignes du Paradis – Pascal Durand** (🖉03 85 36 52 97; www.saint-amour-en-paradis.com; En Paradis; 🕙10am-6pm). This award-winning domaine run by the fifth generation of vintners welcomes visitors to its intimate cellars and sells St-Amour wines at unbeatable prices.

🛏 p221

The Drive » Follow the D186 towards Chânes. In Bourgneuf, take the D31 to St-Vérand. From St-Vérand, follow signs to Chaintré and continue to Fuissé. It's a 10km trip from St-Amour.

TRIP HIGHLIGHT

⑪ Fuissé

If you like peace, quiet and sigh-inducing views, you'll love this absolutely picturesque stone town nestled in a small valley carpeted by manicured vineyards. You've now left Beaujolais – Fuissé is part of Burgundy. It's famous for its prestigious whites

of the Pouilly-Fuissé *appellation*. You can attend tastings at various cellars around town or, for the ultimate experience, at the magnificent **Château de Fuissé** (🖉03 85 35 61 44; www.chateau-fuisse.fr; Le Plan, Pouilly-Fuissé; 🕙by reservation).

The Drive » From Fuissé follow signs to Chasselas along the D172. After about 3.5km, turn right onto the D31 (direction Tramayes). Drive another 2km to a right-hand turn onto the D54 (direction Solutré-Pouilly). Count on 15 minutes for the 7km trip.

TRIP HIGHLIGHT

⑫ Roche de Solutré

A lovely 20-minute walk along the **Sentier des Roches** will get you to the top of the rocky outcrop known as the Roche de Solutré (493m), from where Mont Blanc can sometimes be seen, especially at sunset. For some cultural sustenance, make a beeline for the nearby **Musée Départemental de Préhistoire de Solutré** (🖉03 85 35 85 24; www.musees-bourgogne.org; Solutré; adult/child €3.50/free; 🕙10am-6pm Apr-Sep, 10am-noon & 2-5pm Oct-Mar, closed Dec), which displays finds from one of Europe's richest prehistoric sites.

 p221

Eating & Sleeping

Vaux-en-Beaujolais ❸

🛏 Auberge de Clochemerle   Hotel €€

(📞04 74 03 20 16; www.aubergedeclochemerle.
fr; 12 rue Gabriel Chevallier; d €60-185, q €200,
restaurant menus €42-81; P 🛜) A pleasant
combination of modern and traditional, this
atmospheric hotel smack dab in the centre has
12 stylishly refitted rooms, some with vineyard
views. Dining at its Michelin-starred restaurant is
a treat. Chef Romain creates elaborate Beaujolais
meals using the best local ingredients, and his
wife Delphine is a renowned sommelier – wine
pairings are an adventure. Brilliant value.

Villié-Morgon ❻

🛏 Château de Bellevue   B&B €€

(📞04 74 66 98 88; www.chateau-bellevue.fr;
Bellevue; d incl breakfast €99-160; P 🛜) For the
ultimate château experience, you can't do better
than this attractive venture nestled amid seas
of vineyards. Françoise Barbet will welcome you
in perfect English and offer you a personalised
tour of the winery and the cellars. The five rooms
are spacious and country-chic elegant, with soft-
toned fabrics and sweeping vineyard views.

Fleurie ❼

🍴 Auberge du Cep   French €€

(📞04 74 04 10 77; www.lecep-fleurie.fr; Place de
l'Église; mains €18-28, menus €20-58; 🕐noon-
2pm & 7-8.30pm Tue-Sat, noon-2pm Sun)
Traditional cooking at its best. Feast on regional
specialities such as pike-perch, snails, perfectly
fried frogs' legs, and rosy tenderloin of Charolais
beef (France's best) in a rustic dining room.

Juliénas ❾

🛏 Chez La Rose   Hotel €€

(📞04 74 04 41 20; www.chez-la-rose.fr; Le Bourg;
d €69-125, ste €90-215, mains €17-22, menu €29;

🕐 restaurant noon-2pm Wed, Sat & Sun, 7-9pm
Wed-Sun, closed Dec–mid-Mar; P ❄🛜🛉)
This charming inn features 13 rooms in various
buildings scattered around the village. They're
all equipped to the highest standard, but the
vast suites are the ones to aim for. Dinner at the
restaurant is a gourmet affair, with standouts
like coq au vin de Juliénas (chicken cooked in
Juliénas wine) and Charolais beef fillet.

St-Amour Bellevue ❿

🛏 Le Paradis de Marie   B&B €

(📞03 85 36 51 90; www.leparadisdemarie.com;
Les Ravinets; d €85, caravan €95, incl breakfast;
🕐Apr-Oct; P 🛜) Have a decadently bucolic
rest at this relaxing place, a lovingly restored
stone mansion exquisitely situated not far from
the main street. The five rooms open onto a
courtyard, while the romantically furnished
gypsy caravan in the garden will please those in
search of an offbeat experience.

🛏 L'Auberge du Paradis   Boutique Hotel €€

(📞03 85 37 10 26; www.aubergeduparadis.fr;
Le Bourg; d €145-260, menu €70; 🕐restaurant
7.30-9pm Wed-Sun; P ❄🛜🛉) Beaujolais'
iconic, much-beloved inn occupies a village
house restyled into an urban-chic, design-led
boutique hotel. Oh, and there's the fantastic
restaurant – the creative, inspired cooking
(expect top-quality ingredients served with a
symphony of spices) draws diners from afar.

Solutré ⓬

🍴 La Courtille de Solutré   French €€

(📞03 85 35 80 73; www.lacourtilledesolutre.fr; rte
de la Roche, Solutré-Pouilly; mains €24-25, lunch
menus €16-28, menus €40-44; 🕐noon-2pm &
7-8.30pm Wed-Sat, noon-2pm Sun) Chef Adrien
Yparraguirre does traditional dishes exceptionally
well, with a creative twist. Sit on the shady terrace
or head into the rustic-chic interior.

Rhône Valley

20

The mighty Rhône flows from the Alps to the Mediterranean. Trace its course from Lyon to Provence, visiting gourmet restaurants, Gallo-Roman ruins and spectacular river gorges along the way.

TRIP HIGHLIGHTS

START

0 km — 1

Lyon
Eat like a king and explore secret passageways of the silk weavers

2

35 km

Vienne
A Gallo-Roman treasure trove by the Rhône's river banks

Valence

Mirmande

Montélimar

230 km — 6

Gorges de l'Ardèche
Kayak down this dizzyingly beautiful river gorge

Mornas

8

FINISH

300 km

Orange
Gaze up at Caesar atop an ancient theatre wall

5 DAYS
300KM / 186 MILES

GREAT FOR...

BEST TIME TO GO
June and July for festivals in the Roman theatres of Lyon, Vienne and Orange.

 ESSENTIAL PHOTO
The Pont d'Arc, a stunning stone archway over the Ardèche River.

BEST FOR FOODIES
Lyon's beloved *bouchons* (convivial neighbourhood bistros).

20 Rhône Valley

Food and history are recurring themes on this multifaceted meander down the Rhône, from the fabled eateries of Lyon to the Gallo-Roman museum at Vienne, the nougat factories of Montélimar and the ancient theatre at Orange. As you work your way downriver to Provence, you'll also encounter imposing hilltop fortresses, slow-paced southern villages and one of France's prettiest river gorges.

TRIP HIGHLIGHT

❶ Lyon

This strategic spot at the confluence of the Rhône and Saône Rivers has been luring people ever since the Romans named it Lugudunum in 43 BC. Climb Fourvière hill west of town to witness the successive waves of human settlement, spread out in chronological order at your feet: a pair of Gallo-Roman theatres in the foreground, Vieux Lyon's medieval cathedral on the Saône's near banks, the 17th-century *hôtel de ville* (town hall) on the peninsula between the rivers, and, beyond the Rhône, modern Lyon's skyscrapers backed by the distant Alps.

With its illustrious history and renowned gastronomy, France's third-largest city merits at least a two-day visit. Supplement a walking tour (p230) of Lyon's quintessential sights with a visit to Croix Rousse, the 19th-century silk-weaver's district where Jacquard looms still restore fabrics for France's historical monuments, and don't leave town without eating in at least one of the city's incomparable *bouchons* (small bistros).

✗ 🛏 p45, p229

The Drive » Shoot 33km down the A7 to Vienne, enjoying close-up views of the Rhône en route.

TRIP HIGHLIGHT

❷ Vienne

France's Gallo-Roman heritage is alive and well in this laid-back riverfront city, whose back streets hide a trio of jaw-dropping ruins: the 1st-century-BC **Temple d'Auguste et de Livie**, with its splendid Corinthian columns; the **Pyramide du Cirque**, a 15.5m-tall obelisk that once pierced the centre of a hippodrome; and the 1st-century-AD **Théâtre Romain** (📞04 74 85 39 23; www.musees-vienne. fr; rue du Cirque; adult/child €3/free; ⏰9.30am-1pm & 2-6pm Tue-Sun), which relives its glory days as a performance venue each summer during Vienne's two-week **jazz festival** (www.jazzavienne.com).

Across the river, a treasure trove of Gallo-Roman artefacts is displayed at the **Musée Gallo-Romain** (📞04 74 53 74 01; www.musees-gallo-romains.com; D502, St-Romain-en-Gal; adult/child €6/free; ⏰10am-6pm Tue-Sun).

✗ p229

The Drive » Follow the D386, D1086 and D86 for 48km south, threading the needle between the Rhône and the pretty mountains of the Parc Naturel Régional du Pilat. At Sarras cross the bridge to St-Vallier, then continue 32km south on the N7 through classic Côtes du Rhône wine country around Tain l'Hermitage into Valence.

Valence

With its warm weather, honey-coloured light and relaxed cadence, it's easy to see why Valence advertises itself as the northern gateway to Provence. At lunchtime, make a beeline for André (p229), a stylish eatery with an excellent wine list that's part of the Pic family's award-winning, multigenerational restaurant empire, or pack yourself a picnic at the Pic-affiliated gourmet grocery, **L'Épicerie** (☑04 75 25 07 07; www.anne-sophie-pic.com/content/lepicerie; 210 av Victor Hugo; ☺9.30am-2.30pm & 5-7pm Tue-Sat, 10am-1pm Sun). Afterwards visit **Maison Nivon** (☑04 75 44 03 37; www.maison-nivon-valence.fr; 17 av Pierre Semard; suisses from €1.90; ☺6am 7.30pm Tue-Sun) for a *suisse*, Valence's classic orange-rind-flavoured pastry in the shape of a Swiss Vatican guard. In the old town, gawk at the

LINK YOUR TRIP

13 **Volcanoes of the Auvergne**

Head west of Lyon for this pastoral meander among ancient green peaks.

21 **Roman Provence**

From Orange, head northeast and further south to delve deeper into Roman ruins.

FRANCK GUIZIOU / GETTY IMAGES ©

allegorical sculpted heads adorning the facade of the wonderful 16th-century **Maison des Têtes** (57 Grande Rue).

✗ ⊨ p229

The Drive » Cruise 28km south along the N7, then wind 5km through orchard-covered hills on the D57 into Mirmande.

- - - - - - - - - - - -

❹ Mirmande

Surrounded by pretty orchard country, this hilltop gem of stone houses and sleepy medieval streets was once a major centre of silkworm production. It then became an artists' colony in the 20th century, when cubist painter André Lhote made his home here. Volcanologist-cinematographer Haroun Tazieff later served as the town's mayor, adding to Mirmande's cultural cachet and earning it recognition as one of *les plus beaux villages de la France* (France's prettiest villages).

With a couple of charming hotels, Mirmande makes an inviting overnight stop. Activities include browsing for treasures at **Porte des Gaultiers** (www.porte desgaultiers.fr), an artsy boutique by the arched 14th-century town gate, and wandering up to the 12th-century Roman-esque **Église de Ste-Foy**, where concerts and art exhibits are held in summertime and beautiful Rhône Valley views unfold year-round.

The Drive » Snake 12km southeast on the D57 over Col de la Grande Limite (515m) into medieval Marsanne, then continue 17km southwest into Montélimar on the D105 and D6.

- - - - - - - - - - - -

❺ Montélimar

An obligatory stop for sweet tooths, Montélimar is famous for its delectable nougat made from almonds, lavender honey, pistachios, sugar, egg white and vanilla. To

Montélimar The view from Château des Adhémar

taste this sweet delight at the source, visit one of Montélimar's small producers, such as **L'Artisan Nougatier** (☎04 75 52 01 59; www.lartisannougatier. com; 35 bd Marre Desmarais; ☺9am-7.30pm). Afterwards burn off the calories with a climb to **Château des Adhémar** (☎04 75 00 62 30; www.chateaux.ladrome.fr; adult/child €4/free; ☺10am-12.30pm & 2-6pm Sep-Jun, 10am-6pm Jul-Aug), whose 12th-century fortifications hold a Romanesque chapel and a rotating series of art exhibits.

The Drive ≫ Follow the D73 southwest for 10km across the Rhône into Viviers, follow the river 15km south into Bourg-St-Andéol, then squiggle 30km along the D4 past St-Remèze's lavender museum to Vallon-Pont-d'Arc, western gateway to the Gorges de l'Ardèche.

- - - - - - - - - - - -

`TRIP HIGHLIGHT`

❻ Gorges de l'Ardèche

These steep and spectacular limestone gorges cut a curvaceous swath through the high scrubland along the Ardèche River, a tributary of the Rhône. The real showstopper, near the gorges' western entrance, is the **Pont d'Arc**, a sublimely beautiful natural stone arch. Stop here to camp, swim or join one of the many paddling tours down the river. Further east, the **Sentier Aval des Gorges** descends steeply for 2km to the heart of the gorges, granting hikers access to two primitive campgrounds at Bivouac de Gournier and Bivouac de Gaud. Allow some time to visit the sensational **Caverne du Pont d'Arc** (☎04 75 94 39 40; www. cavernedupontdarc.fr; Plateau du Razal; adult/child €13/6.50; ☺8.30am-8pm May-Sep, 9.30am-6.30pm Oct-Dec & Feb-Apr) museum, which houses replicas of amazing prehistoric paintings.

🛏 p229

BOUCHONS

A *bouchon* might be a 'bottle stopper' or 'traffic jam' elsewhere in France, but in Lyon it's a cosy, traditional bistro specialising in regional cuisine. *Bouchons* originated in the first half of the 20th century when many bourgeois families had to let go their in-house cooks, who then set up their own restaurants.

Kick-start your meal with a *communard,* an aperitif of red Beaujolais wine and *crème de cassis* (blackcurrant liqueur), then move on to a *pot* – a 46cL glass bottle adorned with an elastic band to prevent wine drips – of local Brouilly, Beaujolais, Côtes du Rhône or Mâcon.

Next comes the entrée, perhaps *tablier de sapeur* (breaded, fried tripe), *salade lyonnaise* (green salad with bacon, croutons and poached egg), or lentils in creamy sauce. Hearty main dishes include *boudin noir aux pommes* (blood sausage with apples), *quenelles de brochet* (pike dumplings served in a creamy crayfish sauce) and *andouillette* (sausage made from pigs' intestines).

For the cheese course, choose between a bowl of *fromage blanc* (a cross between cream cheese and natural yoghurt); *cervelle de canut* ('brains of the silk weaver'; *fromage blanc* mixed with chives and garlic, a staple of Lyon's 19th-century weavers); or local St Marcellin ripened to gooey perfection.

Desserts are grandma-style: think *tarte aux pommes* (apple tart), or the Lyonnais classic *tarte aux pralines*, a brilliant rose-coloured confection made with crème fraiche and crushed sugar-coated almonds.

Little etiquette is required in *bouchons*. Mopping your plate with a chunk of bread is fine, and you'll usually sit elbow-to-elbow with your fellow diners at tightly wedged tables (great for practising your French).

The Drive ›› From Vallon-Pont-d'Arc, the breathtaking D290 zigzags for 29km along the canyon's rim, with 11 viewpoints revealing dazzling vistas of horseshoe bends, and kayakers in formation far below. Exiting the gorges, take the D200 for 2km south through pretty medieval Aiguèze, then continue 22km southeast across the Rhône into Mornas via the D901, D6086, D994 and N7.

---

❼ Mornas

Perched on some precipitous cliffs, the 11th- to 14th-century **Forteresse de Mornas** (☎04 90 37 01 26; www.forteresse-de-mornas.com; tours adult/child €9/7; ⊗tours 11am, 2pm, 3pm, 4pm, 5pm daily Jul & Aug, Sat & Sun Apr-Jun & Sep) makes a dramatic backdrop for the pretty village below. Built by the medieval Counts of Toulouse, it commands outstanding views west to the Rhône and east to Mont Ventoux. A trail climbs 137 vertical metres from the village past the 12th-century Romanesque **Église Notre-Dame du Val-Romigier** to the fortress, where costumed guides offer historical re-enactments. Medieval fever also grips Mornas in September during **La Médiévale de Mornas**, a popular annual festival and crafts market.

The Drive ›› Zip 12km southeast down the N7 into Orange, greeted by the magnificent Arc de Triomphe.

TRIP HIGHLIGHT

❽ Orange

Sun-drenched Orange is a dream for fans of ancient ruins. Outstanding **Théâtre Antique** (www.theatre-antique.com; rue Madeleine Roch; adult/child €9.50/7.50; ⊗9am-7pm Jun-Aug, shorter hours rest of year), one of only three Roman theatres in the world with a perfectly preserved stage wall, shines during summer performances such as epic international opera festival **Chorégies d'Orange** (www.choregies.asso.fr; ⊗Jul & Aug). North of town is the exquisite 1st-century-AD **Arc de Triomphe**.

🛏 p245

Eating & Sleeping

Lyon ❶

✕ Daniel et Denise   Bouchon €€

(☏04 78 42 24 62; www.danieletdenise-stjean.
fr; 36 rue Tramassac, 5e; mains €15-25, lunch
menu €21, menus €30-40; ☺noon-2pm &
7.30-9.30pm Tue-Sat) One of Vieux Lyon's most
dependable and traditional eateries, this classic
spot is run by award-winning chef Joseph Viola,
who was elected president of Lyon's *bouchon*
association in 2014. Come here for elaborate
variations on traditional Lyonnais themes.

🛏 Cour des Loges   Hotel €€€

(☏04 72 77 44 44; www.courdesloges.com; 2-8
rue du Bœuf, 5e; d €200-350, ste €250-600;
🌂 @ 🛜 ❄; Ⓜ Vieux Lyon) Four 14th- to 17th-
century houses wrapped around a *traboule*
(secret passage) with preserved features such
as Italianate loggias make this an exquisite
place to stay. Individually decorated rooms
woo with designer bathroom fittings and
bountiful antiques, while decadent facilities
include a spa, a Michelin-starred restaurant
(menus €95 to €115), a swish cafe and a cross-
vaulted bar.

Vienne ❷

✕ L'Espace PH3   Modern French €€

(☏04 74 53 01 96; www.lapyramide.com; 14 bd
Fernand Point; mains €20-23, lunch menu €24;
☺noon-1.30pm & 7.30-9.30pm) Overseen by
two-Michelin-starred chef Patrick Henriroux,
L'Espace PH3 offers an affordable gastronomic
menu, serving a small selection of French
classics with a creative twist. The lunch menu is
an absolute steal. In summer, meals are served
out on the superb garden terrace.

Valence ❸

✕ André   Bistro €€

(☏04 75 44 15 32; www.anne-sophie-pic.com/
content/andre; 285 av Victor Hugo; mains €24-
54, menu €32; ☺noon-2pm & 8-9.30pm) André
is the less formal but still stunning bistro side
of Anne-Sophie Pic's gastronomic empire. The
fabulous-value menu always involves seasonal,
fresh ingredients, and dishes are imaginatively
prepared and artfully presented. The belle
époque–inspired decor, with wooden tables and
old photos of the Pic family adorning the walls,
is equally stunning.

🛏 La Maison de la Pra   B&B €€

(☏04 75 43 69 73; www.maisondelapra.com; 8
rue de l'Équerre; d €145-200, q €240; Ⓟ ❄ 🛜)
Such charm! If you've ever wanted to stay in a
16th-century *hôtel particulier* (master's house),
this bijou B&B enticingly positioned in a quiet
alley near the town hall is the real McCoy. It
shelters five stadium-sized suites with beamed
ceilings, period furniture and artworks. They're
smack in the centre but still feel very quiet.
Good English is spoken.

Gorges de l'Ardèche ❻

🛏 Le Belvédère   Hotel €

(☏04 75 88 00 02; www.hotel-ardeche-belvedere.
com; D290, rte Touristique des Gorges; d €60-125;
☺Apr-Oct; Ⓟ ❄ 🛜 ❄) Just 300m away
from the Pont d'Arc, the aptly named Belvédère
(Lookout) has 30 rooms that have been sleekly
refitted. Half of the rooms have views of the
Gorges, and some come with a balcony. Facilities
include a swimming pool, a canoe/kayak rental
outlet and a well-regarded on-site restaurant
(menus from €23). Fancy a dip? There's direct
access to the river just across the road.

STRETCH YOUR LEGS
LYON

Start/Finish Basilique Notre-Dame de Fourvière

Distance 3km

Duration 2½ hours

Stroll through two millennia of Lyonnais history, from the Gallo-Roman settlement of Lugudunum to Lyon's avant-garde 20th-century opera house; along the way, three secret medieval passageways and a pedestrian bridge across the Saône River are thrown in just for fun.

Take this walk on Trip

Basilique Notre-Dame de Fourvière

Start at this massive hilltop **basilica** (www.fourviere.org; place de Fourvière, 5e; rooftop tours adult/child €7/4; ⏰8am-6.45pm, tours Apr-Nov), whose terrace offers stunning panoramas of Lyon, the Rhône and Saône Rivers, and even distant Mont Blanc on clear days.

The Walk » Head southwest along rue Roger Radisson for 250m to the Gallo-Roman Museum.

Musée Gallo-Romain de Fourvière

Ancient Gallo-Roman artefacts from the Rhône Valley are displayed at this hillside **museum** (📞04 73 38 49 30; 17 rue Cléberg, 5e; adult/child €4/free, Thu free; ⏰10am-6pm Tue-Sun). Next door are two ancient Roman theatres, the 10,000-seat **Théâtre Romain** and the smaller **odéon**.

The Walk » Descend rue Cléberg 200m, then turn left into leafy Parc des Hauteurs, following the main path downhill 400m to Montée St-Barthélémy. Walk downhill about 50m on Montée St-Barthélémy and turn right into Montée des Chazeaux, down to rue du Bœuf. Turn right then immediately left into rue de la Bombarde for about 30m. Take the first street to the right (rue des Antonins) until you reach the cathedral.

Cathédrale St-Jean

This partly Romanesque, partly Flamboyant Gothic **cathedral** (place St-Jean, 5e; ⏰8.15am-7.45pm Mon-Fri, to 7pm Sat & Sun;) was built between the late 11th and early 16th centuries. Don't miss the **astronomical clock** in the north transept, which chimes elaborately at noon, 2pm, 3pm and 4pm daily.

The Walk » Go back to rue du Bœuf and stop at house number 27 (on your right).

Traboules

Throughout Vieux Lyon, secret passages known as **traboules** (from the Latin *transambulare,* 'to walk through') wind through apartment blocks and courtyards, up stairs and down corridors, connecting streets with one another in unexpected ways. In all, 315 passages

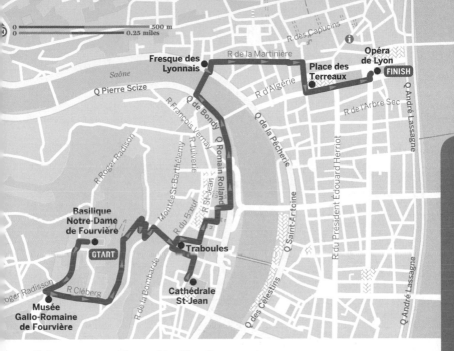

link 230 streets, with a combined length of 50km. Some *traboules* date from Roman times, while others were constructed by *canuts* (silk weavers) in the 19th century to transport silk in inclement weather. Resistance fighters found them equally handy during WWII.

The Walk » Enter the *traboule* at number 27 and navigate to its exit at 54 rue St-Jean; turn left into rue St Jean until you reach number 27. Open the door and cross to 6 rue des Trois Maries. Turn left and walk until you reach Place de la Baleine, which is lined with plenty of eateries and an iconic ice-cream parlour. Take the small alley on your right and you're now on the main road along the Saône River. Now follow the Saône River 600m north and cross the Passerelle St-Vincent pedestrian bridge to Lyon's most famous mural.

Fresque des Lyonnais

Well-known Lyonnais peer out from this seven-storey **mural** (cnr rue de la Martinière & quai St-Vincent, 1er), including loom inventor Joseph-Marie Jacquard, superstar chef Paul Bocuse and the yellow-haired Little Prince, created by author-aviator Antoine de Saint-Exupéry.

The Walk » Head 400m east on rue de la Martinière, then go south one block on rue Paul Chenavard into place des Terreaux.

Place des Terreaux

The centrepiece of Lyon's beautiful **central square** is a 19th-century **fountain** sculpted by Frédéric-Auguste Bartholdi (of Statue of Liberty fame). Fronting the square's eastern edge is the ornate **hôtel de ville** (town hall).

The Walk » From the south side of the square, head 250m east on rue Joseph Serlin to the Opéra.

Opéra de Lyon

Lyon's neoclassical 1831-built **opera house** (www.opera-lyon.com; 1 place de la Comédie, 1er) sports a striking semi-cylindrical glass-domed roof, added in 1993 by renowned French architect Jean Nouvel. On summer evenings, free jazz concerts are performed under the arches up front.

The Walk » From Hôtel de Ville station, where you're now standing, ride the metro three stops back to Vieux Lyon station, then return to Fourvière via funicular.

Provence & Southeast France

WITH ITS SHIMMERING COAST AND RUSTIC PROVENÇAL HEART, the Mediterranean south has a timeless allure. Driving here you'll travel through wildly divergent landscapes: cinematic coastline, rugged hinterland and bucolic valleys. And there are loads of charming villages to explore.

The Cote d'Azur's glamorous cities, deep-blue Med and chic hilltop villages never fail to delight. Inland, you'll weave between fragrant fields, forested gorges and Roman ruins. Skip over the sea to the unspoilt island delights of Corsica or be engulfed in the lush green wetlands of the Camargue.

Along the way you'll connect with the poets, painters and writers who flocked here during the 20th century, chasing sun and inspiration.

Cote d'Azur Corniche de l'Esterel

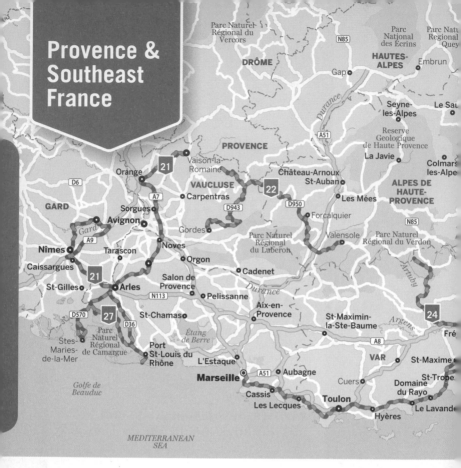

Provence & Southeast France

21 Roman Provence 7 Days
Provence's impressive Roman treasures line up along this leisurely drive. (p237)

22 Lavender Route 4–5 Days
The region at its prettiest, with flowery fields and rustic villages. (p247)

Classic Trip

23 Riviera Crossing 4 Days
The best beaches, cities, villages and nature along the Med coast. (p255)

24 Var Delights 5 Days
Expect an incredible array of viewpoints and spectacular landscapes. (p267)

25 Southern Seduction en Corse 10 Days
This jaunt along Corsica's southern coast takes in plenty of history. (p277)

26 Corsican Coast Cruiser 5 Days
Discover western Corsica's majestic mountain peaks and covetable sandy coves. (p287)

27 The Camargue 4 Days
Loop through the wild, lush wetlands where bulls and white horses roam. (p297)

48km to
Corsica

48km to
Corsica

Mont Ventoux Limestone slopes and stunning vistas

✓ DON'T MISS

The Road up Mt Ventoux

Relive gruelling Tour de France ascents from behind the wheel. Feel the cycling love on Trip 22

Fenocchio

Enjoy some original flavours at this iconic ice cream parlour on Trip 23

Grand Hôtel Nord Pinus, Arles

What other hotel (or city) boasts embedded Roman columns and bullfighters' trophies? Visit on Trip 27

Orange's Roman Arc de Triomphe

This monument's detailed carvings are a fascinating peek into what got your average Roman foot soldier excited. Get close on Trip 21

Pastis

Always ask for this aniseed-flavoured liqueur by brand. We like the herbal Henri Bardouin or the spicy Janot. Sip on Trips 21 24

Roman Provence

21

Survey Provence's incredible Roman legacy as you follow ancient routes through the region's river gorges and vineyards, gathering provisions as you go.

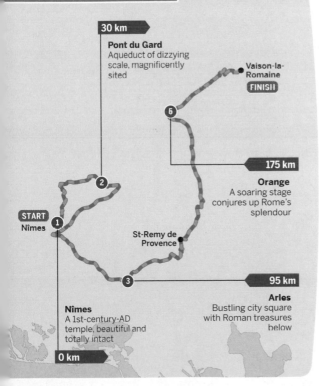

30 km

Pont du Gard
Aqueduct of dizzying scale, magnificently sited

Vaison-la-Romaine

FINISH

175 km

Orange
A soaring stage conjures up Rome's splendour

St-Remy de Provence

START
Nîmes

95 km

Arles
Bustling city square with Roman treasures below

Nîmes
A 1st-century-AD temple, beautiful and totally intact

0 km

7 DAYS
205KM / 127 MILES

GREAT FOR...

BEST TIME TO GO
Ruins open year-round, but avoid August's heat and crush.

 ESSENTIAL PHOTO

The Pont du Gard, illuminated every night in summer.

✓ **BEST FOR CULTURE**

Balmy nights at Orange's Théâtre Antique are magical; July includes the Chorégies d'Orange.

21 Roman Provence

Provence was where Rome first truly flexed its imperial muscles. Follow Roman roads, cross Roman bridges and grab a seat in the bleachers at Roman theatres and arenas. Thrillingly, you'll discover that most of Provence's Roman ruins aren't ruins at all. Many are exceptionally well preserved, and some are also evocatively integrated into the modern city. With Provence's knockout landscape as a backdrop, history never looked so good!

TRIP HIGHLIGHT

1 Nîmes

Nîmes' bizarre coat of arms – a crocodile chained to a palm tree! – recalls the region's first, but definitely not last, horde of sun-worshipping retirees. Julius Caesar's loyal legionnaires were granted land here to settle after hard years on the Nile campaigns. Two millennia later, their ambitious town blends seamlessly with the bustling, workaday French streetscapes of the modern city. An

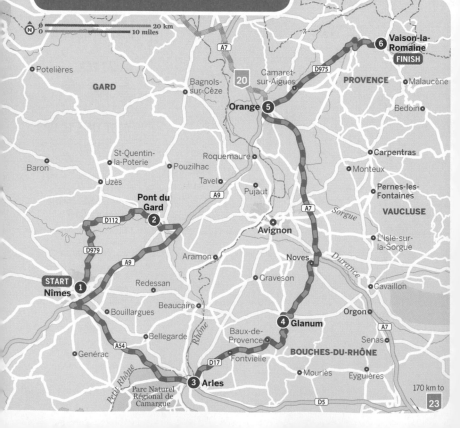

impressively intact 1st-century-AD **amphitheatre** (http://arenes-nimes.com; place des Arènes; adult/child incl audioguide €10/8; ⏱9am-8pm Jul & Aug, shorter hours Sep-Jun) makes for a majestic traffic roundabout. Locals nonchalantly skateboard or window-shop on the elegant place that's home to an astonishingly beautiful and preciously intact 1st-century-AD temple, the **Maison Carrée** (place de la Maison Carrée; adult/child €6/5; ⏱9.30am-8pm Jul & Aug, shorter hours Sep-Jun). Skip the 22-minute film and instead stroll over to the elegant **Jardins de la Fontaine**. The remains of the **Temple de Diane** are in its lower northwest corner and a 10-minute

LINK YOUR TRIP

20 **Rhône Valley**
Join up with this trip in Orange for several great Roman sites in Vienne, and Lyon's Roman theatres and great Gallo-Roman museum.

23 **Riviera Crossing**
The Cote d'Azur shares the Roman treasures, and many of them are in superb locations; head east from Arles to Aix, then take the E80 to Cannes to join this trip.

✓ TOP TIP: PADDLING THE GARD RIVER

Get your first glimpse of the Pont du Gard from the river by paddling 8km downstream from Collias, 4km west of the D981. **Kayak Vert** (☎04 66 22 80 76; www.kayakvert.com; 8 chemin de St-Vincent, Collias; from Collias adult/child €23/19, from Russan €41/37; ⏱9am-6pm mid-May–Oct) and **Canoë Le Tourbillon** (☎04 66 22 85 54; www.canoeletourbillon.com; 3 chemin du Gardon, Collias; from Collias adult/child €23/17, from Russan €36/24; ⏱9am-7pm Apr-Sep), both based near the village bridge, rent out kayaks and canoes (€20 per person for two hours) from March/April to October.

uphill walk brings you to the crumbling, 30m-high **Tour Magne** (quai de la Fontaine; garden free, Tour Magne adult/child €3.50/3; ⏱9am-8pm Jul & Aug, shorter hours Sep-Jun). Built in 15 BC as a watchtower and display of imperial grunt, it is the only one that remains of several that once spanned the 7km-long ramparts.

🍴 🛏 p244

The Drive » The D6086 is direct, but sacrifice 15 minutes, and take route d'Uzès (D979). This way, leave Nîmes' snarly traffic behind and suddenly find yourself on a quiet stretch of winding road skirting grey rocky gorges and honey-stone villages. Cut east via Sanilhac-Sagriès on the D112, then turn off at Begude's roundabout.

TRIP HIGHLIGHT

❷ Pont du Gard

You won't get a sneak peek of the **Pont du Gard** (☎04 66 37 50 99; www.pontdugard.fr; car & up to 5 passengers €18, after 8pm €10, by bicycle or on foot €7, after 8pm €3.50; ⏱visitor centre & museum 9am-8pm Jul & Aug, shorter hours Sep–mid-Jan & mid-Feb–Jun) on approach. Nature (and clever placement of car parks and visitor centres) has created one bravura reveal. Spanning the gorge is a magnificent three-tiered aqueduct, a marvel of 1st-century engineering. It was built around 19 BC by Agrippa, Augustus' deputy, and it's huge: the 275m-long upper tier, 50m above the Gard, has 35 arches. Each block (the largest weighs over 5 tonnes) was hauled in by cart or raft. It was once part of a 50km-long system that carried water from nearby Uzès down to thirsty Nîmes. It's a 400m wheelchair-accessible walk from car parks on both banks of the river to the bridge itself, with a shady cafe en route on the right.

Swim upstream for unencumbered views, though downstream is also good for summer dips, with shaded wooden platforms set in the flatter banks. Want to make a day of it? There's **Museo de la Romanité**, an interactive, information-based museum, plus a children's area, and a peaceful 1.4km botanical walk, Mémoires de Garrigue.

The Drive ›› Kayaking to the next stop would be more fun, and more direct, but you'll need to hit the highway for 40 minutes to Arles – the A9 that skirts back towards Nîmes and then the A54.

TRIP HIGHLIGHT

❸ Arles

Arles, formerly known as Arelate, was part of the Roman Empire from as early as the 2nd century BC. It wasn't until the 49–45 BC civil war, however, when nearby Massalia (Marseille) supported Pompey (ie backed the wrong side), that it became a booming regional capital.

The town today is delightful, Roman cache or no, but what a living legacy it is. **Les Arènes** (Amphithéâtre; ☎08 91 70 03 70; www.arenes-arles.com; Rond-Point des Arènes; adult/child €6/free, incl Théâtre Antique €9/free; ☺9am-8pm Jul & Aug, to 7pm May-Jun & Sep, shorter hours rest of year) is not as larges as Nîmes', but it is spectacularly sited and occasionally

still sees blood spilled, just like in the good old gladiatorial days (it hosts bullfights and *courses Camarguaises,* which is the local variation). Likewise, the 1st-century **Théâtre Antique** (☎04 90 96 93 30; bd des Lices; adult/child €6/free, joint ticket with Les Arènes €9/free; ☺9am-7pm May-Sep, shorter hours rest of year) is still regularly used for alfresco performances.

Just as social, political and religious life revolved around the forum in Arelate, the busy plane-tree-shaded **place du Forum** buzzes with cafe life today. Sip a pastis here and spot the remains of a 2nd-century temple embedded in the facade of the **Hôtel Nord-Pinus**. Under your feet are **Cryptoportiques** (adult/child €4.50/free; ☺9am-noon & 2-7pm) – subterranean foundations and buried arcades. Access the underground galleries, 89m long and 59m wide, at the **hôtel de ville** (Town Hall; place de la République).

Emperor Constantin's partly preserved 4th-century private baths, the **Thermes de Constantin** (rue du Grand Prieuré; adult/child €4/free; ☺9am-7pm Jul & Aug, shorter hours rest of year), are a few minutes' stroll away, next to the *quai.* Southwest of the centre is **Les Alyscamps** (av des Alyscamps; adult/child €4/free; ☺9am-7pm May-Sep, shorter hours rest of year), a necropolis founded by the Romans and adopted

by Christians in the 4th century. It contains the tombs of martyr St Genest and Arles' first bishops. You may recognise it: Van Gogh and Gauguin both captured the avenues of cypresses on canvas (though only melancholy old Van Gogh painted the empty sarcophagi).

✕ ⊨ p244, p303, p409

St-Rémy-de-Provence Roman ruins at Glanum

The Drive » Take the D17 to Fontvielle, then turn off and follow the D78F/D27A to Baux-de-Provence, then the D5. This minor detour takes you past beautiful dry white rocky hills dotted with scrubby pine; the trip will still only take around 45 minutes. There's on-site parking at Glanum. If heading into St-Rémy, there's parking by the tourist office (parking Jean-Jaurès) and north of the periphery (parking Général-de-Gaulle).

④ Glanum

Such is the glittering allure of the gourmet delis, interiors boutiques and smart restaurants that line St-Rémy-de-Provence's circling boulevards and place de la République that a visit to the **Site Archéologique de Glanum** (☎04 90 92 23 79; www.site-glanum.fr; rte des Baux-de-Provence; adult/child €7.50/free, parking €2.70; ⏱9.30am-6.30pm Apr-Sep, 10am-5pm Oct-Mar, closed Mon Sep-Mar) is often an afterthought. But the **triumphal arch** (AD 20) that marks Glanum's entrance, 2km south of St-Rémy, is far from insignificant. It's pegged as one of France's oldest and is joined by a towering **mausoleum** (30–20 BC). Walk down

SALVE, PROVINCIA GALLIA TRANSALPINA

It all starts with the Greeks. After founding the city of Massalia, now Marseille, around 600 BC, they spent the next few centuries establishing a long string of ports along the coast, planting olives and grapes as they went. When migrating Celts from the north joined forces with the local Ligurians, resistance to these booming colonies grew. The Celto-Ligurians were a force to be reckoned with; unfortunately, they were about to meet ancient history's biggest bullies. In 125 BC the Romans helped the Greeks defend Massalia, and swiftly took control.

Thus begins the Gallo-Roman era and the region of Provincia Gallia Transalpina, the first Roman *provincia* (province), the name from which Provence takes it name. Later Provincia Narbonensis, it embraced all of southern France from the Alps to the Mediterranean and the Pyrenees.

Roads made the work of empire possible, and the Romans quickly set about securing a route that joined Italy and Spain. Via Aurelia linked Rome to Fréjus, Aix-en-Provence, Arles and Nîmes; the northbound Via Agrippa followed the Rhône from Arles to Avignon, Orange and onwards to Lyon. The Via Domitia linked the Alps with the Pyrenees by way of the Luberon and Nîmes.

With Julius Caesar's conquest of Gaul (58–51 BC), the region truly flourished. Under the emperor Augustus, vast amphitheatres, triumphal arches and ingenious aqueducts – the ones that propel this trip – were constructed. Augustus celebrated his final defeat of the ever-rebellious Ligurians in 14 BC, with the construction of the monument at La Turbie on the Côte d'Azur.

The Gallo-Roman legacy may be writ large and loud in Provence, but it also persists in the everyday. Look for it in unusual places: recycled into cathedral floors or hotel facades, in dusty cellars or simply buried beneath your feet.

---

the main street and you'll pass the mainstays of Roman life: baths, a forum and marketplace, temples and town villas. And beneath all this Roman handiwork lies the remnants of an older Celtic and Hellenic settlement, built to take advantage of a sacred spring. Van Gogh, as a patient of the neighbouring asylum, painted the olive orchard that covered the site until its excavation in the 1920s.

✕ p245

The Drive » It's the A7 all the way to Orange, 50km of nondescript driving if you're not tempted by a detour to Avignon on the way.

TRIP HIGHLIGHT

❺ Orange

It's often said if you can only see one Roman site in France, make it Orange. And yes, the town's Roman treasures are gobsmacking and unusually old; both are believed to have been built during Augustus Caesar's rule (27 BC–AD 14). Plus, while Orange may not be the Provençal village of popular fantasy, it's a cruisy, decidedly untouristy town, making for good-value accommodation and hassle-free sightseeing (such as plentiful street

parking one block back from the theatre).

At a massive 103m wide and 37m high, the stage wall of the **Théâtre Antique** (Ancient Roman Theatre; ☎04 90 51 17 60; www.theatre-antique.com; rue Madeleine Roch; adult/child €9.50/7.50; ☺9am-7pm Jun-Aug, to 6pm Apr, May & Sep, 9.30am-5.30pm Mar & Oct, 9.30am-4.30pm rest of year) dominates the surrounding streetscape. Minus a few mosaics, plus a new roof, it's one of three in the world still standing in their entirety, and originally seated 10,000 spectators. Admission includes an informative audioguide, and access to the **Musée d'Art et d'Histoire** (☺9.15am-7pm Jun-Aug, to 6pm Apr, May & Sep, shorter hours rest of year) across the road. Its collection includes friezes from the theatre with the Roman motifs we love: eagles holding garlands of bay leaves, and a cracking battle between cavalrymen and foot soldiers.

For bird's-eye views of the theatre – and phenomenal vistas of rocky Mont Ventoux and the Dentelles – follow montée Philbert de Chalons, or montée Lambert, up **Colline St-Eutrope**, once the ever-vigilant Romans' lookout point.

To the town's north, the **Arc de Triomphe** stands on the ancient Via Agrippa (now the busy N7), 19m high and wide, and a stonking 8m thick. Restored in 2009, its richly animated reliefs commemorate 49 BC Roman victories with images of battles, ships, trophies, and chained, naked and utterly subdued Gauls.

🛏 p245

The Drive » Northeast, the D975 passes through gentle vineyard-lined valleys for 40 minutes, with views of the Dentelles de Montmirail's limestone ridges along the way (the D977 and D23 can be equally lovely). Parking in Vaison can be a trial; nab a spot by the tourist office (place du Chanoine Saute), or try below the western walls of the Cité Médiévale, if you don't mind a walk.

---

❻ Vaison-la-Romaine

Is there anything more telling of Rome's smarts than a sturdy, still-used Roman bridge? Vaison-la-Romaine's pretty little **Pont Romain** has stood the test of time and severe floods. Stand at its centre and gaze up at the walled, cobbled-street hilltop Cité Médiévale, or down at the fast-flowing Ouvèze River .

Vaison-la-Romaine is tucked between seven valleys and has long been a place of trade. The ruined remains of **Vasio Vocontiorum**, the Roman city that flourished here between the 6th and 2nd centuries BC, fill two central **Gallo-Roman sites** (☎04 90 36 50 48; www.provenceromaine. com; adult/child incl all ancient sites, museum & cathedral €8/4; ☺9.30am-6.30pm Jun-Sep, 9.30am-6pm Apr & May, 10am-noon & 2-5.30pm Oct-Mar). Dual neighbourhoods lie on either side of the tourist office and av du Général-de-Gaulle. The Romans shopped at the colonnaded boutiques and bathed at **La Villasse**, where you'll find **Maison au Dauphin**, which has splendid marble-lined fish ponds.

In **Puymin**, see noblemen's houses, mosaics, a workmen's quarter, a temple, and the still-functioning 6000-seat **Théâtre Antique** (c AD 20). To make sense of the remains (and gather your audioguide), head for the **archaeological museum**, which revives Vaison's Roman past with an incredible swag – superb mosaics, carved masks, and statues that include a 3rd-century silver bust and marble renderings of Hadrian and his wife, Sabina. Admission includes entry to the soothing 12th-century Romanesque cloister at **Cathédrale Notre-Dame de Nazareth** (cloister only €1.50; ☺10am-12.30pm & 2-6pm Mar-Dec), a five-minute walk west of La Villasse and, like much of Provence, built on Roman foundations.

✕ 🛏 p245

ROMAN PROVENCE READING LIST

» *The Roman Provence Guide* (Edwin Mullins)

» *The Roman Remains of Southern France* (James Bromwich)

» *Southern France: An Oxford Archaeological Guide* (Henry Cleere)

» *Ancient Provence: Layers of History in Southern France* (Jeffrey Wolin)

Eating & Sleeping

Nîmes ❶

✖ Le Cerf à Moustache　　Bistro €€

(☏09 81 83 44 33; www.lecerfamoustache.
com; 38 bd Victor Hugo; 2-/3-course lunch
menus €15.80/19.90, 2-/3-course dinner menus
€25.90/30.90; ☺11.45am-2pm & 7.45-10pm
Mon-Sat) The Deer with the Moustache has
established itself as one of Nîmes' best bistros,
with quirky decor (including reclaimed furniture
and a wall of sketch-covered old books),
matched by chef Julien Salem's creative take on
the classics (Aveyronnais steak with St-Marcellin
cream, rabbit ballotine with crushed potatoes
and garlic, white-chocolate mousse with
mandarin meringue) and 60 wines by the glass.

✖ Vincent Croizard　　Gastronomy €€€

(☏04 66 67 04 99; www.restaurantcroizard.
com; 17 rue des Chassaintes; lunch menus
€23-28, dinner menus €48-70, mains €28;
☺7.45-9.30pm Tue, noon-1.45pm & 7.45-
9.30pm Wed-Sat, noon-1.45pm Sun) From its
discreet facade on a quiet side street you'd
never guess that this restaurant is home to an
impossibly romantic lamplit courtyard garden
and some of Nîmes' most inventive and artistic
high-end cooking. Dishes use premium produce
(black truffles, Aveyron suckling lamb, milk-fed
veal and Bouzigues oysters); rare vintages and
limited releases from small-scale producers
make up the wine list.

⊨ Hôtel des Tuileries　　Hotel €

(☏04 66 21 31 15; www.hoteldestuileries.
com; 22 rue Roussy; d/tr/f from €72/90/115;
P ❀ 🛜) Nîmes' best deal is this delightful,
bargain-priced 11-room hotel strolling distance
from Les Arènes. Individually decorated rooms
are spacious and spotless, and some have
covered balconies. Breakfast costs €8. Its
private parking garage (€10) is located just
down the street, but there are only five car
spaces, so reserve ahead.

⊨ Royal Hôtel　　Hotel €€

(☏04 66 58 28 27; www.royalhotel-nimes.
com; 3 bd Alphonse Daudet; d €85-105, f €190;
❀ 🛜) This upmarket hotel offers grace and

style. Bedrooms have modern-meets-heritage
decor and a choice of street views or an outlook
over the grand place d'Assas. They're split into
standard and superior; it's worth bumping up a
level for extra space and air-con. The downstairs
restaurant, La Boduegita, offers solid Med
dining.

Arles ❸

✖ Le Gibolin　　Bistro €€

(☏04 88 65 43 14; 13 rue des Porcelets; lunch
menu €16, dinner menus €27-34; ☺12.15-2pm
& 8-10.30pm Tue-Sat) After spending three
decades plying Paris with their passion for
organic wines, owners Brigitte and Luc decided
to head south and open a new bistro and wine
bar in Arles. Unsurprisingly, it's become a
much-loved local fixture, known for its hearty
home cooking and peerless wine list (mostly
available by the glass).

✖ L'Atelier Jean-Luc
Rabanel　　Gastronomy €€€

(☏04 90 91 07 69; www.rabanel.com; 7 rue des
Carmes; menus €85-145; ☺ sittings begin noon-
1pm & 8-9pm Wed-Sun) Offering as much an
artistic experience as a meal (and graced with
double Michelin stars), this is the gastronomic
home of charismatic chef Jean-Luc Rabanel.
Many products are sourced from the chef's
veg patch and wine pairings are an adventure
in themselves. Half-day cooking classes are
also available, with/without lunch €200/145.
Next door, Rabanel's **À Côté** (☏04 90 47 61
13; www.bistro-acote.com; 21 rue des Carmes;
menus €32; ☺noon-1.30pm & 7.30-9pm daily)
offers bistro fare.

⊨ Grand Hôtel
Nord Pinus　　Heritage Hotel €€€

(☏04 90 93 44 44; www.nord-pinus.com; place
du Forum; r €170-420) An Arlésian landmark,
this classy hotel has been frequented by
everyone from famous bullfighters to artists
and writers like Picasso, Hemingway, Jean
Cocteau and Fritz Lang. It's chock-full of
heritage: wrought-iron beds, art deco sinks,
20th-century furniture and vintage *féria*

posters, as well as black-and-white photographs by Peter Beard downstairs. Room 10 is the grandest, and the bullfighters' favourite.

Glanum ❹

✕ La Cuisine des Anges
Bistro €€

(📞04 90 92 17 66; www.angesetfees-stremy. com; 4 rue du 8 Mai 1945; 2-course menu €25-27, 3-course menu €29; 🕙 noon-2.30pm & 7.30-11pm Mon, Wed, Sat & Sun, 7.30-11pm Thu & Fri; ❄️🛜) Packed with locals and tourists, this casual *maison d'hôte* (B&B) has been around for an age and just doesn't lose its edge. Light Provençal dishes are derived from organic local ingredients and served in the interior patio or wooden-floored dining room with textured paintings and zinc-topped tables. Upstairs is a cute B&B, **Le Sommeil des Fées** (r incl breakfast €65-85).

Orange ❺

🛏 Hôtel l'Herbier d'Orange
Hotel €

(📞04 90 34 09 23; www.lherbierdorange.com; 8 place aux Herbes; s €57, d €61-70, tr €77, f €90; ❄️🛜@🛜) On a quiet, tree-shaded square, this small, simple hotel makes a pleasant base in Orange, with 20 bright, colourful rooms, livened up with jolly fabrics and tiled floors. The stone-walled breakfast room is attractive too.

Vaison-la-Romaine ❻

✕ Bistro du'O
Bistro €€

(📞04 90 41 72 90; www.bistroduo.fr; rue du Château; lunch/dinner menus from €19/32; 🕙 noon-2pm & 7.30-10pm Tue-Sat) Gosh, this place knows how to impress. First the setting: a vaulted cellar in the medieval city (once the château stables). Then the food: local and seasonal, rooted in the classics but contemporary in style, and dictated by what talented young chef Philippe Zemour has found in the market. The menu's short, but full of surprises: we loved it.

✕ La Lyriste
Provençal €€

(📞04 90 36 04 67; 45 cours Taulignan; menus €14.50-28; 🕙 noon-2.30pm & 7-9.30pm Tue & Thu-Sun, 🍴) Nothing world-changing here, but tasty regional food from *bourride* (fish stew) to *brandade de cabillaud* (cod kebabs), laced with lashings of olive oil, tomatoes and Provençal herbs. Unusually, there's generally a good choice of veggie options on offer. The plane-tree-shaded terrace tables are the ones to ask for.

🛏 Hôtel Burrhus
Hotel €

(📞04 90 36 00 11; www.burrhus.com; 1 place de Montfort; d €65-98, apt €140; 🅿️❄️🛜) As much art gallery as hotel, this imaginative and exciting place zings with modern artwork, sculptures, funky furniture and fun decorative details, like the terracotta pot suspended above the interior patio. Rooms are divided into three size categories, all brimming with interest. Breakfast is copious, and good value at €9.

Lavender Route

22

Banish thoughts of grandma's closet. Get out among the purple haze, sniff the heady summer breezes and navigate picturesque hilltop towns, ancient churches and pretty valleys.

TRIP HIGHLIGHTS

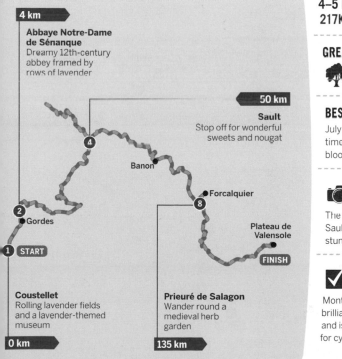

4 km

Abbaye Notre-Dame de Sénanque
Dreamy 12th-century abbey framed by rows of lavender

50 km

Sault
Stop off for wonderful sweets and nougat

Banon

●Forcalquier

4

8

Plateau de Valensole

2
●Gordes

1 START

FINISH

Coustellet
Rolling lavender fields and a lavender-themed museum

0 km

Prieuré de Salagon
Wander round a medieval herb garden

135 km

4–5 DAYS
217KM / 135 MILES

GREAT FOR...

BEST TIME TO GO
July is purple prime time, but June's blooms still impress.

ESSENTIAL PHOTO
The road just north of Sault is a particularly stunning spot.

 BEST FOR OUTDOORS
Mont Ventoux has brilliant hiking trails and is hallowed ground for cycling fans.

ateau de Valensole Lavender fields

22 Lavender Route

The Luberon and Vaucluse may be well-trodden (and driven) destinations, but you'll be surprised at how rustic they remain. This trip takes you to the undoubtedly big-ticket (and exquisitely beautiful) sights but also gets you exploring back roads, sleepy villages, big skies and one stunner of a mountain. And yes, past fields and fields of glorious purple blooms.

TRIP HIGHLIGHT

❶ Coustellet

Our trail begins just outside the village of Coustellet at the **Musée de la Lavande** (☎04 90 76 91 23; www.museedelalavande. com; D2, Coustellet; adult/child €6.80/free; ⊙9am-7pm May-Sep, 9am-noon & 2-6pm Oct-Apr), an excellent eco-museum and working lavender farm, where you can take a guided tour of the lavender fields, learn about extraction methods and buy lavender goodies in the on-site

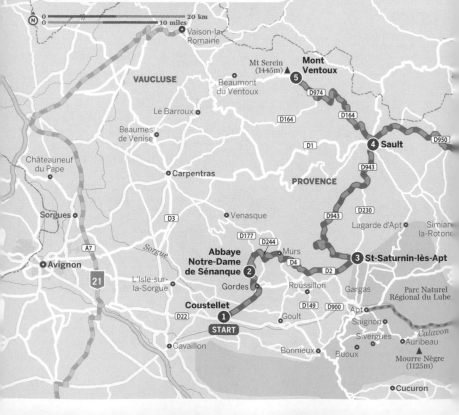

boutique. Afterwards, the hilltop village of Gordes is worth a detour, especially at sunset, followed perhaps by a drink at the newly renovated **Bastide de Gordes** (📞04 90 72 12 12; www.bastide-de-gordes.com; Le Village; r from €346; ❋ 🛜) hotel.

The Drive » The museum is just off the D2. From here, it's another 7km to Gordes along the D2, then a turn-off onto the D177 for 4km till you reach the abbey. You'll pass plenty of lavender photo ops en route, so feel free to stop if you can find an appropriate spot.

TRIP HIGHLIGHT

❷ Abbaye Notre-Dame de Sénanque

Isolated and ridiculously photogenic, this 12th-century Cistercian **abbey** (📞04 90 72 05 72; www.abbayedesenanque.com; adult/child €7.50/3.50; ⏰9.15-11am Mon-Sat, tours by reservation) is famously framed by lavender from mid-June through July. The abbey was founded in 1148 and is still home to a small number of monks. The cloisters have a haunting, severe beauty; reserva-

tions are essential to visit inside but out of high season they can be made on-site (conservative dress and silence are required). Tours begin around 10am, so for some tranquil time with the lavender, arrive well before then.

The Drive » The way out of the abbey has you heading north. Continue up the D177 then turn right onto the D244 and follow the signs to Murs, a very winding 9.5km drive accompanied by wheat fields and vineyards. From here it's about 25 minutes to the next stop.

---

❸ St-Saturnin-lès-Apt

St-Saturnin-lès-Apt is a refreshingly ungentrified village, with marvellous views of the surrounding Vaucluse plateau punctuated by purple fields – climb to the ruins atop

LINK YOUR TRIP

18 Foothills of the Alps

Swap rolling hills for spectacular gorges and then alpine air: take the D6 and D852 to Moustiers-Ste-Marie, or drop in at Sisteron from Forcalquier.

21 Roman Provence

From Roman Provence's last stop in Vaison-la-Romaine, it's a gorgeous drive to Gordes via Carpentras and Venasque.

the village for a knockout vista. At **Moulin à Huile Jullien** (☎04 90 75 56 24; www.moulin-huile-jullien.com; rte d'Apt; ☺10am-noon & 3-7pm Jul & Aug, 10am-noon & 2-6pm rest of year, closed Sun year-round) see how olives are milled into oil (with honey and oil tastings thrown in). See *lavande fine* growing at **Château du Bois** (☎04 90 76 91 23; www.lechateaudubois.com), a winding, but gorgeous, drive 20km to the northeast, with 800,000 sq metres of peaceful plantings. (Note, this is a farm only; the shop and museum is in Coustellet.)

✕ 🛏 p253

The Drive » Spot the pretty 17th-century windmill, Le Château les Moulins, 1km north, off the D943 towards Sault, then look out for the magnificent views of the red-tinged escarpment and the rust-coloured village of Roussillon. The views of Mont Ventoux only get more spectacular as you approach Sault, a 35-minute drive away.

❹ Sault

This drowsily charming, isolated hilltop town mixes its lavender views with plum orchards and scattered forest. Town hot spot is **André Boyer** (☎04 90 64 00 23; www.nougat-boyer.fr; place de l'Europe), keeping farmers, cyclists and mountaineers in honey and almond nougat since 1887; its lavender marshmallows and the local speciality *pognes* (an orange-scented brioche) are also must-tries. Head to **GAEC Champelle** (☎04 90 64 01 50; www.gaec-champelle.fr; rte de Ventoux), a roadside farm stand northwest of town, whose products include great buys for cooks. The lavender up here is known for its dark, OK...deep purple, hue.

The Drive » This is one great 25km. Head out of town on the D164; when you hit the D974, fields give way to dense, fragrant forest (impromptu picnic, perhaps?). Above the tree line, strange spots of Alpine scrub are gradually replaced by pale bald slopes. These steep gradients have often formed a hair-raising stage of the Tour de France – the road is daubed with Tour graffiti and many fans make a brave two-wheeled homage.

❺ Mont Ventoux

If fields of flowers are intoxicating, Mont Ventoux (1912m) is awe-inspiring. Nicknamed *le géant de Provence* – Provence's giant – its great white hulk is visible from much of the region. *Le géant* sparkles all year round – once the snow melts, its lunar-style limestone slopes glimmer in the sun. From its peak, clear-day vistas extend to the Alps and the Camargue.

Even summer temperatures can plummet by 20°C at the top; it's also twice as likely to rain; and the relentless mistrals blow 130 days a year, sometimes exceeding 250km/h. Bring a cardigan and scarf!

The Drive » Go back the way you came to Sault, then head east to Banon on the D950 for another 40 minutes.

❻ Banon

A tasty, nonfloral diversion: little village, big cheese. Bustling Banon is famous for its chèvre de Banon, a goat's-milk cheese wrapped in a chestnut leaf. Fromagerie de Banon sells its cheese at the Tuesday morning market, and at wonderful cheese-and-sausage shop **Brindille Melchio**

Prieure de Salagon Medieval herb gardens of the Jardins Salagon

(☎04 92 73 23 05; place de la République; ⊙8am-12.30pm & 2.30-6.30pm Wed-Sun Sep-Jun, 8am-7pm daily Jul & Aug), which is unbeatable for picnic supplies. Tuck into cheese-and-charcuterie plates at **Les Vins au Vert** (☎04 92 75 23 84; www.lesvinsauvert.com; rue Pasteur; mains €12-16; ⊙10am-7pm Wed, 10am-10pm Thu-Sat, 10am-5pm Sun); make reservations for Thursday to Saturday nights.

The Drive » Follow the D950 southeast for 25km to Forcalquier, as the scenery alternates between gentle forested slopes and fields.

7 Forcalquier

Forcalquier has an upbeat, slightly bohemian vibe, a holdover from 1960s and '70s, when artists and back-to-the-landers arrived, fostering a now-booming organics (*'biologiques'* or bio) movement. Saffron is grown here, absinthe is distilled, and the town is also home to L'Université Européenne des Senteurs & Saveurs (UESS; European University of Scents and Flavours). To see it all in action, time your visit for the Monday morning market.

Climb the steep steps to Forcalquier's gold-topped **citadel** and octagonal **chapel** for more sensational views; on the way down note the once-wealthy seat's ornately carved wooden doorways and grand bourgeois town houses. Prefer to work your senses overtime? UESS' **Couvent des Cordeliers** (☎04 92 72 50 68; www.couventdescordeliers.com; workshops €40-50) conducts workshops (€40 to €50) in perfume making, wine tasting, and aromatherapy in Forcalquier's 13th-century convent.

p253

The Drive » Find yourself in a gentle world of plane-tree arcades, wildflowers and, yes, lavender. Around 4km south on the D4100 you'll come to our next stop, just before the pretty town of Mane.

⑧ Prieuré de Salagon

This beautiful 13th-century priory, located on the outskirts of Mane, is home to a garden museum, the **Jardins Salagon** (www. musee-de-salagon.com; adult/child/family €8/6/22; ⊘10am-8pm Jun-Aug, to 7pm May & Sep, to 6pm Oct–mid-Dec & Feb-Apr;). This is ethno-botany at its most poetic and sensual: wander through

recreated medieval herb gardens, fragrant with native lavender, mints and mugworts. The bookshop is inviting, too.

The walled town of **Mane** is lovely for strolling. Or for a mysterious, potentially curative detour, visit remote **Église de Châteauneuf**, where a hermit church sister concocts natural remedies and makes jam. Head 800m south of Mane to the Hôtel Mas du Pont Roman, then turn right and either park and walk, or drive the bumpy final 3km. Be warned: the good sister doesn't always reveal herself. Just in case, bring a picnic and consider it an adventure.

🡒 DETOUR: THE LUBERON

Start: ⑧ Prieuré de Salagon

The Luberon's other, southern, half is equally as florally blessed. Lavender carpets the **Plateau de Claparèdes** between **Buoux** (west), **Sivergues** (south), **Auribeau** (east) and **Saignon** (north). Cycle, walk or motor through the lavender fields and along the northern slopes of **Mourre Nègre** (1125m) – the Luberon's highest point, accessible from **Cucuron**. The D113 climbs to idyllic lavender distillery **Les Agnels** (☏04 90 74 34 60; www.lesagnels.com; rte de Buoux, btwn Buoux & Apt; adult/child €6/free; ⊘10am-7pm Apr-Sep, to 5.30pm Oct-Mar), which distils lavender, cypress and rosemary. The small on-site spa has a lavender-scented swimming pool. Stay at **Chambre avec Vue** (☏04 90 04 85 01; www.chambreavecvue.com; rue de la Bourgade; r €90-110; ⊘closed Dec-Feb) in tiny, hip Saignon, which perches on high rocky flanks, its narrow streets crowning a hill ringed with craggy scrub and petite lavender plots, with incredible vistas across the Luberon to Mont Ventoux.

The Drive » Get on the D13, then follow the signs to the D5 for the drive to Manosque (roughly 30 minutes in total).

---

⑨ Manosque

Manosque has two lovely fountains and a historic cobblestoned core, but traffic and suburban nothingness make visiting a nuisance. But just southeast is the home of **l'Occitane**, the company that turned traditional lavender-, almond- and olive oil–based Provençal skincare into a global phenomenon. Factory tours can be booked through the **tourist office**; the shop offers a flat 10% discount, and the odd bargain.

The Drive » Leave the freeways and ring roads behind and cross the Durance River towards the quieter D6 (from where it will take around 20 minutes to reach the town of Valensole); check the rear-view mirrors for mountain views.

---

⑩ Plateau de Valensole

Things get very relaxed once you hit the D6, and the road begins a gentle climb. This dreamily quiet plateau has Provence's greatest concentration of lavender farms, and a checkerboard of waving wheat and lavender rows stretch to the horizon, or at least until Riez. Fine picnic spots and photo ops are not hard to find.

Eating & Sleeping

St-Saturnin-lès-Apt ③

✕ La Coquillade   French €€€

(☎04 90 74 71 71; www.coquillade.fr; Le Perrotet, Gargas; menus lunch €39, dinner €72-90, d €325-390; ⏱12.30-1.30pm & 7.30-9.30pm mid-Apr–mid-Oct) Overnighting at this luxurious hilltop estate won't suit everyone's budget, but everyone should try to fork out for the great-value Bistrot lunch menu. Michelin-starred and run by renowned chef Christophe Renaud, it'll be one of the most memorable meals you'll have in the Luberon. It's a 13km drive west from St-Saturnin, near the village of Lioux; there are plenty of signs, but phone ahead to confirm directions.

🛏 Le Mas Perréal   B&B €€

(☎04 90 75 46 31; www.masperreal.com; Quartier la Fortune; d €130-140, self-catering studio €100-150; 🖥🏊) Surrounded by vineyards, lavender fields and cherry orchards, on a vast 7-hectare property outside St-Saturnin-lès Apt, this farmhouse B&B offers a choice of cosy rooms or self-catering studios, both filled with country antiques and Provençal fabrics. There's a heavenly pool and big garden with mountain views. Elisabeth, a long-time French teacher, offers cooking and French lessons. It's 2km southwest of town along the D2.

Forcalquier ⑦

✕ Restaurant Le 9   Provencal €€

(☎04 92 75 03 29; www.le9-forcalquier.fr; av Jean Giono; menus €22-28; ⏱noon-2.30pm & 7.30-10pm Wed-Mon) High in Forcalquier, behind the Citadel with a panoramic terrace, Le 9 (say luh-nuf) is the town's most reliable address for earthy, market-driven cooking, incorporating fresh-from-the-farm ingredients in simple bistro fare, like honey-braised rabbit or grilled lamb with tomato and basil. The best idea is usually just to go for whatever is on the blackboard. Reservations recommended.

✕ Les Petites Tables   Provencal €€

(☎04 86 68 53 14; lespetitestables@gmail.com; lunch mains €10-16; ⏱noon-3pm Tue-Sat) This Provençal restaurant at the **Ecomusée l'Olivier** (☎04 92 72 66 91; www.ecomusee-olivier.com) near Volx is only open for lunch. It makes full use of its own olive oils, which are used to make homemade salad dressings and tomato dishes.

🛏 Relais d'Elle   B&B €

(☎04 92 75 06 87, 06 75 42 33 72; http://relaisdelle.com; rte de la Brillane, Niozelles; s/d/tr/q from €60/75/90/115; 🖥🏊) What a stunner of a B&B this is, 8km from Forcalquier in a delightful ivy-covered farmhouse dating from 1802, surrounded by tended gardens, bucolic countryside and a grand pool. The sweet, feminine rooms all have views – we liked Collines for its cosiness and Pierres for its atmosphere. The owners are passionate about horses. They also offer a delicious dinner by reservation.

🛏 Couvent des Minimes   Hotel €€€

(☎04 92 74 77 77; www.couventdesminimes-hotelspa.com; chemin des Jeux de Maï, Mane; r from €275; ❄🖥🏊) A real budget-buster, but boutique in every sense of the word. Housed in a converted convent, it pulls out all the luxury stops: beautiful rooms, an indulgent spa and a superb restaurant, all wrapped up in wonderful medieval architecture. Low-season and last-minute deals often bring prices down a notch. It's in the village of Mane on the D4100.

Classic Trip

Riviera Crossing

23

French road trips just don't get more glamorous than this: cinematic views, searing sunshine, art history aplenty and the Med around every turn.

TRIP HIGHLIGHTS

110 km
Èze
End with a sundowner
in a dreamy hilltop village

62 km
La Grande Corniche
Cruise the Côte d'Azur's
most famous road

FINISH
Menton

Roquebrune-
Cap-Martin
Monaco

Nice
Delve into busy markets
and an atmospheric
old town
48 km

**St-Paul de
Vence**
Paint your own pictures
in this hilltop artists'
hideaway
28 km

START
Antibes
Juan-les-Pins

Cannes
Cinematic heritage
and cinematic views
to match
0 km

**4 DAYS
110KM / 68 MILES**

GREAT FOR...

BEST TIME TO GO

Anytime, but avoid
July and August's
heavy traffic.

**ESSENTIAL
PHOTO**

Standing beneath
Augustus'
monumental Trophée
des Alpes, with
Monaco and the Med
far below.

**BEST FOR
GLAMOUR**

Strolling the Croisette
in Cannes and fulfilling
those film-star fantasies.

Menton Seaside town of peaceful gardens and belle-époque mansions

Classic Trip

23 Riviera Crossing

Cruising the Côte d'Azur is the French road trip everyone has to do at least one in their lifetime. From film town Cannes to down-to-earth Nice via the corkscrew turns of the Corniches and into millionaire's Monaco, it's a drive that you'll remember forever (and hopefully not because of the dreadful summer traffic). Filmmakers, writers, celebs and artists have all had their hearts stolen by this glittering stretch of coastline: by the end of this trip, you'll understand why.

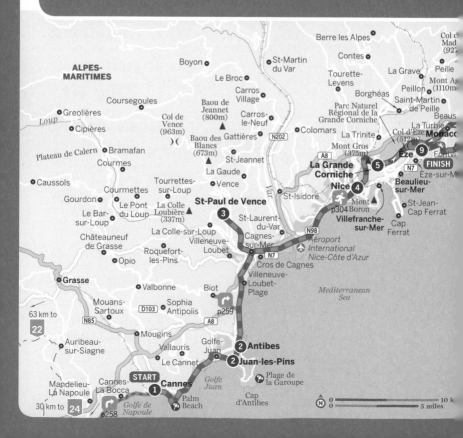

❶ Cannes

What glitzier opening could there be to this Côte d'Azur cruise than Cannes, which is just as cinematic as its reputation suggests. Come July during the film festival, the world's stars descend on **boulevard de la Croisette** (aka La Croisette) to stroll beneath the palms, plug their latest opus and hobnob with the media and movie moguls. Getting your picture snapped outside the **Palais des Festivals** is a must-do, as is a night-time stroll along the boulevard, illuminated by coloured lights.

Outside festival time, Cannes still feels irresistibly ritzy. Private beaches and grand hotels line the seafront; further west lies old Cannes. Follow rue St-Antoine and snake your way up **Le Suquet**, Cannes' atmospheric original village. Pick up the region's best produce at **Marché Forville**, a couple of blocks back from the port.

Not seduced? Then head to the **Îles de Lérins**, two islands a 20-minute boat ride away. Tiny and traffic-free, they're perfect for walks or a picnic. Boats for the islands leave from quai des Îles, on the western side of the harbour.

🍴 🛏 p264

The Drive » The most scenic route to Antibes is via the coastal D6007. Bear right onto av Frères Roustan before Golfe Juan. With luck and no tailbacks, you should hit Juan-les-Pins in 30 minutes or so.

❷ Antibes & Juan-les-Pins

A century or so ago, Antibes and Juan-les-Pins were a refuge for artists, writers, aristocrats and hedonistic expats looking to escape the horrors of post-WWI Europe. They came in their droves – F Scott Fitzgerald wrote several books here, and Picasso rented a miniature castle (it's now a museum dedicated to him).

First stop is the beach resort of **Juan-les-Pins**. It's a long way from the fashionable resort of Fitzgerald's day, but the beaches are still good for sun-lounging (even if you do have to pay).

Then it's on around the peninsula of **Cap d'Antibes**, where many of the great and good had their holiday villas. the Hotel Cap du Eden Roc was one of their favourite fashionable haunts. Round the peninsula is pretty **Antibes**, with a harbour full of pleasure boats and an old town ringed by medieval ramparts. Aim to arrive before lunchtime, when

Castellar
gnès
Garavan
brune ❼ **Menton**
Carnolès
Roverino
LIGURIA
Ventimiglia
Mortola
❻ **Roquebrune-Cap-Martin**
Cap
Martin
Azur

LINK YOUR TRIP

22 Lavender Route
After the coast, head into the lavender-filled hills of Haute-Provence.

24 Vars Delights
Mediterranean coast and Provençal countryside: a natural extension west.

the atmospheric **Marché Provençal** will still be in full swing, and then browse the nearby **Musée Picasso** (☎04 92 90 54 20; www.antibes-juanlespins.com/culture/musee-picasso; Château Grimaldi, 4 rue des Cordiers; adult/concession €6/3; ☺10am-6pm Tue-Sun mid-Jun–mid-Sep, 10am-noon & 2-6pm Tue-Sun mid-Sep–mid-Jun) to see a few of the artist's Antibes-themed works.

✖ ⏸ p264

The Drive » Brave the traffic on the D6007 and avoid signs to turn onto the A8 motorway: it's the D2 you want, so follow signs for Villeneuve-Loubet. When you reach the town, cross the river. You'll pass through a tunnel into the outskirts of Cagnes-sur-Mer; now start following signs to St-Paul.

TRIP HIGHLIGHT

❸ St-Paul de Vence

Once upon a time, hilltop St-Paul de Vence was just another village like countless others in Provence. But then the artists moved in: painters such as Marc Chagall and Pablo Picasso sought solitude here, painted the local scenery and traded canvases for room and board (this is how the **Colombe d'Or** (☎04 93 32 80 02; www.la-colombe-dor.com; place de Gaulle; d €250-430; ☺restaurant noon-2.30pm & 7.30-10.30pm late Dec-Oct; ✳🛜🏊) hotel came by its stellar art collection).

It's now one of the Riviera's most exclusive locations, a haven for artists, film stars and celebrities, not to mention hordes of sightseers, many of whom are here to marvel at the incredible art collection at the **Fondation Maeght** (☎04 93 32 81 63; www.fondation-maeght.com; 623 chemin des Gardettes; adult/child €15/10; ☺10am-7pm Jul-Sep, to 6pm Oct-Jun). Created in 1964 by collectors Aimé and Merguerite Maeght, it boasts works by all the big 20th-century names – Miró sculptures, Chagall mosaics, Braque windows and canvases by Picasso, Matisse and others.

While you're here, it's worth taking a detour northwards to Vence, where the marvellous **Chapelle du Rosaire** (Rosary Chapel; ☎04 93 58 03 26; 466 av Henri Matisse; adult/child €6/3; ☺2-5.30pm Mon, Wed & Sat, 10-11.30am & 2-5.30pm Tue & Thu, closed mid-Nov–early Dec) was designed by an ailing Henri Matisse. He had a hand in everything here, from the stained-glass windows to the altar and candlesticks.

The Drive » Return the way you came, only this time follow the blue signs onto the A8 motorway to Nice. Take exit 50 for Promenade des Anglais, which will take you all 18km along the Baie des Anges. The views are great, but you'll hit nightmare traffic at rush hour.

DETOUR: CORNICHE DE L'ESTÉREL

Start: ❶ Cannes

West of Cannes, the winding coast road known as the **Corniche de l'Estérel** (sometimes known as the Corniche d'Or, the Golden Road) is well worth a side trip if you can spare the time. It's also a natural link with our Var Delights itinerary (p267). Opened in 1903 by the Touring Club de France, this twisting coast road is as much about driving pleasure as getting from A to B; it runs for 30 unforgettable coastal kilometres all the way to St-Raphael. En route you'll pass seaside villages, secluded coves (sandy, pebbled, nudist, cove-like, you name it) and the rocky red hills of the Massif de l'Estérel, dotted with gnarly oaks, juniper and wild thyme. Wherever you go, the blue Mediterranean shimmers alongside, tempting you to stop for just one more swim. It's too much to resist.

❹ Nice

With its mix of real-city grit, old-world opulence and year-round sunshine, Nice is the undisputed capital of the Côte d'Azur. Sure, the traffic's horrendous and the beach is made entirely of pebbles (not a patch of sand in sight!), but that doesn't detract from its charms. It's a great base, with loads of hotels and restaurants, and character in every nook and cranny.

Start with a morning stroll through the huge food and flower markets on **cours Saleya**, then delve into the winding alleyways of the old town, **Vieux Nice**, with many backstreet restaurants where you can try local specialities such as *pissaladière* (onion tart topped with olives and anchovies) and *socca* (chickpea-flour pancake). Stop for an ice cream at famous Fenocchio (p264) – flavours include tomato, lavender, olive and fig – then spend the afternoon sunbathing on the beaches along the seafront **Promenade des Anglais** before catching an epic sunset.

If you have the time, the city has some great museums too – you'll need at least an afternoon to explore all of the modern masterpieces at the **Musée d'Art Moderne et d'Art Contemporain** (MAMAC;

☑04 97 13 42 01; www.mamac-nice.org; place Yves Klein; ⏰10am-6pm Tue-Sun).

✕ 🛏 p264, p409

The Drive » Head out of the city through Riquier on the D2564. You don't want the motorway – you want to hit bd Bischoffsheim, which becomes bd de l'Observatoire as it climbs up to the summit of Mont Gros. Take it all in, stop for the pan-city views, then get ready to really drive. The next 12km are thrilling, twisting past the Parc Naturel Régional de la Grande Corniche. Pull over and make use of the picnic tables if you wish, or take a break for a hilly hike, then continue to La Turbie.

❺ La Grande Corniche

Remember that sexy scene from Hitchcock's *To Catch A Thief*, when Grace Kelly and Cary Grant cruised the hills in a convertible, enjoying sparkling banter and searing blue Mediterranean views? Well you're about to tackle the very same drive – so don your shades, roll down the windows and hit the asphalt.

It's a roller coaster of a road, veering through hairpins and switchbacks as it heads into the hills above Nice. There are countless picnic spots and photo opportunities along the way, including the **Col d'Èze**, the road's highest point at 512m. Further on you'll pass the monumental Roman landmark known as the **Trophée des Alpes** (☑04 93 41 20 84; http://la-turbie. monuments-nationaux.fr; 18 av Albert Ier, La Turbie; adult/child

➦ DETOUR: BIOT

Start: ❷ Antibes & Juan-les-Pins

This 15th-century hilltop village was once an important pottery-manufacturing centre. The advent of metal containers brought an end to this, but Biot is still active in handicraft production, especially glassmaking. At the foot of the village, the **Verrerie de Biot** (☑04 93 65 03 00; www.verreriebiot.com; chemin des Combes; museum adult/child €3/1.50; ⏰9.30am-7.30pm Mon-Sat, 10.30am-1pm & 2.30-7.30pm Sun Apr-Sep, to 6pm Oct-Mar) produces bubbled glass by rolling molten glass into baking soda; bubbles from the chemical reaction are then trapped by a second layer of glass. You can watch skilled glass-blowers at work and browse the adjacent art galleries and shop. There are also guided tours (€6), during which you get the chance to try your hand at a spot of glass-blowing – and learn why it's probably best left to the professionals.

Classic Trip

WHY THIS IS A CLASSIC TRIP
OLIVER BERRY, WRITER

If there were a top 10 of French road trips, this would have to figure near the top. It takes in most of the quintessential sights of the Côte d'Azur, from seaside cities to hilltop villages, and tackles the hairpin turns and hair-raising drops of the three clifftop roads known as the Corniches. The views are simply stunning – simply put, it's one of the world's must-do drives.

Top: St-Paul de Vence
Left: Èze
Right: Harbour, Cannes

€5.50/free; ⊘9.30am-1pm & 2.30-6.30pm Tue-Sun mid-May–mid-Sep, 10am-1.30pm & 2.30-5pm rest of year), a magnificent triumphal arch built to commemorate Augustus' victory over the last remaining Celtic-Ligurian tribes who had resisted conquest. The views from here are jaw-dropping, stretching all the way to Monaco and Italy beyond.

The Drive » Monte Carlo may sparkle and beckon below, but keep your eyes on the road; the principality will keep for another day. Stay on the D2564 to skirt Monaco for another amazing 10km, then turn right into the D52 to Roquebrune.

⑥ Roquebrune-Cap-Martin

This village of two halves feels a world away from the glitz of nearby Monaco: the coastline around **Cap Martin** remains relatively unspoilt, as if Roquebrune had left its clock on medieval time. The historic half of the town, Roquebrune itself, sits 300m high on a pudding-shaped lump. It towers over the Cap, but they are, in fact, linked by innumerable, very steep steps.

The village is delightful, free of tack, and there are sensational views of the coast from the main village square, **place des Deux Frères**. Of all Roquebrune's steep streets, **rue Moncollet** –

with its arcaded passages and stairways carved out of rock – is the most impressive. Scurry upwards to find architect Le Corbusier's grave at the cemetery at the top of the village (in section J, and, yes, he did design his own tombstone).

The Drive » Continue along the D52 towards the coast, following promenade du Cap-Martin all the way along the seafront to Menton. You'll be there in 10 minutes, traffic permitting.

❼ Menton

Last stop on the coast before Italy, the beautiful seaside town of Menton offers a glimpse of what the Riviera once looked like, before the high rises, casinos and property developers moved in. It's ripe for wandering, with peaceful gardens and belle-èpoque mansions galore, as well as an attractive yacht-filled harbour. Meander the historic quarter all the way to the **Cimetière du Vieux Château** (montée du Souvenir; ⊙7am-8pm May-Sep, to 6pm Oct-Apr) for the best views in town.

Menton's miniature microclimate enables exotic plants to flourish here, many of which you can see at the **Jardin Botanique Exotique du Val Rahmeh** (☑04 93 35 86 72; http://jardinvalrahmeh. free.fr; av St-Jacques; adult/ child €6.50/5; ⊙10am-12.30pm & 3.30-6.30pm Wed-Mon May-Aug, 10am-12.30pm & 2-5pm Wed-Mon Sep-Apr), where terraces overflow with fruit trees, and the beautiful, once-abandoned **Jardin de la Serre de la Madone** (☑04 93 57 73 90; www.serredelamadone. com; 74 rte de Gorbio; adult/ child €8/4; ⊙10am-6pm Tue-Sun Apr-Oct, to 5pm Jan-Mar, closed Nov-Dec), overgrown with rare plants. The tourist office's garden website (www.jardins-

---

PERFUME IN GRASSE

Up in the hills to the north of Nice, the town of Grasse has been synonymous with perfumery since the 16th century, and the town is still home to around 30 makers – several of which offer guided tours of their factories, and the chance to hone your olfactory skills.

It can take up to 10 years to train a *perfumier*, but since you probably don't have that much time to spare, you'll have to make do with a crash course. Renowned maker **Molinard** (☑04 93 36 01 62; www.molinard.com; 60 bd Victor Hugo; 30min/1hr workshops €30/69; ⊙9.30am-6.30pm) runs workshops ranging from 30-minute sessions to two hours, during which you get to create your own custom perfume (sandalwood, vanilla, hyacinth, lily of the valley, civet, hare and rose petals are just a few of the potential notes you could include). At the end of the workshop, you'll receive a bottle of *eau de parfum* to take home. **Galimard** (☑04 93 09 20 00; www.galimard.com; 73 rte de Cannes; workshops from €49; ⊙9am-12.30pm & 2-6pm) and **Fragonard's Usine Historique** (☑04 93 36 44 65; www.fragonard.com; 20 bd Fragonard; ⊙9am-7pm Jul & Aug, 9am-12.30pm & 2-6pm Sep-Jun) offer similar workshops.

For background, it's also worth making time to visit the **Musée International de la Parfumerie** (MIP; ☑04 97 05 58 11; www.museesdegrasse.com; 2 bd du Jeu de Ballon; adult/ child €4/free; ⊙10am-7pm May-Sep, 10.30am-5.30pm Oct-Apr; 🖈) and its nearby **gardens** (☑04 92 98 62 69; www.museesdegrasse.com; 979 chemin des Gourettes, Mouans-Sartoux; adult/child €4/free; ⊙10am-7pm May-Aug, 10am-5.30pm mid-Mar–Apr & Sep–mid-Nov, closed mid-Nov–mid-Mar), where you can see some of the many plants and flowers used in scent-making. Needless to say, the bouquet is overpowering.

menton.fr) has a list and opening times.

Spend your second night in town.

✕ ⊨ p265

The Drive › Leave Menton on the D6007, the Moyenne Corniche, skirting the upper perimeter of Monaco. When you're ready turn off into Monaco, take your pick of the car parks (they all charge the same rate, capped at €20 per day). Good options include the Chemin des Pêcheurs and Stade Louis II for old Monaco, or the huge underground Casino car park by allées des Boulingrins for central Monte Carlo.

---

⑧ Monaco

This pint-sized principality (covering barely 200 hectares) is ridiculous, absurd, ostentatious and fabulous all at once. A playground of the super-rich, with super-egos to match, it's the epitome of Riviera excess – especially at the famous **Casino de Monte Carlo**, where cards turn, roulette wheels spin and eye-watering sums are won and lost.

For all its glam, Monaco's not all show. Up in the hilltop quarter of **Le Rocher**, shady streets surround the **Grimaldi Palace**, the wedding-cake castle of Monaco's royal family (time your visit for the pomptastic changing of the guard at 11.55am). Nearby is the impressive **Musée Océanographique de Monaco**, stocked with all kinds of deep-sea denizens. It even has a 6m-deep lagoon complete with circling sharks.

Round things off with a stroll around the cliffside **Jardin Exotique** and the obligatory photo of Monaco's harbour, bristling with over-the-top yachts.

The Drive › Pick up where you left off on the Moyenne Corniche (D6007), and follow its circuitous route back up into the hills all the way to Èze.

TRIP HIGHLIGHT

⑨ Èze

This rocky little village perched on an impossible peak is the jewel in the Riviera crown. The main attraction is technically the medieval village, with small higgledy-piggledy stone houses and winding lanes (and, yes, galleries and shops). It's undoubtedly delightful but it's the ever-present views of the coast that are truly mesmerising. They just get more spectacular from the **Jardin Exotique d'Èze** (📞04 93 41 10 30; adult/child €6/2.50; ⏰9am-7.30pm Jul-Sep, to 6.30pm Apr-May & Jun, to 5.30pm rest of year), a surreal cactus garden at the top of the village, so steep and rocky it may have been purpose-built for mountain goats. It's also where you'll find the old castle ruins; take time to sit, draw a deep breath and gaze, as few places on earth offer such a panorama.

Èze gets very crowded between 10am and 5pm; if you prefer a quiet wander, plan to be here early in the morning or before dinner. Or even better, treat yourself to a night and a slap-up supper at the swish **Château Èza**, a fitting finish to this most memorable of road trips.

⊨ p265

Eating & Sleeping

Cannes ❶

✗ Bobo Bistro   Mediterranean €

(☎04 93 99 97 33; 21 rue du Commandant
André; pizza €12-16, mains €15-20; ☻noon-3pm
& 7-11pm Mon-Sat, 7-11pm Sun) Predictably,
it's a 'bobo' (bourgeois bohemian) crowd that
gathers at this achingly cool bistro in Cannes'
fashionable Carré d'Or (Golden Sq). Decor is
stylishly retro, with attention-grabbing *objets
d'art* like a tableau of dozens of spindles of
coloured yarn. Cuisine is local, seasonal and
invariably organic: artichoke salad, tuna
carpaccio with passion fruit, roasted cod with
mash *fait masion* (homemade).

🛏 Hôtel Le
Mistral   Boutique Hotel €€

(☎04 93 39 91 46; www.mistral-hotel.com; 13
rue des Belges; s €89-109, d €99-129; ❄🞧)
For super-pricey Cannes, this little 10-roomer
is quite amazing value. Rooms are small but
decked out in flattering red and plum tones –
Privilege rooms have quite a bit more space,
plus a fold-out sofa bed. There are sea views
from the top floor, and the hotel is just 50m
from La Croisette. There's no lift, though.

🛏 Villa Garbo   Boutique Hotel €€€

(☎04 93 46 66 00; www.villagarbo-cannes.com;
62 bd d'Alsace; d from €230; ❄@🞧) For a
taste of Cannes' celeb lifestyle, this indulgent
stunner is hard to beat. Rooms are more like
apartments, offering copious space, plus
kitchenettes, king-size beds, sofas and more.
The style is designer chic – acid tones of puce,
orange and lime contrasted with blacks and
greys, supplemented by quirky sculptures and
objets d'art. Unusually, rates include breakfast.

Antibes ❷

✗ La Badiane   Fusion €

(☎04 93 34 45 41; 3 traverse du 24 Août; lunch
menus €17-18.50, mains €13-15; ☻lunch Mon-Fri)
This little side street behind Antibes' bus station
has a clutch of great lunchtime restaurants,
including this exotic Moroccan-tinged diner,
which serves up yummy treats like chicken tagine,
crispy *pastillas* (filled pastries) and spicy quiches.
Shame it's only open for lunch on weekdays.

🛏 Hôtel La Jabotte   B&B €€

(☎04 93 61 45 89; www.jabotte.com; 13 av Max
Maurey; d from €120; ❄@🞧) A couple of
kilometres south of the old town on the coastal bd
James Wyllie towards Cap d'Antibes, this pretty
little hideaway makes a cosy base. Hot pinks,
sunny yellows and soothing mauves dominate the
homey, feminine decor, and there's a sweet patio
where breakfast is served on sunny days. There's
a minimum stay of three nights in summer.

Nice ❹

✗ Fenocchio   Ice Cream €

(☎04 93 80 72 52; www.fenocchio.fr; 2 place
Rossetti; 1/2 scoops €2.50/4; ☻9am-midnight
Feb-Oct) There's no shortage of ice-cream sellers
in the old town, but this *maître glacier* (master
ice-cream maker) has been king of the scoops
since 1966. The array of flavours is mind-
boggling – olive, tomato, fig, beer, lavender and
violet are just a few to try. Dither too long over
the 70-plus flavours and you'll never make it to
the front of the queue. For a Niçois twist, ask for
tourte de blette (a sweet chard tart with raisins,
pine kernels and parmesan).

✕ Le Bistrot d'Antoine
Modern French €€

(📞04 93 85 29 57; 27 rue de la Préfecture; menus €25-43, mains €15-25; 🕑 noon-2pm & 7-10pm Tue-Sat) A quintessential French bistro, right down to the checked tablecloths, streetside tables and impeccable service – not to mention the handwritten blackboard, loaded with classic dishes like rabbit pâté, pot-cooked pork, blood sausage and duck breast. If you've never eaten classic French food, this is definitely the place to start; and if you have, you're in for a treat.

🛏 Hôtel Le Genève
Hotel €€

(📞04 93 56 84 79; www.hotel-le-geneve-nice.com; 1 rue Cassini; r €135-169; ❄🛜) Situated just off place Garibaldi, this renovated corner hotel is bang in the middle of Nice's lively Petit Marais *quartier*. Bedrooms look sleek in cool greys, crimsons and charcoals; bathrooms are modern and well-appointed. Breakfast is served in the ground-floor cafe, brimful of vintage bric-a-brac and mismatched furniture. Bars and cafes abound here.

🛏 Hôtel Villa Rivoli
Boutique Hotel €€

(📞04 93 88 80 25; www.villa-rivoli.com; 10 rue de Rivoli; s €96, d €116-178, f €254; ❄🛜) This charming but strangely shaped villa dates back to 1890, and it's packed with period detail – gilded mirrors, fireplaces, cast-iron balconies and old-world wallpapers, as well as little conifer trees on the balconies and a sweeping marble staircase. Rooms are on the small side, and some are showing their age. There's a small garden and car park beside the hotel.

Menton ❼

✕ Le Cirke
Seafood €€

(📞04 89 74 20 54; www.restaurantlecirke.com; 1 square Victoria; menus lunch €26 & €29, dinner €30 & €45, mains €18-35; 🕑 noon-1.30pm & 7.15-9.30pm Wed-Mon) From paella to bouillabaisse, grilled fish to fried calamari, this smart Italian-run restaurant is the place to turn to for delicious seafood. The wine list is a mix of Italian and French wines, and the service is as sunny as Menton itself.

🛏 Hôtel Napoléon
Boutique Hotel €€

(📞04 93 35 89 50; www.napoleon-menton.com; 29 porte de France; d €95-330; ❄@🛜❄) Standing tall on the seafront, the Napoléon is Menton's most stylish sleeping option. Everything from the pool, the restaurant-bar and the back garden (a heaven of freshness in summer) has been beautifully designed. Rooms are decked out in white and blue, with Cocteau drawings on headboards. Sea-facing rooms have balconies but are a little noisier because of the traffic.

Èze ❾

🛏 Château Eza
Luxury Hotel €€€

(📞04 93 41 12 24; www.chateaueza.com; rue de la Pise; d from €360; ❄🛜) If you're looking for a place to propose, well, there can be few more memorable settings than this wonderful clifftop hotel, perched dramatically above the glittering blue Mediterranean. There are only 12 rooms, so it feels intimate, but the service is impeccable, and the regal decor (gilded mirrors, sumptuous fabrics, antiques) explains the sky-high price tag.

Var Delights

24

Varied is the Var: on this drive you'll encounter bleached cliffs, tropical gardens, idyllic islands, pristine forests, secret beaches and a few gorges for good measure.

TRIP HIGHLIGHTS

128 km

St-Tropez
Watch old men play pétanque near place des Lices

Moustiers-Ste-Marie

FINISH

95 km

Bormes-les-Mimosas
Wander the streets of this atmospheric village

St-Raphaël

START
Marseille

7

Bandol

2

5

Sanary-sur-Mer

Domaine du Rayol

The Calanques
Explore this wild and spectacular protected area near Marseille

9 km

5 DAYS
310KM / 192 MILES

GREAT FOR...

BEST TIME TO GO
Early spring and late autumn to dodge summer tailbacks.

ESSENTIAL PHOTO
Standing on the dazzling white cliffs above the Calanque d'En Vau.

BEST FOR FAMILIES
Snorkelling in sapphire waters at the Domaine du Rayol.

24 Var Delights

This is the other side of the Côte d'Azur, snazzy in spots, stark and wild in others, taking in everything from seaside towns to hilltop villages and big, busy cities. While many sections of the coast have been heavily developed (especially around the big cities of Marseille and Toulon) that doesn't mean solitude is impossible to find — you can hike to deserted coves in the Calanques, explore the forested trails of the Massif des Maures or get well and truly lost in the wild hills of the Var.

❶ Marseille

Long dismissed as the Riviera's troublesome cousin – crime-ridden, industrial, downright dirty – Marseille has enjoyed a long-overdue renaissance since its stint as European Capital of Culture in 2013. Though it's true it has a much grittier, rough-and-ready feel compared to the coast's more genteel towns, it also has character in abundance.

Take a stroll around the **Vieux Port**, then swing by the city's

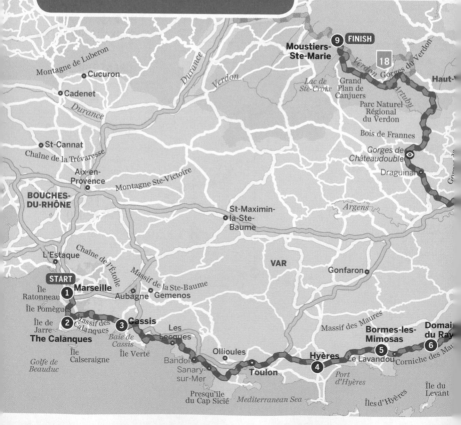

spangly Mediterranean-themed museum, **Musée des Civilisations de l'Europe et de la Méditerranée** (MuCEM, Museum of European & Mediterranean Civilisations; 04 84 35 13 13; www.mucem.org; 7 Promenade Robert Laffont; adult/family/child incl exhibitions €9.50/14/free, 1st Sun of month free; ⊙10am-8pm Wed-Mon Jul & Aug, 11am-7pm Wed-Mon Sep, Oct, May & Jun, 11am-6pm Wed-Mon Nov-Apr; ♿; Ⓜ Vieux Port or Joliette), which helped kickstart the city's revival in 2013. It's attached to the formidable **Fort St-Jean**,

which once protected the city's harbour from attack. Afterwards, head uphill to the city's oldest quarter, **Le Panier** (from the French for basket), criss-crossed by graffiti-clad alleyways, quirky shops and neighbourhood cafes. Reward yourself with a black vanilla ice cream from **Vanille Noire** (☎07 77 33 68 19; 13 rue Caisserie; ice cream €2; ⊙12.30-6.45pm), then head off for dinner at one of the city's excellent bistros around rue Sainte.

✕ 🍴 p274

The Drive ≫ To get to the Calanques, follow av du Prado south from the Vieux Port; it winds up into the hills behind the city and becomes the D559, the main road through the national park. There are loads of places to stop, but you'll have to do some walking if you want to see any coves. Things get very hot and sweaty in summer, so set out early.

 TRIP HIGHLIGHT

❷ The Calanques

East of Marseille, a range of bone-white, parched cliffs towers above glittering turquoise coves. Known as the **Calanques**

(www.calanques-parcnational. fr), these craggy inlets run for around 20km all the way to the seaside village of Cassis. They've been protected since 1975, and were designated as a national park in 2014. They're a favourite place for Marseillais to hike and picnic; Marseille's tourist office runs regular guided hikes, although trails are closed in July and August due to fire risk.

Of the many *calanques* along the coastline, the most accessible are **Calanque de Sormiou** and **Calanque de Morgiou**, while remote inlets such **Calanque d'En Vau** and **Calanque de Port-Miou** take dedication and time to reach – either on foot or by kayak. The roads into each *calanque* are usually closed to drivers, but a sneaky workaround is to make a booking at one of the cove restaurants: good options are **Le Château** (☎04 91 25 08 69; http://lechateausormiou. fr; Calanque de Sormiou; mains €19-25; ⊙noon-2.30pm & 7.30-9.30pm Apr-Sep) in Sormiou and **Nautic Bar** (☎04 91 40 06 37; Calanque

PROVENCE & SOUTHEAST FRANCE **24** VAR DELIGHTS

 LINK YOUR TRIP

18 **Foothills of the Alps**
From Haute-Provence on into the wilds of the Vercors.

23 **Riviera Crossing**
Cut out the gorges and stick to the coast for Cannes.

de Morgiou; mains €18-27; ⏱noon-2.30pm & 7.30-9.30pm May-Oct, closed Sun evening & Mon Apr) in Morgiou.

The Drive » You'll see signs for Cassis not long after you drive out of the national park. Bandol is another 25km along the D559, and Sanary-sur-Mer is 8km further on.

- - - - - - - - - - - -

❸ Cassis, Bandol & Sanary-sur-Mer

East of Marseille, the coast road passes a handful of lovely seaside villages, all with their own reason for a stop, not least the area's excellent wines. First comes **Cassis**, nestled at the foot of a dramatic rocky outcrop crowned by a 14th-century château (now a hotel). Still a working fishing port, its harbourside is crammed with seafood restaurants, perfect for a plate of grilled sardines or a copious shellfish platter. Neighbouring **Bandol** is well-known for its wines, too: stop in at the **Maison des Vins** (Oenothèque des Vins du Bandol; ☎04 94 29 45 03; www.maisondesvins-bandol.com; place Lucien Artaud, Bandol; ⏱10am-1pm & 3-6.30pm Mon-Sat, 10am-1pm Sun), where manager Pascal Perier will happily give you a crash course, and recommend local vineyards. Last comes seaside **Sanary-sur-Mer**, perhaps the prettiest and most authentic of all: here you can still watch the fishers unload their catch on the quayside, and pick up local produce at the lively **Wednesday market**.

✖ p274

The Drive » There's no compelling reason to make a detour via run-down Toulon, so skip it and zoom past on the motorway (A50, A57 and A570). Take exit 7 to Hyères.

- - - - - - - - - - - -

❹ Hyères

The coastal town of Hyères is split in two: there's the attractive **old town**, centring around a medieval castle, and the T-shaped **peninsula**, home to a busy pleasure port and some fine sandy beaches (perfect for a day's leisurely swimming and sunbathing). In between are several lagoons that are great for birdwatchers. But the main reason to visit Hyères is (rather ironically) to leave: it's the main harbour for trips over to the idyllic **Îles d'Hyères**, a tiny archipelago of islands fringed by white sand and criss-crossed by nature trails. **Transport Littoral Varois** (☎04 94 58 21 81; www.tlv-tvm.com) runs ferries, including a two-island day trip (return €31.50) to Île de Port-Cros and Le Levant.

✖ 🛏 p274

The Drive » It's an easy 21km along the D98 to Bormes-les-Mimosas, although the climb up to the village can be trafficky in summer. There's a large car park on the edge of the village beneath the *pétanque* pitch.

- - - - - - - - - - - -

TRIP HIGHLIGHT

❺ Bormes-les-Mimosas

This 12th-century hilltop village is heralded for its horticultural splendour: dazzling yellow mimosas in winter, deep-fuchsia bougainvilleas in summer. Generally, though, it's just a lovely place to stop for a wander: a browse around the many art galleries, a spot of souvenir shopping in the smart boutiques, or a leisurely lunch at a village bistro. On the peninsula, there's also an 11th-century fortress to visit, the **Fort de Brégançon** (www.bormeslesmimosas.com; Hameau de Cabasson, Bormes-les-Mimosas; adult/child €10/free; ⏱9am-7pm Jul-Sep, shorter hours rest of year), used to as a private state residence for the French president since 1968, and opened to the public in July 2014. Book a ticket at Bormes' tourist office, which also arranges guided nature walks in the nearby forests.

The Drive » Pick up the coast road again (D559) and follow its curves as it becomes the Corniche des Maures. There are numerous swimming spots along here, so keep your eyes peeled and your bathing suit to hand. The Domaine du Rayol is clearly signed when you hit Le Rayol-Canadel.

Le Rayol-Canadel Coastal gardens at Domaine du Rayol

271

❻ Domaine du Rayol

East of Bormes, the coastal Corniche des Maures twists past sandy beaches and seaside settlements like Le Lavandou and Le Rayol-Canadel, where you'll find one of the gems of this stretch of the coastline: the dazzling gardens of the **Domaine du Rayol** (☎04 98 04 44 00; www.domainedurayol.org; av des Belges, Rayol-Canadel-sur-Mer; adult/child €10.50/7.50; ⏱9.30am-7.30pm Jul & Aug, to 6.30pm Apr-Jun, Sep & Oct, to 5.30pm Nov-Mar), stocked with plants from Mediterranean climates from across the globe. It's a riot of fragrance and colour, best visited in April and May when the flowers are in full bloom. In summer, the estate's lovely beach also runs guided snorkelling ses-sions, during which you get to spot some of the colourful flora and sea life that lie beneath the Mediterranean waves.

The Drive » The D559 meanders all the way to swish St-Tropez, although, unfortunately, if you're here in summer, you're pretty much guaranteed to hit jams the nearer you get to town. There's a big car park by the port.

TRIP HIGHLIGHT

❼ St-Tropez

Sizzling sexpot Bri-gitte Bardot came to St-Tropez in the '50s and transformed the peaceful fishing village into a jet-set favourite. Tropeziens have thrived on their sexy image ever since. At the **Vieux Port**, yachts like spaceships jostle for millionaire moorings, while out on the beaches, cashed-up kids dance until dawn and the restaurants are really fabulous, if only you weren't picking up the tab.

Swamped by more than 100,000 visitors a day in summer, outside the peak season St-Tropez rediscovers its soul. Now's the time to wander the cobbled lanes in the old fishing quarter of **La Ponche**, or sip a pastis and watch a game of *pétanque* on lovely **place des Lices** – prefer-ably with a generous slice of *tarte Tropézinenne,* the town's famous orange-perfumed cake.

✕ ⊨ p274

The Drive » Back onto the our old friend again, the D559, through Port-Grimaud and Ste-Maxime, along the coast, and into Fréjus after 38km. Allow more time than you think you'll need; traffic's inevitable. St-Raphaël is just round the bay.

MASSIF DES MAURES

A wild range of wooded hills rumpling the landscape inland between Hyères and Fréjus, the **Massif des Maures** is a pocket of surprising wilderness just a few kilometres from the summer hustle of the Côte d'Azur. Shrouded by pine, chestnut and cork oak trees, its near-black vegetation gives rise to its name, derived from the Provençal word *mauro* (dark pine wood). Traditional industries (chestnut harvests, cork, pipe-making) are still practised here, and the area is criss-crossed by hiking trails that offer wraparound views of the coastline. From June to September, access to many areas is limited due to the risk of forest fire, but at other times of year, it's a haven of peace and nature.

The leafy village of **Collobrières** (population 1950) is worth a detour: it's renowned for its chestnuts and hosts its own chestnut festival in August. The tourist office offers guided forest walks and can point you in the direction of the Châtaignier de Madame, the biggest chestnut tree in Provence, measuring a mighty 10.4m round.

Epic roads are ten-a-penny here: the D27 via the **Col du Canadel** and the tortuous **route des Crêtes** nearby are the stuff of *Top Gear* dreams.

8 Fréjus & St-Raphaël

They might not be quite on a par with many of Provence's Roman ruins, but the little town of **Fréjus** is still worth a detour if you're an archaeology enthusiast, with the remains of an amphitheatre, Roman theatre and various arches and portals.

Even if you're not, the old town is lovely: make sure you stop in at Le Fromager for a gourmet tour of local cheeses. Just along the coast is Fréjus' sister town, **St-Raphaël**, a beachy, boaty kind of place, and a good overnight base.

🍴 🛏 p275

The Drive >> Get the quick stretch along the A8 out of the way, exiting onto the D1555 northwards towards Draguignan. Turn off onto the D955 before you reach town, which will take you via the Gorges de Chateaudouble, and stay on the road all the way to Comps-sur-Artuby. Here you turn left onto the D71 and enter the wild, sky-high world of the Gorges du Verdon.

9 Haut-Var

From the coast, it's time to head inland into the hills of the Haut-Var, a rocky, wild landscape

THE VILLAGE OF TORTOISES

About 20km north of Collobrières, this wildlife reserve protects one of France's most endangered species, the Hermann tortoise (*Testudo hermanni*). Once common along the Mediterranean coast, it is today found only in the Massif des Maures and Corsica. A viewing trail travels through the reserve (look out for vicious-looking models of the tortoise's ancestors lurking among the bushes). Along the way, you'll also visit the tortoise clinic, where wounded tortoises are treated before being re-released back into the wild, and the nurseries, where precious eggs are hatched and young tortoises spend the first three of their 60 to 100 years.

In summer, the best time to see the tortoises is in the morning and late afternoon. Hatching season is from mid-May to the end of June; from November through early March, they're all tucked up during hibernation.

that feels a world away from the chichi towns of the coast. Dry and sparsely populated, studded with hill villages and riven by gorges, it makes for spectacular driving. Your ultimate destination is the majestic **Gorges du Verdon**, sometimes called Europe's Grand Canyon – but it's worth making a detour via one of the lesser-known valleys, like the **Gorges de Chateaudouble**, 12km north of the military town of Draguignan.

From the coast, it's about a 90-minute drive before you enter the gorges near Comps-sur-

Artuby, then climb past the impressive **Pont d'Artuby**, Europe's highest bridge, and track the southern side of the gorges along a route that's sometimes known (appropriately enough) as **La Corniche Sublime** (D955 to D90, D71 and D19). The drops are dizzying and it's single-file most of the way, but there aren't many more memorable drives. Eventually, you'll pass the emerald-green waters of the Lac de Ste-Croix before reaching the journey's end in **Moustiers-Ste-Marie**.

🍴 🛏 p275

Eating & Sleeping

Marseille ❶

✗ Les Buffets du Vieux Port   French €

(☑04 13 20 11 32; www.clubhousevieuxport.com; 158 quai du Port; adult/child menu €23/13; ⊗noon-2.30pm & 7.30-10.30pm; 🚲; ⓂVieux Port) What a great idea – a high-class, on-trend self-service canteen, with a vast array of starters, mains, salads and desserts laid out like a banquet for diners to help themselves to. Premium cold cuts, fresh seafood, bouillabaisse, mussels, fish soup – it's all here and more. Portside tables go fast, but there's plenty of room inside.

🛏 Hôtel Edmond Rostand   Design Hotel €€

(☑04 91 37 74 95; www.hoteledmondrostand.com; 31 rue Dragon; d €99, tr €114; ❄@🛜; ⓂEstrangin-Préfecture) Ignore the grubby outside shutters of this excellent-value Logis de France hotel in the Quartier des Antiquaires. Inside, decor is a hip mix of contemporary design and vintage, with a great sofa area for lounging and 16 rooms dressed in crisp white and soothing natural hues. Some rooms overlook a tiny private garden, others the Basilique Notre Dame de la Garde.

🛏 Mama Shelter   Design Hotel €€

(☑01 43 48 48 48; www.mamashelter.com; 64 rue de la Loubière; d €79-129; ❄🛜; ⓂNotre Dame du Mont-Cours Julien) This funky mini-chain of design-forward hotels recently opened its outpost in Marseille, and if you're a cool kid in search of sexy sleeps, this is the address for you. It's all about the details here – Philippe Starck furniture, sleek white-and-chrome colour schemes, in-room iMacs. Smaller rooms are oddly shaped, though, and it's a walk from the old port.

Cassis ❸

✗ La Villa Madie   Gastronomy €€€

(☑04 96 18 00 00; www.lavillamadie.com; av de Revestel-anse de Corton; menus €75-145, mains €54-72; ⊗noon-1.15pm Wed-Sun & 7-9.15pm Wed-Sat) Overseen by Marielle and

Dimitri Droisneau, this double Michelin-starred restaurant has become one of the destination addresses on the Riviera, renowned for its creative seafood and refined sea-view setting. Top-drawer ingredients like Aubrac beef, sea urchins, turbot and blue lobster form the core of the menu. There's a cheaper bistro on the 1st floor that's only open for lunch on weekdays (menus €37 to €45).

Hyères ❹

✗ Joy   Provencal €€

(☑04 94 20 84 98; www.restaurant-joy.com; 24 rue de Limans; lunch/dinner menus from €22.50/45; ⊗noon-1.30pm & 7-9.30pm Tue-Sat, noon-1.30pm Sun) In the old town, this intimate bistro is indeed a culinary joy. Fresh, seasonal menus change constantly and could include anything from seafood-stuffed ravioli to cinnamon-spiced foie gras.

🛏 Hôtel Bor   Boutique Hotel €€€

(☑04 94 58 02 73; www.hotel-bor.com; 3 allée Émile Gérard, Hyères Beach; d from €150; ⊗Mar-Oct; ❄@🛜🏊) Right beside the main beach, this Scandi-tinged hotel is a stylish place to stay, with its cedar-clad exterior, sun-loungers, potted plants and seafront deck. Rooms are modern and minimal with gloss-wood floors, monochrome photos and steel-grey walls.

St-Tropez ❼

✗ La Tarte Tropézienne   Cafe €

(☑04 94 97 04 69; www.latartetropezienne.fr; place des Lices; mains €13-15, cakes €3-5; ⊗6.30am-7.30pm & noon-3pm) This newly renovated cafe-bakery is the creator of the eponymous sugar-crusted, orange-perfumed cake. There are smaller branches on **rue Clémenceau** (☑04 94 97 71 42; www.latartetropezienne.fr; 36 rue Clémenceau; mains €13-15, cakes €3-5; ⊗7am-7pm) and near the **new port** (☑04 94 97 19 77; www.latartetropezienne.fr; 9 bd Louis Blanc; mains €13-15, cakes €3-5; ⊗6.30am-7.30pm), plus various other towns around the Côte d'Azur.

✖ Bistro Canaille Fusion €€

(☎04 94 97 75 85; 28 rue des Remparts; plates €8-24; ⏰7-11pm Fri & Sat Mar-May & Oct-Dec, 7-11pm Tue-Sun Jun-Sep) Probably the pick of the places to eat in town – creative, cosy and great value while still hitting the gourmet heights. It's got the soul of a bistro, but specialises in fusion-style tapas dishes inspired by the owners' travels. More filling mains are chalked on the board. It's on the street leading up to the château.

🛏 B Lodge Hôtel Hotel €€€

(☎04 94 97 58 72; www.hotel-b-lodge.com; 23 rue de l'Aïoli; d €200-450; ⏰Dec-Oct; ❄🛜) Just downhill from the Citadelle, this swanky design pad looks old from the outside, but inside it's a model modern hotel: minimalist furniture, exposed stone walls, muted tones and all. Some rooms don't have air-con – which feels stingy – but at least breakfast is included. Obviously those with balconies and Citadelle views are fabulous. Prices drop significantly in winter.

Fréjus ➑

✖ Mon Fromager Deli €

(☎04 94 40 67 99; www.mon-fromager.fr; 38 rue Sieyès; plat du jour €13.90, 5-cheese platter €10.90; ⏰shop 9am-7pm Tue-Sat, lunch noon-2pm Tue-Sat; 🍴) Enterprising cheesemonger Philippe Daujam not only sells cheese – he also cooks it into tasty lunches in his deli-style restaurant arranged in front of the cheese counter and on the street outside. Locals flock for the excellent-value plat du jour and can't go wrong cheese platters with salad. The faux cow-skin table mats are a fun touch, and Philippe is a fount of fromage knowledge.

🛏 Hôtel L'Aréna Hotel €€

(☎04 94 17 09 40; www.hotel-frejus-arena. com; 145 rue du Général de Gaulle; d €63-201, tr €97-253, f €104-298; ❄🛜🏊) One of Fréjus's fanciest options, a traditional family hotel bedecked in Provençal decor complete with garden, pool and upmarket restaurant. The duplexes are ideal for families (with two single beds on a mezzanine). Breakfast is a juicy €17.

Moustiers-Ste-Marie ➒

✖ La Grignotière Provencal €

(☎04 92 74 69 12; rte de Ste-Anne; mains €6-15; ⏰11.30am-10pm May-Sep, to 6pm Feb–mid-May) Hidden behind the soft pink facade of Moustiers's Musée de la Faïence is this utterly gorgeous, blissfully peaceful garden restaurant. Tables sit between olive trees and the colourful, eye-catching decor – including the handmade glassware – is the handiwork of talented, dynamic owner Sandrine. Cuisine is 'picnic chic', meaning lots of creative salads, tapenades, quiches and so on.

🛏 Ferme du Petit Ségriès Farmstay €

(☎04 92 74 68 83; www.chambre-hote-verdon. com; d incl breakfast €74-84; 🛜) Friendly hosts Sylvie and Noël offer five colourful, airy rooms in their rambling farmhouse, 5km west of Moustiers on the D952 to Riez. Family-style tables d'hôte (€30 with wine, served daily except on Wednesday and Sunday) are served at a massive chestnut table, or outside beneath a foliage-covered pergola in summer. Bikes are available for hire (from €15 per day).

Southern Seduction en Corse

25

From edgy urban vibe to tranquil green lanes and cliff-carved coastline, this trip takes history fiends and culture-vultures on a dramatic spin around the best of southern Corsica.

TRIP HIGHLIGHTS

150 km

Plage de Palombaggia
Slip into serene turquoise waters on Corsica's most photographed beach

Ajaccio
START

FINISH
Solenzara

Sartène

Porto-Vecchio

Col de Bavella
Hike below the majestic sawtooth spires of Aiguilles de Bavella

230 km

Filitosa
Admire the handiwork of prehistoric man on Corsica

50 km

Bonifacio
Test your nerves and fitness on the terrifying Aragon staircase

130 km

10 DAYS
260KM / 160 MILES

GREAT FOR...

BEST TIME TO GO
Spring or late summer to beat the crowds on the coast road and heat on the beach.

ESSENTIAL PHOTO
The cliffs of Bonifacio snapped afloat a boat.

BEST FOR HEART-POUNDING HIKES
The Col de Bavella is hot, but nothing beats the hike down the king's staircase in Bonifacio.

Corsica Swimmers enjoy cliff-fringed Mediterranean waters

25 Southern Seduction en Corse

Starting with your foot on the pedal in the Corsican capital, this 10-day journey ducks and dives along the island's most dramatic coastal roads and mountain passes in southern Corse (Corsica). Mellow green hikes, gold-sand beaches and crisp turquoise waters to break the drive and stretch your legs are never far away, and for archaeology buffs there's the added bonus of some of France's most extraordinary prehistoric sites.

❶ Ajaccio

Napoléon Bonaparte's hometown and the capital of France's ravishing Île de Beauté (aka Corsica), this charismatic city on the sea thoroughly spoils with fine art in **Palais Fesch – Musée des Beaux-Arts** (☎04 95 26 26 26; www.musee-fesch.com; 50-52 rue du Cardinal Fesch; adult/child €8/5; ⏰10.30am-6pm Mon, Wed & Sat, noon-6pm Thu, Fri & Sun May-Sep, to 5pm Oct-Apr) and a beautiful bay laced with palm trees. Afterwards hike 12km west to **Pointe de la Parata** to

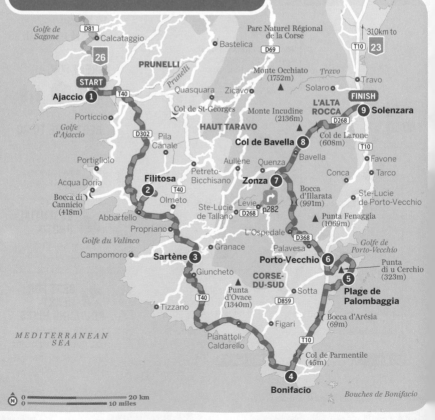

watch the sunset turn the **Îles Sanguinaires** (Bloody Islands) vivid crimson. Later, savour drinks beneath the stars on a trendy waterfront terrace at Port Tino Rossi.

 p284, p295

The Drive » From Ajaccio port, pick up the N193 and subsequent T40 to Bonifacio. After 12km turn right onto the D302, direction Pila Canale (a brown sign reads 'Filitosa'), and prepare for the sudden grand view of Ajaccio city below as the road climbs. Bear right onto the D266 and wind along peaceful green lanes via the D55, D355, D757 and D57 to Filitosa.

- - - - - - - - - - - - - -

TRIP HIGHLIGHT

❷ Filitosa

Nowhere is more evocative of ancient Corsican civilisation than this archaeological site, ripe

LINK YOUR TRIP

23 **Riviera Crossing**
Pop your car on the ferry in Bastia and sail to Nice for more mountainous, hairpin-laced corniches (coastal roads) with giant blue views.

26 **Corsican Coast Cruiser**
Completely smitten? Motor north from Ajaccio and up to Île Rousse to cruise the island's west coast.

with olive trees, pines and the intoxicating scent of maquis (herbal scrub). Visit around noon when the sun casts dramatic shadows on the carved statues and menhirs woven around trees and circling sheep pastures.

Corsica developed its own megalithic faith around 4000 BC to 3000 BC, and many of the stones at **Filitosa** (☎04 95 74 00 91; www.filitosa.fr; D57; €7; ◷9am-sunset Apr-Oct) date from this period. The menhirs are particularly unusual, including some with detailed faces, anatomical features like rib cages, even swords and armour.

The Drive » Wind your way back to the D57 and meander south to the sea along the D157 to join the southbound T40 just north of Propriano. Count on about 40 minutes to cover the 30km trip to Sartène.

- - - - - - - - - - - - - -

❸ Sartène

With its ramshackle granite houses, shaded shabby streets and secretive alleys, this sombre town evokes the rugged spirit of rural Corsica, notorious for banditry and bloody vendettas in the 19th century.

A colourful time to motor in is on Good Friday during the **Procession du Catenacciu**, celebrated since the Middle Ages. Barefoot, red-robed and cowled, the Catenacciu (literally 'chained one'; penitent) lugs a

massive 35kg wooden cross through town in a re-enactment of Christ's journey to Calvary. The rest of the year, cross and 17kg penitent chain hang inside **Église Ste-Marie** (place Porta).

Don't leave town without filling your picnic hamper with cheese, sausage, honey and wine from **La Cave Sartenaise** (☎04 95 77 12 01; www.lacavesartenaise.com; place Porta; ◷10am-noon & 3-6pm May–mid-Oct).

 p284

The Drive » From Sartène it is an easy one hour drive along the southbound T40 to Bonifacio. Slow down along the final leg – coastal views are glittering and you might well want to jump out for a dip.

- - - - - - - - - - - - - -

TRIP HIGHLIGHT

❹ Bonifacio

With its glittering harbour, incredulous clifftop perch and stout citadel teetering above the cornflower-blue waters of the **Bouches de Bonifacio**, this Italianate port is an essential stop. Sun-bleached town houses, dangling washing lines and murky chapels secreted in a postcard web of alleyways hide within the old citadel, while down at the harbour, kiosks tout must-do boat trips through gin-clear waters to **Îles Lavezzi**.

Park at the harbour and walk up **montée du Rastello** and

montée St-Roch to the citadel gateway with 16th-century drawbridge. Inside is the 13th-century **Bastion de l'Étendard** (adult/child €2.50/free, incl Escalier du Roi d'Aragon €3.50/free; 🕙9am-8pm mid-Apr–Sep, 10am-5pm rest of year) with a history museum. Stroll the ramparts to **place du Marché** and **place de la Manichella** for jaw-dropping views of the legendary cliffs. Then hike down the **Escalier du Roi d'Aragon** (adult/child €2.50/free, incl Bastion de l'Étendard €3.50/free; 🕙9am-sunset Apr-Oct), a steep staircase cut into the southern cliff-face to the water. Legend says its 187 steep steps were carved in a single night by Aragonese troops during the siege of 1420. In truth, the steps led to an underground freshwater well, in a cave on the seashore.

✗ 🛏 p284

The Drive ❯❯ From the harbour, head north along the T10 towards Porto-Vecchio. Count on about 45 minutes to cover the 35km from Bonifacio to the Plage de Palombaggia turn-off, signposted on the large roundabout south of Porto-Vecchio town proper.

- - - - - - - - - - -

TRIP HIGHLIGHT

❺ Plage de Palombaggia

When it comes to archetypal 'idyllic beach', it's impossible to think past immense Plage de Palombaggia, the pine-fringed beach on most Corsica postcards. Imagine

MICHAEL BUSSELLE / GETTY IMAGES ©

Bonifacio Harbour and citadel

DETOUR: PREHISTORIC CORSICA

Start: ❼ Zonza

This short but startling loop dives into the heart of ancient Corsica. To create a perfect weekend, combine it with an overnight stay at the island's best boutique-farm spa.

From Zonza drive 9km south along the D268 to **Levie**, unexpected host to the **Musée de l'Alta Rocca** (Site Archéologique Cucuruzzo Capula; ☑04 85 78 00 78; www. cg-corsedusud.fr/patrimoine-et-culture/musee-de-levie; av Lieutenant de Peretti, Levie; adult/ child €4/free; ⏰10am-5pm Tue-Sat Oct-May, to 6pm daily Jun-Sep), a local history and ethnographical museum.

Continue south along the D268 and after 3km turn right onto rte du Pianu (D20), a narrow lane signposted 'Cucuruzzu Capula Site Archéologique'. Soon after you arrive at **A Pignata** (☑04 95 78 41 90; www.apignata.com; rte du Pianu, Levie; d €200-360, ste €280-400, all incl half-board; ⏰late Mar-Dec; ❄️🛜🏊), a chic mountain retreat where you can gorge on Alta Rocca mountain views crossed by swirling clouds from a poolside chaise longue. Fronted by brothers Antoine and Jean-Baptiste, the farmhouse spa with vegetable garden and pigs (and the most mouth-melting charcuterie) is first-class. Its 18 rooms are contemporary and its restaurant (*menu* €40) is the best in southern Corsica. For heaven on earth, go for the impossibly romantic tree house for two.

Next morning, continue along the same D20 road for five minutes to the **Site Archéologique Cucuruzzu Capula** (Site Archéologique Cucuruzzu Capula; ☑04 95 78 48 21; Levie; adult/child €4/free; ⏰9.30am-7pm Jun-Sep, to 6pm Apr, May & Oct), 3.7km in all from the D268. Allow two hours to explore the archaeological site. Enthralling for kids and adults alike, an evocative 3km interpretive trail takes you on foot between giant boulders coloured bright green with moss to the Bronze Age *castelli* (castles) of Cucuruzzu and Capula. Along the way kids can duck into the earliest natural-rock shelters used by prehistoric humans (who were small in stature) and poke around the remaining rooms of a stronghold where, a few centuries later, they would butcher wild boar, cooked broth, spun wool and fashioned thongs from stretched animal skins.

Backtrack to the D268 and turn left (north) back to Levie and beyond to Zonza.

---

sparkling turquoise water, long stretches of sand edged with pine trees and splendiferous views over the **Îles Cerbicale**. Melting into its southern fringe are the equally picture-perfect expanses of sand and lapping shallow waters of **Plage de la Folacca**. This irresistible duo is sure to set your heart aflutter.

🍴 🛏 p284

The Drive » Join rte de Palombaggia in its anticlockwise loop around the peninsula, afterwards joining the busy T10 briefly for its final sprint into Porto-Vecchio. Spend a pleasant hour mooching along at a relaxed, view-savouring pace.

- - - - - - - - - - - -

❻ Porto-Vecchio

Shamelessly seductive and fashionable, Porto-Vecchio is the Corsican St-Tropez, the kind of place that lures French A-listers and wealthy tourists. Its picturesque backstreets, lined with restaurant terraces and designer shops, has charm in spades – presided over with grace by the photogenic ruins of an old Genoese **citadel**.

Small and sleepy by day, Porto-Vecchio sizzles in season when its party reputation dons its dancing shoes and lets rip for a hot night out. Cafes and bars cluster place de la République and along the seafront. On the town's southern outskirts, **Via Notte** (☎04 95 72 02 12; www.vianotte.com; rte de Porra; ☺8pm-5am daily Jun-Sep), with 5000-odd revellers and superstar DJs most summer nights, is the hottest club in Corsica and one of the most famous in the Med.

✖ p285

The Drive » Leave Porto-Vecchio by the winding D368 and follow it through the heavily wooded Forêt de l'Ospédale – excellent walks and picnic spots – to the rural hamlet of L'Ospédale (1000m), 18km northeast. Continue on the same road through more forest and loads more exhausting wiggles to Zonza, 20km north again. It'll take a good hour for the entire journey.

- - - - - - - - - - - -

7 Zonza

The chances are you've had a temporary surfeit of superb seascapes, so take a couple of days out to explore the **Alta Rocca** wilderness, a world away from the bling and glitz of the coast. At the south of the long spine that traverses Corsica, the area is a bewildering combination of dense, mixed evergreen–deciduous forests and granite villages strung over rocky ledges.

No mountain village plunges you more

dramatically into its heart than Zonza, a hamlet overshadowed by the iconic **Aiguilles de Bavella** (Bavella Needles), granite pinnacles like shark's teeth that jab the skyline at an altitude of more than 1600m. Hiking is the thing to do in this wild neck of the woods.

🛏 p285

The Drive » Allow up to 20 minutes for the go slow, bend-laced D268 that climbs slowly and scenically up from Zonza to the mountain pass at 1218m, 9km north.

- - - - - - - - - - - -

TRIP HIGHLIGHT

8 Col de Bavella

No number of hairpins or sheer drops can prepare you for the spectacular drama that awaits you atop the Bavella Pass (1218m), the perfect perch for marvelling close-up at the Aiguilles de Bavella. Depending on the time of day and weather, these gargantuan granite spikes glimmer red, gold, crimson, ginger or dark broody burgundy.

Short and long hikes are a dime a dozen, and when the drinking in of outdoor action and intoxicating alpine views is done, there is unforgettable feasting on roasted baby goat and wild pig stew at the **Auberge du Col de Bavella** (☎04 95 72 09 87; www.auberge-bavella. com; Col de Bavella, D268; mains €11-23; menu €24;

☺noon-3pm & 7-9.30pm Apr-Oct) on the pass. If you want to stay overnight, this Corsican inn has dorm beds (per person including half-board €40).

The Drive » Steady your motoring nerves for relentless hairpins on the perilously steep descent along the D268 from the Col de Bavella to the Col de Larone, 13km northeast, and onwards north through the hills to Solenzara on the coast. Allow at least an hour for the entire 30km trip.

- - - - - - - - - - - -

9 Solenzara

The town itself is not particularly worthy of a postcard home. What gives this seaside resort on Corsica's eastern coast natural appeal is its handsome spread of sandy beaches and the journey to it – one of the most stunning (and nail-biting) drives on Corsica. So steep and narrow is the road in places that it's not even single lane, while hazy views of the tantalising Mediterranc far below pose an unnerving distraction. Once through the thick pine forest of the **Forêt de Bavella**, the road drops across the **Col de Larone** (608m) to eventually meet the banks of the **River Solenzara**. When the extreme driving gets too much, pull over and dip your toes in the crystal-clear river water – there are swimming and picnic spots aplenty.

Eating & Sleeping

Ajaccio ❶

✕ **Le 20123**   Traditional Corsican €€

(🖉04 95 21 50 05; www.20123.fr; 2 rue du Roi de Rome; menu €35; ⏰7-11pm Tue-Sun) This fabulous, one-of-a-kind eatery started life in the village of Pila Canale (postcode 20123, get it?), and when the owner upped sticks to Ajaccio, he decided to take the old village with him – water pump, washing line, life-sized dolls in traditional dress, central square and all. It may sound tacky, but you won't find many more character-filled places in Corsica. Everyone feasts on the same four-course menu, built solely from local produce and traditional recipes, and, amazingly, unchanged for 25 years.

🛏 **Hôtel Marengo**   Hotel €

(🖉04 95 21 43 66; www.hotel-marengo.com; 2 rue Marengo; d €78-98; ⏰Apr-Oct; ✽🛜) For something near to the sand, try this charmingly eccentric small hotel. Rooms have a balcony, there's a quiet flower-filled courtyard and reception is an agreeable clutter of tasteful prints and personal objects. Find it down a cul-de-sac off bd Madame Mère.

🛏 **Hôtel San Carlu Citadelle**   Hotel €€

(🖉04 95 21 13 84; www.hotel-sancarlu.com; 8 bd Danièle Casanova; d €85-157, f €158-248; ✽🛜) Located smack opposite the citadel, this cream-coloured town house with oyster-grey shutters is a solid bet. Rooms are clean and modern and views get better with every floor. Traffic noise could be an issue for light sleepers. The family room sleeps up to five comfortably.

Sartène ❸

🛏 **Domaine de Croccano**   B&B €€

(🖉04 95 77 11 37; www.corsenature.com; rte de Granace/D148, km 3; d €92-120, q €142-180; ⏰Jan-Nov; ✽🛜) This charming stone farmhouse, set among 10 hectares of rolling maquis, makes a blissful getaway for those seeking end-of-the-road tranquillity. The rooms are very old-fashioned but the welcome couldn't be warmer, and the pastoral views are stunning.

The Domaine also offers picnic facilities and horse-riding excursions for guests. From Sartène's town square, follow the green signs 3.5km towards Granace.

Bonifacio ❹

✕ **Kissing Pigs**   Corsican €

(🖉04 95 73 56 09; 15 quai Banda del Ferro; mains €11-23, menus €20-22; ⏰noon-2.30pm & 7-10.30pm Tue-Sun) Soothingly positioned by the harbour, this widely acclaimed restaurant and wine bar serves savoury fare in a seductively cosy interior, complete with wooden fixtures and swinging sausages. It's famed for its cheese and charcuterie platters; for the indecisive, the combination *moitié-moitié* (half-half) is perfect. The Corsican wine list is another hit.

🛏 **Hôtel Le Colomba**   Hotel €€

(🖉04 95 73 73 44; www.hotel-bonifacio-corse. fr; 4-6 rue Simon Varsi; d €112-167; ✽🛜) Occupying a tastefully renovated 14th-century building, this hotel enjoys a prime location on a picturesque (steep) street, bang in the heart of the old town. Rooms are simple and smallish, but fresh and individually decorated with amenities including wrought-iron bedsteads, country fabrics, carved bedheads and/or checkerboard tiles. Other pluses include friendly staff and breakfast served in a medieval vaulted cellar.

Plage de Palombaggia ❺

✕ **Tamaricciu**   Mediterranean €€

(🖉04 95 70 49 89; www.tamaricciu.com; plage de Palombaggia; mains €16-32; ⏰12.30-6pm May–mid-Jun & Sep–mid-Oct, to 10.30pm mid-Jun–Aug) Among the various beach restaurants scattered along the Palombaggia sands south of Porto-Vecchio, Tamaricciu has that hip St-Tropez-chic touch. With its wooden decking terrace and first-class views of the turquoise surf, dining really does not get better than this. Cuisine is Mediterranean, with lots of grilled fish and meat and pasta, all beautifully presented.

A Littariccia
B&B €€

(☎04 95 70 41 33; www.littariccia.com; rte de Palombaggia; d €100-215; ❄☎☎) This B&B's trump card is its *fabulous* location, in the hills overlooking Plage de Palombaggia, with a dreamy pool. The rooms are pretty but simple and not all come with a sea view – or wi-fi.

Le Belvédère
Hotel €€€

(☎04 95 70 54 13; www.hbcorsica.com; rte de Palombaggia; d €250-300, ste €380-510; ☺May Nov; ❄☎☎) Built out of an old family estate tucked between eucalyptus, palm and pine on the seashore, this 15-room hotel is quite divine, darling. Decor is modern and exotic: a gregarious mix of traditional stone, wood, marble and wrought iron. Public areas lounge between natural rock and sand, and as for the sea-facing pool, you'll be hard-pushed to move. Rates tumble by 50% in the low season, making Le Belvédère a real bargain.

Porto-Vecchio ❻

✗ A Cantina di l'Orriu
Corsican €

(☎04 95 25 95 89; www.orriu.com; 5 cours Napoléon; mains €15-29; ☺noon-2pm Wed-Sun, 7-10pm Tue-Sun mid-Mar–Oct) Gourmets will be in heaven at this wonderful *bar à vin*, its atmospheric old-stone interior packed to the rafters with sausages and cold meats hung up to dry, cheeses, jars of jam and honey, and other tasty Corsican produce. Lunch platters range from light to feisty – raviolis are one of the house specialities – and desserts are sumptuous.

Zonza ❼

Hameau de Cavanello
B&B €

(☎04 95 78 66 82; www.locationzonza.com; Hameau de Cavanello; s €72-87, d €79-94; ☺May mid Oct; ❄☎☎) For a rural setting, Hameau de Cavanello, 2km towards the Col de Bavella, has a handful of cosy rooms (equipped with fridges and TVs) and a pool nesting in hectares of green meadows and forests with magical views of the Aiguilles de Bavella.

Chez Pierrot
B&B €€

(☎04 95 78 63 21; www.gitechezpierrot.free. fr; Plateau de Ghjallicu, Quenza; dm/d incl half-board €45/120) If you're after a typically Corsican atmosphere and the most tranquil location imaginable, at an altitude of about 1200m, bookmark Chez Pierrot, southern Corsica's most idiosyncratic venture. This multifaceted place – *gîte,* B&B, restaurant and equestrian centre – is run by charismatic Pierrot, a local character who's been living here since his early childhood. It's on Plateau de Ghjallicu, about 5km uphill from Quenza. Horse-riding excursions (€45, 1½ hours) are available April to October.

Corsican Coast Cruiser

26

Few coastlines are as ravishing or varied as the seashore ribbon that unfurls on this five-day trip around western Corsica. For some daredevil action, detour inland to the island's deepest canyon.

TRIP HIGHLIGHTS

5 DAYS
185KM / 115 MILES

10 km

Algajola
Discover the secret cove of your dreams aboard the rickety Trembler

Île Rousse START

Calvi

20 km

Plage de l'Arinella
Lunch on the sand at one of Corsica's most coveted beach dining spots

90 km

Porto
Cruise from Porto to the dazzling Réserve Naturelle de Scandola

100 km

Les Calanques de Piana
See red, blazing red, between fantastic rock formations

185 km

Ajaccio
Enjoy sweeping bay views and explore the sights of Napoléon Bonaparte's hometown

FINISH

GREAT FOR...

BEST TIME TO GO

April to July and September for quiet roads and blue-sky views.

ESSENTIAL PHOTO

Snap blazing-red rock formations at Les Calanques de Piana.

BEST FOR BOAT TRIPS

Set sail from Porto for some of Corsica's most breathtaking coastal scenery.

Corsican Coast Cruiser

Keep both hands firmly on the wheel during this high-drama ride along Corsica's hairpin-laced west coast. Dangerously distracting views out the window flit from glittering bay and bijou beach to sawtooth peak, blazing-red rock and maquis-cloaked mountain; while the road — never far from the dazzling big blue — gives a whole new spin to the concept 'Go Slow': you won't average much more than 35km/h for the duration of the trip.

❶ Île Rousse

Sun-worshippers, celebrities and holiday-ing yachties create buzz in this busy beach town straddling a long, sandy curve of land backed by mountains and herb-scented maquis.

Begin the day on Île Rousse's central tree-shaded square, **place Paoli**, overlooked by the 21 classical columns of the Greek Temple–styled **food market**, built around 1850. Get lost in the rabbit warren of old-town alleys around the square, and at noon sip a pre-lunch aperitif on the terrace of venerable **Café des Platanes** (place Paoli; ◷6am-2am Jun-Sep, 7am-8.30pm Oct-May) and watch old men play boules.

Later, take a sunset stroll past a Genoese watchtower and light-house to the russet-coloured rock of **Île de la Pietra**, from which the town, founded by Pascal Paoli in 1758, gets its colourful name. **Sea kayaking** (☏04 95 60 22 55; www.cnir.org; rte du Port; ◷9am-6pm Jul & Aug, by arrangement Sep-Jun) around the promontory and its islets is an outdoor delight.

✖ ⊨ p294

The Drive » From the roundabout at the western end of town, pick up the T30 towards Calvi; buy fresh fruit for the journey from the open-air stall signposted 'Marche Plein Air' on the roundabout.

TRIP HIGHLIGHT

❷ Algajola

This gloriously old-fashioned, bucket-and-spade address makes a great base. Its golden-sand beach is one of Corsica's longest and loveliest, and budget accommodation options are superb. If your idea of luxury is drifting off to the orchestra of crashing waves, and frolicking on the sand in pyjamas fresh out of bed at dawn, there is no finer place to stay.

Next morning, jump aboard the *trinighellu* (trembler), aka the **Tramway de la Balagne**, a dinky little seaside train that trundles along sand-covered tracks between Île Rousse and Calvi, stopping on request only at hidden coves and bijou beaches en route.

✖ ⊨ p294

The Drive » Continue towards Calvi on the coastal T30 and in the centre of Lumio, 6km south of Algajola, turn right following signs for 'Plage de l'Arinella'. Twist 2.6km downhill past leafy walled-garden *residences secondaires* to the turquoise water lapping onto Plage de l'Arinella.

TRIP HIGHLIGHT

❸ Plage de l'Arinella

If there is one crescent of sand in Corsica you must not miss, it's this serene, rock-clad cove with one of Corsica's finest beach

restaurants and dramatic views of the citadel of Calvi. Lunch here is a trip highlight.

From the stylish, shabby-chic interior of **Le Matahari** (📞04 95 60 78 47; www.lematahari.com; Plage de l'Arinella; mains €25-35; ⏲noon-3pm mid-Apr–Sep, 7-10.30pm Tue-Sun late May–mid-Sep) to the big windows looking out to Calvi beyond the waves, this hip beach spot is one very special hideaway. Wooden tables, strung on the sand and topped with straw parasols, immediately evoke a tropical paradise, while cuisine is creative – think penne *à la langouste* (lobster), squid, fresh *morue* (codfish) or a simple tuna steak panfried to pink perfection.

The Drive ❯❯ Motor back up the hill to join the coastal T30 and continue south for another

LINK YOUR TRIP

24 **Var Delights**
Sail by car ferry to Marseille and enjoy the coastal treasures of the Var.

25 **Southern Seduction en Corse**
Corsica is so seductive you might well find yourself extending your trip with this 10-day motor from Ajaccio around the island's southern tip to Porto-Vecchio on the east coast and beyond.

289

15 minutes, around the Golfe de Calvi, to Calvi. The best spot to park is at the top of town, across from the entrance to the citadel.

square shaded by rare Ombu trees with gnarled and knotted trunks, and sweet honey-producing flowers.

4 Calvi

Basking between the fiery orange bastions of its 15th-century citadel and the glittering waters of a moon-shaped bay, Calvi feels closer to the chichi sophistication of a French Riviera resort than a historic Corsican port. Palatial yachts and private cruisers jostle for space along its harbour-side, while high above the quay the watchtowers and battlements of the town's Genoese stronghold stand guard, proffering sweeping views inland to Monte Cinto (2706m).

Set atop a lofty promontory, Calvi's massive fortified **citadel** has fended off everyone down the centuries, from Franco-Turkish raiders to Anglo-Corsican armies. Wraparound views from its five feisty bastions certainly have the wow-factor, and **Chez Tao** (www.cheztao.com; rue St-Antoine; ⏰6pm-5am Jun-Sep), a wildly hip and lavish music bar around since 1935, is the spot to lap them up, cocktail in hand.

✗ ⌷ p294

The Drive » Across from the citadel, pick up the coastal road D81B signposted 'Rte de Porto – Bord de Mer'. Before driving off, don't miss the old shabby

5 Pointe de la Revellata

Within seconds of leaving town, you're deep in the hot sun-baked maquis (herbal scrubland), with a low stone wall being the only separator between white-knuckled passenger and green drop down to emerald water below. After 4km the magnificent cape of Pointe de la Ravelleta – the nearest Corsican point to the French mainland – pops into view, with a toy-like white lighthouse at its tip and dusty walking trails zigzagging between the scrub and the ocean. Park and indulge in a signposted 1.5km hike to **Chapelle Notre Dame de la Serra** or a 20-minute sea-bound stroll for lunch at **Mar A Beach** (📞06 33 62 17 64; Plage de l'Alga; mains €12-25; ⏰restaurant noon-4pm May-Oct, bar noon-7pm May-Oct), a Robinson Crusoe–style beach hut in a turquoise-water creek.

The Drive » Continue south on the D81B. After the *champ de tir* (military shooting range), savour a brief reprieve from the big coastal views as the road ducks inland between the mountainous 703m hulk of Capu di a Veta and fields of grazing sheep. At the first road fork, 35km south of Calvi, bear right along the D81 signposted

Calvi The 15th-century citadel towers over the town

DETOUR:
GORGES DE SPELUNCA

Start: ❼ Porto

If you crave a break from blue, head inland to the hills to **Ota** and **Évisa**, a twin set of enigmatic mountain villages that dangle defiantly above a plunging canyon blanketed with thick woods of pine, oak and chestnut. Quintessentially Corsican, these magical mountain hideaways are a haven for hikers, positioned halfway along the **Mare e Monti hiking trail** and within striking distance of Corsica's answer to the Grand Canyon, the unforgettable **Gorges de Spelunca**.

Until the D84 was carved out from the mountainside, the only link between the two villages was a tiny mule track via two Genoese bridges, the **Ponte Pianella** (also called **Ponte Vecchju**) and **Ponte Zaglia**. The trail between the villages is a fantastic day hike (five hours return), winding along the valley floor past the rushing River Porto and soaring orange cliffs, some more than 1km high. Or follow the shorter two-hour section between the bridges; pick up the trail at the arched road-bridge 2km east of Ota.

Carpeting the slopes east of Évisa is **Forêt d'Aïtone**, home of Corsica's most impressive stands of *laricio* pines. These arrow-straight, 60m-high trees once provided beams and masts for Genoese ships.

South of Porto, the D84 wiggles direct to Évisa, 22km east and a good 30 minutes of go-slow, blind-bend driving. Or opt for the narrower, slower D124 to the north that detours to the village of Ota before hooking up with the same D84.

'Galeria 5km, Porto 49km', and at the second fork, bear left.

----

❻ Col de la Croix

Having driven for a good hour around relentless hairpins, you might be tempted to stop on **Col de Palmarella** (405m), a mountain pass with fine views of the W-shaped bay of the Golfe de Girolata far below. Pull over to photograph the blazing blue Mediterranean ensnared by the flaming-red rock of **Punta Rossa**, the dollhouse-sized hamlet of Girolata tucked in the creek of the bay, and the menacing dark green of forested **Capo d'Osani**. But save the picnic lunch

and sun-fuelled siesta for **Col de la Croix** (260m), about 10km further south.

Park in the car park and pick up the dusty footpath behind the snack bar signposted *'Panorama – Table d'Orientation'*. Climbing gently uphill for 20 minutes through typical Corsican maquis, the path suddenly staggers out of the Mediterranean bush into a mind-blowing panorama of fiery red and smouldering black-green capes, blue bay and the spaghetti road you've successfully navigated to get here. An orientation table tells you what's what.

Back at the roadside *buvette* (snack bar), longer

walking trails lead downhill to the seaside hamlet of **Girolata** (1¾ hours, 7km) and to **Plage de Tuara** (45 minutes, 3km).

The Drive ›› Count on a good half-hour of relentlessly bend-laced motoring to cover the 25km from Col de la Croix south to Porto. The final five minutes reward you with a sudden narrowing of the road and dramatic roadside rock formations that flame a brilliant red. Go even slower than slow.

TRIP HIGHLIGHT

❼ Porto

The crowning glory of the west coast, Porto sits sweet at the foot of a thickly forested valley trammelled on either side by crimson peaks. Split by a promontory, the village itself is topped by a restored **Genoese tower** (€2.50; 9am-6pm mid-Apr–mid-Oct) built in the 16th century to protect the gulf from Barbary incursions. Scale the russet-coloured rocks up to the square tower, take in the tiny local-history exhibition inside, then stroll to the bustling marina where a footbridge crosses the estuary to a eucalyptus grove and pebble beach. April to October, boats sail from the marina to the shimmering seas around the magnificent, Unesco-protected marine reservation of the **Réserve Naturelle de Scandola**.

✕ 🛏 p294

The Drive » Cruise 12km south along the same coastal D81 towards the village of Piana. When you see red you know you've hit the next stop.

❽ Les Calanques de Piana

No amount of hyperbole can capture the astonishing beauty of these sculpted cliffs teetering above the Golfe de Porto. Rearing up from the sea in staggering scarlet pillars, teetering columns, towers and irregularly shaped boulders of pink, ochre and ginger, Les Calanques flames red in the sunlight and is among Corsica's most

iconic, awe-inspiring sights. And as you sway around switchback after switchback along the rock-riddled 12km stretch of the D81 south of Porto towards the village of **Piana**, one mesmerising vista piggy backs another.

For the full technicolour experience of this natural ensemble of gargantuan proportion, park up and savour Les Calanques on foot. Several trails wind their way around these dramatic rock formations unwittingly shaped like dogs' heads, dinosaurs and all sorts; trails start near **Pont de Mezzanu**, a road bridge on the D81 about 3km north of Piana. Afterwards, splurge on lunch at Corsica's most mythical hotel, **Les Roches Rouges** (☎04 95 27 81 81; www.lesrochesrouges. com; D81; s €130, d €125-145; ☀Apr-Oct; ✱🕾).

The Drive » Driving drama done with, it is a relatively easy 70km drive south along the D81 to the Corsican capital of Ajaccio.

TRIP HIGHLIGHT

❾ Ajaccio

Corsica's capital is all class – and seduction. Commanding a lovely sweep of the bay, the city breathes confidence and has a real whiff of the Côte d'Azur. Mosey around the centre with its mellow-toned buildings and vibrant cafe

culture, stroll the marina and trendy beach-clad rte des Sanguinaires area, and congratulate yourself on arriving in the city – several hundred hairpin bends later – in one piece!

Napoléon Bonaparte was born here in 1769, and the city is dotted with sites relating to the diminutive dictator. The **Salon Napoléonien** (☎04 95 51 52 62; www.musee-fesch. com; Hôtel de Ville, av Antoine Sérafini; adult/child €2.50/ free, ☀9-11.45am & 2-5.45pm Mon-Fri mid-Jun–mid-Sep. to 4.45pm rest of year) displays Napoléonic medals, portraits, busts and a frescoed ceiling of Napoléon and entourage; and his childhood home is now the **Maison Bonaparte** (☎04 95 21 43 89; www. musees-nationaux-napoleoniens.org; rue St-Charles; adult/child €7/ free; ☀10.30am-12.30pm & 1.15-6pm Tue-Sun Apr-Sep, to 4.30pm Oct-Mar).

The Oscar for most fascinating museum goes to Ajaccio's fine arts museum, established by Napoléon's uncle, inside **Palais Fesch** (☎04 95 26 26 26; www.musee-fesch.com; 50-52 rue du Cardinal Fesch; adult/child €8/5; ☀10.30am-6pm Mon, Wed & Sat, noon-6pm Thu, Fri & Sun May-Sep, to 5pm Oct-Apr). France's largest collection of Italian paintings outside the Louvre hangs here.

✕ 🛏 p284, p295

Eating & Sleeping

Île Rousse ❶

✖ A Casa Corsa   Corsican €

(📞04 95 60 23 63; 6 place Paoli; sandwiches & salads €5-10; ⏱8am-11pm Tue-Sun mid-Mar–Oct; 🍴) With a prime location on the gorgeous place Paoli, this wine bar makes a brisk trade in salads, cheese and charcuterie platters and other stalwart Corsican fare. As expected, the wine selection, including by the glass, and advice is excellent and all Corsican.

🛏 L'Escale Côté Sud   Hotel €€

(📞04 95 63 01 70; www.hotel-ilerousse.com/escale-cote-sud; 22 rue Notre-Dame; r €95-195) Open year-round, this centrally located, recently remodelled three-star with attached restaurant is an excellent midrange option, especially if you can snag one of the four sea-facing rooms with dreamy views of limpid turquoise waters lapping the beach across the street.

Algajola ❷

✖ Le Padula   Seafood, Pizza €€

(📞04 95 60 75 22; Plage d'Aregno; pizza from €10, mains €15-24; ⏱8am-11pm Easter-Oct) Spectacular views and tasty, unpretentious food are the twin drawcards at this informal beach terrace restaurant on Plage d'Aregno, just east of Algajola. The menu ranges from pizza (served day and night) to the daily *plat du jour* (€14.90) to classic seafood snacks like *moules marinière* (mussels cooked with garlic, shallots and white wine) and *friture de calamars* (fried squid).

🛏 U Castellu   B&B €€

(📞04 95 36 26 13; www.ucastelluchambresdhotes.com; 8 place du Château; d €90-166; ⏱Apr-Oct; ❄🛜) U Castellu will win you over with its location on the village's square in the shade of the ancient castle. Set in an old village home, the five rooms are a wonderful blend of old and new. Maud's welcome is another drawcard, as is the panoramic rooftop terrace where the copious buffet breakfast is served. The adjoining **restaurant** (📞04 95 60 78 75; 10 place du Château; mains €12-20, menus €20-25; ⏱noon-2.30pm & 7-10.30pm Apr-Sep) comes equally recommended for its sunny, reliable Mediterranean cuisine.

Calvi ❹

✖ A Candella   Corsican €€

(📞04 95 65 42 13; 9 rue St-Antoine; mains €16-25; ⏱noon-2pm & 7-10pm mid-May–Sep) One of a handful of addresses at which to eat within the citadel, A Candella stands out for its romantic, golden-hued terrace of stone strung with pretty flowers in pots and olive trees. The food is Corsican hearty, and the sea view is the most marvellous you could hope for.

✖ U Casanu   Corsican €€

(📞04 95 65 00 10; 18 bd Wilson; mains €15-22; ⏱noon-1.30pm & 8-10pm Mon-Sat Jan-Oct) For an unforgettable lunch, grab a booth at this cosy hole-in-the-wall, decorated in cheery yellow and green, and hung with watercolours painted by septuagenarian artist-owner Monique Luciani. Tuck into home-cooked fish couscous, roast lamb, codfish aioli or octopus salad, and don't miss the exquisite *fiadone*, a classic Corsican cheesecake made with lemon-scented *brocciu* cheese soaked in *eau de vie* (brandy).

🛏 Hôtel Le Magnolia   Hotel €€

(📞04 95 65 19 16; www.hotel-le-magnolia.com; rue Alsace Lorraine; d €110-155; ⏱Apr-Oct; ❄🛜) An oasis from the harbourside fizz, this attractive mansion sits behind a beautiful high-walled courtyard garden pierced by a handsome magnolia tree. Pretty much every room has a lovely outlook – Calvi rooftops, garden or sea – and connecting doubles make it an instant hit with families.

Porto ❼

✖ Le Maquis   Corsican €€

(📞04 95 26 12 19; cnr D124 & D81; mains €19-24, menus €23-25; ⏱noon-2pm & 7-10pm, closed Dec) This character-filled eatery in a granite house high above the harbour is much loved by locals and tourists alike. The food's a delight, with a tempting menu based on traditional Corsican cooking. Sit in the cosy wood-beamed interior or reserve a table on the balcony for brilliant views.

Hôtel-Restaurant Le Belvédère — Hotel €€

(04 95 26 12 01; www.hotelrestaurant-lebelvedere-porto.com; Porto Marine; r €65-135, q €116-146;) Brilliantly located down by Porto's harbour, near the steps to the Genoese watchtower, this small hotel has many rooms with direct sea views, including some with private terraces. Family rooms sleep up to five, with a double bed, two bunks and a trundle bed.

Ajaccio 7

L'Altru Versu — Bistro €€

(04 95 50 05 22; rte des Sanguinaires; mains €20-29; 12.30-2pm Thu-Mon & 7.30-10.30pm daily mid-Jun–mid-Oct, 12.30-2pm Thu-Tue & 7.30-10.30pm Mon, Tue & Thu-Sat rest of year) A phoenix rising from the ashes, this perennial favourite reopened in 2015 on Ajaccio's western waterfront after suffering two devastating winter storms and a fire. Magnificent sea views complement the exquisite gastronomic creations of the Mezzacqui brothers (Jean-Pierre front of house, David powering the kitchen), from crispy minted prawns with pistachio cream to pork with honey and clementine zest.

Hôtel Demeure Les Mouettes — Boutique Hotel €€€

(04 95 50 40 40; www.hotellesmouettes.fr; 9 cours Lucien Bonaparte; d €170-520; Apr-Oct;) This peach-coloured 19th-century colonnaded mansion right on the water's edge is a dream. Views of the bay of Ajaccio from the (heated) pool and terrace are exquisite: dolphins can often be spotted very early in the morning or in the evenings. Inside, the decor is one of understated elegance and service is four stars.

Hôtel Marengo — Hotel €

(04 95 21 43 66; www.hotel-marengo.com; 2 rue Marengo; d €78-98; Apr-Oct;) For something near to the sand, try this charmingly eccentric small hotel. Rooms have a balcony, there's a quiet flower-filled courtyard and reception is an agreeable clutter of tasteful prints and personal objects. Find it down a cul-de-sac off bd Madame Mère.

The Camargue

27

Take this semicircular tour from Arles to the coast and loop back again to experience Provence at its most wild, lush and lovely. Welcome to a watery, dreamlike landscape that's like no other.

TRIP HIGHLIGHTS

35 km

Stes-Maries-de-la-Mer
A 12th-century church houses the town's namesakes

START/FINISH
1

0 km

Arles
Home to Provence's hippest square

Etang de Vaccarès

Le Sambuc

5

3

105 km

Salin de Badon
Flamingos swoop over wetlands as you walk

Le Point de Vue

7

125 km

Plage de Piémanson
End-of-the-earth feel with miles of windswept beach

4 DAYS
190KM / 118 MILES

GREAT FOR...

BEST TIME TO GO
May, July and September – if you like it hot and can handle mosquitoes.

 ESSENTIAL PHOTO
Point de Vue for its salty backdrop and flamingos taking flight.

BEST FOR ROMANTICS
Dinner by the hearth in the timber-beamed 17th-century kitchen of Mas de Peint.

rc Ornithologique de Pont de Gau Wading flamingos

27 | The Camargue

Leave Arles and the highway behind and suddenly you're surrounded by the Camargue's great yawning green, and an equally expansive sky. It won't be long until you spot your first field of cantering white horses, or face off with a black bull. This is not a long trip, but one that will plunge you into an utterly unique world of cowboys, fishers, beachcombers, the Roma and all their enduring traditions.

TRIP HIGHLIGHT

❶ Arles

Befitting its role as gateway to the Camargue, Arles has a delightfully insouciant side. Long home to bohemians of all stripes, it's a great place to hang up your sightseeing hat for a few languorous hours (or days). Soak it in from the legendary bar at the Hôtel Nord-Pinus, with its bullfighting trophies and enthralling photography collection, or pull up a table on lively **place Paul Doumer**, where Arles'

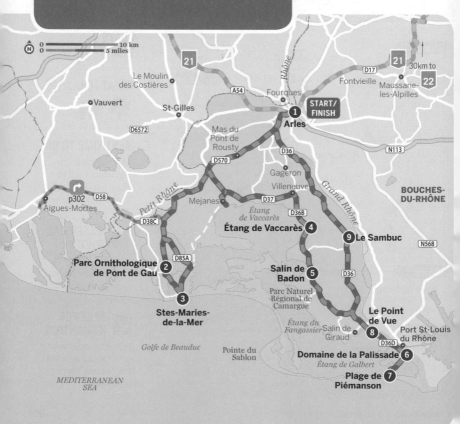

new generation makes its mark. Make a beeline for the Saturday-morning **market** (bd des Lices) and pack a Camargue-worthy picnic basket with local goats' cheese, olives and *saucisson d'Arles* (bull-meat sausage), or do likewise on Wednesday mornings on bd Émile Combes.

With precious little parking within the old town, unless you're staying at a hotel with a garage (usually an expensive extra), opt for the secure municipal facilities on bd des Lices (€7 per day).

✕ 🛏 p244, p303, p409

The Drive » Take the D35A across the Grand Rhône at the Pont de Trinquetaille, then follow signs to the D570 – you'll soon be in no doubt you've entered the Camargue. Continue south on the D570 until Pont de Gau, 4km before you hit the coast, around 30 minutes all up.

LINK YOUR TRIP

 21 Roman Provence
Slot in the Camargue trip's loop south from either Nîmes or Arles.

22 Lavender Route
From Arles, take the 570N and the D28 (direction Châteaurenard), then the D900 to Coustellet.

---

② Parc Ornithologique du Pont de Gau

Itching to get in among all that green? **Parc Ornithologique de Pont de Gau** (☎04 90 97 82 62, www.parcornithologique.com; D570, Pont du Gau; adult/child €7.50/5; ☀9am-sunset Apr-Sep, from 10am Oct-Mar), a 60-hectare bird park, makes for a perfect pit stop. As you meander along 7km of trails, flamingos pirouette overhead; the pink birds can't help play diva. Secreted away in the marshes, though, is every bird species that calls the Camargue wetlands home, including herons, storks, egrets, teals and raptors.

The Drive » Continue south on the D570. The last stretch of road into Stes-Maries-de-la-Mer is dotted with stables – little-white-horse heaven, so get out your camera.

TRIP HIGHLIGHT

③ Stes-Maries-de-la-Mer

Apart from a stretch of fine sand beaches – some 30km – the main attraction at this rough-and-tumble beach resort is the hauntingly beautiful **Église des Stes-Maries** (www.sanctuaire-des-saintesmaries.fr; place Jean XXIII; ☀rooftop 10am-noon & 2-5pm Mon-Sat, 2-5pm Sun), a 12th-century church that's home to a statue of Sara-la-Kali, or black Sara. The crypt

houses her alleged remains, along with those of Marie-Salomé and Sainte Marie-Jacobé, the Maries of the town's name. Shunned by the Vatican, this paleo-Christian trio has a powerful hold on the Provençal psyche, with a captivating back story involving a boat journey from Palestine and a cameo from Mary Magdalene. Sara is the patron saint of the *gitans* (Roma people), and each 24 May, thousands come to town to pay their respects and party hard. Don't miss the ex-voto paintings that line the smoke-stained walls, personal petitions to Sara that are touching and startlingly strange in turns.

This town is the easiest spot to organise *promenades à cheval* (horseback riding); look for Fédération Française d'Equitation (FFE) accredited places, such as the friendly **Les Cabanes de Cacharel** (☎04 90 97 84 10, 06 11 57 74 75; www cabanesdecacharel.com; rte de Cacharel, D85A; 1/2/3hr horse trek €20/30/40) on the easterly D85A.

✕ 🛏 p303

The Drive » The scenic D85A rejoins the D570, then, after 10 minutes or so, turn right into the D37. Stop at Méjanes for supplies or to visit the legendary fish restaurant Le Mazet du Caccarés. The D36B dramatically skims the eastern lakeshore; it's a 20-minute journey but is worth taking your time over.

❹ Étang de Vaccarès

This 600-sq-km lagoon, with its watery labyrinth of peninsulas and islands, is where the wetlands are at their most dense, almost primordial. Much of its tenuous shore forms the **Réserve National-ale Camargue** and is off-limits, making the wonderful nature trails and wildlife observatories at **La Capelière** (☎04 90 97 00 97; www.reserve-camargue. org; permits adult/child €3/1.50; ⏰9am-1pm & 2-6pm daily Apr-Sep, 9am-1pm & 2-5pm Wed-Mon Oct-Mar; 🚲) particularly precious. The 1.5km-long **Sentier des Rainettes** (Tree-Frog Trail) takes you through tamarisk wood-lands and the grasses of brackish open meadows.

The Drive » Continue on the D36B past Fiélouse for around 10 minutes.

TRIP HIGHLIGHT

❺ Salin de Badon

Before you leave **La Cape-lière**, grab your permits for another outstanding reserve site, once the **royal salt works** (adult/child €3/1.50). Around the picturesque ruins are a number of observatories and 4.5km of wild trails – spy on flamingos wad-ing through springtime iris. True birdwatchers mustn't miss a night in the **gîte** (dorms €12) here, a bare-bones cottage in a priceless location.

The Drive » Continue south until you meet the D36, turning right. Stop in Salin de Giraud for bike hire and fuel (there's a 24/7 gas station) or visit the salt works. The D36 splits off to cross the Rhône via punt, but you continue south on the D36D, where it gets exciting: spectacular saltpans appear on your right, the river on your left.

❻ Domaine de la Palissade

Along the D36D, **Domaine de la Palissade** (☎04 42 86 81 28; www.palissade.fr; rte de la Mer; adult/child €3/free; ⏰9am-6pm mid-Jun–mid-Sep, to 5pm Mar–mid-Jun & mid-Sep–Oct, 9am-5pm Wed-Sun Feb & Nov, closed Dec-Jan) organises horse treks (€18 per hour) where you'll find yourself wading across brackish lakes and through a pur-ple haze of sea lavender. It will also take you around lagoons and scrubby glasswort on foot, or give you a free map of the estate's marked walking trails. Don't forget to rent binoculars; best €2 you'll spend this trip!

The Drive » The next 3.7km along the rte de la Mer is equally enchanting, with flocks of birds circling and salt crystals flashing in the sun. Stop when you hit the sea.

TRIP HIGHLIGHT

❼ Plage de Piémanson

Just try to resist the urge to greet the Med with a wild dash into the waves at this lovely, windswept

DANITA DELIMONT / GETTY IMAGES ©

beach. Unusually, camp-ing is allowed here from May to September, and hundreds of campervans line up along the dunes for the duration of the *belle saison*. It's a scene that's as polarising of opinion as it is spectacu-lar. Basic facilities and a patrolled section of sand are right at the end of rte de la Mer; head east for the popular nudist beach.

Stes-Maries-de-la-Mer White horses on the beach

The Drive » Backtrack north along the D36. Just before Salin de Giraud, look for a car park and a small black shack on your right.

- - - - - - - - - - - -

8 Le Point de Vue

This lookout provides a rare vantage point to take in the stunning scene of pink-stained *salins* (saltpans) and soaring crystalline mountains. As fruitful as it is beguiling, this is Europe's largest salt works, producing some 800,000 tonnes per year. A small shop (the aforementioned black shack) sells *sel de Camargue* (Camargue salt) by the pot or sack, bull sausages and tins of fragrant local olive oil.

The Drive » Heading north on D36 for 20 minutes, Le Mas de Peint is on your right before Le Sambuc, while La Chassagnette's fork and trowel shingle is on the left to its north.

- - - - - - - - - - - -

9 Le Sambuc

This sleepy town's outskirts hide away a couple of the region's best restaurants and its most upscale lodgings. *Manadier* (bull estate owner) Jacques Bon, son of the family who owns

301

DETOUR:
AIGUES-MORTES

Start: ❸ Stes-Maries-de-la-Mer

Located over the border from Provence in the Gard, Aigues-Mortes sits a winding 28km northwest of Stes-Maries-de-la-Mer at the Camargue's far western extremity. Its central axis of streets often throngs with tourists, and shops spill out Camargue-themed tack, but the town is none the less magnificent, set in flat marshland and completely enclosed by rectangular ramparts and a series of towers. Come sundown, things change pace, and its squares are a lovely place to join locals for a relaxed *apéro* (pre-dinner drink). Established by Louis IX in the mid-13th century to give the French crown a Mediterranean port, it was from here that the king launched the seventh Crusade (and persecuted Cathars). The **Tour de Constance** (www.tourdeconstance.com; adult/child €7.50/free; ⏰10am-7pm May-Aug, 10am-5.30pm Sep-Apr) once held Huguenot prisoners; today it's the start of the 1.6km wall-top circuit, a must-do for heady views of salt mountains and viridian plains. Park on bd Diderot, on the outside of the northwestern wall.

hotel Le Mas de Peint, hosts Camargue farm-life demonstration days, **Journées Camarguaises** (📞04 90 97 28 50; www.manade-jacques-bon.com; adult/child incl lunch €38/19; ⏰monthly in summer), with music, *gardians* (cowboys) doing their thing and *taureau au feu de bois* (bull on the barbie). But if it's boots-'n'-all *gardian* style you're after, pull up a stool at the roadside **Café du Sambuc** (rte de Sambuc): bull couscous and a jug of rosé for loose change, *and* staff adorned with

horse and Camargue cross tattoos.

🍴 p303

The Drive » Continue north on the D36, where you'll re-meet the D570 heading to Arles, a 25km stretch in all.

- - - - - - - - - - - - - -

❿ Arles

Back in Arles, last stop is **Les Arènes** (Amphithéâtre; 📞08 91 70 03 70; www.arenes-arles.com; Rond-Point des Arènes; adult/child €6/free, incl Théâtre Antique €9/free; ⏰9am-8pm Jul & Aug, to 7pm May-Jun & Sep, shorter hours rest of year), the town's fabulous amphitheatre,

which still hosts bloody bullfights as well as less grisly *courses Camarguaises*. Rather than poking the bull to death, these traditional spectacles are a test of bravery, in which amateur *razeteurs* wearing skin-tight white shirts and trousers snatch rosettes and ribbons tied to the horns of the *taureau* with a sharp comb. Victory is never as certain as the fact that, at some point, the bull will charge, the *razeteurs* will leap the arena's barrier and the crowd will cheer.

🍴 🛏 p303, p409

Eating & Sleeping

Arles ❶

✗ Le Comptoir du Calendal — Cafe €

(📞04 90 96 11 89; www.lecalendal.com; 5 rue
Porte de Laure; mains €12-18; ⏱8am-8.30pm;
📶) Based on the ground floor of Le Calendal
hotel, this bright and breezy cafe does a nice
line in lunchtime sandwiches and salads, plus a
tempting choice of cakes and teas.

⮕ Le Cloître — Design Hotel €€

(📞04 88 09 10 00; www.hotel-cloitre.com;
18 rue du Cloître; s €105, d €130-185; @📶)
Proving you don't need to spend a fortune for
originality and imagination, the 19 rooms at this
zingy hotel next to the Cloître Ste-Trophime
combine history and modern design to winning
effect: bold colours, funky patterns and retro
furniture abound, and the rooftop terrace is a
stunning sundowner spot. The lavish breakfast
spread is (unusually) worth the €14 price tag.

⮕ Grand Hôtel Nord Pinus — Heritage Hotel €€€

(📞04 90 93 44 44; www.nord-pinus.com; place
du Forum; r €170-420) An Arlésian landmark,
this classy hotel has been frequented by
everyone from famous bullfighters to artists
and writers like Picasso, Hemingway, Jean
Cocteau and Fritz Lang. It's chock-full of
heritage: wrought-iron beds, art deco sinks,
20th-century furniture and vintage *féria*
posters, as well as black-and-white photographs
by Peter Beard downstairs. Room 10 is the
grandest, and the bullfighters' favourite.

Stes-Maries-de-la-Mer ❸

✗ La Cabane aux Coquillages — Seafood €

(📞06 10 30 33 49; www.degustationcoquillages-
lessaintesmariesdelamer.com; 16 av Van Gogh;
shellfish €8.50-12.50; ⏱noon-3pm & 5-11pm
Apr-Nov) Seafood is the only thing worth its salt
in Stes-Maries. Part of the excellent **Ô Pica
Pica** (mains €17-25; ⏱noon-3pm & 7-11pm
Mar-Nov) restaurant, this attractive little shack
specialises in *coquillages* (shellfish), including
oysters, *palourdes* (clams), *coques* (cockles),
tellines (a type of local shellfish known
elsewhere in France as *pignons*) and *tritures*
(deep-fried and battered baby prawns, baby
squid or anchovies).

⮕ Lodge Sainte Hélène — Boutique Hotel €€€

(📞04 90 97 83 29; www.lodge-saintehelene.
com; chemin Bas des Launes; d €150-190;
❄ @📶📺) These designer-chic, pearly white
terraced cottages strung along a lake edge are
prime real estate for birdwatchers and romance
seekers. The mood is exclusive, remote and
so quiet you can practically hear the flamingo
wings flapping overhead. Each room comes
with a birdwatchers' guide and binoculars, and
dynamic owner Benoît Noel is a font of local
knowledge. Breakfast €15.

Le Sambuc ❾

✗ La Chassagnette — Gastronomy €€€

(📞04 90 97 26 96; www.chassagnette.fr; rte
du Sambuc, 7-course menu €95, 5-course
menu with wine €125, mains €36-42; ⏱noon-
1.30pm & 7-9.30pm Thu-Mon Mar-Jun, Sep &
Oct, daily Jul & Aug, reduced hours Nov-Mar)
Surrounded by a vast *potager* (kitchen garden),
which supplies practically all the restaurant's
produce, this renowned gourmet table is run by
Armand Amal, a former pupil of Alain Ducasse.
The multi-course menus are full of surprises,
and the bucolic setting is among the loveliest
anywhere in the Camargue.

STRETCH YOUR LEGS
NICE

Start Hotel Negresco, Promenade des Anglais

Finish Promenade des Anglais

Distance 5.8km

Duration 2 hours

Get to know Nice's bustling heart with this walk that begins with a seaside stroll, then takes you into the tangled alleys of the old town, and finally up and over the city's soaring headland to the port. Along the way shop, eat and drink with the fun-loving Niçois.

Take this walk on Trips

23 38

Promenade des Anglais

Nice personified, the Prom seductively blends hedonism with history, pumping beach clubs with quiet seaside gazing. English expats paid out-of-work citrus farmers to build the Prom in 1822 – a civic win-win. Don't miss the palatial facades of belle époque **Hôtel Negresco** and art deco **Palais de la Méditerranée**.

The Walk » Turn up av de Verdun past palms and posh shops to place Masséna. Take in the elegant Italian architecture, then head down the steps. Take rue de l'Opéra, a quick walk to our next stop.

Rue St-François de Paule

Window-shop, pick up snacks or shop for gifts on this elegant street just back from the seaside. First stop: **Moulin à Huile d'Olive Alziari** (www.alziari.com.fr; 14 rue St-François de Paule; ⊘8.30am-12.30pm & 2.15-7pm Mon-Sat) for superb local olive oil, tapenade (olive spread) and olives. Head west to the florid **Opera House**; across the road is **Henri Auer Confiserie** (www.maison-auer.com; 7 rue St-François de Paule; ⊘9am-6pm Tue-Sat), a film-set-perfect sweet shop; pick up *amandes enrobé* (cocoa-dredged chocolate-covered almonds).

The Walk » Continue on past soap sellers and wine bars and into the open square. This eventually becomes cours Saleya.

Cours Saleya

A top tourist destination that remains Niçois to the core, this bustling market square does different moods according to the hour. Greet the day with espresso and a banter with the produce and flower sellers, lunch with locals or get rowdy after dark with the town's cool kids and students.

The Walk » Any of the streets running away from the beach take you to rue de la Préfecture.

Vieux Nice

Soak in the labyrinthine streets of Nice's old town, stumbling upon Baroque gems like **Cathédrale Ste-Réparate** (place Rossetti). Stop to eat – book **Le Bistrot d'Antoine** (☎04 93 85 29 57; 27 rue de la Préfecture; menus €25-43,

mains €15-25; ⊙noon-2pm & 7-10pm Tue-Sat),
or grab an aperitif at **Les Distilleries
Idéales** (www.lesdistilleriesideales.fr; 24 rue
de la Préfecture; ⊙9am-12.30am) and snack
at **Lou Pilha Leva** (✆04 93 13 99 08; 10 rue
du Collet, small plates €3-5, ⊙9am-midnight,
✎). Grab a delicious ice-cream cone at
Fenocchio (www.fenocchio.fr; 2 place Rossetti;
1/2 scoops €2.50/4, ⊙9am-midnight Feb-Oct).

The Walk » Take the stairs at rue Rossetti, or
the lift at rue des Ponchettes to avoid the climb.

Colline du Château

On a rocky outcrop towering over Vieux
Nice, the **Parc du Château** (⊙8.30am-
8pm Apr-Sep, to 6pm Oct-Mar) offers a panorama of the whole city – Baie des Anges
on one side, the port on the other. Fabulous for picnics (there's a waterfall) or to
let the kids loose in the playground.

The Walk » Follow the path north through the
park towards the cemetery, then follow Allée
Font aux Oiseaux and the Montée du Château
back into the old town. Find your way along the
backstreets to bd Jean Jaurès, and cross the road
into Promenade du Paillon.

Promenade du Paillon

It's hard to imagine that this beautifully
landscaped park was once a bus station
and multi-storey car park. The park
unfolds from the Théâtre National to
place Masséna with a succession of green
spaces, play areas and water features,
and is now a favourite among Niçois for
afternoon or evening strolls. Local kids
love playing in the fountains, too.

The Walk » Follow the park as it heads
northeast and exit onto av St-Sébastien.

Musée d'Art Moderne et d'Art
Contemporain (MAMAC)

Nice's flagship modern art **museum**
(www.mamac-nice.org; place Yves Klein;
⊙10am-6pm Tue-Sun) focuses is on European and American avant-garde from
the 1950s to the present, with works
by leading artists such as Niki de Saint
Phalle, César, Arman and Yves Klein.
The building's rooftop is also an exhibition space (with knockout panoramas
of the city). Then it's back to the Prome-
dade des Anglais for a post-walk *pastis*.

Pyrenees & Southwest France

PEAKS TO PLAINS, VALLEYS TO VILLAGES, MOUNTAINS TO MED:
the southwest encompasses the French landscape in all its drama and diversity. Stretching from the dog's-tooth peaks of the Pyrenees all the way to the scrubby, sun-baked plains of the Languedoc, it's a region that's made for driving, with lots of scenic roads punctuated by fabulous viewpoints.

In the west, you'll meander across mountain passes and delve into remote valleys where life still feels timeless and traditional. As you move east, you'll discover the two sides of the Languedoc: Bas-Languedoc, with its flat plains, sprawling vineyards and laid-back coastal cities, and Haut-Languedoc, home to the wild hills and rocky gorges of the Parc National des Cévennes.

Le Pays Cathare Hillside village on the Cathar Trail

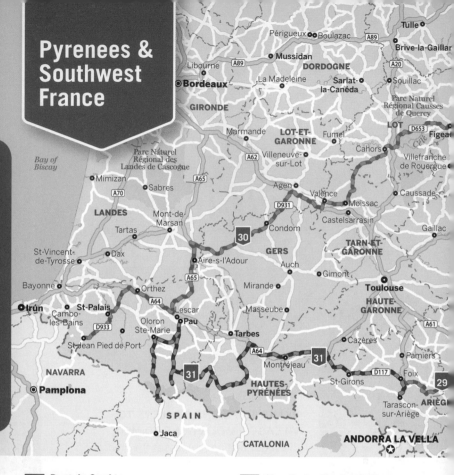

Pyrenees & Southwest France

28 Pont du Gard to Viaduc de Millau 5 Days
Traverse the crags and *causses* of the Cévennes, with a landmark bridge at either end. (p311)

29 The Cathar Trail 3 Days
Head into Bas-Languedoc's backcountry to discover its Cathar castles. (p319)

30 Cheat's Compostela 7 Days
Take a spiritual trip along one of France's oldest pilgrimage routes. (p327)

Classic Trip 31 The Pyrenees 7 Days
Explore the majestic mountain landscape, easily the equal of the Alps. (p335)

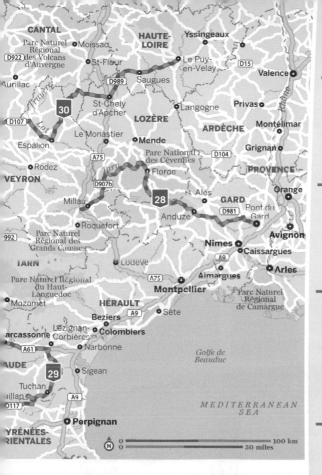

DON'T MISS

Le Puy-en-Velay
Climb inside a giant statue of the Virgin Mary for views across this Auvergnat town. Take them in on Trip 30

Lac de Gaube
One of the Pyrenees' finest trails leads to the glittering Lac de Gaube. Catch the cable car to the trail on Trip 31

Chaos de Montpellier-le-Vieux
An otherworldly landscape of limestone pillars has been created here by centuries of natural erosion. Walk it on Trip 28

Col d'Aubisque
The col is one of the Pyrenees' highest road passes. Competitors in the Tour de France have to pedal it, so count yourself lucky to just drive it on Trip 31

Roquefort
Descend into murky, mould-covered cellars to find out how this pungent fromage is made. Sample a piece on Trip 28

Languedoc Bridge over the Hérault River between Anduze and Florac

Pont du Gard to Viaduc de Millau

28

This trip begins and ends with a river, traversing hills and gorges in between. Start at the Pont du Gard, France's greatest Roman aqueduct, and finish by crossing the space-age Viaduc du Millau.

TRIP HIGHLIGHTS

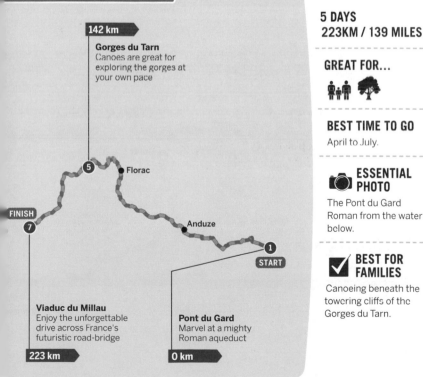

142 km

Gorges du Tarn
Canoes are great for exploring the gorges at your own pace

5

● Florac

FINISH
7

● Anduze

1
START

Viaduc du Millau
Enjoy the unforgettable drive across France's futuristic road-bridge

223 km

Pont du Gard
Marvel at a mighty Roman aqueduct

0 km

5 DAYS
223KM / 139 MILES

GREAT FOR...

BEST TIME TO GO
April to July.

ESSENTIAL PHOTO

The Pont du Gard Roman from the water below.

BEST FOR FAMILIES

Canoeing beneath the towering cliffs of the Gorges du Tarn.

28 Pont du Gard to Viaduc de Millau

Languedoc's known for its fine coastline and even finer wines, but on this trip you'll explore a different side to this peaceful corner of France. Inland, the landscape climbs into the high hills and river ravines of the Parc National des Cévennes, beloved by walkers, kayakers and nature-lovers alike. The scenery is truly grand, but keep your eyes on the tarmac, as some of the roads are hairy.

TRIP HIGHLIGHT

❶ Pont du Gard

The trip begins 21km northeast of Nîmes at the **Pont du Gard** (📞04 66 37 50 99; www.pontdugard.fr; car & up to 5 passengers €18, after 8pm €10, by bicycle or on foot €7, after 8pm €3.50; ⊗ site 24hr year-round, visitor centre & museum 9am-8pm Jul & Aug, shorter hours Sep–mid-Jan & mid-Feb–Jun), France's finest Roman aqueduct. At 50m high and 275m long, and graced with 35 arches, it was built around 19 BC to transport water from Uzès to Nîmes. A

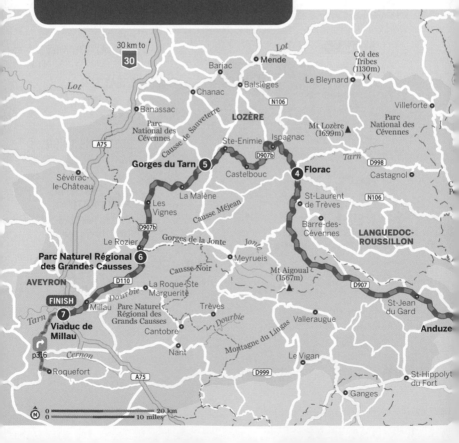

museum explores the bridge's history. You can walk across the tiers for panoramic views over the Gard River, but the best perspective on the bridge is from downstream, along the 1.4km Mémoires de Garrigue walking trail.

For a unique perspective on the Pont du Gard, you need to see it from the water. Canoe and/or kayak rental companies are plentiful.

There are large car parks on both banks of the river, a 400m level walk from the Pont du Gard. Early evening is a good time to visit, as admission is cheaper and the bridge is stunningly illuminated after dark.

The Drive » Drive northwest from the Pont du Gard along the D981 for 15km to Uzès.

- - - - - - - - - - - -

❷ Uzès

Northwest of the Pont du Gard is Uzès, a once-wealthy medieval town that grew rich on the proceeds of silk, linen and liquorice. It's also home to the **Duché Château** (www.duche-uzes.fr; place du Duché; €13, incl tour €18; ⏲10am-12.30pm & 2-6.30pm Jul & Aug, 10am-noon & 2-6pm Sep-Jun), a castle that belonged to the powerful Dukes of Uzès for more than 1000 years. You can climb 135 steps to the top of the Tour Bermonde for a magnificent view across the town's rooftops.

Built in 1090 on the site of a Roman temple, Uzès' **Cathédrale St-Théodont** (http://nimes. catholique.fr; place de l'Évêché; ⏲9am-6pm May-Sep, to 5pm Oct-Apr) was partially destroyed in both the 13th and 16th centuries and stripped during the French Revolution. All that remains of the 11th-century church is its 42m-high round tower, Tour Fenestrelle, the only round bell tower in France, which resembles an upright Leaning Tower of Pisa.

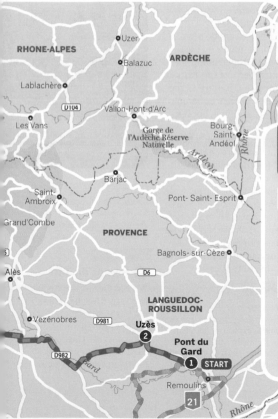

LINK YOUR TRIP

21 Roman Provence
Our tour through southern France's Gallo-Roman legacy also passes through Pont du Gard, so it's a perfect add-on.

30 Cheat's Compostela
Our Chemin de Compostela drive is an ideal route to the Atlantic Coast. It starts 180km northeast of Millau in Le Puy-en-Velay.

If you've got a sweet tooth, don't miss the nearby **Musée du Bonbon Haribo** (Sweets Museum; www.museeharibo.fr; Pont des Charrettes; adult/child €7/5; ☺9.30am-7pm Jul & Aug, 10am-1pm & 2-6pm Tue-Sun Sep-Jun), a candy museum belonging to the Haribo brand. Join in with a tasting session, or just pick up some treats for the road.

✖ ⊨ p317

The Drive » From Uzès, travel 44km west on the D982 and D907 to Anduze; the Train à Vapeur des Cévennes is well signposted.

❸ Anduze

If you fancy a break from driving, a trip aboard the **Train à Vapeur des Cévennes** (☎04 66 60 59 00; www.trainavapeur. com; adult/child/bike return €15.50/10.50/3; ☺Apr-Oct) is just the ticket. This vintage steam train chugs 13km between Anduze and St-Jean du Gard, a journey of 40 minutes. each way. En route, you'll stop at a 150-year-old bamboo garden, the **Bambouseraie de Prafrance** (www.bambouseraie. com; adult/child €9.60/5.60; ☺9.30am-7pm mid-Mar–Sep, to 6pm early–mid-Mar & Oct, to 5pm early–mid-Nov, closed mid-Nov–Feb).

The Drive » The 74km stretch between Anduze and Florac along the D907 follows the river and slowly loops up through the forested hillsides into the high Cévennes. Petrol stations

are few and far between, so remember to fill your tank.

❹ Florac

It's a long, winding drive up into the **Parc National des Cévennes** (www.ceven nesparcnational.fr). Created in 1970, this wild expanse of hills, gorges and empty plateaus covers a core 937 sq km of Upper Languedoc. Famously featured in Robert Louis Stevenson's classic 1878 travelogue, *Travels with a Donkey in the Cévennes,* it's still a remote and sparsely populated landscape, home to rare species including vultures, beavers, otters, roe deer and golden eagles.

The riverside town of Florac makes an ideal base, draped along the west bank of the Tarnon River, a tributary of the Tarn. There's not much to see in town, but it's a good place to stretch your legs: Florac's **Maison du Parc National des Cévennes** (☎04 66 49 53 00; www.cevennes-parc national.fr; 6bis place du Palais; ☺9am-noon & 2-6pm Mon-Fri, 10am-1pm & 3-6pm Sat & Sun Apr-Sep, shorter hours Oct-Mar) has comprehensive information on hiking and other activities.

✖ p317

The Drive » Head on from Florac along the N106, and keep your eyes open for the sharp left turn onto the D907B towards Ispagnac. The road teeters along the edge of the gorge as

WESTEND61 / GETTY IMAGES ©

it passes through Ispagnac and tracks the river to Ste-Énimie, 28km northwest of Florac.

TRIP HIGHLIGHT

❺ Gorges du Tarn

West of Florac, the rushing Tarn River has carved out a series of sheer slashes into the limestone known as the Gorges du Tarn. Running southwest for 50km from Ispagnac,

Gorges du Tarn Kayaking on the Tarn River

this spectacular ravine provides one of Languedoc's most scenic drives. In summer the cliffside road becomes one long traffic jam, though – you'll find spring or autumn are more relaxing times to travel.

Until the road was constructed in 1905, the only way through the gorges was by boat. Piloting your own kayak is still the best way to experience the scenery; the villages of **Ste-Énimie** and **La Malène** both have lots of companies offering river trips.

The Drive » The cliff-side D907B runs all the way to Le Rozier, 36km to the southwest of Ste-Énimie. It's a superbly scenic drive, so don't rush, and leave ample time for photo ops. When you get to Le Rozier, crawl your way up the hairpin bends of the D29 and turn left onto the D110 to the Chaos de Montpellier-le-Vieux, another 9km.

----

⑥ Parc Naturel Régional des Grandes Causses

Around the gorges of the western Cévennes, the Tarn, Jonte and Dourbie Rivers have created four high *causses* ('plateaux'

DETOUR: ROQUEFORT

Start: **7** Millau

The village of Roquefort, 25km southwest of Millau via the D992 and the D999, is synonymous with its famous blue cheese, produced from the milk of ewes who live in natural caves around the village. Marbled with distinctive blue-green veins caused by microscopic mushrooms known as *Penicillium roquefort,* this powerfully pungent cheese has been protected by royal charter since 1407, and was the first cheese in France to be granted AOC (Appéllations d'Origines Contrôlées) status in 1925.

There are seven AOC-approved producers in the village, two of which (La Société and and Gabriel Coulet) offer cellar visits and tasting sessions. The cellars of five other producers (Roquefort Carles, Le Paipillon, Le Vieux Berger, Vernières Frères and Les Fromageries Occitanes) aren't open to the public, but they all have shops where you can sample the village's illustrious cheese.

in the local lingo): Sauveterre, Méjean, Noir and Larzac, each slightly different in geological character. You could spend several days touring along the tangled roads that cut between them, but the D996 along the **Gorges de la Jonte** is particularly detour-worthy.

South of Le Rozier is the **Chaos de Montpellier-le-Vieux** (www.montpellier levieux.com; Montpellier-le-Vieux; adult/child €6.80/5.40, combination ticket with Aven Armand €15.80/11.50; ⏰9am-7pm Jul & Aug, 9.30am-5.30pm late Mar-Jun & Sep-early Nov), where centuries of erosion have carved out a landscape of amazing limestone formations, often given fanciful names, such as the Sphinx and the Elephant. Three walking trails cover the site, or you can cheat and catch the **Chaos de**

Montpellier-le-Vieux Tourist Train (www.montpel lierlevieux.com; Montpellier-le-Vieux; adult/child €4.40/3.60; ⏰9am-7pm Jul & Aug, 9.30am-5.30pm late Mar-Jun & Sep-early Nov) instead.

The Drive » Continue along the narrow D110 towards Millau, 18km to the southwest. There are a couple of great roadside lookouts on the way, as well as a trail to the top of the local peak known as Puncho d'Agast.

TRIP HIGHLIGHT

7 Viaduc de Millau

Finish your road trip with a spin over the gravity-defying **Viaduc de Millau** (www.leviaducde millau.com; A75, Millau; toll Jul & Aug €9.80, Sep-Jun €7.80; ⏰24hr), the famous road bridge that hovers 343m above the Tarn River. Designed by the British architect Norman Foster, the bridge contains over 127,000 cu metres of concrete and 19,000 tonnes

of steel, but somehow still manages to look like a gossamer thread, seemingly supported by nothing more than seven needle-thin pylons.

It's such a wonderful structure, it's worth seeing it twice. Begin with the drive across: head north of Millau on the D911, and then turn south onto the A75 motorway.

Once you've crossed the bridge, turn off at exit 46, and loop back to Millau along the D999 and D992, which passes directly underneath the bridge and gives you an unforgettable ant's-eye view. En route, you'll pass the bridge's visitor centre, **Viaduc Éspace** (☎05 65 61 61 54; www. leviaducdemillau.com; D992, Millau; guided tours adult/child €6/3.50; ⏰10am-7pm Apr-Oct, to 5pm Nov-Mar).

⚒ 🛏 p317

Eating & Sleeping

Uzès ➋

✕ Le Tracteur
Bistro €€

(☎04 66 62 17 33; www.lucietestud.com/letracteur; Argilliers; 3-course lunch/dinner menus €25/29.50; ☺ kitchen noon-2pm Mon-Thu, noon-2pm & 7-10pm Fri, 7-10pm Sat) A converted warehouse in Argilliers, 8km southeast of Uzès via the D981, is the setting for this offbeat, and brilliant, dining destination – part wine shop, part art gallery, part deli, part bistro with a tree-shaded courtyard. Filled with battered furniture and abstract art, it's a fantastic space for dining on inspired Mediterranean creations. Look out for the namesake tractor outside.

🛏 Château d'Arpaillargues
Hotel €€€

(☎04 66 22 14 48; http://hp360.fr; rue du Château, Arpaillargues-et-Aureillac; d €160-315; P ❄ 🛜 ☀) Inside an 18th-century château once occupied by Franz Liszt's muse, Marie de Flavigny, rooms at this regal residence range from large to vast and come with period features such as fireplaces, beams and flagstone floors. All are decorated in restrained country style. There's a wonderful swimming pool and an excellent restaurant. It's 5km west of Uzès off the D982.

Florac ➍

✕ Les Tables de la Fontaine
Traditional French €€

(☎04 66 65 21 73; www.tables-de-la-fontaine.com; 31 rue du Therond; 2-/3-course menus €21/24; ☺ noon-2pm & 7-9.30pm Mon-Sat, noon-2pm Sun Apr-Sep; 🐾) Red-umbrella-shaded tables are scattered around a natural spring in the courtyard adjoining this ivy-clad restaurant. River trout with preserved lemon, Lozère lamb with potato gratin, vegetable tart with Cévennes goat's cheese, and red wine–marinated pears are among the daily-changing dishes incorporating locally sourced produce. Wines are also local and beers are artisanal. Live music often plays of an evening.

Millau ➐

✕ La Mangeoire
Regional Cuisine €€

(☎05 65 60 13 16; www.restaurantmillau.com; 10 bd de la Capelle; 2-/3-course lunch menus €16/23, 3-/4-/5-course dinner menus €24/33/49.50, mains €17-26; ☺ noon-2pm & 7-10pm Tue-Sun) Fronted by a shady pavement terrace strung with fairy lights and opening to a romantic vaulted-stone dining room, Millau's best restaurant refines the rich flavours of the region: wood-fire-grilled Trénels sheep-stomach sausage with *aligot* (mashed potato and melted sheep's cheese); Aubrac beef ribs with Roquefort sauce; spicy spit-roasted local hare; lamb sweetbreads in parsley-butter sauce; and chestnut sorbet in Armagnac.

🛏 Château de Creissels
Hôtel €€

(☎05 65 60 16 59; www.chateau-de-creissels.com; place du Prieur, Creissels; d €86-120, ste €132; ☺ early Mar-late Dec; P ❄ 🛜 ☀) In Creissels, 2km southwest of Millau on the D992, this castle's rooms are split between the 12th-century tower (parquet floors, fireplaces, oil paintings) and modern wings (sleek showers, stripped-wood floors, designer lamps; some have balconies overlooking the large garden). Excellent regional cuisine is served in the restaurant's brick-vaulted cellar and panoramic terrace. Breakfast costs €11.50; half-board is €74 per person.

The Cathar Trail

29

From the fairy-tale towers of Carcassonne to the tumbledown walls of Montségur, this cross country trip explores the main Cathar strongholds of sunbaked southwest France.

TRIP HIGHLIGHTS

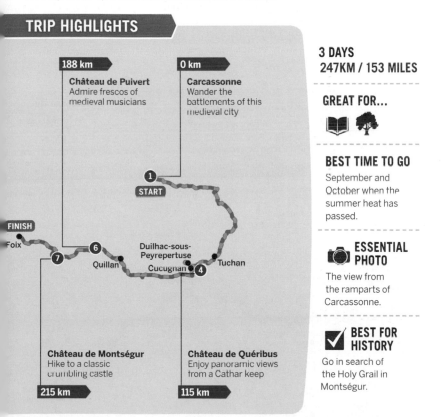

188 km

Château de Puivert
Admire frescos of medieval musicians

0 km

Carcassonne
Wander the battlements of this medieval city

START

FINISH
Foix

6

Duilhac-sous-Peyrepertuse

7

Quillan

Cucugnan

4

Tuchan

Château de Montségur
Hike to a classic crumbling castle

215 km

Château de Quéribus
Enjoy panoramic views from a Cathar keep

115 km

3 DAYS
247KM / 153 MILES

GREAT FOR...

BEST TIME TO GO
September and October when the summer heat has passed.

ESSENTIAL PHOTO
The view from the ramparts of Carcassonne.

BEST FOR HISTORY
Go in search of the Holy Grail in Montségur.

The Cathar Trail

The parched land between Perpignan and the Pyrenees is known as Le Pays Cathare (Cathar Land), a reference to the Christian order that escaped persecution here during the 12th century. Its legacy remains in a string of hilltop castles, flanked by sheer cliffs and dusty scrubland. Most can be reached after a short, stiff climb, but this is wild country and fiercely hot in summer, so be sure to pack a hat.

TRIP HIGHLIGHT

❶ Carcassonne

Jutting from a rocky spur of land, and ringed by battlements and turrets, the fortress of Carcassonne was one of the Cathars' most important strongholds. After a notorious siege in August 1209, the castle crumbled into disrepair, but was saved from destruction in the 19th century by Viollet-le-Duc, who rebuilt the ramparts and added the turrets' distinctive pointy roofs.

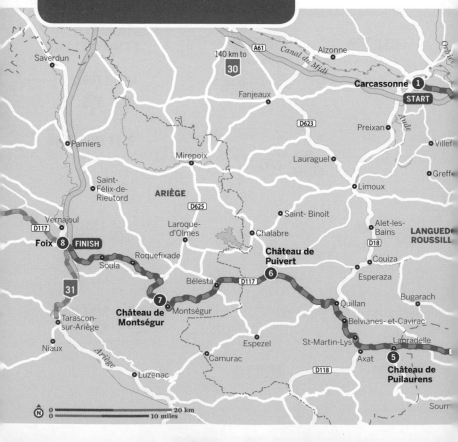

These days Carcassonne is one of the Languedoc's biggest tourist draws, which means its cobbled streets can feel uncomfortably crowded in summer. Try to time your visit for early or late in the day when it's at its most peaceful.

✕ 🛏 p325

The Drive » From Carcassonne, take the A61 east for 36km towards Narbonne. Turn off at exit 25, signed to Lezignan-Corbières, and follow the D611 across the sunbaked countryside for 46km. Just before you reach Tuchan, look

out for a white sign with a blue castle pointing to 'Aguilar'. Drive along this minor track to the car park.

- - - - - - - - - - - - -

❷ Château d'Aguilar

When the Albigensian Crusade forced the Cathars into the mountains between France and the province of Aragon, they sought refuge in a line of frontier strongholds. The first of these sites is the **Château d'Aguilar** (☎04 68 45 51 00, www.tuchan. fr; Tuchan; adult/child €4/2; ⏰9am-7pm Jun-Aug, shorter

hours Sep–mid-Nov & mid-Feb–May), which squats on a low hill near the village of Tuchan. It's the smallest of the castles, and it is crumbling fast – but you can still make out the six corner turrets as well as the hexagonal outer wall.

The Drive » Take the D611 through Tuchan, emerging from the narrow streets onto dry, vine-covered slopes. You'll reach a roundabout; turn left onto the D14, signed to Padern and Cucugnan. (After 15km, take note of the turn-off to the Château de Quéribus on the D123 as you bypass Cucugnan; you'll be returning here following your next stop.) Continue 9km northwest towards Duilhac-sous-Peyrepertuse.

🔗 LINK YOUR TRIP

30 **Cheat's Compostela**

Make a longish detour off our version of the Chemin de St-Jacques by driving southeast of Moissac for 165km to Carcassonne, with an optional stop in Toulouse en route.

31 **The Pyrenees**

Foix sits on the eastern edge of the Pyrenees, so our Pyrenean tour makes a natural next stage – although you'll have to do it in reverse.

③ Château de Peyrepertuse

The largest of the Cathar castles is **Peyrepertuse** (📞04 82 53 24 07; www.chateau-peyrepertuse.com; Duilhac-sous-Peyrepertuse; adult/child Jul & Aug €9/3.50, rest of year €6.50/3.50; ⏰9am-8pm Jul & Aug, shorter hours rest of year), with a dizzying drop of 800m on either side. Several of the original towers and many sections of ramparts are still standing. In mid-August, the castle holds falconry displays and a two-day medieval festival, complete with knights in armour.

The Drive » Backtrack along the D14 for 9km to the turn-off onto the D123 near Cucugnan. The road twists and turns steeply into the dusty hills. Keep your eyes peeled for the Quéribus turn-off as you drive another 3km uphill.

TRIP HIGHLIGHT

④ Château de Quéribus

Perilously perched 728m up on a rocky hill, **Quéribus** (📞04 68 45 03 69; www.cucugnan.fr; Cucugnan; adult/child €6.50/3.50; ⏰9am-8pm Jul & Aug, shorter hours rest of year) was the site of the Cathars' last stand in 1255. Its interior structure is fairly well preserved: the **Salle du Pilier** inside the central keep still features its original Gothic pillars, vaulting and archways. There's also a small house

that has been converted into a theatre, and shows a film documenting the story of the castle through the eyes of one of the castle's curates.

The top of the keep is reached via a narrow staircase and offers a truly mind-blowing view stretching to the Mediterranean and the Pyrenees on a clear day.

The Drive » Drive back down to the turn-off, and turn left. Continue along this road (the D19) for 8km to the small town of Maury. Take the D117 for 25km to Puilaurens. The next castle is signed from here, another 3km south.

---

⑤ Château de Puilaurens

If it's the classic hilltop castle you're after, **Puilaurens** (📞04 68 20 65 26; www.pays-axat.org; Lapradelle; adult/child €5/3; ⏰9am-8pm Jul & Aug, shorter hours Sep–mid-Nov & Feb-Jun) is it. With its turrets and lofty location, it's perhaps the most dramatic of the Cathar fortresses, with all the classic medieval defences: double defensive walls, four corner towers and crenellated battlements. It's also said to be haunted by the White Lady, a niece of Philippe le Bel.

The Drive » Backtrack to the D117 and follow it west for 36km to Puivert, skirting through hills, fields and forests. Just before you reach the village, there's a sharp right turn to the château,

TUUL AND BRUNO MORANDI / GETTY IMAGES ©

Carcassone A 12th-century Cathar stronghold

TOP TIP: PASSEPORT DES SITES DU PAYS CATHARE

The **Passeport des Sites du Pays Cathare** (www.payscathare.org/passeport-des-sites; €2) gives a €1 reduction off 21 local sites, including medieval abbeys at St-Hilaire, Lagrasse and Villelongue. Pick it up at tourist offices throughout the region.

near a white barn. It is 1km further up a steep track.

TRIP HIGHLIGHT

⑥ Château de Puivert

Built during the late 12th century, the **Château de Puivert** (☎04 68 20 81 52; www.chateau-de-puivert.com; Puivert; adult/child €5/3; ⏰9am-7pm Easter–mid-Nov, 10am-5pm Sun-Fri mid-Dec–Easter) belonged to the aristocratic Congost family, who were high-profile members of the Cathar movement. It was besieged in 1210 by Thomas Pons de Bruyères-le-Chatel, who subsequently took control of the castle and oversaw its redevelopment.

Camped on a 605m-high promontory, Puivert still boasts much of its medieval footprint. Five of the eight corner towers remain, and the central keep has four vaulted rooms including the **Salle des Musiciens**, decorated with frescos of medieval troubadours – including a flautist, guitarist, bagpiper, tambourine man and hurdy-gurdy player.

The Drive » Take the D117 west of Puivert for 13km to Bélesta. As you drive through town, spot signs to 'Fougax et B/Querigut/Château de Montségur'. The village is another 14km further, spectacularly perched above the forested slopes; follow the winding road past the village until you see the castle's roadside car park.

TRIP HIGHLIGHT

⑦ Château de Montségur

For the full Monty Python medieval vibe – not to mention a good workout (bring your own water!) – tackle the steep 1207m climb to the ruins of the **Château de Montségur** (www.montsegur.fr; adult/child Jul & Aug €6.50/3.50, other times €5.50/3; ⏰9am-7pm Jul & Aug, 10am-6pm Apr-Jun & Sep, 10am-5pm Mar & Oct, 11am-4pm Nov-Feb). It was here, in 1242, that the Cathar movement suffered its heaviest defeat; attacked by a force of 10,000 royal troops, the castle fell after a gruelling nine-month siege, and 220 of the defenders were burnt alive when they refused to renounce their faith.

Montségur has also been cited as a possible location for the Holy Grail, which was supposedly smuggled out of the castle in the days before the final battle.

The original castle was razed to rubble after the siege, and the present-day ruins largely date from the 17th century.

The Drive » Continue on the D117, turning onto the busy N20 to Foix, 32km northwest.

⑧ Foix

Complete your trip through Cathar country with a visit to the **Château de Foix** (☎05 61 05 10 10; adult/child €5.60/3.80; ⏰19am-6pm in summer, shorter hours rest of year), nestled among the foothills of the Pyrenees. It's in a more complete state of repair than many of the Cathar fortresses you've seen, and gives you some idea of how they may have looked in their medieval heyday.

🛏 p325, p343

Eating & Sleeping

Carcassonne ❶

✗ Au Comte Roger   Modern French €€

(☎04 68 11 93 40; www.comteroger.com; 14
rue St-Louis, La Cité; 2-/3-course lunch menus
€24/30, 3-course dinner menu €41, mains
€20-32; ☺noon-1.30pm & 7-9.30pm Tue-Sat)
The citadel location bumps up the prices
considerably, but this is one of the better
establishments for traditional *cassoulet* (stew
with white beans, Toulouse sausage and duck).
The restaurant's smart dining room has cream-
coloured chairs and tables and polished wooden
floors, but the best seats are in the vine-draped
courtyard beside an old well.

✗ La Barbacane   Gastronomy €€€

(☎04 68 71 98 71; www.hoteldelacite.fr;
place Auguste-Pierre-Pont, La Cité; 3-course
lunch menu €38, 6-course dinner menu €85,
mains €40-60; ☺12.30-2pm & 7.30-9.30pm)
Carcassonne's finest dining is inside the
Hôtel de la Cité at chef Jérôme Ryon's
Michelin-starred premises. Opulent carved
woodwork and stained glass set the stage for
unforgettable dishes utilising some of France's
finest produce: poached Bouzigues oysters with
preserved lemon; Charolais beef with potato
churros and Périgord sauce; and Languedoc-
grown saffron, white asparagus and black-garlic
risotto with Cévennes goat's cheese.

🛏 La Maison Vieille   B&B €€

(☎06 23 40 65 34; www.la-maison-vieille.com;
8 rue Trivalle; d €90-95, f €105-125; 🙴) As
charming a B&B as you'll find in Carcassonne,
this old mansion's beautiful rooms include
Barbacane in blues, Cité with exposed brick,
Prince Noir with an in-room bath, and vintage-
furnished Dame Carcas. Filled with fig trees,
olive trees and lavender, its walled courtyard is
idyllic for breakfast. It's handy for the walled city
and Ville Basse; families are warmly welcomed.

🛏 Hôtel de la Cité   Historic Hotel €€€

(☎04 68 71 98 71; www.hoteldelacite.fr;
place Auguste-Pierre-Pont, La Cité; s/d/f from
€230/270/350; ❄🙴🛏) Built in the 19th
century in the Gothic Revival style, this is
Carcassonne's most magnificent place to stay.
Palatial rooms are individually appointed, many
with wood panelling and/or timber beams, and
some have panoramic private terraces. Floor-
to-ceiling bookshelves line the private library,
which has its own bar, and there's a topiary-
flanked swimming pool. Its Michelin-starred
restaurant, La Barbacane (p325), is sublime.

Foix ❽

🛏 Château de Beauregard   Hotel €€

(☎05 61 66 66 64; www.chateaubeauregard.net;
av de la Résistance, St-Girons; r €100-220, d incl
half-board €180-300; 🅿🙴🛏) In St-Girons,
halfway between St-Gaudens and Foix along the
D117, this grand château is ideal for playing lord
of the manor: the house is topped by turrets and
surrounded by 2.5 hectares of gardens, with
grand rooms named after writers (some have
their bathrooms hidden in the castle's corner
towers) There's also a pool, spa and a great
Gascon restaurant.

🛏 Hôtel les Remparts   Hotel €€

(☎05 61 68 12 15; www.hotelremparts.com; 6
cours Louis Pons Tarde, Mirepoix; s €68-78, d
€82-98; 🙴) Built into the bastide architecture
of Mirepoix, this is a smart option, with a mixed-
bag of nine rooms that combine modern design
with the building's centuries-old heritage – a
patch of exposed stone here, a wonky wooden
doorway there. The excellent restaurant is one
of Mirepoix's best, serving fine French cuisine
(*menus* €26 to €37) under stone arches and
great oak beams.

Cheat's Compostela

30

Follow in the footsteps of pilgrims on this holiest of road trips, which follows one of the main routes across France en route to Santiago de Compostela in Spain.

TRIP HIGHLIGHTS

0 km

Le Puy-en-Velay
Puff your way around this volcanic town in the Massif Central

349 km

Cahors
Explore Cahors' shady old city and Romanesque cathedral

Sauguea ①
START
② ● Espalion
④ ● Agen
FINISH ⑦ ● Pau

St-Jean Pied de Port
Look out from the ramparts towards the Spanish border
725 km

Conques
Wander around the classic pilgrimage church of St-Foy
220 km

**7 DAYS
725KM / 450 MILES**

GREAT FOR...

BEST TIME TO GO
May to September, to make the most of the summer sunshine.

ESSENTIAL PHOTO
Being dwarfed beside Le Puy's huge statue of the Virgin Mary.

BEST FOR CULTURE
Comparing the tympanum (decorative arch) of churches in Condom, Cahors and Moissac.

30 | Cheat's Compostela

During the Middle Ages, countless pilgrims undertook the long trek along the Chemin de St-Jacques, as it's known in France, in the hope of earning spiritual salvation and favour in the afterlife. We've chosen to follow one of the oldest routes between Le Puy-en-Velay and St-Jean Pied de Port: on the way you'll visit iconic churches, historic cities and a giant iron statue of the Virgin Mary.

TRIP HIGHLIGHT

❶ Le Puy-en-Velay

Your journey begins at the striking town of Le Puy-en-Velay, where pilgrims would traditionally have earned a blessing at the Unesco-listed **Cathédrale Notre-Dame** (www.cathedraledupuy. org; rue de la Manécanterie; ⊙6.30am-7pm). Among the Romanesque archways and Byzantine domes is a statue of St Jacques himself, the patron saint of Compostela pilgrims.

While you're here, it's well worth visiting Le

Puy's other ecclesiastical sights. Perched on the top of an 85m-high volcanic pillar is the **Chapelle St-Michel d'Aiguilhe** (www.rochersaintmichel.fr; adult/child €3.50/2; 9am-6.30pm May-Sep, shorter hours rest of year, closed mid-Nov–Jan), Le Puy's oldest chapel (established in the 10th century). Carved directly into the rock, its cave-like atmosphere and 12th-century frescos create an otherworldly atmosphere.

On another nearby peak is an enormous cast-iron statue of the Virgin Mary, aka **Notre Dame de France** (adult/child €4/2; 9am-7pm May-Sep, 10am-5pm Feb-Apr & Oct–mid-Nov). A creaky spiral staircase winds its way to the top of the 22.7m-tall, 835-tonne statue, including the pedestal; you can peep out through portholes for dizzying vistas over the town.

🍴 🛏 p333

The Drive ››› From Le Puy to Conques, it's a scenic half-day drive of around 220km. Take the twisty D589, passing through the spectacular Gorges de l'Allier to Saugues. Follow the D989 under the A75 highway, then join the D921 to Espalion.

The last stretch along the D920, D107 and D141 tracks the course of the Lot River, turning briefly onto the D901 to Conques.

- - - - - - - - - - - - -

TRIP HIGHLIGHT

② Conques

The next stop for medieval pilgrims would have been Conques – or more specifically, the **Abbey Church of Ste-Foy**, built to house the holy relics of its namesake saint, a young woman martyred during the 4th century. In fact, the relics proved so popular that the original 8th-century church had to be rebuilt with extra chapels, a higher roof and a viewing gallery to accommodate the pilgrim traffic.

It's a classic example of a pilgrimage church: simple and serene, with architectural flourishes kept to a minimum. It's laid out to a cruciform (cross-shaped) design,

LINK YOUR TRIP

The Pyrenees
31 For fantastic mountain scenery, veer off 140km south of Condom at Pau to begin our Pyrenees trip.

The Lot Valley
37 You can do two trips in one by incorporating our trip through the beautiful Lot Valley as your route from Cahors to Figeac.

CHEMIN DE ST-JACQUES

Ever since the 9th century, when a hermit named Pelayo stumbled across the tomb of the Apostle James (brother of John the Evangelist), the Spanish town of Santiago de Compostela has been one of Christendom's holiest sites. The pilgrimage to Santiago de Compostela is traditionally known as the Camino de Santiago (Chemin de St-Jacques in French; Way of St James in English). Early pilgrims were inspired to undertake the arduous journey in exchange for fewer years in purgatory. Today the reward is also more tangible: walkers or horse riders who complete the final 100km to Santiago (cyclists the final 200km) qualify for a Compostela Certificate, issued on arrival at the cathedral. The modern-day GR36 roughly follows the Via Podensis route from Le Puy. Find out more at www.webcompostella.com and www.csj.org.uk.

the traditional layout for pilgrimage churches. Also note the elegant columns, decorated with scenes from the life of Ste Foy.

Outside, look out for the tympanum (decorative arch) above the main doorway depicting the Day of Last Judgment – a popular theme for Compostela churches.

The Drive >> Backtrack north to the Lot River and turn left onto the D42. Follow signs to Decazeville, then turn west onto the D840 to Figeac, just over 52km from Conques.

- - - - - - - - - - - - - - - - -

❸ Figeac

During the Middle Ages, riverside Figeac was a major ecclesiastical centre. All the four monastic orders (Franciscans, White Friars, Dominicans and Augustinians) were established here, and the

town had a large hospice for accommodating pilgrims (later turned into Figeac's hospital, appropriately named Hôpital St-Jacques).

Though most of Figeac's monastic buildings were torn down during the Revolution, a few still remain. On place Vival, there's an arcaded 13th-century building that was part of Figeac's lost abbey; it's now home to the tourist office.

You can pick up a leaflet called *Les Clefs de la Ville* (€0.30), which details the town's other medieval buildings. **Rue de Balène** and **rue Caviale** offer rich pickings; they're lined with 14th- and 15th-century houses, many with stone carvings and open-air galleries on the top floor, once used for drying leather.

✂ 🛏 p399

The Drive >> The prettiest drive to Cahors is along the D662, which runs for a scenic but slow 75km along a dramatic gorge carved out by the Lot River. A faster alternative is via the D13 and D653, which takes about an hour from Figeac.

- - - - - - - - - - - - - - -

TRIP HIGHLIGHT

❹ Cahors

Now best known for its wine, the walled city of Cahors once earned a lucrative trade from passing pilgrims. A prosperous (and well-protected) city, Cahors also has an impressive Romanesque cathedral, the **Cathédrale St-Étienne** (place de la Cathédrale; ⏰7am-6pm). Consecrated in 1119, the cathedral's airy nave is topped by two huge cupolas which, at 18m wide, are the largest in France.

Some of the frescos are from the 14th century, but the side chapels and carvings in the cloister mainly date from the 16th century. On the cathedral's north façade is another carved tympanum, depicting Christ surrounded by fluttering angels and pious saints.

At the top of the old city, the **Tour du Pape Jean XXII** (3 bd Léon Gambetta) was part of a 14th-century mansion belonging to Jacques Duèse, who went on to become Pope John XXII.

Cahors' medieval bridge, the **Pont Valentré**, was part of the town's

Conques Decorative arch on the Abbey Church of Ste-Foy

defences during the 14th century.

✕ 🛏 p399

The Drive » The D653 travels part of the 61km southwest towards Moissac, passing through a delightful landscape of woods, fields and sleepy villages. After about 39km, turn south on the D2 to connect with the D16 and D957 into Moissac.

- - - - - - - - - - - -

⑤ Moissac

Moissac's crowning glory is the monumental **Abbaye St-Pierre** (place Durand de Bredon; adult/child €6.50/4; ◷9am-7pm Jul & Aug, 9am-noon & 2-7pm Sep-Jun), one of France's finest Romanesque abbeys. Above the south portal is yet another marvellous **tympanum**: completed in 1130, it depicts St John's vision of the Apocalypse, with Christ flanked by the Apostles, angels and 24 awestruck elders.

Outside, the columns of the cloister are topped with carved capitals depicting foliage, figures and biblical scenes. Sadly, the Revolution took its toll – almost every face has been smashed.

Entry to the abbey is via the **tourist office** (☎05 63 04 01 85; http://tourisme.moissac.fr; 6 place Durand de Bredon; ◷9am-noon & 2-6pm Apr-Oct, 9am-7pm Jul & Aug, shorter hours Nov-Mar).

✕ 🛏 p333

The Drive » The easiest route for the 85km trip to Condom travels west on the D813 to

Valence, crosses the river and then joins the A62 highway (toll charge). Take exit 7 onto the D931, a much quieter road that meanders through rural countryside to Condom.

- - - - - - - - - - - -

⑥ Condom

Despite its snigger-inducing name, Condom actually has nothing to do with contraceptives – its name dates from Gallo-Roman times, when it was known as Condatomagus.

Established as a Roman port on the Baïse River, the town's Flamboyant Gothic **Cathédrale St-Pierre** (place St-Pierre; ◷8am-6pm daily) was the main point of interest for pilgrims. The tent-like cloister, covered by a vaulted roof, was designed to offer wet-weather protection while pilgrims waited to pay their religious dues.

Condom's other claim to fame is as the home of Armagnac, a potent brandy brewed since medieval times as a medicinal tonic, but now drunk as an after-dinner *digestif*. There are many distilleries around town, but one of the best is **Armagnac Ryst-Dupeyron** (☎05 62 28 08 08; 36 rue Jean Jaurès; ◷10am-noon & 2-5pm Mon-Fri), where you can taste vintage brandies in a turn-of-the-century cellar.

Nearby, the teeny **Musée de l'Armagnac** (2 rue Jules Ferry; adult/child €2.20/1.10; ◷10am-noon

& 3-6pm Wed-Mon Apr-Oct, 2-5pm Wed-Sat Nov & Dec, Feb & Mar, closed Jan) has a small collection of vintage Armagnac-making equipment.

✕ p333

The Drive » The last stretch to St-Jean Pied de Port is an epic 255km via the A65 and A64 highways, so you might like to break it up by combining it with stops detailed in our tours of the Pyrenees or the Atlantic Coast.

- - - - - - - - - - - -

TRIP HIGHLIGHT

⑦ St-Jean Pied de Port

Your pilgrimage ends at the walled town of St-Jean Pied de Port, the last stop for Compostela pilgrims on French soil before crossing the Spanish border, 8km away.

With its cobbled lanes and impressive ramparts, it's one of southwest France's most authentically medieval towns, so it makes a fitting end to your trip. The foundations of the **Église Notre Dame du Bout du Pont** are said to be as old as the town itself, but the building itself was rebuilt in the 17th century.

While you might be ending your pilgrimage here, spare a thought for the real pilgrims – for them, there's still another 800km to go before they reach journey's end at Santiago de Compostela's famous cathedral.

✕ p357

Eating & Sleeping

Le Puy-en-Velay ❶

✕ Restaurant Tournayre — Auvergnat Cuisine €€

(📞04 71 09 58 94; www.restaurant-tournayre. com; 12 rue Chênebouterie; mains €25; ☻noon-1.30pm & 7.30-9.30pm Wed-Sat, 12-1.30pm Sun) This is one of the best addresses in Le Puy for food and form. Its atmospheric setting, within a 12th- to 16th-century *hôtel particulier* (historic town house), sets the tone. But the four-course *menus* will dominate conversation. Savour seared cod or succulent lamb on the great-value lunchtime *menu du marché* (€29) or try the 'Compostelle *menu*', featuring scallops and zander with gnocchi (€42).

⯿ L'Epicurium — Guesthouse €

(📞06 24 41 56 10; 5 rue du Bessat; s/d/ tr incl breakfast from €58/64/99; 📶) This gastronomy-obsessed guesthouse in the city's historic centre is Le Puy-en-Velay's trendiest address. Its five spacious rooms have been freshly renovated in minimalist chic: ceilings are high, bathrooms are vast, breakfast involves a toothsome range of fancy jams, and you can add a three-course meal of local specialities to your stay (€18). Wooden floors are rather creaky, but background din is part of L'Epicurium's old-world charm.

Moissac ❺

✕ Le Table de Nos Fils — French €€

(www.le-pont-napoleon.com; 2 allée Montebello; menus €29-45; ☻noon-1.30pm & 7.30-10.30pm; ☝) The restaurant attached to hotel

Le Pont Napoléon (📞05 63 04 01 55; r/ste €62/75; 🅿 📶) is one of the best places in town to dig into beautifully presented Tarn produce, such as duck nestled in a bed of artichokes or scallops surfing an asparagus risotto. Talented chef Patrick Delaroux runs occasional Saturday **cooking courses** (€55), from Lebanese food to the art of macaron-making; enquire in advance via the website.

⯿ Le Moulin de Moissac — Hotel €€

(📞05 63 32 88 88; www.lemoulindemoissac. com; 1 promenade Sancert; d €105-179, ste from €164; 🅿 ❄ 📶) Housed in a 15th-century grain mill overlooking the Tarn, this hotel is a riverside treat. Rooms with distressed wallpaper, lovingly painted furniture and tall French windows open onto river-view balconies. The restaurant (lunch/dinner *menu* €25.50/43) dishes up duck tartare and beef in miso soup, among other French-Asian fusions. There's a smart sauna-spa and a romantic Jacuzzi, too.

Condom ❻

✕ La Table des Cordeliers — Gastronomy €€€

(📞05 62 68 43 82; www.latabledescordeliers. com; 1 rue des Cordeliers; menus €23-75; ☻noon-2pm & 7-9pm Tue-Sat) Condom's premier restaurant is run by Michelin-starred Eric Sampietro, a culinary magician known for seasonal ingredients assembled in surprising combinations. Tasting *menus* come at a price, but the adjoining bistro offers a three-course *menu* for just €23, with beguiling dishes such as ricotta-and-lobster ravioli. The setting is gorgeous: it's inside a 13th-century chapel, complete with cloister garden.

The Pyrenees

31

Traversing hair-raising roads, sky-top passes and snow-dusted peaks, this trip ventures deep into the unforgettable Pyrenees. Buckle up – you're in for a roller coaster of a drive.

TRIP HIGHLIGHTS

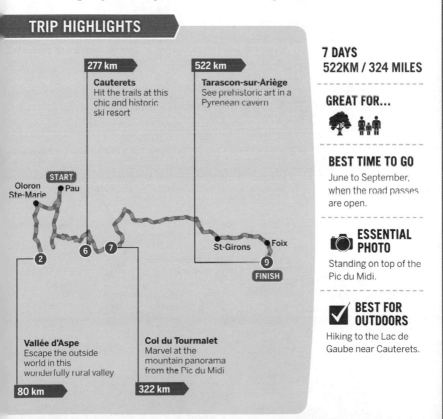

277 km

Cauterets
Hit the trails at this chic and historic ski resort

522 km

Tarascon-sur-Ariège
See prehistoric art in a Pyrenean cavern

Oloron Ste-Marie
START
● Pau

2 — 6 — 7

St-Girons ● ● Foix
9
FINISH

Vallée d'Aspe
Escape the outside world in this wonderfully rural valley

80 km

Col du Tourmalet
Marvel at the mountain panorama from the Pic du Midi

322 km

**7 DAYS
522KM / 324 MILES**

GREAT FOR...

BEST TIME TO GO
June to September, when the road passes are open.

ESSENTIAL PHOTO
Standing on top of the Pic du Midi.

BEST FOR OUTDOORS
Hiking to the Lac de Gaube near Cauterets.

31 The Pyrenees

They might not have the altitude of the Alps, but the Pyrenees pack a mighty mountain punch, and if you're an outdoors-lover, you'll be in seventh heaven here. With quiet villages, rustic restaurants, spectacular trails and snowy mountains galore, the Pyrenees are a wild adventure – just remember to break in your hiking boots before you arrive.

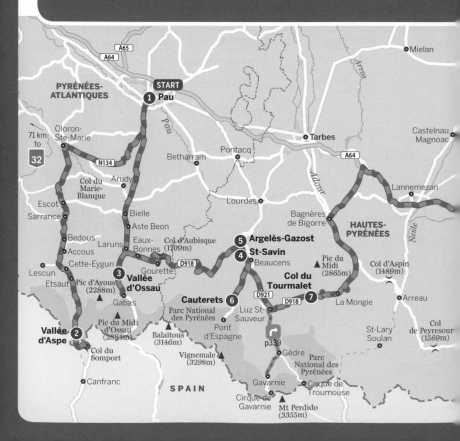

❶ Pau

Palm trees might seem out of place in this mountainous region, but Pau (rhymes with 'so') has long been famed for its mild climate. In the 19th century this elegant town was a favourite wintering spot for wealthy Brits and Americans, who left behind many grand villas and smart promenades.

Its main sight is the **Château de Pau** (☎05 59 82 38 00; www.chateau-pau. fr; 2 rue du Château; adult/child €7/free; ⏰9.30am-12.15pm & 1.30 5.45pm, gardens open longer hrs), built by the monarchs of Navarre and transformed into a Renaissance château in the 16th century. It's home to a fine collection of Gobelins tapestries and Sevres porcelain.

Pau's tiny old centre extends for around 500m around the Château de Pau, and boasts many attractive medieval and Renaissance buildings.

LINK YOUR TRIP

29 The Cathar Trail
From Foix, it's only a short drive from the mountains before you reach the heart of the Cathar lands and their amazing châteaux.

32 Basque Country
This Pyrenean trip makes a natural extension of our themed trip through the French Basque country. From St-Jean Pied de Port, it's 71km to Oloron-Ste-Marie, or 103km to Pau.

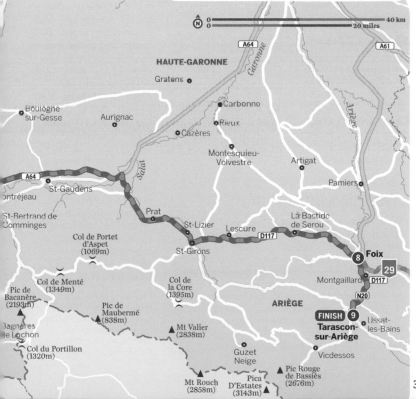

Classic Trip

Central street parking is mostly *payant* (chargeable), but there's free parking on place de Verdun and the street leading west of there (av du 18 Régiment d'Infanterie).

✕ ⊨ p343

The Drive ≫ To reach the Vallée d'Aspe from Pau, take the N193 to Oloron-Ste-Marie. The first 30km are uneventful, but over the next 40km south of Oloron the mountain scenery unfolds in dramatic fashion, with towering peaks stacking up on either side of the road.

TRIP HIGHLIGHT

② Vallée d'Aspe

The westernmost of the Pyrenean valleys makes a great day trip from Pau. Framed by mountains and bisected by the Aspe River, it's awash with classic Pyrenean scenery. The main attraction here is soaking up the scenery.

Allow yourself plenty of time for photo stops, especially around pretty villages such as **Sarrance**, **Borcé** and **Etsaut**.

Near the quiet village of **Bedous**, it's worth detouring up the narrow road to **Lescun**, a tiny hamlet perched 5.5km above the valley, overlooking the peak of **Pic d'Anie** (2504m) and the cluster of mountains known as the **Cirque de Lescun**.

The valley ends 25km further south near the **Col du Somport** (1631m), where a controversial tunnel burrows 8km under the Franco-Spanish border. The return drive to Pau is just over 80km.

The Drive ≫ To reach the Vallée d'Ossau from Pau, take the N134 south of town, veering south onto the D934 towards Arudy/Laruns. From Pau to Laruns, it's about 42km.

③ Vallée d'Ossau

More scenic splendour awaits in the Vallée d'Ossau, which tracks the course of its namesake river for a spectacular 60km. The first part of the valley as far as Laruns is broad, green and pastoral, but as you travel south the mountains really start to pile up, before broadening out again near Gabas.

Halfway between Arudy and Laruns, you can spy on some of the Pyrenees' last griffon vultures at the **Falaise aux Vautours** (Cliff of the Vultures; ☎ 05 59 82 65 49; www.falaise-aux-vautours.com; adult/child €6/4; ⊗ 10.30am-12.30pm & 2-6.30pm Jul & Aug, 2-5.30pm Apr-Jun & Sep). Once a common sight, these majestic birds have been decimated by habitat loss and hunting; they're now protected by law. Live CCTV images are beamed from their nests to the visitors centre in Aste-Béon.

The ski resort of **Artouste-Fabrèges**, 6km east of Gabas, is linked by cable car to the **Petit Train d'Artouste** (☎ 05 59 05 36 99; www.altiservice. com/excursion/train-artouste; adult/child €25/21; ⊗ Jun– mid-Sep), a miniature mountain railway built for dam workers in the 1920s. The train is only open between June and September; reserve ahead and allow four hours for a visit.

The Drive ≫ The D918 between Laruns and Argelès-Gazost is one of the Pyrenees' most breathtaking roads, switchbacking over the lofty Col d'Aubisque. The road feels

THE TRANSHUMANCE

If you're travelling through the Pyrenees between late May and early June and find yourself stuck behind a cattle-shaped traffic jam, there's a good chance you may have just got caught up in the Transhumance, in which shepherds move their flocks from their winter pastures up to the high, grassy uplands.

This ancient custom has been a fixture on the Pyrenean calendar for centuries, and several valleys host festivals to mark the occasion. The spectacle is repeated in October, when the flocks are brought back down before the winter snows set in.

exposed, but it's a wonderfully scenic drive. You'll cover about 52km, but allow yourself at least 1½ hours. Once you reach Argelès-Gazost, head further south for 4km along the D101 to St-Savin.

---

❹ St-Savin

After the hair-raising drive over the Col d'Aubisque, St-Savin makes a welcome refuge. It's a classic Pyrenean village, with cobbled lanes, quiet cafes and timbered houses set around a fountain-filled main square.

It's also home to one of the Pyrenees' most respected hotel-restaurants, **Le Viscos** (☎05 62 97 02 28; www.hotel-leviscos.com; 1 rue Lamarque, St-Savin; menus €49-75; ⊗12.30-2.30pm Tue-Sun & 7.30-9.30pm daily; P ❋ 🛜), run by celeb chef Jean-Pierre St-Martin, known for his blend of Basque, Breton and Pyrenean flavours (as well as his passion for foie gras). After dinner, retire to one of the cosy country rooms and watch the sun set over the snowy mountains.

🛏 p343

The Drive ≫ From St-Savin, travel back along the D101 to Argelès-Gazost. You'll see signs to the Parc Animalier des Pyrénées as you approach town.

---

❺ Argelès-Gazost

Spotting wildlife isn't always easy in the Pyrenees, but thankfully the

Parc Animalier des Pyrénées (☎05 62 97 91 07; www.parc-animalier-pyrenees.com; adult/child €18/13; ⊗9.30am-6pm or 7pm Apr-Oct) does all the hard work for you. It's home to a menagerie of endangered Pyrenean animals including wolves, marmots, lynxes, giant ravens, vultures, racoons, beavers and even a few brown bears (the European cousin of the grizzly bear).

The Drive ≫ Take the D921 south of Argelès-Gazost for 6km to Pierrefitte-Nestalas. Here, the road forks: the southwest branch (the D920) climbs up a lush, forested valley for another 11km to Cauterets.

TRIP HIGHLIGHT

❻ Cauterets

For alpine scenery, the century-old ski resort of Cauterets is perhaps the signature spot in the Pyrenees. Hemmed in by mountains and forests, it

has clung on to much of its *fin-de-siècle* character, with a stately spa and grand 19th-century residences.

To see the scenery at its best, drive through town along the D920 (signed to the 'Pont d'Espagne'). The road is known locally as the **Chemins des Cascades** after the waterfalls that crash down the mountainside; it's 6.5km of nonstop hairpins, so take it steady.

At the top, you'll reach the giant car park at **Pont d'Espagne** (cable cars adult/child €13/10.50). From here, a combination *télécabine* and *télésiege* (adult/child €13/10.50) ratchets up the mountainside allowing access to the area's trails, including the popular hike to the sapphire tinted **Lac de Gaube**.

🍴 🛏 p343

↱ **DETOUR:**
CIRQUE DE GAVARNIE

Start: ❻ Cauterets

For truly mind-blowing mountain scenery, it's well worth taking a side trip to see the Cirque de Gavarnie, a dramatic amphitheatre of mountains 20km south of Luz-St-Saveur. It's a return walk of about two hours from the village, and you'll need to bring sturdy footwear.

There's another spectacular circle of mountains 6.5km to the north, the **Cirque de Troumouse**. It's reached via a hair-raising 8km toll road (€5 per vehicle; open April to October). There are no barriers and the drops are really dizzying, so drive carefully.

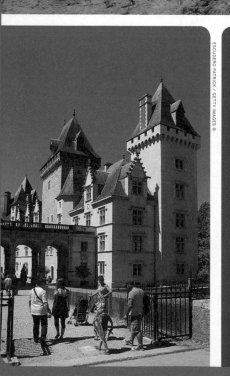

PHILIPPE COHAT / GETTY IMAGES ©

ESCUDERO PATRICK / GETTY IMAGES ©

WHY THIS IS A CLASSIC TRIP
OLIVER BERRY, WRITER

The craggy peaks of the Pyrenees are home to some of France's rarest wildlife and most unspoilt landscapes, and every twist and turn in the road seems to reveal another knockout view – one of my personal favourites is the amazing road over the Col d'Aubisque, which feels closer to flying than driving. I love the traditional way of life here, too. Visit during the Transhumance to be treated to one of France's great rural spectacles.

Top: Col d'Aubisque
Left: Château de Pau
Right: Cauterets ski resort

FELIX ALAIN / GETTY IMAGES ©

The Drive › After staying overnight in Cauterets, backtrack to Pierrefitte-Nestalas, and turn southeast onto the D921 for 12km to Luz-St-Saveur. The next stretch on the D918 is another mountain stunner, climbing up through Barèges to the breathtaking Col du Tourmalet.

- - - - - - - - -

TRIP HIGHLIGHT

⑦ Col du Tourmalet

Even in the pantheon of Pyrenean road passes, the Col du Tourmalet commands special respect. At 2115m, it's the highest road pass in the Pyrenees, and usually only opens between June and October. It's often used as a punishing mountain stage in the Tour de France, and you'll feel uncomfortably akin to a motorised ant as you crawl up towards the pass.

From the ski resort of La Mongie (1800m), a cable car climbs to the top of the soaring **Pic du Midi** (www.picdumidi.com; adult/child €36/23; ⊙9am-7pm Jun-Sep, 10am-5.30pm Oct, Dec-Apr). This high-altitude observatory commands otherworldly views – but it's often blanketed in cloud, so make sure you check the forecast before you go.

The Drive › The next stage to Foix is a long one. Follow the D918 and D935 to Bagnères-de-Bigorre, then the D938 and D20 to Tournay, a drive of 40km. Just before Tournay, head west onto the A64 for 82km. Exit onto the D117, signed to St-Girons. It's another 72km to Foix.

ROAD PASSES IN THE PYRENEES

The high passes between the Vallée d'Ossau, the Vallée d'Aspe and the Vallée de Gaves are often closed during winter. Signs are posted along the approach roads indicating whether they're *ouvert* (open) or *fermé* (closed). The dates given below are approximate, and depend on seasonal snowfall.

Col d'Aubisque (1709m, open May–Oct) The D918 links Laruns in the Vallée d'Ossau with Argèles-Gazost in the Vallée de Gaves. An alternative that's open year-round is the D35 between Louvie-Juzon and Nay.

Col de Marie-Blanque (1035m, open most of year) The shortest link between the Aspe and Ossau valleys is the D294, which corkscrews for 21km between Escot and Bielle.

Col du Pourtalet (1795m, open most of year) The main crossing into Spain generally stays open year-round except during exceptional snowfall.

Col du Tourmalet (2115m, open Jun–Oct) Between Barèges and La Mongie, this is the highest road pass in the Pyrenees. If you're travelling east to the Pic du Midi (for example from Cauterets), the only alternative is a long detour north via Lourdes and Bagnères-de-Bigorre.

8 Foix

Foix is a quiet mountain town, but it's an excellent base for exploring the eastern Pyrenees. Looming above town is the triple-towered **Château de Foix** (📞05 61 05 10 10; adult/child €5.60/3.80; ⏰10am-6pm summer, shorter hours rest of year), constructed in the 10th century as a stronghold for the counts of Foix. The interior is rather bare, but there's a small museum, and the view from the battlements is glorious. There's usually at least one daily tour in English in summer.

Afterwards, head 4.5km south to **Les Forges de Pyrène** (📞05 34 09 30 60; adult/child €9/6; ⏰10am-6.30pm), a fascinating 'living museum' exploring Ariège folk traditions. Spread over 5 hectares, it illustrates traditional trades such as glass blowing, tanning, thatching and nail making, and even has its own blacksmith, baker and cobbler.

🍴 🛏 p325, p343

The Drive » Spend the night in Foix, then head for Tarascon-sur-Ariège, 17km south of Foix on the N20. Look out for brown signs to the Parc de la Préhistoire.

TRIP HIGHLIGHT

9 Tarascon-sur-Ariège

Thousands of years ago, the Pyrenees were home to thriving communities of hunter-gatherers, who used the area's caves as shelters and left behind many stunning examples of prehistoric art.

Near Tarascon-sur-Ariège, the **Parc de la Préhistoire** (📞05 61 05 10 10; adult/child €11/8.30; ⏰10am-7pm, closed Nov-Mar) provides a handy primer on the area's ancient past. It's a mix of multimedia exhibits and hands-on outdoor displays, exploring everything from prehistoric carving to the art of animal-skin tents and ancient spear-throwing.

About 6.5km further south, the **Grotte de Niaux** (www.sites-touristiques-ariege. fr; adult/child €12/8) is home to the Pyrenees' most precious cave paintings. The centrepiece is the **Salon Noir**, reached after an 800m walk through the darkness and decorated with bison, horses and ibex. To help preserve the delicate paintings, there's no artificial light inside; you're given a torch as you enter. The cave can only be visited with a guide. From April to September there's usually a daily tour in English at 1.30pm. Bookings advised.

Eating & Sleeping

Pau ❶

✕ Les Papilles
Insolites   Bistro €€

(📞05 59 71 43 79; www.lespapillesinsolites.
blogspot.co.uk; 5 rue Alexander Taylor; lunch/
dinner menu €22/45, mains around €23;
⏰12.15-2pm & 8-9.30pm Wed-Sat) Run by a
former Parisian sommelier, this cosy bar-bistro
pitches itself between a bistro and a wine shop.
It serves beautifully prepared, ingredient-rich
dishes like Galician-style octopus with potatoes,
fennel and olive tapenade, or beef with leeks,
tempura and lemongrass-raspberry reduction.
Complete the experience with the owner's
choice of one of the 350-odd wines stacked
around the shop. Gorgeously Gallic.

🛏 Hôtel Bristol   Hotel €€

(📞05 59 27 72 98; www.hotelbristol-pau.
com; 3 rue Gambetta; s €55-100, d €80-110,
f €120-130; 🅿🛜) A classic old French hotel
with surprisingly up-to-date rooms, all wrapped
up in a fine 19th-century building. Each room
is uniquely designed, with stylish decor,
bold artwork and elegant furniture; while big
windows fill the rooms with light. Ask for a
mountain-view room with balcony. Breakfast
costs €12.

St-Savin ❹

🛏 Hôtel des Rochers   Hotel €€

(📞05 62 97 09 52; www.lesrochershotel.com; 1
place du Castillou; d €60-68, tr €95-100; 🅿🛜)
In the idyllic village of St-Savin, 16km south of
Lourdes, this handsomely landscaped hotel
makes a perfect mountain retreat. It's run by an
expat English couple, John and Jane, who have
renovated the rooms in clean, contemporary
fashion – insist on one with a mountain view.
Half-board is available.

Cauterets ❻

✕ La Grande
Fache   Traditional French €€

(📞06 08 93 76 30; 5 rue Richelieu; fondue per
person €18-23; ⏰noon-2.30pm & 7-10pm)
You're in the mountains, so really you should be
eating artery-clogging, cheese-heavy dishes
such as *tartiflette* (potatoes, cheese and bacon
baked in a casserole), *raclette* and fondue. This
family-run restaurant crammed with mountain
memorabilia will oblige.

🛏 Hôtel du Lion d'Or   Hotel €€

(📞05 62 92 52 87; www.liondor.eu; 12 rue
Richelieu; s €76-86, d €80-162, with half-board s/d
from €119/144; 🛜) This Heidi-esque hotel oozes
mountain character from every nook and cranny.
In business since 1913, it is deliciously eccentric,
with charming old rooms in polkadot pinks, sunny
yellows and duck-egg blues, and mountain-
themed knick-knacks dotted throughout, from
antique sleds to snowshoes. Breakfast includes
homemade honey and jams, and the restaurant
serves hearty Pyrenean cuisine.

Foix ❽

🛏 Hôtel Eychenne   Hotel €€

(📞05 61 65 00 04; www.hotel-eychenne.com;
11 rue Peyrevidal; s/d €50/60; 🛜) In a good
location in the centre of Foix, Hôtel Eychenne
has simple, carpeted rooms with wooden
shutters and bathrooms of a vaguely futuristic
(circa 1960s) design, with capsule-like showers.
There's an easygoing bar downstairs.

🛏 Hôtel Restaurant Lons   Hotel €€

(📞05 34 09 28 00; www.hotel-lons-foix.com; 6
place Dutilh; r €79-103) One of the better hotels
in Foix is an old-fashioned affair with rambling
corridors and functional but comfy rooms, some
of which look onto the river, while the others face
Foix's shady streets. The riverside restaurant
offers good-value half-board (*menus* €18 to €36).

STRETCH YOUR LEGS
TOULOUSE

Start Place Wilson

Finish Quai de la Daurade

Distance 3km

Duration 3 hours

Known to locals as *'La Ville Rose'* (the pink city), Toulouse has the same sun-baked air as the Languedoc to its southeast. As France's fourth-largest city, it's a vibrant place, refreshed by waterways and well worth a stroll for its buzzing markets and atmospheric old quarter.

Take this walk on Trip

38

Les Halles Victor Hugo

Start on place Wilson and head along rue Victor Hugo to Toulouse's covered **food market** (☎05 61 22 76 92; www.marchevictorhugo.fr; place Victor Hugo; ⏰7am-1.30pm Tue-Sun), where shoppers stock up on cheeses, fresh meat and veg. Look out for the long, curly *saucisse de Toulouse,* the city's trademark sausage.

For a memorable local experience, bump elbows with Toulouse's foodie crowd at the busy restaurants on the 1st floor.

The Walk ≫ Follow rue du Périgord, then head north along rue du Taur.

Basilique St-Sernin

This **basilica** (place St-Sernin; ambulatory €2.50; ⏰8.30am-6pm Mon-Sat, to 7.30pm Sun) is one of France's finest Romanesque structures. It's topped by a soaring spire and octagonal tower, and inside is the tomb of St Sernin himself, sheltered beneath a sumptuous canopy. The basilica is a key stop along one of the four French Chemin de St-Jacques pilgrimage routes.

The Walk ≫ Head south on rue du Taur all the way to place du Capitole.

Place du Capitole

At the end of rue du Taur, you'll emerge onto **place du Capitole**, Toulouse's grand main square, where Toulousiens turn out on sunny evenings to sip a coffee or an early aperitif.

On the eastern side is the 128m-long façade of the **Capitole**, a neoclassical masterpiece in Toulouse's characteristic pink, built in the early 1750s. Inside is the spectacular Salle des Illustres (Hall of the Illustrious), decorated by artists including post-impressionist Henri Martin. To the south are the alleys of the **Vieux Quartier**, the heart of old Toulouse.

The Walk ≫ Take rue de la Pomme, which runs southeast to another cafe-lined square, place St-Georges. Before you reach it, turn right onto rue des Arts, then right onto rue de Metz, where you'll find the museum entrance.

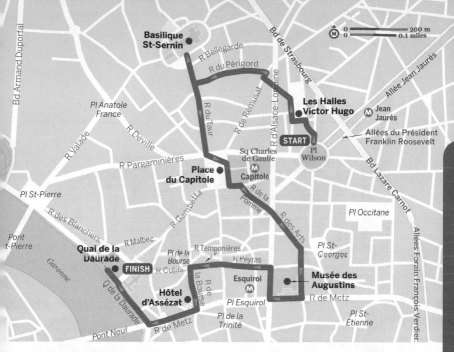

Musée des Augustins

Toulouse's fabulous fine arts **museum** (www.augustins.org; 21 rue de Metz; adult/child €5/free; ☺10am-6pm Thu-Mon, to 9pm Wed) spans the centuries from the Roman era through to the early 20th century. The highlights are the French rooms, with 18th-to-20th-century masterpieces from Delacroix, Ingres, Toulouse-Lautrec and Monet. It's housed within a former Augustinian monastery and its 14th-century cloister gardens are richly decorated with sculptures.

The Walk » Turn right onto rue d'Alsace-Lorraine, then left onto rue Peyras. Follow this street to place de la Bourse, then turn left along rue de la Bourse.

Hôtel d'Assézat

This area has some of Toulouse's most elegant *hôtels particuliers,* private mansions built during the 16th and 17th centuries. Among the finest is the **Hôtel d'Assézat**, built for a woad merchant in 1555. It now houses a private art collection belonging to the **Fondation**

Bemberg (www.fondation-bemberg.fr; place d'Assézat; adult/child €8/5; ☺10am 12.30pm & 1.30-6pm Tue-Sun, to 8.30pm Thu). On the 1st floor, velvet-walled rooms are packed with period furniture. The 2nd floor exhibits artworks spanning impressionist to expressionist schools of thought.

The Walk » Walk onto rue de Metz and follow it west to the elegant Pont Neuf, spanning the Garonne. Turn right onto quai de la Daurade.

Quai de la Daurade

Toulouse looks best when seen from the water. From March to October, scenic **boat cruises** run along the Garonne from the quai de la Daurade; in summer, some boats also travel onto the Canal du Midi. The two main companies are **Les Bateaux Toulousains** (www.bateaux-toulousains.com) and **Toulouses Croisières** (www.toulouse-croisieres.com). Trips cost around €10/5 per adult/child for an hour's cruise.

The Walk » From quai de la Daurade, follow rue Malbec and rue Gambetta back towards place Wilson.

Atlantic Coast

THE ATLANTIC COAST IS WHERE FRANCE GETS BACK TO NATURE. Much more laid-back than the Med, this is the place to slow the pace right down.

Driving through this region is all about quiet country roads winding through vine-striped hills, glimpsed views of dead-at-noon villages and the occasional foray into energetic cities such as Bordeaux.

The region's wine is famous worldwide, and to wash it down you'll find fresh-from-the-ocean seafood wherever you go, plus plenty of regional delicacies including snails in the north, foie gras further south and, in the unique Basque regions, chilli-tinted dishes filled with hints of Spain.

Biarritz Waves weather the coastal houses
SHAUN EGAN / GETTY IMAGES ©

Atlantic Coast

✓ DON'T MISS

St-Cyprien

An expert resident in the village offers truffle hunts. Accompany the hounds on Trip **34**

Musée National de Préhistoire

A brilliant place to do your homework on the Vézère Valley's cave art. Bone up on Trip **35**

Domme

Explore this spectacular hilltop village, with its views over the Dordogne valley. Take it all in on Trip **36**

Najac

This fairy-tale castle offers some of the most breathtaking views in southwest France. Explore it on Trip **36**

Tapas

Tuck into these tasty bites and wonder whether you're in France, Spain or somewhere else altogether. Indulge yourself on Trip **32**

La Roque Gageac Boating on the Dordogne River

Basque Country **32**

Feisty and independent, the Basque Country is famous for the glitzy resort of Biarritz. But on this tour you'll also fall for delightful fishing ports, chocolate-box villages and jade-green rolling hills.

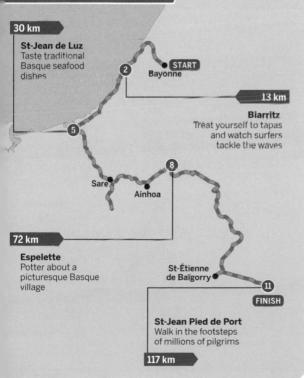

30 km

St-Jean de Luz
Taste traditional Basque seafood dishes

2 **START**
Bayonne

13 km

Biarritz
Treat yourself to tapas and watch surfers tackle the waves

5

8

Sare

Ainhoa

72 km

Espelette
Potter about a picturesque Basque village

St-Étienne de Baïgorry

11

FINISH

St-Jean Pied de Port
Walk in the footsteps of millions of pilgrims

117 km

7 DAYS
117KM / 73 MILES

GREAT FOR...

BEST TIME TO GO

September and October offer the best combination of weather and low crowds.

ESSENTIAL PHOTO

Looking across Grande Plage in Biarritz from the southern headland.

BEST FOR CULTURE

Absorbing the Basque spirit of old Bayonne.

32 Basque Country

Driving into the village of Espelette you'll be struck by how different everything is from other parts of the country. The houses are all tarted up in the red and white of Basque buildings, streamers of chilli peppers hang from roof beams, and from open windows comes a language you don't recognise. As you'll discover on this tour, being different from the rest of France is exactly how the proud Basques like it.

❶ Bayonne

Surrounded by sturdy fortifications and splashed in red and white paint, Bayonne is one of the most attractive towns in southwest France. Its perfectly preserved old town and riverside restaurants are an absolute delight to explore, but the town is best known to French people for producing some of the nation's finest chocolate and ham.

Inside the **Musée Basque et de l'Histoire de Bayonne** (☎05 59 59 08 98;

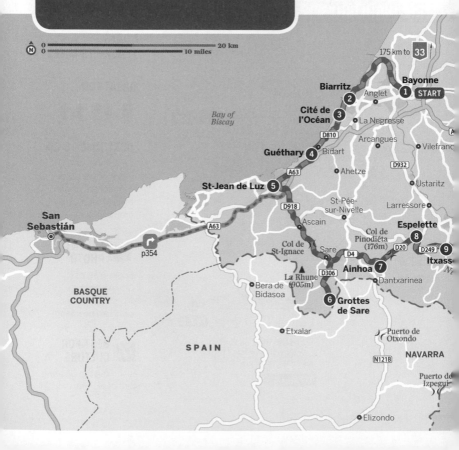

www.musee-basque.com; 37 quai des Corsaires; adult/child €6.50/free; ⊙10am-6.30pm Jul & Aug, closed Mon rest of year) the seafaring history, traditions and cultural identity of the Basque people are all explored.

Also worth a visit is Bayonne's Gothic **Cathédrale Ste-Marie** (place Louis Pastour; ⊙10-11.45am & 3-6.15pm Mon-Sat, 3.30-6.15pm Sun, cloister 9am-12.30pm & 2-6pm), whose twin towers soar elegantly above the old city.

✗ p357

The Drive » Bring a towel because we're taking the 13km (25 minute) beach-bums' route to Biarritz. Follow the Adour River out of Bayonne down allée Marines and av de l'Adour. At the big roundabout turn left onto bd des Plages and take your pick from any of the beaches along this stretch. This road will eventually lead into Biarritz.

– – – – – – – – –

❷ Biarritz

As ritzy as its name suggests, this stylish coastal town took off as a resort in the mid-19th century when Napoléon III and his Spanish-born wife, Eugénie, visited regularly. Along its rocky coastline are architectural hallmarks of this golden age, and the belle-époque and art-deco eras that followed. Although it retains a high glamour quotient (and high prices to match), it's also a magnet for vanloads of surfers, with some of Europe's best waves.

Biarritz's *raison d'être* is its fashionable beaches, particularly the central **Grande Plage** and

Plage Miramar, which are lined end to end with sunbathing bodies on hot summer days.

For a look under the waves, check out the **Musée de la Mer** (☎05 59 22 75 40; www.museedelamer. com; esplanade du Rocher de la Vierge; adult/child/family €14.50/9.80/50, joint ticket with Cité de l'Océan €18.50/13/63; ⊙9.30am-midnight Jul & Aug, 9.30am-8pm Apr, Jun, Sep & Oct, shorter hours rest of year), rich in underwater life from the Bay of Biscay and beyond.

For life further afield, have a poke about the stunning collections of Asian art at the **Musée d'Art Oriental Asiatica** (☎05 59 22 78 79; www. museeasiatica.com; 1 rue Guy Petit; adult/child €10/2; ⊙10.30am-6.30pm Mon-Fri, 2-7pm Sat & Sun Jul, Aug & during French school holidays, shorter hours rest of year).

✗ ⊨ p357

The Drive » It's a 4km, 10-minute drive south out of Biarritz down rue Gambetta and rue de Madrid to the Cité

LINK YOUR TRIP

30 **Cheat's Compostela**

From St-Jean Pied de Port work your way in reverse through our cheat's version of this ancient spiritual journey.

33 **Heritage Wine Country**

From Bayonne it's a 192km pine-tree-scented drive to the capital of wine, Bordeaux, and the start of our wine tour.

de l'Océan. On the way you'll pass some fantastic stretches of sand just calling for you to dip a toe in the sea or hang ten on a surfboard.

③ Cité de l'Océan

We don't really know whether it's fair to call Biarritz's new showpiece, **Cité de l'Océan** (☎05 59 22 75 40; www.citedelocean. com; 1 av de la Plage; adult/child/family €11.50/7.50/39, joint ticket with Musée de la Mer €18.50/13/63; ☉10am-10pm Jul & Aug, 10am-7pm Easter, Apr-Jun, Sep & Oct, shorter hours rest of year), a mere 'museum'. At heart it's a museum of the ocean, but in reality this is entertainment, cutting-edge technology, theme park and science museum all

rolled into one spectacular attraction. Inside the eye-catching building you'll learn how the ocean was born and watch giant squid and sperm whales do battle.

The Drive » It's an easy 6km drive down the D911 (av de Biarritz) and the D810, passing through the village of Bidart, to the ocean views of pretty Guéthary. Traffic can be awful.

④ Guéthary

Built onto cliffs overlooking the ocean south of Biarritz, this red-and-white seaside village has gained a reputation as the Basque Country's chichi resort of choice for the jet set. The pebble beach below the village offers safe bathing for all the family,

while the offshore reefs offer some exceptional surf for the brave.

The Drive » It's another seriously traffic-clogged 7km down the D810 to St-Jean de Luz. This short hop should only take 10 minutes but it rarely does! Sadly, there's no worthwhile alternative route.

TRIP HIGHLIGHT

⑤ St-Jean de Luz

If you're searching for the quintessential Basque seaside town – with atmospheric narrow streets and a lively fishing port pulling in large catches of sardines and anchovies that are cooked up at authentic restaurants – you've found it.

St-Jean de Luz's beautiful banana-shaped sandy **beach** sprouts stripy bathing tents from June to September. The beach is sheltered from Atlantic swells and is among the few child-friendly beaches in the Basque Country.

With plenty of boutique shops, little cafes and pretty buildings, walking the streets of the pedestrianised town centre is a real pleasure. Don't miss the town's finest church, the **Église St-Jean Baptiste** (rue Gambetta; ☉8.30am-noon & 2-7pm), which has a splendid interior with a magnificent baroque altarpiece.

✗ 🛏 p357

DETOUR: SAN SEBASTIÁN, SPAIN

Start: ⑤ St-Jean de Luz

Spain, and the elegant and lively city of San Sebastián, is just a few kilometres along the coast from St-Jean de Luz and put simply, San Sebastián is not a city you want to miss out on visiting. The town is set around two sickle-shaped beaches, at least one of which, **Playa de la Concha**, is the equal of any city beach in Europe. But there's more to the city than just looks. With more Michelin stars per capita than anywhere else in the world, and arguably the finest tapas in Spain, many a culinary expert has been heard to say that San Sebastián is possibly the world's best food city.

By car from St-Jean de Luz, it's just a short 20-minute jump down the A64 (and past an awful lot of toll booths!), or you can endure the N10, which has no tolls but gets so clogged up that it will take you a good couple of hours to travel this short distance.

BY RUHEY / GETTY IMAGES ©

St-Jean de Luz Houses on the waterfront

The Drive » The 15km, 20-minute drive down the D918 and D4 to Sare is a slow road through the gorgeous gentle hills of the pre-Pyrenees. From the village of Sare, which is well worth a wander, hop onto the D306 for a further 7km (10 minutes) to the Grottes de Sare.

- - - - - - - - - - - - -

⑥ Grottes de Sare

Who knows what the first inhabitants of the **Grottes de Sare** (www. grottesdesare.fr; adult/child €8.50/4.50; ⊙10am-7pm Aug, 10am-6pm Apr-Jul & Sep, closed Jan–mid-Feb) – who lived some 20,000 years ago – would make of today's whiz-bang technology, including lasers and holograms, during the sound-and-light shows at these caves. Multilingual 45-minute tours take you through a gaping entrance via narrow pas-

sages to a huge central cavern adorned with stalagmites and stalactites.

The Drive » To get to our next stop, Ainhoa, retrace your steps to Sare and then jump onto the D4. After 14km and 20 minutes it's job done. If you're feeling adventurous, you could weave your way there on any number of minor back roads or even cross briefly into Spain and drive via the lovely village of Zugarrmurdi.

7 Ainhoa

Beautiful Ainhoa's elongated main street is flanked by imposing 17th-century houses, half-timbered and brightly painted. The fortified **church** has the Basque trademarks of an internal gallery and an embellished altarpiece.

The Drive » It's 6km down the D20 to our next halt, Espelette.

TRIP HIGHLIGHT

8 Espelette

The whitewashed Basque town of Espelette is famous for its dark-red chillies, which are an integral ingredient in traditional Basque cuisine. In autumn, the walls of the houses are strung with rows of chillies drying in the sun.

To learn more about the chillies, and taste and buy chilli products, visit **l'Atelier du Piment** (☏05 59 93 90 21; www.atelier dupiment.com; ☺9am-8pm Apr-Oct, to 6pm Nov-Mar) on the edge of town.

The Drive » The next leg is an exceedingly pretty 6km (10 minutes) down the D249 to the cherry capital, Itxassou.

9 Itxassou

Famed for its cherries, as well as the beauty of its surrounds, Itxassou is a classic Basque village that well rewards a bit of exploration. The cherries are used in the region's most famous cake, gateau Basque, which is available pretty much everywhere you look throughout the Basque Country.

The Drive » It's 28km (about 30 minutes) down the D918 and D948 to St-Étienne de Baïgorry. On the way you'll pass the village of Bidarry, renowned for its white-water rafting, and some pretty special mountain scenery.

10 St-Étienne de Baïgorry

The riverside village of St-Étienne de Baïgorry is tranquillity itself. Like so many Basque settlements, the village has two focal points: the **church** and the **fronton** (court for playing *pelota,* the local ball game). It's the kind of place to while away an afternoon doing nothing very much at all.

The Drive » It's a quiet 11km (20 minute) drive along the rural D15 to our final stop St-Jean Pied de Port. The thirsty will be interested to know that the hills around the village of Irouléguy, which you pass roughly around the halfway point, are home to the vines that produce the Basque Country's best-known wine.

TRIP HIGHLIGHT

11 St-Jean Pied de Port

At the foot of the Pyrenees, the walled town of St-Jean Pied de Port was for centuries the last stop in France for pilgrims heading south over the Spanish border and on to Santiago de Compostela in western Spain. Today it remains a popular departure point for hikers attempting the same pilgrim trail.

St-Jean Pied de Port isn't just about hiking boots and religious pilgimage, though; its old core, sliced through by the Nive River, is an attractive place of cobbled streets and geranium-covered balconies.

Specific sights worth seeking out include **Église Notre Dame du Bout du Pont**, which was thoroughly rebuilt in the 17th century. Beyond Porte de Notre Dame (the main gate into the old town) is photogenic **Vieux Pont** (Old Bridge), the town's best-known landmark.

✕ p357

Eating & Sleeping

Bayonne ❶

✗ Table de Pottoka   Gastronomy €€

(☏05 59 46 14 94; www.pottoka.fr; 21 quai Amiral Dubourdieu; lunch menu €15, dinner menu €35, à la carte mains €20; ⊘ noon-2pm & 7-10pm Mon-Tue & Thu-Sat) Run by renowned chef Sebastien Gravé (who also runs a place in Paris), this is Bayonne's hottest new table. It's committed to big Basque flavours, but explores them in all kinds of innovative ways. Inside things are sleek and minimal, with plain wooden tables and pop-art prints on the walls, and there are dreamy river views through the plate-glass windows

Biarritz ❷

✗ Le Clos Basque   Basque €€

(☏05 59 24 24 96; 12 rue Louis Barthou; menus €26, mains €14.50; ⊘ noon-1.30pm & 7.45-9.30 Tue-Sat, noon-1.30pm Sun) One of Biarritz's more traditional tables, with a sweet front patio sheltered by climbing plants and an awning. The menu is proudly Basque, so expect classic dishes such as axoa (mashed veal, onions and tomatoes spiced with red Espelette chilli). It gets very busy, so service can be slow.

⌂ Hôtel de Silhouette   Boutique Hotel €€€

(☏05 59 24 93 82; www.hotel-silhouette-biarritz. com; 30 rue Gambetta; d from €200; ❄ 🛜) The address if you want to splash in Biarritz, just steps from the covered market, but surprisingly secluded thanks to its set-back-from-the-street setting. It's full of fun, from the weird faces on the wallpaper to the odd sculptures of bears and sheep dotted round, and there's a gorgeous garden. The building dates from 1610, but it's metropolitan modern in style.

St-Jean de Luz ❺

✗ Buvette des Halles   Seafood €

(☏05 59 26 73 59; bd Victor Hugo; dishes €7-14; ⊘6am-2pm & dinner, closed Tue Sep-Jun) For the full-blown French market experience, this tiny corner restaurant hidden away in Les Halles is a must. Pull up a stool at the counter under its collection of vintage tea-pots, and tuck into plates of Bayonne ham, grilled sardines, mussels, fish soup and local cheeses. In summer there are tables outside.

⌂ Les Almadiès   Hotel €€

(☏05 59 85 34 48; www.hotel-les-almadies. com; 58 rue Gambetta; d €100-135; 🛜) Summer bargains are hard to come by in St-Jean de Luz, but this pretty little streetside hotel definitely ranks as one. It's in a great location on the lively thoroughfare of rue Gambetta, overlooking a little square, and though the rooms are a bit generic – beige carpets, white bathrooms, identikit furniture – there's no doubting the deal here.

St-Jean Pied de Port ⓫

✗ Chez Arrambide   Gastronomy €€€

(☏05 59 37 01 01; www.hotel-les-pyrenees. com; 19 place Charles de Gaulle; menus €42-110, mains €34-52; ⊘12.15-1.45pm & 7.45-9pm Jul & Aug, Wed-Mon Sep-Jun) This twin Michelin-starred restaurant at the Hôtel des Pyrénées is renowned for miles around, and is where chef Firmin Arrambide works wonders with market produce. It's a high-class treat, where dishes are as arty as they are edible. Pricey rooms (r €105 to €225) are available upstairs.

Heritage Wine Country

33

This is the trip for those who appreciate the finer things in life: great wine, fabulous regional cuisine and gentle driving through glorious vine-ribboned countryside studded with grand châteaux.

TRIP HIGHLIGHTS

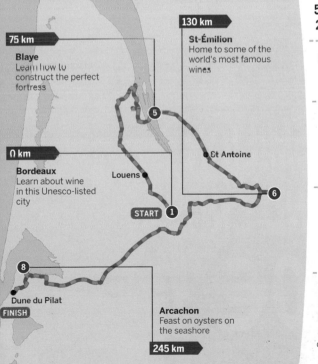

130 km

St-Émilion
Home to some of the world's most famous wines

75 km

Blaye
Learn how to construct the perfect fortress

0 km

Bordeaux
Learn about wine in this Unesco-listed city

Louens

St Antoine

START ❶

❺

❻

8

Dune du Pilat
FINISH

Arcachon
Feast on oysters on the seashore

245 km

---

5 DAYS
257KM / 160 MILES

GREAT FOR...

BEST TIME TO GO
September and October: the grape harvest takes place, oysters are in season.

 ESSENTIAL PHOTO

Red roofs of St-Émilion from place des Créneaux.

✓ **BEST FOR FOODIES**

Slurping fresh oysters at Bordeaux's Marché des Capucins.

---

t-Émilion Wine shops line the cobbled streets

33 Heritage Wine Country

10am: the southern sun warms your face and you're standing in a field surrounded by vines heavy with ready-to-burst grapes. 1pm: cutlery clinks, tummies sigh in bliss and you're on a gastronomic adventure in a top-class restaurant. 7pm: toes in the sand, Atlantic breezes in your hair and you down an oyster in one. All this and more awaits on this refined culinary trip.

TRIP HIGHLIGHT

1 Bordeaux

Gourmet Bordeaux is a city of sublime food and long, lazy sun-drenched days. Half the city (18 sq km) is Unesco-listed, making it the largest urban World Heritage site – and an absolutely delight to wander around (p410). Barista-run coffee shops, super-food food trucks, an exceptional dining scene and more fine wine than you could ever possibly drink make it a city hard to resist.

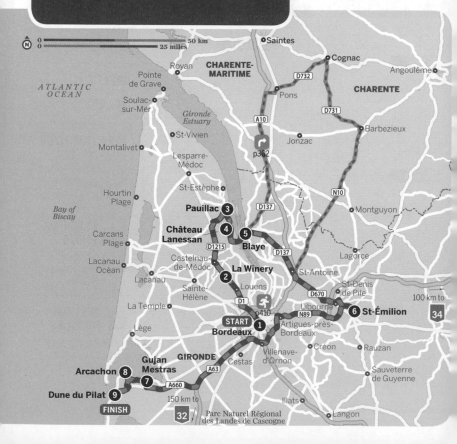

Wine aficionados will adore **La Cité du Vin** (☎05 56 81 38 47; www.laciteduvin.com; 1 Esplanade de Pontac; adult/child €20/free; ☺9.30am-7.30pm daily Apr-Oct, 9.30am-7.30pm Tue-Sun Nov-Mar), a stunning contemporary building designed to resemble a (very modern) wine decanter on the banks of the River Garonne. The curvaceous gold building glitters in the sun and its 3000 sq metres of exhibits inside, dedicated to immersing visitors in the complex world of wine, are equally sensational. Tours end with a glass of wine in the panoramic Latitude 20 wine bar on the 8th floor.

The **tourist office** (☎05 56 00 66 00; www.bordeaux-tourisme.com; 12 cours du 30 Juillet; ☺9am-7.30pm Mon-

> ✔ **TOP TIP: OYSTERS AT CAPUCINS**
>
> A classic Bordeaux experience is a Saturday morning spent slurping oysters and white wine from one of the seafood stands at **Marché des Capucins** (http://marchedescapucins.com; place des Capucins; ☺6am-1pm Tue-Sun). Afterwards you can peruse the stalls while shopping for the freshest ingredients to take on a picnic.

Sat, 9.30am-6.30pm Sun Jul & Aug, shorter hours Sep-Jun) runs a packed program of city tours in English, including gourmet and wine tours, river cruises in the warmer months, and child-friendly tours. All tours take a limited number of participants; reserve ahead.

🍴 🛏 p44, p366

The Drive >> It's a 24km trip along the D1 from Bordeaux to La Winery in Arsac. Technically this should take around 40 minutes, but traffic around Bordeaux can be dreadful so allow longer.

- - - - - - - - - - - -

② La Winery

Part giant wine shop, part grape-flavoured theme park, and part wine museum, **La Winery** (☎05 56 39 04 90; www.winery.fr; rte du Verdon, Rond-point des Vendangeurs, Arsac-en-Médoc; ☺10.30am-7.30pm Tue-Sun, boutique 10am-8pm Jun-Sep, to 7.30pm Oct-May) is a vast glass-and-steel wine centre that mounts concerts and contemporary-art exhibits alongside

various fee-based tastings, including innovative ones that determine your *signe œnologique* ('wine sign') costing from €16 (booking required). It stocks more than 1000 different wines.

The Drive >> It's 29km (30 minutes) from Arsac to Pauillac along the D1215, which becomes ever more rural. From the centre of Pauillac continue 2km south to get to Bages and Café Lavinal.

- - - - - - - - - - - -

③ Pauillac

Northwest of Bordeaux, along the western shore of the Gironde Estuary – formed by the confluence of the Garonne and Dordogne Rivers – lie some of Bordeaux's most celebrated vineyards. On the banks of the muddy Gironde, the port town of Pauillac is at the heart of the wine country, surrounded by the distinguished Haut-Médoc, Margaux and St-Julien appellations. Extraordinary châteaux pepper these parts, including Château Margaux with striking new cellars that

§ LINK YOUR TRIP

32 Basque Country
From Arcachon drive 182km through the forests of Les Landes to Bayonne and our Spanish-flavoured Basque Country tour.

34 Gourmet Dordogne
Slip some truffle hunting into your wine tour. From St-Émilion it's a mere 100km to Périgueux and our Gourmet Dordogne drive.

were designed by Lord Norman Foster in 2015.

The Pauillac wine appellation encompasses 18 *crus classés* in all, including the world-renowned Mouton Rothschild, Latour and Lafite Rothschild. The town's tourist office houses the **Maison du Tourisme et du Vin** (☏05 56 59 03 08; www. pauillac-medoc.com; La Verrerie; ☻9.30am-7pm Mon-Sat, 10am-1pm & 2-6pm Sun), with information on châteaux and how to visit them.

Essential is lunch at **Café Lavinal** (www.jmcazes. com/en/cafe-lavinal; Passage du Desquet, Bages; menus €28 & €38, mains €12-25; ☻noon-2pm & 7.30-9pm, cafe from 8am), a mind-blowing village bistro in Bages with retro red banquet seating and

zinc bar, and a menu of French classics overseen by twin Michelin-starred chef Jean-Luc Rocha from nearby Château Cordeillan-Bages.

The Drive ≫ Count no more than 15 minutes to cover the 9km between Bages and the next stop. Follow the D2 south out of Pauillac for almost 7km, turn right towards Lachesnaye, and continue for another 1.5km then turn right to Château Lanessan.

– – – – – – – – – – – – – –

❹ Château Lanessan

There are so many châteaux around here with such a confusing web of opening times and visiting regulations that it can be hard to know where to begin. One of the easiest to visit is

Château Lanessan (☏05 56 58 94 80; www.lanessan. com; Cussac-Fort-Medoc; adult/child €8/2; ☻9am-noon & 2-6pm by advance reservation), whose daily hour-long guided tours take in the neoclassical château, its English-style gardens with magnificent 19th-century greenhouse, the stables built in 1880 in the shape of a horseshoe with marble feed troughs, the pine-panelled tack room and a horse museum with several 19th-century horse-drawn carriages. Tours end with wine tasting. Advance reservations, at least one day before, are obligatory.

The Drive ≫ Getting to Blaye involves splashing over the Gironde River on a car ferry – how exciting! Return to the D2 and head south to Lamarque where you hop on board the ferry (passenger/car €2.70/14.10, departures every 1½ hours in July and August) for the short crossing to Blaye. It's 11km from the château to the ferry.

– – – – – – – – – – – – – –

TRIP HIGHLIGHT

❺ Blaye

If you want a lesson in how to build a protective citadel, then the spectacular **Citadelle de Blaye** is about as good an example as you could hope to find. Largely constructed by that master fortress-builder Vauban in the 17th century, it was a key line of defence protecting Bordeaux from naval

---

↱ DETOUR: COGNAC

Start: ❺ **Blaye**

On the banks of the Charente River amid vine-covered countryside, the picturesque town of Cognac, home of the double-distilled spirit that bears its name, proves that there's more to southwest France than just wine.

The best-known Cognac houses are open to the public, running tours of their cellars and production facilities, and ending with a tasting session. The **tourist office** (☏05 45 82 10 71; www.tourism-cognac. com; 16 rue du 14 Juillet; ☻9am-7pm Mon-Sat, 10am-5pm Sun Jul-Aug, shorter hours rest of year) can give advice on current opening hours of each Cognac house. It's 85km from Blaye to Cognac, much of which is along the A10 highway. From Cognac you can cut down to stop 6, St-Émilion, in two hours on the D731 followed by the busy N10.

St-Émilion Vineyards outside the village

attack. It was inscribed onto the Unesco World Heritage List in 2008.

The Drive >> From Blaye to St-Émilion is a 50km drive. From Blaye take the D137 toward St-André de Cubzac, where you join the D670 to Libourne. After a bit of time stuck in traffic you continue down to St-Émilion. It should take an hour but traffic means it will probably take longer!

TRIP HIGHLIGHT

⑥ St-Émilion

The medieval village of St-Émilion perches above vineyards renowned for producing full-bodied red wines and is easily the most alluring of all the region's wine towns.

The only way to visit the town's most interesting historical sites is with one of the tourist office's varied **guided tours** (adult/child from €8/free).

The tourist office also organises two-hour afternoon **château visits** (adult/child €12/free), and runs various events throughout the year, such as **Les Samedis de l'Oenologie** (tours €77), which combines a vineyard visit, lunch, town tour and wine-tasting course on Saturdays.

For a fun and informative introduction to wine tasting, get stuck into some 'blind' tastings at L'École du Vin de St-Émilion. The adjacent **Maison du Vin** (📞05 57 55 50 55; www.maisonduvin saintemilion.com; place Pierre Meyrat; ⏰9.30am-12.30pm & 2-6.30pm) also offers bilingual 1½-hour wine-tasting classes. Reserve all tours in advance.

🍴🛏️ p366, p409

The Drive » To get to the next stop you've simply no option but to endure the ring road around Bordeaux – avoid rush hour! Head toward Bordeaux on the

N89, then south down the A63 following signs to Arcachon and then Gujan Mestras. It's a 100km journey that should, but probably won't, take an hour.

- - - - - - - - - -

➐ Gujan Mestras

Take a break from the grape and head to the seaside to eat oysters in the area around Gujan Mestras. Picturesque oyster ports are dotted around the town, but the best one to visit is **Port de Larros**, where locally harvested oysters are sold from wooden shacks. To learn more about these delicious shellfish, the

small **Maison de l'Huître** (www.maison-huitre.fr; rue du Port de Larros; adult/child €5.80/3.80; ⏰10am-12.45pm & 2.15-6.30pm Jul & Aug, 10am-12.30pm & 2.30-6pm Mon-Sat Sep-Jun) has a display on oyster farming, including a short film in English.

The Drive » It's 10 sometimes-traffic-clogged but well-signposted kilometres from Gujan Mestras to Arcachon.

- - - - - - - - - -

TRIP HIGHLIGHT

➑ Arcachon

The seaside town of Arcachon has lured bourgeois Bordelaises since the end of the 19th

ON THE WINE TRAIL

Thirsty? The 1000-sq-km wine-growing area around the city of Bordeaux is, along with Burgundy, France's most important producer of top-quality wines.

The Bordeaux region is divided into 57 appellations (production areas whose soil and microclimate impart distinctive characteristics to the wine produced there) that are grouped into seven families, and then subdivided into a hierarchy of designations (eg *premier grand cru classé*, the most prestigious) that often vary from appellation to appellation. The majority of the Bordeaux region's reds, rosés, sweet and dry whites and sparkling wines have earned the right to include the abbreviation AOC (Appellation d'Origine Contrôlée) on their labels, indicating that the contents have been grown, fermented and aged according to strict regulations that govern such viticultural matters as the number of vines permitted per hectare and acceptable pruning methods.

Bordeaux has more than 5000 châteaux, referring not to palatial residences but rather to the properties where grapes are raised, picked, fermented and then matured as wine. The smaller châteaux sometimes accept walk-in visitors, but at many places, especially the better-known ones, you have to make advance reservations. Many close during the *vendange* (grape harvest) in October.

Whet your palate with the Bordeaux tourist office informal introduction to wine and cheese courses (adult €25) where you sip three different wines straight from the cellar and sup on cheese.

Serious students of the grape can enrol at the **École du Vin** (Bordeaux Wine School; 📞05 56 00 22 85; www.bordeaux.com; 3 cours du 30 juillet), within the Maison du Vin de Bordeaux, across the street from the tourist office. Introductory two-hour courses (adult €25) are held Monday to Saturday from 10am to noon between July and September.

century. Its four little quarters are romantically named for each of the seasons, with villas that evoke the town's golden past amid a scattering of 1950s architecture.

Arcachon's sandy beach, **Plage d'Arcachon**, is flanked by two piers. Lively **Jetée Thiers** is at the western end. In front of the eastern pier, **Jetée d'Eyrac**, stands the town's turreted **Casino de la Plage**, built by Adalbert Deganne in 1953 as an exact replica of Château de Boursault in the Marne. Inside, it's a less-grand blinking and bell-ringing riot of poker machines and gaming tables.

On the tree-covered hillside south of the Ville d'Été, the century-old **Ville d'Hiver** (Winter Quarter) has more than 300 villas ranging in style from neo-Gothic through to colonial.

For a different view of Arcachon and its coastline, take to the ocean waves on one of the boat cruises organised by **Les Bateliers Arcachonnais** (☎08 25 27 00 27; www. bateliers-arcachon.com; 75 bd de la Plage; 🚻). It offers daily, year-round cruises around the **Île aux Oiseaux**, the uninhab-

✓ **TOP TIP: OYSTER TASTE TEST**

Oysters from each of the Bassin d'Arcachon's four oyster-breeding zones hint at subtly different flavours. See if you can detect these:
Banc d'Arguin – milk and sugar
Île aux Oiseaux – minerals
Cap Ferret – citrus
Grand Banc – roasted hazelnuts

ited 'bird island' in the middle of Arcachon bay. It's a haven for tern, curlew and redshank, so bring your binoculars. In summer there are regular all-day excursions (11am to 5.30pm) to the **Banc d'Arguin**, the sand bank off the Dune du Pilat.

✕ 🛏 p367

The Drive » Dune du Pilat is 12km south of Arcachon down the D218. There are restrictions on car access in summer for the last part of the route.

– – – – – – – – – – – –

9 Dune du Pilat

This colossal sand dune (sometimes referred to as the Dune de Pyla because of its location in the resort town of Pyla-sur-Mer) stretches from the mouth of the Bassin d'Arcachon southwards for almost 3km. Already the largest in Europe, it's

spreading eastwards at 4.5m a year – it has swallowed trees, a road junction and even a hotel.

The view from the top approximately 114m above sea level – is magnificent. To the west you can see the sandy shoals at the mouth of the Bassin d'Arcachon, and dense dark-green pine forests stretch from the base of the dune eastwards almost as far as the eye can see. The only address to have a drink or dine afterwards is **La Co(o)rniche** (☎05 56 22 72 11; www.lacoorniche-pyla. com; 46 av Louis Gaume, Pyla-sur-Mer; 2-/3-course lunch menu €53/58, seafood platters €40-85), a 1930s hunting lodge transformed by French designer Philippe Starck into one of France's most stunning seaside restaurants.

Eating & Sleeping

Bordeaux ❶

✕ Magasin Général — International €

(☎05 56 77 88 35; www.magasingeneral.camp/; 87 quai des Queyries; 2-/3-course menu €14/18, mains €9-19; ☺8.30am-6pm Wed-Fri, 8.30am-midnight Sat, 10am-midnight Sun, kitchen noon-2.15pm & 7-10pm; 🛜) Follow the hip crowd across the river to this huge industrial hangar on the right bank, France's biggest and best organic restaurant with gargantuan terrace complete with vintage sofa seating, ping-pong table and table football. Everything here, from the vegan burgers and super-food salads to smoothies, pizzas, wine and French bistro fare, is *bio* (organic) and sourced locally. Sunday brunch (€24) is a bottomless feast.

✕ Le Petit Commerce — Seafood €€

(05 56 79 76 58; 22 rue Parlement St-Pierre; 2-course lunch menu €14, mains €15-25; ☺noon-midnight) This iconic bistro, with dining rooms both sides of a narrow pedestrian street and former Michelin-starred chef Stéphane Carrade in the kitchen, is the star turn of the trendy St-Pierre quarter. It's best known for its excellent seafood menu that embraces everything from Arcachon sole and oysters to eels, lobsters and *chipirons* (baby squid) fresh from St-Jean de Luz.

✕ La Tupina — Regional Cuisine €€€

(☎05 56 91 56 37; www.latupina.com; 6 rue Porte de la Monnaie; lunch menu €18, dinner menus €39 & €74; ☺noon-2pm & 7-11pm Tue-Sun) Filled with the aroma of soup simmering inside a *tupina* ('kettle' in Basque) over an open fire, this iconic bistro is feted for its seasonal southwestern French fare: think foie gras and egg *cassoullette* (mini casserole), milk-fed lamb, tripe and goose wings. Hopefully nothing will change following the 2016 retirement of the gregarious Jean-Pierre Xiradakis, life and soul of La Tupina since 1968.

🛏 Chez Dupont — B&B €€

(☎05 56 81 49 59; www.chez-dupont.com; 45 rue Notre Dame; s/d from €85/100) Five impeccably decorated rooms, peppered with a wonderful collection of vintage curiosities, inspires love at first sight at this thoroughly contemporary, design-driven B&B in the trendy former wine-merchant quarter of Chartrons. Across the road from, and run by, the bistro of the same name, Chez Dupont is one of the best deals in town.

🛏 L'Hôtel Particulier — Boutique Hotel €€€

(☎05 57 88 28 80; www.lhotel-particulier.com; 44 rue Vital-Carles; d €189-299; 🛜) Step into this fabulous boutique hotel and be wowed by period furnishings mixed with contemporary design, extravagant decorative touches and an atmospheric courtyard garden. Its five individually designed hotel rooms (breakfast €12) match up to expectations with vintage fireplaces, carved ceilings and bathtubs with legs. Exceptional value are the suite of equally well-furnished self-catering apartments, sleeping one (€89), two (€109) or four people (€179).

St-Émilion ❻

✕ L'Envers du Decors — French €€

(☎06 57 74 48 31; www.envers-dudecor.com; 11 rue du Clocher; mains €17.50-35; ☺noon-2.30pm & 7-10.30pm) A few doors down from the tourist office, this wine bar is one of the best places to eat – and inevitably drink – in this tasteful wine town. The kitchen cooks up fabulous local classics like *lamproie à la Bordelaise* (a local eel-like fish simmered in red wine), duck liver pan-fried in Sauternes and oysters by the dozen.

✕ La Table de Plaisance — Gastronomy €€€

(Hostellerie de Plaisance; ☎05 57 55 07 55; www.hostelleriedeplaisance.com; place du Clocher; menus €78-134, mains €49-57; ☺noon-1.30pm Sat, 7.30-9.30pm Tue-Sat) Wine pairings are naturally in a league of their own at this exquisite Michelin-starred restaurant, in the heart of the village in luxurious, five-star Hostellerie de Plaisance. Tasting *menus* include a mystery eight-course extravaganza served to the whole table or more modest three- and five-course feasts. Advance reservations essential.

Maison de la Commanderie

B&B €€

(☎05 57 24 26 59; www.maisondelacommand erie.com; 3bis rue de la Porte Brunet; d €155-235; 🛜) Snug in a traditional ginger-stone *maison de village* across the road from 14th-century Cloître de Cordeliers, this four-room guesthouse enchants. Rooms mix original features (like exposed stone walls) and period furniture with stylish contemporary fabrics and other decorative touches. Two overlook the cloister and vineyards, and two have a majestic panorama of burnt-red rooftops and the green Dordogne Valley beyond.

Grand Barrail

Chateau €€€

(☎05 57 55 37 00; www.grand-barrail.com; rte de Libourne; d €320; 🌡🛜🏊) Grand doesn't even begin to describe this immense château, built in 1850, with its 46 antique-dressed rooms, spa, stone-flagged heated swimming pool, vast park and helipad on the front lawn. Undoubtedly the best seat in its gastronomic restaurant (*menus* €55 and €65) is the corner table framed by exquisite 19th-century stained glass. Find the castle 3km from St-Émilion village, signposted off the D243. Breakfast €24.

Arcachon ⑧

✖ Club Plage Pereire

Seafood €€

(☎05 57 16 59 13; www.clubplagepereire.com; 12 bd de la Mer; mains €20; 🕙10am-midnight Apr-Oct) Each year this pop-up beach hut on sandy Plage Pereire is built afresh, much to the joy of local foodies and bons vivants who flock here for tasty seafood cuisine, the buzzing beach vibe, impossible romantic drinks on the sand and stunning sunset views. To get here from Jetée Thiers, follow the coast west along bd de la Plage and bd de l'Océan, for 2km. Reservations essential.

Hôtel Villa d'Hiver

Boutique Hotel €€

(☎05 56 66 10 36; www.hotelvilledhiver.com; 20 av Victor Hugo; d from €165; 🕙reception 8am-10pm; 🌡@🛜🏊) In the heart of Arcachon's stylish 1860s Ville d'Hiver district, this 12-room boutique hotel seduces with a trio of garden-clad houses a 10-minute walk from the train station. Pricier, balcony-clad rooms on the 1st floor can glimpse the sea and the hotel's pop-up Club Plage Pereire is one of the hottest addresses in town.

Gourmet Dordogne

34

The Dordogne is definitely a place that thinks with its stomach. On this foodie tour you'll indulge in the region's gastronomic goodies, from walnuts and truffles to fine wine and foie gras.

TRIP HIGHLIGHTS

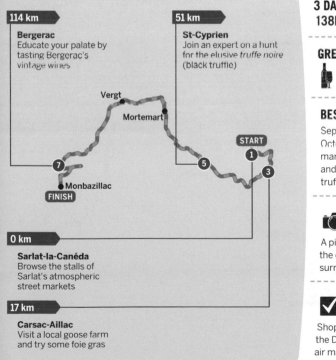

114 km

Bergerac
Educate your palate by tasting Bergerac's vintage wines

51 km

St-Cyprien
Join an expert on a hunt for the elusive *truffe noire* (black truffle)

Vergt

Mortemart

START

7

5

1

3

Monbazillac
FINISH

0 km

Sarlat-la-Canéda
Browse the stalls of Sarlat's atmospheric street markets

17 km

Carsac-Aillac
Visit a local goose farm and try some foie gras

3 DAYS
138KM / 85 MILES

GREAT FOR...

BEST TIME TO GO

September and October for harvest markets; December and February for truffle season.

ESSENTIAL PHOTO

A picnic among the endless vines surrounding Bergerac.

BEST FOR FOODIES

Shop till you drop at the Dordogne's open-air markets.

34 Gourmet Dordogne

If you enjoy nothing better than soaking up the sights, sounds and smells of a French market, you'll be in seventh heaven in the Dordogne. This region is famous for its foodie traditions, and immersing yourself in its culinary culture is one of the best — and tastiest — ways to experience life in rural France.

TRIP HIGHLIGHT

❶ Sarlat-la-Canéda

Start in the honey-stoned town of Sarlat-la-Canéda, which hosts a busy **outdoor market** on Saturday mornings. Local farmers set up their stalls on the cobbled place de la Liberté, selling seasonal treats such as cèpe mushrooms, duck terrines, foie gras, walnuts and even *truffes noires* (black truffles). There's also an atmospheric **night market** (🕐6-10pm) on Thursdays from mid-June to September, and **truffle markets**

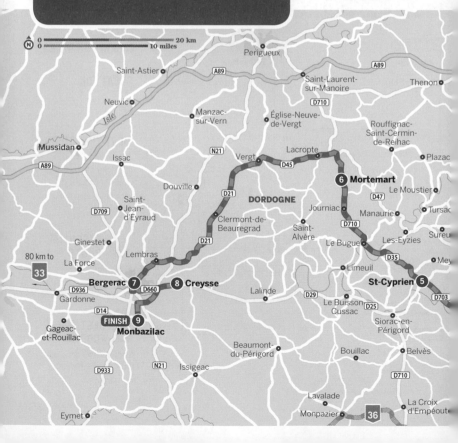

(🕑 mornings from 9am Sat Dec-Feb) **from December to February.**

Even if you're not here on market day, you can shop for foodie souvenirs at Sarlat's **covered market** (🕑8.30am-2pm daily mid-Apr– mid-Nov, closed Mon, Thu & Sun rest of year), **housed in the converted Église Ste-Marie** (place de la Liberté). While you're here, don't miss a trip up the tower in the **panoramic lift**, overlooking Sarlat's slate rooftops.

✕ 🛏 p375

The Drive » Travel 9km east of Sarlat on the D47 towards the village of Ste-Nathalène. You'll pass walnut groves and wooded copses lining the roadsides. The Moulin de la Tour is on a back road north of the village, signed to Proissans, Salignac and St-Crépin-et-Carlucet; you'll see the sign after another 1.5km.

- - - - - - - - - - -

❷ Ste-Nathalène

One of the Dordogne's most distinctive flavours is the humble *noix* (walnut). It's been a prized product of the Dordogne for centuries, and is still used in many local recipes – cakes, puddings, pancakes and breads, as well as liqueurs and *huile de noix* (walnut oil). At the **Moulin de la Tour** (🎧05 53 59 22 08; www.moulindelatour.com, Ste-Nathalene; 🕑9.30am-noon & 2-6.30pm Mon, Wed & Fri, 2-6.30pm Sat Apr-Sep, Wed & Fri only rest of year), **the region's last working watermill,** you can watch walnut oil being made and stock up with nutty souvenirs. Don't miss the *cerneaux*

de noix au chocolat (chocolate-covered walnuts) and *gâteau de noix* (walnut cake).

The Drive » Backtrack to the junction in Ste-Nathalène, turn left and follow road signs to St-Vincent-Le-Paluel/D704. Continue along this minor road until you reach the D704A. Cross straight over and follow white signs to Le Bouyssou. It's a drive of 8km or 15 minutes.

- - - - - - - - - - -

TRIP HIGHLIGHT

❸ Carsac-Aillac

Alongside black truffles, the Dordogne is famous for its foie gras (fattened goose liver). As you drive around, you'll see duck and goose farms dotted all over the countryside, many of which offer guided tours and *dégustation* (tasting).

L'Elevage du Bouyssou (🎧05 53 31 12 31, www.elevagedubouyssou. com; Le Bouyssou, Carsac Aillac; 🕑 shop 8am-6pm, tours 6.30pm daily Jul & Aug, Mon-Sat rest of year) is a family-run farm to the north of Carsac-Aillac. If it's your

---

🔗 LINK YOUR TRIP

33 **Heritage Wine Country**

The hallowed vineyards of Bordeaux lie 96km to the west of Bergerac along the D936.

36 **Dordogne's Fortified Villages**

Most of the region's best *bastides* (fortified towns) lie to the south of the Dordogne River. Head south from La Roque Gageac for 6km to begin in Domme.

kind of thing, owners Denis and Nathalie Mazet run tours and demonstrate *la gavage* – the controversial force-feeding process that helps fatten up the goose livers. You can also buy homemade foie gras in the shop.

The Drive » Travel south from Carsac-Aillac and turn left onto the D703 for 13km towards La Roque Gageac. You'll have lovely views across the river, and the banks are lined with medieval villages dangling over the water. Stop for photos at the Cingle de Montfort viewpoint, which overlooks a picturesque bend backed by a medieval château.

- - - - - - - - - - - -

❹ La Roque Gageac

The lovely D703 tracks the course of the Dordogne River and passes through a string of lovely riverside villages, including La Roque Gageac.

If you feel like burning off some of the calories acquired on this trip, the village is an ideal place to do it: several companies hire out kayaks and canoes for exploring the river, including **Canoë Vacances** (📞05 53 28 17 07; www.canoe vacances.com; Lespinasse; self-guided canoeing per person €14-22) and **Canoë Dordogne** (📞05 53 29 58 50; www. canoesdordogne.fr; self-guided canoeing per person €7-24). Or cruise on a flat-bottomed *gabarre* with **Gabarres Norbert** (📞05 53 29 40 44; www.gabarres.com; 1hr trip adult/child €9/7; ⏰Apr-Oct).

 p375

CHARLIEPHOTOX / GETTY IMAGES ©

The Drive » From La Roque Gageac, St-Cyprien is 15km further west along the river. It's a gorgeous drive that passes several medieval châteaux en route. Once you reach St-Cyprien, continue north on the D49 for another 6.5km, and look out for the easy-to-miss right turn to Lussac/Péchalifour.

- - - - - - - - - - - -

TRIP HIGHLIGHT

❺ St-Cyprien

In the village of St-Cyprien you can indulge in another of the Dordogne's great gastronomic gems – the *perle noire* of the Périgord, otherwise known as the black truffle. At **Truffière de Péchalifour** (📞05 53 29 20 44; www.truffe-perigord.com; tours adult €8-10, child free-€5; ⏰tours 10.45am Wed-Sat Jul & Aug, by reservation rest of year), expert Édouard Aynaud offers hour-long truffle-hunting trips (11am Tuesday to Saturday July and August) assisted by his keen-nosed hounds. The best time to visit is during truffle season from December to March, when he runs half-/full-day trips around the *truffières* (truffle-growing areas) that include a chance to try the rarefied fungi over a picnic lunch.

If you have time, stop at the nearby **Domaine de la Voile Blanche** (📞05

Dordogne Dog hunting for truffles

53 29 20 36; www.domaine-voie-blanche.com; St-Cyprien; ⊙1-7pm Jul & Aug, by reservation rest of year), where the Dalbavie family run tours around their vineyard.

The Drive 》 From Lussac, backtrack to the D35 and turn northwest towards the bustling town of Le Bugue, following signs to Périgueux onto the D710. From Le Bugue it's about 13km to Mortemart; there's a sign to the boar farm just before the village.

- - - - - - - - - - - - -

❻ Mortemart

Next up is **Les Sangliers de Mortemart** (☎05 53 03 21 30; www.elevage-sangliers-mortemart.com; St-Felix-de-Reilhac; adult/child €3/1.50;

⊙10am-7pm Jul & Aug, 1-5pm Sep-Jun), where you can see wild boars being raised in semi-freedom on a farm just outside Mortemart. These porky cousins of the modern pig were once common across France, but their numbers have been reduced by habitat restriction and hunting.

The boars are fed a rich diet of *châtaignes* (chestnuts), which gives the meat a distinctive nutty, gamey flavour. It's a key ingredient in the hearty stew known as *civet de sanglier*, as well as pâtés and country terrines. Naturally enough, there's

a farm shop where you can buy boar-themed goodies.

The Drive 》 From Mortemart, the nicest drive to Bergerac follows the D45 and D21, a drive of 53km through classic Dordogne countryside. Once you reach town, leave your car in the car park on quai Salvette, and walk towards the centre along rue des Récollets.

- - - - - - - - - - - - -

TRIP HIGHLIGHT

❼ Bergerac

It's not as famous as Bordeaux and St-Émilion, but Bergerac is still an essential stop for wine-lovers. Vineyards carpet the countryside around town, producing rich reds,

TRUFFLE SECRETS

Few ingredients command the same culinary cachet as the *truffe noire* (black truffle), variously known as the *diamant noir* (black diamond) or, hereabouts, the *perle noire du Périgord* (black pearl of the Périgord). The gem references aren't just for show, either: a high-end truffle crop can fetch as much as €1000 per kg at seasonal markets.

A subterranean fungus that grows naturally in chalky soils (especially around the roots of oak trees), this mysterious mushroom is notoriously capricious; a good truffle spot one year can be bare the next, which has made farming them practically impossible.

The art of truffle-hunting is a closely guarded secret; it's a matter of luck, judgement and experience, with specially trained dogs (and occasionally pigs) to help in the search.

The height of truffle season is between December and March, when special truffle markets are held around the Dordogne, including in Périgueux and Sarlat.

fragrant whites and fruity rosés – but with 13 AOCs (Appéllations d'Origines Contrôlées), and more than 1200 wine-growers, the choice is bewildering.

Thankfully, the town's **Maison des Vins** (📞05 53 63 57 55; www.vins-bergerac.fr; Cloître des Récollets; ⊗10am-12.30pm & 2-7pm Tue-Sat, daily Jul & Aug, closed Jan) **knows** all the best vintages, offers wine-tasting courses and organises vineyard visits. You could spend at least another couple of days touring the local vineyards, using Bergerac as a base.

✕ ⌂ p375

The Drive ⟫ Creysse is 8km east of Bergerac along the D660.

– – – – – – – – – – – –

⑧ Creysse

Many Bergerac vineyards are open to the public, including the prestigious **Château de Tiregand** (📞05 53 23 21 08; www. chateau-de-tiregand.com; tours adult/child €3/2; ⊗10am-6.30pm Jul & Aug, shorter hours rest of year), which is mainly known for its Pécharmant wines; it runs tours and tasting sessions in its cellars. English tours run at 2.30pm from June to August.

The Drive ⟫ South of Bergerac, you'll really start to get out into wine country, with vineyards and châteaux lining the roadsides. Monbazillac is 8km south of Bergerac on the D13. Take the D936E around the southern edge of Bergerac, and look out for the left turn onto the D13.

– – – – – – – – – – – –

⑨ Monbazillac

Driving round among the rows of vines south of Bergerac is a pleasure in itself, especially if you indulge in a bit of *dégustation*. **Château de Monbazillac** (📞05 53 63 65 00; www.chateau-monbazillac. com; château adult/child €7.50/3.75; ⊗10am-noon & 2-5pm Jun-Sep, shorter hours rest of year, closed Dec & Jan) is often crowded because of its grand 16th-century château (best seen from outside). This vineyard specialises in sweet white Monbazillac AOC, as does nearby family-run **Château Montdoyen** (📞05 53 58 85 85; www. chateau-montdoyen.com; Le Puch; ⊗9.30am-1pm & 2-7pm). Montdoyen also makes excellent Bergerac AOC reds, whites with intriguing names like Divine Miséricorde (sauvignon blanc and sauvignon gris), and a delicious rosé.

Eating & Sleeping

Sarlat-la-Canéda ❶

✘ Le Petit Manoir — Regional Cuisine €€

(☎05 53 29 82 14; 13 rue de la République; mains €20; ⏰12.40-2pm & 7-9pm Tue-Sun; 🛜🍴) Book ahead for a seat in the ornate 15th-century mansion where the cuisine combines creative Dordogne specialities with a touch of Asian fusion. The Vietnamese chef creates a menu that changes with the seasons, and there are always vegetarian options (menu €27).

✘ Le Grand Bleu — Gastronomy €€€

(☎05 53 31 08 48; www.legrandbleu.eu; 43 av de la Gare; menus lunch €36, dinner €54-125; ⏰12.30-2pm Thu-Sun, 7.30-9.30pm Tue-Sat) This eminent Michelin-starred restaurant run by chef Maxime Lebrun is renowned for its creative cuisine with elaborate menus making maximum use of luxury produce: truffles, lobster, turbot and scallops, with a wine list to match. Cooking courses (€40) are also available. Located 1.5km south of the centre.

🛏 La Maison des Peyrat — Hotel €€

(☎05 53 59 00 32; www.maisondespeyrat.com; Le Lac de la Plane; r €70-112) This beautifully renovated 17th-century house, formerly a nuns' hospital and later an aristocratic hunting lodge, is set on a hill about 1.5km from Sarlat centre. Eleven generously sized rooms are decorated in modern farmhouse style; the best have views over gardens and the countryside beyond. Good restaurant, too.

🛏 Villa des Consuls — B&B €€

(☎05 53 31 90 05; www.villaconsuls.fr; 3 rue Jean-Jacques Rousseau; d €95-110, apt €150-190; @🛜) Despite its Renaissance exterior, the enormous rooms here are modern through and through, with shiny wood floors and sleek furnishings. Several delightful self-contained apartments dot the town, all offering the same mix of period plushness – some also have terraces overlooking the town's rooftops.

La Roque Gageac ❹

✘ La Belle Étoile Restaurant — Traditional French €€

(www.belleetoile.fr; menus from €32; ⏰noon-1.30pm Tue & Thu-Sun, 7.30-9.30pm Tue-Sun) This restaurant in a riverside hotel has the best position in La Roque, lodged in a solid stone building with river vistas. It is renowned for its sophisticated French food, and opens onto a vine-shaded terrace with a fabulous view.

Bergerac ❼

✘ Villa Laetitia — Regional Cuisine €€

(☎05 53 61 00 12; laetitiajustino@hotmail.com; 21 rue de l'Ancien Port; menus lunch €17-22, dinner €25-38; ⏰noon-2pm Tue-Sun, 7-9pm Tue-Sat) Book ahead for a seat with in-the-know locals in the soft, cream-stone dining room where charming waitstaff serve delicious local cuisine, made in the open kitchen at the rear. Expect farm-fresh ingredients and delicious Périgord classics exquisitely presented.

🛏 Château les Merles — Boutique Hotel €€€

(☎05 53 63 13 42; www.lesmerles.com; Tuilières, Mouleydier; d €190-210, ste €250, apt €350; @🛜🏊) Behind its 19th-century neoclassical facade, this château 15km east of Bergerac is a study in modish minimalism. Monochrome colour schemes including black-and-white sofas and artfully chosen antiques run throughout the rooms, most of which would look more at home in Paris than deep in the Dordogne. From the nine-hole golf course to the ravishing fusion **restaurant** (lunch/dinner menus from €20/30), it's a royal retreat.

Cave Art of the Vézère Valley

35

The limestone caves of southwest France contain some of Europe's finest examples of prehistoric art. This tailored trip explores the most famous ones, including the frescos of the Grotte de Lascaux.

TRIP HIGHLIGHTS

50 km

Le Thot
Get up close to some of the wildlife depicted by prehistoric painters

Rouffignac-Saint-Cermin-de-Reihac

Plazac

6 **7** FINISH

55 km

Grotte de Lascaux
Marvel at the modern-day replica of France's finest ancient artwork

1 **2**

START

Les-Eyzies-de-Tayac
Explore a treasure trove of prehistoric artefacts

Grotte de Font de Gaume
A multicoloured menagerie of animals adorns this impressive cave

0 km

2 km

3 DAYS
55KM / 34 MILES

GREAT FOR...

BEST TIME TO GO
April to June, when most caves are open, but the summer crowds haven't arrived.

ESSENTIAL PHOTO
The minimalist façade of the Musée National de Préhistoire.

BEST FOR FAMILIES
The prehistoric zoo at Le Thot, to see bison, reindeer and ibex.

35 Cave Art of the Vézère Valley

This trip feels like opening a time capsule into the prehistoric past. Hidden deep underground in the murky caves of the Vézère and Lot Valleys, a spectacular legacy of ancient artworks, ranging from rock sculptures to multicoloured murals, was left behind by Cro-Magnon people – and this is one of the few places in the world where it's possible to see their work up close.

TRIP HIGHLIGHT

❶ Les-Eyzies-de-Tayac

This small one-street tourist town is right in the middle of the Vézère Valley, 20km northwest of Sarlat-la-Canéda. Most of the area's major caves are within half-an-hour's drive, so it makes a useful base for exploring, and for a quick primer on prehistoric art there's nowhere better than the **Musée National de Préhistoire** (☏ 05 53 06 45 65; www.musee-prehistoire-

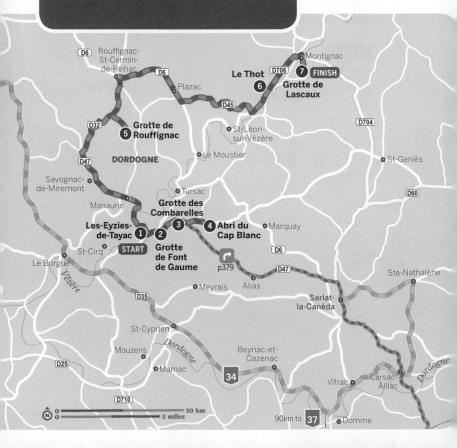

eyzies.fr; 1 rue du Musée; adult/child €6/4.50, 1st Sun of month free; ⊙9.30am-6.30pm daily Jul & Aug, 9.30am-6pm Wed-Mon Jun & Sep, 9.30am-12.30pm & 2-5.30pm Wed-Mon Oct-May), home to France's most comprehensive collection of prehistoric artefacts. Inside you'll find lots of fascinating Stone Age tools, weapons and jewellery, as well as animal skeletons and original rock friezes taken from the caves themselves: look out for the famous one of a bison licking its flank. Panels are mostly in French, but explanatory sheets in English are available.

✕ 🍴 p383

The Drive » To get to Font de Gaume from Les-Eyzies, follow the D47 east towards Sarlat, and look out for the brown signs pointing to Font de Gaume.

LINK YOUR TRIP

34 Gourmet Dordogne

It's easy to combine this trip with our gourmet guide to the Dordogne – take the D47 to Sarlat-la Canéda.

37 The Lot Valley

From Cabrerets, you'll be roughly halfway along our Lot Valley route, 3km west of St-Cirq-Lapopie and 32km east of Cahors.

DETOUR: GROTTE DE PECH MERLE

Start: ❶ Les-Eyzies-de-Tayac

To complete your cave tour, it's worth taking the longish 92km trip southeast to the **Grotte de Pech Merle** (📞05 65 31 27 05; www.pechmerle.com; adult/child €11/7; ⊙9.30-noon & 1.30-5pm Apr-Oct, greatly reduced rest of year), one of only a handful of decorated caves to be discovered around the Lot Valley. It contains galleries of mammoths, goats and bison, as well as a famous panel featuring two dappled horses. Most haunting of all, the cave's walls are covered with human hand tracings, as well as a set of footprints, left behind by an adolescent artist between 15,000 BC and 10,000 BC.

Guided tours are in French, but explanatory sheets in English are available. Reserve ahead, as visitor numbers are limited to 700 per day.

- - - - - - - - - - - -

TRIP HIGHLIGHT

❷ Grotte de Font de Gaume

Now you've got the background, it's time to see some real cave art. Just 1km northeast of Les-Eyzies is **Font de Gaume** (📞05 53 06 86 00; www.eyzies.monuments-nationaux.fr; 4 av des Grottes; adult/child €7.50/free; ⊙guided tours 9.30am-5.30pm Sun-Fri mid-May–mid-Sep, 9.30am-12.30pm & 2-5.30pm Sun-Fri mid-Sep–mid-May), an underground cavern that contains the only multicoloured paintings still open to the public. Around 14,000 years ago, the prehistoric artists created a gallery of more than 230 animals, including reindeer, horses, mammoths and bears, as well as a dramatic

'Chapelle des Bisons' (Bison Chapel). Reservations are essential, with only 78 people allowed in per day. The 8-person 45-minute tours are usually in French, but English tours are offered in summer.

The Drive » Continue along the D47 for 1km from Font de Gaume and turn off at the brown sign for the Grotte de Combarelles.

- - - - - - - - - - - -

❸ Grotte des Combarelles

Prehistoric artists weren't just skilful painters – they also knew how to sculpt. About 1.5km further east of Font de Gaume, this narrow **cave** (📞05 53 06 86 00; www.eyzies.monuments-nationaux.fr; adult/child €7.50/free; ⊙guided tours 9.30am-5.30pm Sun-Fri

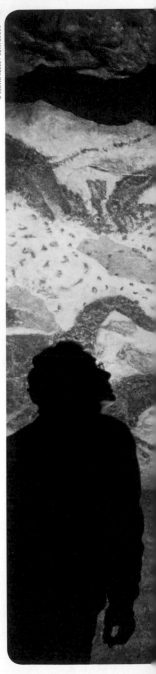

mid-May–mid-Sep, 9.30am-12.30pm & 2-5.30pm Sun-Fri mid-Sep–mid-May) contains many engravings that cleverly use the natural contours of the rock to sculpt the animals' forms: look out for mammoths, horses, reindeer and a mountain lion that seems to leap out from the rock face. The cave's walls are also covered with geometric symbols and shapes that have so far eluded interpretation. Six- to eight-person group tours last about an hour and can be reserved through the Font de Gaume ticket office.

The Drive » Travel 1km further east of Combarelles, then turn left onto the twisty D48. You'll travel into a pleasant wooded valley. Continue for 7km, following the road up the hillside towards the Cap Blanc car park. The museum entrance is a short walk downhill along a rough track.

❹ Abri du Cap Blanc

This ancient **sculpture gallery** (☎05 53 06 86 00; www.eyzies.monuments-natio naux.fr; adult/child €7.50/free; ☉ guided tours 10am-6pm Sun-Fri mid-May–mid-Sep, 10am-12.30pm & 2-5.30pm Sun-Fri mid-Sep–mid-May) makes a fascinating comparison with Combarelles. It was used as a natural shelter 14,000 years ago by Cro-Magnon people, who left behind an amazing 40m-long frieze of horses and bison, carved directly

into the rear wall of the overhang using flint tools. Originally the cave would have been open to the elements, but it's now housed inside a modern museum.

The Drive » Backtrack to Les-Eyzies, then follow the D47 northwest along the valley, turning right onto the D32 after about 11km. The road becomes narrower and travels through woodland. Follow the signs to the 'Grotte Préhistorique de Rouffignac' for another 7km.

❺ Grotte de Rouffignac

After staying overnight in Les-Eyzies, get an early start at the astonishing **Grotte de Rouffignac** (☎05 53 05 41 71; www.grotte derouffignac.fr; Rouffignac-St-Cernin-de-Reilhac; adult/child €7.50/4.80; ☉9-11.30am & 2-6pm Jul & Aug, 10-11.30am & 2-5pm Apr-Jun, Sep & Oct, closed Nov-Mar), often known as the 'Cave of 1000 Mammoths' thanks to its plethora of painted pachyderms. The paintings are spread along the walls of a subterranean cavern that stretches for 10km – fortunately, you visit aboard a rickety electric train, so there's no chance of getting lost. Along the way is an amazing frieze of 10 mammoths in procession. You'll also see many hollows in the cave floor, scratched out by long-extinct cave bears. Tickets are sold at the cave entrance; wrap up

Grotte de Lascaux France's most famous prehistoric paintings

PREHISTORY 101

If you're visiting the cave paintings around the Vézère, it helps to know a little about the artists who created them. Most of the paintings date from the end of the last ice age, between 20,000 BC and 10,000 BC, and were painted by Cro-Magnon people – descendants of the first *Homo erectus* settlers who arrived from North Africa between 700,000 BC and 100,000 BC.

Cro-Magnon people lived a hunter-gatherer lifestyle, using the mouths of caves as temporary hunting shelters (not the deep interiors, where you often find the art) while they followed their prey, including mammoths, woolly rhinoceros, reindeer and aurochs, an ancestor of the modern cow.

Generally, they painted geometric forms, the occasional stylised human form, and the animals they hunted using mineral paints derived from magnesium and charcoal (black), ochre (red/yellow) and iron (red). Although no one is certain what the purpose of the paintings was, it's assumed they held some kind of magical, religious or shamanic significance.

Painting seems to have ceased around 10,000 BC, about the same time that humans settled down to a more fixed lifestyle of farming and agriculture.

warm, as it's chilly below ground.

The Drive >> From the Grotte de Rouffignac, retrace your route to the D32, and follow signs to Montignac, making turns onto the D6 and D45. Northeast of Thonac, turn left onto the D706 and look out for the sign to Le Thot shortly afterwards.

- - - - - - - - - -

TRIP HIGHLIGHT

❻ Le Thot

It's well worth visiting **Le Thot** (☎05 53 50 70 44; www.semitour.com; Thonac; adult/child €9/5.90, joint ticket with Lascaux II €14.50/9.80; ◷10am-7pm Jul & Aug, to 6pm Apr-Jun, Sep & Oct, shorter hours rest of year), where you can see some of the real-life beasts depicted by prehistoric artists – including reindeer, stags, horses, ibex and

European bison. Sadly, though, you'll have to put up with fibreglass models of extinct species such as woolly mammoths.

The Drive >> Turn back onto the D706 and head towards Montignac, about 7km northeast, where there are dining and accomodation options (see p383). Once you reach town, cross the bridge and follow av du 4 Septembre, then look out for brown signs to the Grotte de Lascaux, perched on a hilltop 1km south of town.

- - - - - - - - - -

TRIP HIGHLIGHT

❼ Grotte de Lascaux

Sometimes known as the Sistine Chapel of cave art, the **Grotte de Lascaux** (☎05 53 51 95 03; www.semi tour.com; Montignac; adult/child €9.90/6.40, combined ticket with Le Thot €13.50/9.40; ◷guided tours 9am-7pm Jul &

Aug, 9.30am-6pm Apr-Jun, Sep & Oct, 10am-12.30pm & 2-5pm Nov-Mar, closed Jan) is home to France's most famous – and finest – prehistoric paintings.

The 600-strong menagerie is vividly depicted in shades of red, black, yellow and brown, ranging from reindeer, aurochs, mammoths and horses to a huge 5.5m-long bull, the largest cave drawing ever found.

The original cave has been closed to the public since 1963, but a painstakingly precise replica has been created nearby. There are several guided tours every hour, including some in English. From April to September, tickets are sold *only* at the ticket office next to Montignac's tourist office.

Eating & Sleeping

Les-Eyzies-de-Tayac ❶

✖ Moulin de la Beaune
Regional Cuisine €€

(Au Vieux Moulin; ☎05 53 06 94 33; www.
moulindelabeune.com; menus €21-58; ⊗mid-
Apr–Oct) Reserve ahead for a spot at one of
the river-front terrace tables at this renovated
water mill converted into a lovely restaurant and
hotel (doubles €70 to €80). The most charming
family-run establishment in Les-Eyzies, it's also
the most beautifully situated, and serves up
authentic, seasonal local fare.

🛏 Hôtel des Glycines
Hotel €€

(☎05 53 06 97 07; www.les-glycines-dordogne.
com; 4 av de Laugerie; d €144-199, ste €270-345;
⊗Jan–mid-Nov; ❄ 🤶 ⛱) Les-Eyzies' top posh
pad: plush rooms range from cream-and-check
'classics' to full-blown suites with terraces and
garden views. Beware 'courtyard rooms' which
overlook the main road. The hotel's gastronomic
restaurant (lunch *menus* €19, dinner *menus*
€62 to €110) is a pampering affair.

🛏 Hôtel des Roches
Hotel €

(☎05 53 06 96 59; www.roches-les-eyzies.com;
15 av de la Forge; d/tr €90/140; ⊗mid-Apr–mid
Oct; 🤶⛱) This smart pale stone hotel set
back from the main road is decorated in simple
pastoral style. Rear rooms overlook the garden
and swimming pool.

🛏 Hôtel Le Cro-Magnon
Hotel €

(☎05 53 06 97 06; www.hostellerie-cro-
magnon.com; 54 av de la Préhistoire; d €85-100;
⊗Mar-Nov; 🤶⛱) This pretty wisteria-clad
hotel has been around since the 1850s and
was often used as a base by pioneering
prehistorians. Flowery rooms are a touch bland,
but corridors built straight into the rock face

add quirky appeal. Dining is good value in the
lovely beam-ceilinged restaurant.

Montignac ❻

✖ La Chaumière
Regional Cuisine €

(☎05 53 50 14 24; 53 rue du 4 Septembre;
menu €18.90; ⊗noon-2pm Sun-Tue & Thu-Fri,
7.30-9.30pm Wed-Mon) A simple menu of
charcuterie, cut by the friendly proprietor at the
back of the small dining room, or large portions
of duck confit, cassoulet and duck-fat roasted
potatoes are the order of the day.

✖ Le Tourny
Cafe €

(☎05 53 51 59 95; place Tourny; lunch/dinner
menus €13.50/17; ⊗noon-2pm daily, 7-9.30pm
Mon-Sat) Locals flock here for cheap, no-frills
daily specials and omelettes or snacks.

🛏 Hotel Le Lascaux
Hotel €

(☎05 53 51 82 81; http://hotel-lascaux.jimdo.
com; 109 av Jean-Jaurès; d €73-95; ⊗Apr-Sep;
🤶) Despite the old-timey candy-stripe awnings,
rooms at this family-owned hotel are bang up
to date, with cool colour schemes, distressed
wood furniture and sparkling bathrooms.
Superior rooms have more space, and some
overlook the shady back garden.

🛏 Hostellerie La Roseraie
Hotel €€

(☎05 53 50 53 92; www.laroseraie-hotel.com;
11 place des Armes; d €80-164, ste/q from
€200/220; ⊗Apr-Oct; 🤶⛱) This mansion
in Montignac boasts its own gorgeous rose
garden, set around a palm-fringed pool. Rococo
rooms are lovely if you like rosy pinks, floral
patterns and garden views. Truffles, chestnuts,
pork and guinea fowl find their way onto the
seasonal menu in the restaurant, and on warm
summer nights the terrace is a delight.

Dordogne's Fortified Villages

36

The Dordogne spoils for choice with its hilltop history. This trip links some of the region's distinctive bastides (fortified villages) and medieval castles, and takes in holy Rocamadour.

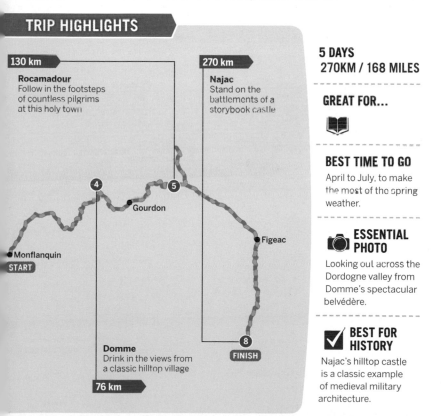

130 km

Rocamadour
Follow in the footsteps of countless pilgrims at this holy town

270 km

Najac
Stand on the battlements of a storybook castle

4

Gourdon

5

Figeac

Monflanquin
START

Domme
Drink in the views from a classic hilltop village

76 km

8
FINISH

5 DAYS
270KM / 168 MILES

GREAT FOR...

BEST TIME TO GO

April to July, to make the most of the spring weather.

ESSENTIAL PHOTO

Looking out across the Dordogne valley from Domme's spectacular belvédère.

BEST FOR HISTORY

Najac's hilltop castle is a classic example of medieval military architecture.

amadour Stone paths lead up to the 14th-century château

385

36

Dordogne's Fortified Villages

The Dordogne may be a picture of tranquillity now, but during the Middle Ages it was frequently a battleground. The Dordogne River marked an important strategic frontier between English and French forces during the Hundred Years War, and the area's many châteaux and fortified villages remain as a reminder of this war-torn past. Most distinctive of all are the *bastide* towns, encircled by defensive walls and protected by sturdy ramparts.

❶ Monflanquin

Founded in 1256, this small *bastide* makes an excellent place to start your tour of France's defensive architecture. It has the classic *bastide* structure: a rectangular layout, a grid of straight streets, and an arcaded market square, with a church tucked into one corner. Originally the town would have also been ringed by ramparts, but these have long since been plundered. The central place des Arcades still hosts its weekly market

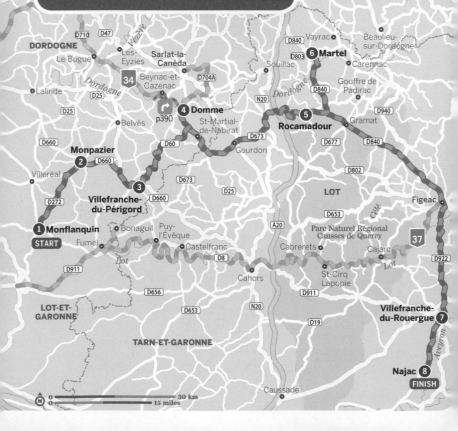

on Thursday morning, just as it has done since the Middle Ages.

The Drive » The quickest route to Monpazier heads 22km northwest across quiet farmland, following the minor D272. You'll pass into woodland near Vergt-de-Biron, and then turn right onto the D2 towards Monpazier.

② Monpazier

Monpazier is perhaps the best example of *bastide* architecture in southwest France. It's crisscrossed by arrow-straight streets, all of which lead to the market square on **place Centrale**, lined by arcaded walkways and tall houses built from lemon-yellow stone. In one corner, there's an old *lavoir* (wash house) that was still being used for washing clothes right up to the end of the 19th century.

LINK YOUR TRIP

34 **Gourmet Dordogne**

Head north from Domme for 14km along the D46 to link up with our gastronomic road trip around the Dordogne.

37 **The Lot Valley**

This trip combines well with our route along the Lot Valley – just turn off at Figeac.

The town itself was founded in 1284 by a representative of Edward I (king of England and duke of Aquitaine). It had a turbulent time during the Wars of Religion and the Peasant Revolts of the 16th century, but despite numerous assaults it survived the centuries remarkably unscathed. Most unusually of all, its defensive walls are still largely intact.

The Drive » Take the D660 east from Monpazier, and follow it for 21km through the countryside.

③ Villefranche-du-Périgord

The amber town of Ville-franche-du-Périgord once occupied an important strategic position on the frontier between the historic regions of Agen and Quercy. It was founded in 1261 by Alphonse de Poitiers, a brother of the French king Louis IX, and still possesses most of its medieval layout, including the original arcaded square, pillared marketplace and fortified church, all of which date from the 13th century. It's a bit off the beaten track and a touch neglected in spots, which means its often much quieter than some of the area's better-known *bastides*.

The Drive » The drive to Domme is particularly pleasant, veering across hilltops and passing through oak and beech

woodland. Start on the minor D57 towards Besse, turning onto the D60 at St-Pompont, followed by the D46 to Domme – it's just over 33km in all, or 40 minutes. Parking is tricky in the village, so leave your car outside the walls and walk up.

TRIP HIGHLIGHT

④ Domme

For panoramic views, there's nowhere in the Dordogne that can top Domme. Teetering on an outcrop high above the river valley, this hilltop *bastide* still boasts most of its 13th-century ramparts as well as three original fortified gateways.

Approached via a tortuous switchback road from the valley below, it's the perfect defensive stronghold – a fact not lost on Philippe III of France, who founded the town in 1281 as a bastion against the English. The town's clifftop position is best appreciated from the esplanade du Belvédère and the adjacent promenade de la Barre, which both offer an unforgettable outlook across the valley.

✗ ⊨ p391

The Drive » The most pleasant route to Rocamadour travels southeast via the D46 and the towns of St-Martial-de-Nabirat and Gourdon. From here, pick up the twisty D673, which crosses underneath the A20 motorway. Soon afterwards there's a wonderful windy section with fine views across the Ouysse River and the cliffs around Rocamadour. Most of

Rocamadour's car parks are above the old city in L'Hospitalet. All in, the journey covers 54km.

TRIP HIGHLIGHT

⑤ Rocamadour

Clinging precariously to a rocky cliffside, the holy town of Rocamadour looks like something out of *Lord of the Rings*. It's been an important pilgrimage destination since the Middle Ages thanks to the supposedly miraculous powers of its Vierge Noire (Black Madonna), which is now housed in the Chapelle de Notre Dame, one of several chapels that make up the town's **Sanctuaires** (Sanctuaries).

The old town itself (known as La Cité) consists of one long medieval thoroughfare, overflowing (just as in the pilgrims' day) with souvenir shops and touristy restaurants. One of the medieval gateways is still standing at the end of the Grande Rue.

From here, a stone staircase leads to the Sanctuaries, and a Stations of the Cross path switchbacks up the cliff emerging next to Rocamadour's 14th-century **château** (€2; ⊙8am-8pm). During the Middle Ages, pilgrims would have climbed the steps on their knees as a demonstration of piety, but these days you can cheat by catching a lift and then a cable car.

The Drive ≫ From the town's main car parks in L'Hospitalet, head north along the D673 and follow the signs to Martel, 22km away.

---

⑥ Martel

Known as *la ville aux sept tours* (the town of seven towers) thanks to its turret-topped skyline, this delightful village was the ancient capital of the Vicomte de Turenne. It's crammed with fascinating architecture, best seen around the place de la Halle. The **covered market** still boasts many of its medieval roof beams, and one of the town's namesake towers can be seen above the **Palais de la Raymondi** (built for a 13th-century tax collector but now home to the village's tourist office). You'll spot the other towers as you wander round town, including **La Tour Tournemire**, a square tower which once served as a prison, and the **Cordeliers Tower**, the only remains of a 13th-century Franciscan monastery. Try to time your visit with the lively markets on Wednesday and Saturday.

✕ 🍴 p391

The Drive ≫ Spend the night in Martel, then pick up the D840 all the way to Figeac, a historic riverside town that makes a good spot to stop for coffee and cake. From here, continue south on the D922 to Villefranche de Rouergue. Plan on covering the 95km in 1¾ hours.

GUY CHRISTIAN / GETTY IMAGES ©

Martel The covered market

DETOUR: CHÂTEAU DE BEYNAC

Start: ④ Domme

The riverbanks of the Dordogne are lined with medieval châteaux, mostly built as defensive fortresses during the 12th and 13th centuries. One of the most dramatic is the **Château de Beynac** (☎05 53 29 50 40; www.beynac-en-perigord.com; Beynac-et-Cazenac; adult/child €8/3.50; ☀10am-6.30pm May-Aug, to 5pm Jan-Apr, Sep & Oct, closed Nov & Dec), a clifftop castle 10km northwest of La Roque, protected by 200m cliffs, a double wall and double moat. From the battlements, there's a dizzying view over the picture-perfect village of **Beynac-et-Cazenac**, which featured in the Lasse Hallström movie *Chocolat* (2000), starring Johnny Depp and Juliette Binoche.

There are several other châteaux to explore nearby. Situated 4.5km southwest is the **Château de Castelnaud** (www.castelnaud.com/uk; Castelnaud-la-Chapelle; adult/child €9.60/4.80; ☀9am-8pm Jul & Aug, 10am-5pm Feb-Jun, 2-5pm Nov-mid-Jan), another quintessential castle that houses a museum of medieval warfare.

Another 4km further is the **Château de Milandes** (☎05 53 59 31 21; www.milandes. com; Castelnaud-la-Chapelle; adult/child €10/6.50; ☀9.30am-7.30pm Jul & Aug, 10am-6.30pm Apr-Jun & Sep–mid-Nov), which was famously owned by the glamorous American music-hall star Josephine Baker (1906–75), who bought it in 1936.

---

❼ Villefranche de Rouergue

Villefranche's origins as a *bastide* are barely recognisable beneath the modern roads and busy shopping streets – it's only once you get right into the old town that they become apparent. At the centre is the arcaded **place Notre Dame** – another typical example of a *bastide* square. Nearby is the square-pillared 15th-century **Collégiale Notre Dame**, with its never-completed bell tower and choir stalls, ornamented with a menagerie of comical and cheeky figures.

The Drive ❯❯ The D922 continues south toward Najac, 23km south of Villefranche.

TRIP HIGHLIGHT

❽ Najac

If you were searching for a film set for Camelot, you've found it. Najac's soaring hilltop **castle** (☎05 65 29 71 65; adult/child €5.50/4; ☀10.30am-7pm Jul & Aug, 10.30am-1pm & 3-5.30pm Mar-Jun, Sep & Oct) looks as if it's fallen from the pages of a fairy tale: slender towers and fluttering flags rise from the battlements, surrounded on every side by dizzying *falaises* (cliffs) dropping to the Aveyron River far below.

The castle is reached via a steep 1.2km-long cobbled street from **place du Faubourg**, the village's central square. It's a masterpiece of military planning: its clifftop position meant it was practically unassailable, and it became a key stronghold during the Middle Ages. Its architecture is beautifully preserved, and the view from the central keep is simply superb.

🛏 p391

Eating & Sleeping

Domme ❶

✕ Le Petit Paris Regional Cuisine €€

(📞05 53 28 41 10; www.le-petit-paris.fr; Daglan; menus €29-39; ⏰ noon-1.30pm Tue-Sun & 7-8.45pm Tue-Sat late-Feb–mid-Nov) Friendly staff serve you on little Daglan's central square, promoting an elegant 'there's all the time in the world' feel, while wowing with impeccable seasonal local cuisine. Spring brings lovely asparagus, the rest of the year find tender Limousin beef, falling off the bone, or foie gras that melts in your mouth. It's 11km south of Domme.

🛏 La Guérinière B&B €€

(📞05 53 29 91 97; www.la gueriniere-dordogne. com; Cénac et St-Julien; d incl breakfast €105, q €175; 🖥🚲) Surrounded by 6-hectare grounds in the valley 5km south of Domme along the D46, this family-friendly B&B's rooms are all named after flowers: our faves are Mimosa, with its sloping roof and chinoiserie wardrobe, and the supersized Bleuet room. Book ahead for tables d'hôte (set menus; €28 including wine) that use mostly organic produce.

🛏 Château de Maraval Design Hotel €€€

(📞06 06 94 37 61; www.chateaudemaraval. fr; Cénac-et-Saint-Julien; d €195; ⏰Feb-Dec, 🅿❄🖥🚲) Here's your chance to combine historic elegance (a grand château in lush grounds) with contemporary luxury (mod rooms kitted out with design tapestries, sleek furnishings and high-concept bathrooms). This friendly escape just south of Domme in Cénac pampers with high-threadcount linens, spa facilities and an idyllic pool.

Martel ❻

✕ Au Hasard Balthazar Regional Cuisine €€

(📞05 65 37 42 01; www.auhasardbalthazar. fr; rue Tournemire; lunch/dinner menus from €19/28; ⏰ noon-1.30pm Tue-Sun & 7.30-9.30pm Tue-Sat May-Aug, shorter hours Apr & Sep) Local farm Les Bouriettes operates this wonderful shop and restaurant filled with their super products. Friendly proprietors serve regional specialities in the courtyard below the Tour Tournemire, or in the intimate stone dining room. Imagine ingredients like walnut oil, pigeon confit, foie gras and wine mustard.

🛏 Manoir de Malagorse B&B €€

(📞05 65 27 14 83; www.manoir-de-malagorse. fr; Cuzance; d incl breakfast €160-200, ste €290-320; ⏰mid-Mar–mid-Dec, 🖥🚲) In quiet Cuzance, 8km northwest of Martel, this beauty of a B&B offers luxury normally reserved for top-end hotels. Owners Anna and Abel's period house is a chic combo of sleek lines, soothing colours and fluffy fabrics. It's surrounded by 10 private acres, and the four-course home-cooked dinner (€42) is superb. Hosts winter truffle weekends.

Najac ❽

🛏 Oustal del Barry Hotel €

(📞05 65 29 74 32; www.oustaldelbarry.com; place du Faubourg; s €54, d €65-70; ❄🖥) The best hotel in town is this wonderfully worn and rustic auberge, with haphazard rooms filled with trinkets and solid furniture to match its venerable timber-framed facade. Try for a room with a balcony. Visit its renowned country restaurant (menus €22 to €56) for traditional southwest cuisine.

The Lot Valley

37

This scenic drive snakes along a plunging canyon carved out by the Lot River. It's bookended by the riverside towns of Figeac and Villeneuve-sur-Lot, and veers through wine country.

TRIP HIGHLIGHTS

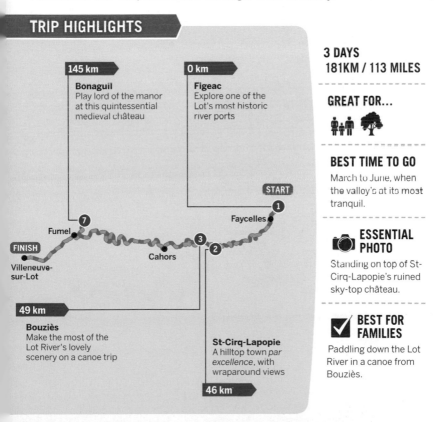

145 km

Bonaguil
Play lord of the manor at this quintessential medieval château

0 km

Figeac
Explore one of the Lot's most historic river ports

START

Faycelles

Fumel

FINISH

Villeneuve-sur-Lot

Cahors

49 km

Bouziès
Make the most of the Lot River's lovely scenery on a canoe trip

St-Cirq-Lapopie
A hilltop town *par excellence*, with wraparound views

46 km

**3 DAYS
181KM / 113 MILES**

GREAT FOR...

BEST TIME TO GO
March to June, when the valley's at its most tranquil.

ESSENTIAL PHOTO
Standing on top of St-Cirq-Lapopie's ruined sky-top château.

BEST FOR FAMILIES
Paddling down the Lot River in a canoe from Bouziès.

Cirq-Lapopie Hilltop village above the Lot River

37 The Lot Valley

For river scenery, the Lot is right up there alongside the Loire and the Seine. Over countless millennia, it's carved its way through the area's soft lemon-yellow limestone, creating a landscape of canyons, ravines and cliffs, best seen on the zigzagging 80km-odd section between Figeac and Cahors. It's a journey to savour: take your time, pack a picnic and soak up the vistas.

TRIP HIGHLIGHT

❶ Figeac

Riverside Figeac has a lived-in charm that is unlike many of the Lot's prettified towns. Traffic buzzes along the river boulevards and the old town has an appealing atmosphere, where shady streets are lined with ramshackle medieval and Renaissance houses, many with open-air galleries on the top floors (once used for drying leather). Founded by Benedictine monks, the town was later an important

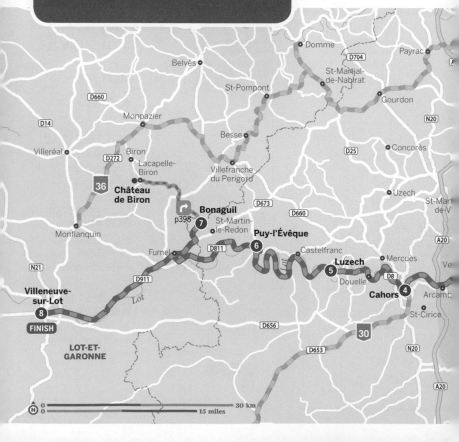

medieval trading post and pilgrims' stopover.

Figeac is also famous as the birthplace of François Champollion (1790–1832), the Egyptologist and linguist whose efforts in deciphering the Rosetta Stone provided the key for cracking Egyptian hieroglyphics. Explore his story at the **Musée Champollion** (☎05 65 50 31 08; www.musee-champollion.fr; place Champollion; adult/child €5/2.50; ⏰10.30am-6.30pm daily Jul & Aug, shorter hours rest of year).

✗ 🛏 p399

The Drive ≫ The corkscrew drive west of Figeac along the D662 is a classic, tracking the course of the Lot River all the way to Cahors. The 46km stretch to St-Cirq-Lapopie is particularly scenic, at some points cut directly into the cliffside, at others snaking along the peaceful riverbanks. Take it slow and enjoy the drive.

- - - - - - - - - - - - -

TRIP HIGHLIGHT

② St-Cirq-Lapopie

This famously photogenic hilltop village teeters at the crest of a sheer cliff, high above the Lot. It's a delightful tangle of red-roofed houses, cobbled streets and medieval buildings, many of which now house potters' and artists' studios. The village is essentially one long, steep main street; at the top is the ruined **château**, which has a magnificent viewing terrace that overlooks the whole Lot Valley. It's a magical setting, but be warned: if it's peace and tranquillity you're looking for, you won't find it in high summer.

There are car parks at the top of the village and at the bottom of the hill.

✗ 🛏 p399

The Drive ≫ Head downhill from St-Cirq-Lapopie, cross the river and rejoin the D662. Bouziès is 4km west.

- - - - - - - - - - - - -

TRIP HIGHLIGHT

③ Bouziès

Just west of St-Cirq, this riverside hamlet is an ideal place to get out on

LINK YOUR TRIP

30 Cheat's Compostela

This route intersects with our road-trip version of the Chemin de St-Jacques at Cahors and Figeac.

36 Dordogne's Fortified Villages

Our *bastides* tour begins at Monflanquin, 20km north of Villeneuve-sur-Lot.

the water – either on a boat cruise or under your own steam. **Les Croisères de St-Cirq-Lapopie** (☑05 65 31 72 25; www.croisieres-saint-cirq-lapopie.com; 1hr tours adult/child €11/8) runs regular river cruises on its small fleet of boats, including aboard an open-topped *gabarre,* a flat-bottomed barge that was once the traditional mode of river transport in this region of France.

Alternatively, if you prefer to be your own captain, **Kalapca** (☑05 65 24 21 01; www.kalapca.com/uk; half-/full day €30/45; ☻Apr-Sep) rents kayaks and canoes, perfect for experiencing

the gorgeous river scenery at your own pace. Trip lengths range from 4km to 22km; rates include minibus transport to your chosen starting-point.

The Drive >> The twisty route west to Cahors is another fine drive, travelling for 28km along the gorge and affording dramatic views nearly all the way. There are plenty of pleasant places to stop for a picnic by the river. Once you reach Cahors, follow signs to the 'Centre-Ville'. Parking is free along the river and on place Charles de Gaulle.

- - - - - - - - - - - -

❹ Cahors

Nestled in a U-shaped *boucle* (curve) in the Lot, Cahors is the area's

main city. With its balmy weather and scarlet-stone buildings, it has the air of a sunbaked Mediterranean town. Pastel-coloured buildings line the shady squares of the old medieval quarter, crisscrossed by a labyrinth of alleyways, cul-de-sacs and medieval quays. It's also an important winegrowing area, with vineyards stretching out across the surrounding hills.

The town's main landmark is the impressive **Pont Valentré**, one of France's most iconic medieval bridges. Built as part of the town's defenc-

Figeac Inside the Musée Champollion

es in the 14th century, the parapets projecting from two of its three tall towers were designed to allow defenders to drop missiles on attackers below. It's also worth stepping inside the beautiful 12th-century **Cathédrale St-Étienne**, a harmonious blend of Romanesque and Gothic styles.

✗ 🛏 p399

The Drive » Head west of town via the D8, following signs to Luzech and Pradines.

- - - - - - - - - -

⑤ Luzech

Downstream from Cahors, the lower Lot twists its way through the rich **vineyards** of the Cahors AOC region. It's up to you whether you wish to take advantage of the signs offering *dégustation* (tasting). Otherwise, carry on along the road, passing the dams at Luzech, whose medieval section sits at the base of a *donjon* (keep), and **Castelfranc**, with a dramatic suspension bridge.

The Drive » West of Luzech, stay on the minor D8, which hugs the south bank of the river. The road affords super vistas of the local vineyards and the river's many hairpin curves. You'll reach Puy l'Évêque after 26km, or around 35 minutes' driving.

⑥ Puy l'Évêque

On a rocky hillside above the northern bank of the Lot, Puy l'Évêque was one of the most important medieval ports in the Lot Valley, and its quays are lined with once-grand merchants' houses – some have been carefully restored; others are a little worse for wear. The old town is also well worth a stroll, with many fine stone mansions and tumble-down medieval buildings, best appreciated from the road bridge that spans the Lot just outside town.

DETOUR:
CHÂTEAU DE BIRON

Start: ❼ Bonaguil

If you enjoyed the castle architecture of Bonaguil, you might like to cut across country to the nearby **Château de Biron** (☎ 05 53 63 13 39; www.semitour.com; D53; adult/child €8.20/5.30, joint ticket with Cadouin €11.90/7; ☺10am-7pm daily Jul & Aug, 10am-1pm & 2-6pm Apr-Jun & Sep-Oct, Tue-Sun Nov-May, closed Jan), a glorious mishmash of styles, having been fiddled with by eight centuries of successive heirs. It's particularly notable for its slate turrets, state rooms and double loggia staircase, supposedly modelled on one at Versailles; the oldest part of the castle is the 12th-century keep.

It's had mixed fortunes over the centuries, and was finally sold in the early 1900s to pay for the extravagant lifestyle of a particularly irresponsible heir. It's since featured in countless films, including Luc Besson's *Jeanne d'Arc* (Joan of Arc; 1999) and Bernard Tavernier's *La Fille d'Artagnan* (D'Artagnan's Daughter; 1994).

The Drive » To get to the Château de Bonaguil, continue west along the D811 for 14km towards Fumel. About 1km east of town, there's a right turn onto the D673, signed to Gourdon/Bonaguil. Follow signs for another 8km, making sure not to miss the left turn onto the D158.

- - - - - - - - - - - -

TRIP HIGHLIGHT

❼ Bonaguil

There's one unmistakeable reason to stop in the village of Bonaguil, and that's to wander round its imposing feudal **château** (☎ 05 53 71 90 33; www.chateau-bonaguil.com; adult/child €8/4; ☺10am-7pm Jul & Aug, 10am-5.30pm Apr-Jun, Sep & Oct), a fine example of late-15th-century

military architecture, with towers, bastions, loopholes, machicolations and crenellations built directly into the limestone cliffs. Guided tours in English run several times daily in July and August.

The Drive » Loop back onto the D673, making a short detour via the pretty little village of St-Martin-le-Redon if you wish. Follow signs through Fumel onto the D911 all the way to Villeneuve-sur-Lot.

- - - - - - - - - - - -

❽ Villeneuve-sur-Lot

Last stop on the trip is the river town of Villeneuve-sur-Lot, which began life as a *bastide*

but has long since been swallowed up by more modern architecture. The centre of the old town is guarded by two medieval gateways, the **Porte de Paris** and the **Porte de Pujols** (the other six are no longer standing); in between runs the main thoroughfare of rue de Paris and the arcaded *bastide*-style square of place Lafayette, surrounded by shops and cafes. Along the river, look out for the **Pont Vieux**, a 13th-century bridge that was supposedly modelled on the Pont Valentré in Cahors, although its defensive towers have disappeared.

Eating & Sleeping

Figeac ❶

✘ La Dinée du Viguier   Gastronomy €€

(☎05 65 50 05 05; www.chateau-viguier-figeac.fr; 4 rue Boutaric; menus lunch €23, dinner €32-80; ⊙noon 2pm & 7.45 9pm) Figeac's top table is a must for foodies into creative cuisine incorporating fresh, regional ingredients. Choose between beautifully prepared dishes including lobster, oysters, and locally reared duck.

⊨ Hôtel La Grézalide   Hotel €€

(☎05 65 11 20 40; www.grezalide.com; Grèzes; d €105-188, tr/f €145/185; [P][⊛][≋][⊛]) You'll need a car to reach this beautiful country estate, 21km west of Figeac in the quaint village of Grèzes, but it's worth the drive. Rooms in the 17th-century manor make maximum use of its architecture, with solid stone and original floorboards. Public rooms display art collections, and the courtyard garden, pool, and fantastic regional restaurant (*menus* €26 to €45) round it all out.

St-Cirq-Lapopie ❷

✘ Le Gourmet Quercynois   Regional Cuisine €€

(☎05 65 31 21 20; www.restaurant-legourmetquercynois.com; rue de la Peyrolerie; menus €21-38; ⊙noon-2pm & 7.30-9.30pm mid-Feb–Dec) St-Cirq's top table offers an enormous menu, ranging from *nougat de porc* (pork medallions) to country *cassoulet* (stew). Escape to the little patio to catch evening rays setting over town.

⊨ Hôtel Le Saint Cirq   Hotel €€

(☎05 65 30 30 30; www.hotel-lesaintcirq.com; Tour de Faure; d €88-128, d €108-148, f/ste from €158/218; [@][⊛][≋]) This luxurious hotel in the valley below St-Cirq boasts one of the best views of its hilltop profile. Lovely, traditional rooms have terracotta-tiled floors and French windows onto the garden. 'Seigneurale' rooms boast sunken baths, slate bathrooms and the like.

Cahors ❹

✘ L'Ô à la Bouche   Modern French €€

(☎05 65 35 65 69; www.loalabouche-restaurant.com; 56 allée Fénelon; menus lunch €22-40, dinner €28-45; ⊙noon-2pm & 7.30-9.30pm Tue-Sat) Book ahead to get a seat in this small, contemporary restaurant that takes its creative, local cuisine quite seriously. The welcome is warm and the ingredients are the finest the region has to offer.

✘ Le Marché   Regional Cuisine €€

(☎05 65 35 27 27; www.restaurantlemarche.com; 27 place Jean-Jacques Chapou; lunch menu from €20, dinner menus €27-42; ⊙noon-2pm & 7.30-9pm Tue-Sat) Food sourced from the region stars at this urbane bistro. Puce-and-cream armchairs set the designer tone; the short menu changes with the seasons.

⊨ Hôtel Jean XXII   Hotel €

(☎05 65 35 07 66; www.hotel-jeanxxii.com; 2 rue Edmond-Albé; s €57, d €68-77, q €89; ⊙reception closes 10.30am-4.30pm; [⊛]) Next to the Tour du Pape Jean XXII, this excellent nine room hotel mixes original stone, greenery and well-worn wood with a dash of metropolitan minimalism. Rooms sleep one to four people; there's a reading area on the 1st floor where you can unwind in leather armchairs.

⊨ Grand Hôtel Terminus   Hotel €€

(☎05 65 53 32 00; www.balandre.com; 5 av Charles de Freycinet; d €75-115, ste €150; [❋][⊛]) Built c 1920, Cahors's original railway-station hotel evokes an air of faded grandeur. Most of the rooms are large and comfortable, with hefty radiators, claw foot baths and king size beds.

Classic Trip

Atlantic to Med

38

Salty Atlantic ports, pristine mountain vistas, the heady bouquet of fine wine, reminders of Rome and Hollywood glam. this classic sea-to-sea trip takes you through the best of southern France.

TRIP HIGHLIGHTS

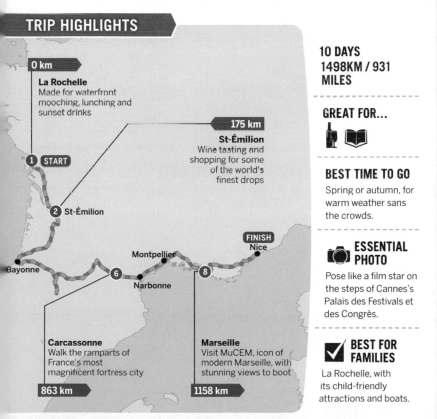

0 km

La Rochelle
Made for waterfront mooching, lunching and sunset drinks

175 km

St-Émilion
Wine tasting and shopping for some of the world's finest drops

1 START

2 St-Émilion

FINISH
Nice

Montpellier

6

8

Bayonne

Narbonne

Carcassonne
Walk the ramparts of France's most magnificent fortress city

863 km

Marseille
Visit MuCEM, icon of modern Marseille, with stunning views to boot

1158 km

10 DAYS
1498KM / 931 MILES

GREAT FOR...

BEST TIME TO GO

Spring or autumn, for warm weather sans the crowds.

ESSENTIAL PHOTO

Pose like a film star on the steps of Cannes's Palais des Festivals et des Congrès.

BEST FOR FAMILIES

La Rochelle, with its child-friendly attractions and boats.

Rochelle Seafaring centre built from limestone

401

Classic Trip

38 Atlantic to Med

In May the film starlets of the world pour into Cannes to celebrate a year of movie-making. Let them have their moment of glam — by the time you've finished scaling Pyrenean highs, chewing Basque tapas, acting like a medieval knight in a turreted castle and riding to the moon in a spaceship, you too will have the makings of a prize-winning film.

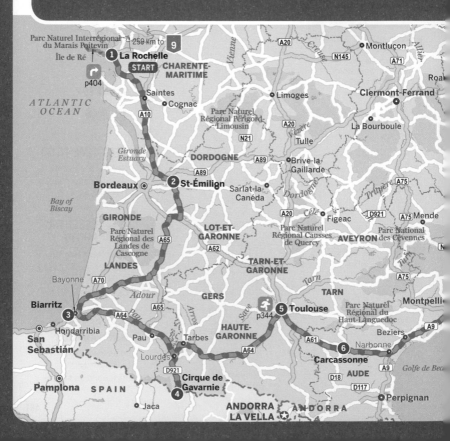

❶ La Rochelle

Known as La Ville Blanche (the White City), La Rochelle is home to luminous limestone facades, arcaded walkways, half-timbered houses and ghoulish gargoyles glowing in the bright coastal sunlight. One of France's foremost seaports from the 14th to the 17th centuries, it remains a great seafaring centre and one of France's most attractive cities.

There are several defensive towers around the **Vieux Port** (Old Port), including the lacy **Tour de la Lanterne** (rue sur les Murs; adult/child €6/free, 3 towers €8.50/free; ◷10am-1pm & 2.15-6.30pm Apr-Sep, to 5.30pm Oct-Mar), that once served to protect the town at night in times of war. Scale their sturdy stone heights for fabulous city and coastal views.

La Rochelle's number-one tourist attraction is its state-of-the-art **aquarium** (www.aquarium-larochelle.com; quai Louis Prunier; adult/child €16/12; ◷9am-11pm Jul & Aug, 9am-8pm Apr-Jun & Sep, 10am-8pm Oct-Mar) with UFO-like rays and fearsome sharks, teeth-gnashing piranhas, timid turtles and the bizarre half-newt. Equally fun for families is the **Musée Maritime** (Maritime Museum; ☎05 46 28 03 00; www.museemaritimelarochelle.fr; place Bernard Moitessier; adult/child €8/5; ◷10am-7pm Jul & Aug, to 6.30pm Apr-Jun & Sep, shorter hours rest of year), with its fleet of boats to explore; and a trip out to sea with **Croisières Inter-Îles** (☎08 25 13 55 00; www.inter-iles.com; cours des Dames) to admire the unusual iceberg of an island fortress, Fort Boyard.

🛏 p409

The Drive 》 Using the main A10 toll road it's 187km (about 2½ hours) to St-Émilion. Turn off the A10 at exit 39a, signed for Libourne. Skirt this industrial town and follow the D243 into St Émilion.

LINK YOUR TRIP

9 **Breton Coast**
The wind-swept coast of Brittany is a wild tonic to the south's refined atmosphere. Drive three hours north of La Rochelle to start the trip in Vannes.

23 **Riviera Crossing**
Starting in Nice, this drive takes you through the glitzy, glam French Riviera.

Classic Trip

has a superb exhibition covering wine essentials.

Guided tours of the town (adult/child from €8/free) and surrounding chateaux are run by the **tourist office** (☏05 57 55 28 28; www.saint-emilion-tourisme. com; place des Créneaux; ☺9.30am-7.30pm Jul & Aug, shorter hours rest of year); reserve ahead in season. Several tours include tastings and vineyard visits.

✕ 🛏 p366, p409

The Drive » Leave St-Émilion on the D243 to Libourne, cross the town, then pick up the D1089 signposted 'Agen, Bergerac, Bordeaux'. Continue on the N89 towards Bordeaux until you see signs for the A630 toll road – at which point sit back and hit cruise control for the remaining 226km to Biarritz. Count 240km and about 2½ hours in all.

TRIP HIGHLIGHT

② St-Émilion

Built of soft honey-coloured rock, medieval St-Émilion produces some of the world's finest red wines. Visiting this pretty town, and partaking in some of the tours and activities on offer, is the easiest way to get under the (grape) skin of Bordeaux wine production. The **Maison du Vin de St-Émilion** (www. maisonduvinsaintemilion.com; place Pierre Meyrat; ☺9.30am-12.30pm & 2-6.30pm) runs wine-tasting classes and

---

③ Biarritz

Biarritz is as ritzy as its name suggests. This coastal town boomed as a resort in the mid-19th century, when regularly visited by Napoléon III and his Spanish-born wife, Eugénie. Along its rocky coastline are architectural hallmarks of this golden age, and the belle-époque and art-deco eras that followed.

Biarritz is all about its fashionable beaches, especially the central **Grande Plage** and **Plage Miramar**. In the heat of summer you'll find them packed end to end with sun-loving bathers.

✕ 🛏 p357

↪ DETOUR: ÎLE DE RÉ

Start: ① La Rochelle

Bathed in the southern sun, drenched in a languid atmosphere and scattered with villages of green-shuttered, whitewashed buildings with red Spanish-tile roofs, Île de Ré is one of the most delightful places on the west coast of France. The island spans just 30km from its most easterly and westerly points, and just 5km at its widest section. But take note: the secret's out and in high season it can be almost impossible to move around and even harder to find a place to stay.

On the northern coast about 12km from the toll bridge that links the island to La Rochelle is the quaint fishing port of **St-Martin-de-Ré**, the island's main town. Surrounded by 17th-century fortifications (you can stroll along most of the ramparts) constructed by Vauban, the port town is a mesh of streets filled with craft shops, art galleries and sea-spray ocean views.

The island's best beaches are along the southern edge – including unofficial naturist beaches at **Rivedoux Plage** and **La Couarde-sur-Mer** – and around the western tip (northeast and southeast of Phare-des-Baleines). Many beaches are bordered by dunes that have been fenced off to protect the vegetation.

From La Rochelle it's 24km and a half-hour drive to St-Martin-de-Ré via the toll bridge, Pont de l'Île de Ré (www.pont-ile-de-re.com; return ticket €16 mid-June to mid-September, €8 rest of the year).

The Drive » It's 208km (2¾ hours) to the village of Gavarnie. Take the A63 and A64 toll roads to exit 11, then the D940 to Lourdes (worth a look for its religious Disneyland feel). Continue south along D913 and D921.

---

④ Cirque de Gavarnie

The Pyrenees doesn't lack impressive scenery, but your first sight of the Cirque de Gavarnie is guaranteed to raise a gasp. This breathtaking mountain amphitheatre is one of the region's most famous sights, sliced by thunderous waterfalls and ringed by sawtooth peaks, many of which top out at above 3000m.

There are a couple of large car parks in the village of Gavarnie, from where it's a two-hour walk to the amphitheatre. Wear proper shoes, as snow lingers along the trail into early summer. Between Easter and October you can go by horse or donkey (around €25 return).

The Drive » Retrace your steps to Lourdes, then take the N21 toward Tarbes and veer onto the A64 to reach Toulouse. It takes nearly three hours to cover the 228km.

---

⑤ Toulouse

Elegantly sited at the confluence of the Canal du Midi and Garonne River, the vibrant southern city of Toulouse is often known as La Ville Rose, a reference to the distinc-

tive pink stone used in many of its buildings.

Toulouse's magnificent main square, **place du Capitole**, is the city's literal and metaphorical heart. To its south is the city's **Vieux Quartier** (Old Quarter), a tangle of lanes and leafy squares that beg exploration on foot (p344). Then, of course, there are the soothing twists and turns of the Garonne River and mighty Canal du Midi – laced with footpaths and likewise clearly created with stretching your legs in mind.

The sky's the limit at the fantastic **Cité de l'Espace** (www.cite-espace. com/en; av Jean Gonord; adult €21-25.50, child €15.50-19; ⏰10am-7pm daily Jul & Aug, to 5pm or 6pm Sep-Dec & Feb-Jun, closed Mon Feb, Mar & Sep-Dec, closed Jan). Since WWII, Toulouse has been the centre of France's aerospace industry, developing many important aircraft (including Concorde and the Airbus A380) as well as components for many international space programs. The museum brings this interstellar industry vividly to life through hands-on exhibits including a shuttle simulator, a planetarium, a 3D cinema and a simulated observatory.

✕ 🛏 p409

The Drive » It's an easy 95km (one hour) down the fast A61 to Carcassonne. Notice how the vegetation becomes suddenly much more Mediterranean about 15 minutes out of Toulouse.

TRIP HIGHLIGHT

⑥ Carcassonne

Perched on a rocky hilltop and bristling with zigzagging battlements, stout walls and spiky turrets, from afar the fortified city of Carcassonne is most people's perfect idea of a medieval castle. Four million tourists a year stream through its city gates to explore **La Cité** (enter via Porte Narbonnaise or Porte d'Aude; ⏰24hr), visit **Château Comtal** (place du Château, La Cité; adult/child €8.50/free; ⏰10am-6.30pm Apr-Sep, 9.30am-5pm Oct-Mar) and ogle at stunning views along the city's ancient ramparts.

✕ 🛏 p325

The Drive » Continue down the A61 to the Catalan-flavoured town of Narbonne, where you join the A9 (very busy in summer) and head east to Nîmes. From there the A54 will take you into Arles. Allow just over two hours to cover the 223km and expect lots of toll booths.

---

⑦ Arles

Arles' poster boy is the celebrated impressionist painter Vincent van Gogh. If you're familiar with his work, you'll be familiar with Arles: the light, the colours, the landmarks and the atmosphere, all faithfully captured. But long before Van Gogh rendered this grand Rhône River locale on canvas, the Romans valued its worth. Today it's the reminders of Rome that are probably

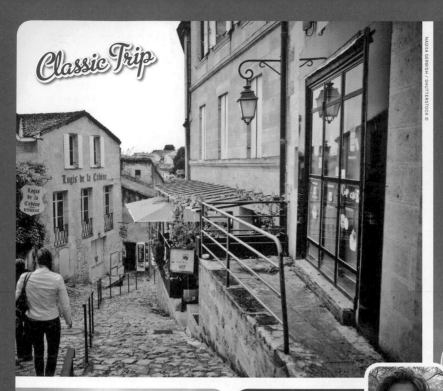

NADIIA GERBISH / SHUTTERSTOCK ©

Classic Trip

DELPIXEL / SHUTTERSTOCK ©

WHY THIS IS A CLASSIC TRIP
NICOLA WILLIAMS, WRITER

I'm a sucker for the big blue and fine wine, so this seafaring trip is right up my alley. Feasting on fresh oysters on the seashore aside, I strongly advise lingering over lunch at La Terrasse Rouge (p409) near St-Émilion. This spectacular vineyard restaurant was borne out of Jean Nouvel's designer revamp of Château La Dominique's wine cellars: dining on its uber-chic terrace overlooking a field of dark-red glass pebbles is the ultimate French road-trip reward.

Top & Left: St-Emilion
Right: Cathedral & MuCEM, Marseilles

JEAN-PIERRE LESCOURRET ©

the town's most memorable attractions.

At **Les Arènes** (Amphithéâtre; www.arenes-arles.com; Rond-Point des Arènes; adult/child €6/free, incl Théâtre Antique €9/free; ⊙9am-8pm Jul & Aug, to 7pm May-Jun & Sep, shorter hours rest of year) slaves, criminals and wild animals (including giraffes) met their dramatic demise before a jubilant 20,000-strong crowd during Roman gladiatorial displays.

The **Théâtre Antique** (☑04 90 96 93 30; bd des Lices; ⊙9am-7pm May-Sep, shorter hours rest of year), which dates from the 1st century BC, is still regularly used for al fresco concerts and plays.

✕ ⊨ p244, p303, p409

The Drive » From Arles take the scenic N568 and A55 route into Marseille. It's 88km (an hour's drive) away.

- - - - - - - - - - - -

TRIP HIGHLIGHT

⑧ Marseille

With its history, fusion of cultures, *souq*-like markets, millennia-old port and *corniches* (coastal roads) along rocky inlets and sun-baked beaches, Marseille is a captivating and exotic city.

Ships have docked for more than 26 centuries at the city's birthplace, the colourful Vieux Port (Old Port), which remains a thriving harbour to this day. Guarding it are **Bas Fort St-Nicolas** on the

south side and, across the water, **Fort St-Jean**, founded in the 13th century by the Knights Hospitaller of St John of Jerusalem. A vertigo-inducing footbridge links the latter with the stunning **Musée des Civilisations de l'Europe et de la Méditerranée,** (MuCEM; www.mucem. org; 7 Promenade Robert Laffont; adult/family/child €9.50/14/ free; ⏰10am-8pm Wed-Mon Jul & Aug, 11am-7pm Wed-Mon Sep, Oct, May & Jun, 11am-6pm Wed-Mon Nov-Apr) the icon of modern Marseille. Its vast anthropological collection is housed in a bold, contemporary building known as J4, designed by Algerian-born, Marseille-

educated architect Rudi Ricciotti.

From the Vieux Port, hike up to the fantastic history-woven quarter of **Le Panier**, dubbed Marseille's Montmartre as much for its sloping streets as its artsy ambience. It's a mishmash of lanes hiding artisan shops, *ateliers* (workshops) and terraced houses strung with drying washing.

✕ ⮕ p274

The Drive » To get from Marseille to Cannes, take the northbound A52 and join the A8 toll road just east of Aix-en-Provence. It's 181km and takes just under two hours.

----

⑨ Cannes

The eponymous film festival only lasts for two weeks in May, but thanks to regular visits from cele-

brities the buzz and glitz are in Cannes year-round.

The imposing **Palais des Festivals et des Congrès** (1 bd de la Croisette; guided tour adult/child €4/ free) is the centre of the glamour. Climb the red carpet, walk down the auditorium, tread the stage and learn about cinema's most prestigious event on a 1½-hour guided tour run by the **tourist office** (☏04 91 13 89 00; www.marseille-tourisme.com; 11 La Canebière; ⏰9am-7pm Mon-Sat, 10am-5pm Sun).

✕ ⮕ p264

The Drive » Weave along the D6007 to Nice, taking in cliffs, turquoise waters and the yachties' town of Antibes. It's 31km and, on a good day, takes 45 minutes.

----

⑩ Nice

You don't need to be a painter or artist to appreciate the extraordinary light in Nice. Matisse, Chagall et al spent years lapping up the city's startling luminosity and radiance, and for most visitors to Nice, it is this magical light that seduces. The city has a number of world-class sights, but the star attraction is probably the seafront **Promenade des Anglais**. Atmospheric, beautiful and photogenic, it's a wonderful place to stroll (p304) or watch the world go by, so make sure you leave yourself plenty of time to soak it all in.

✕ ⮕ p264, p409

DETOUR: AIX-EN-PROVENCE

Start: ⑦ Arles

Aix-en-Provence is to Provence what the Left Bank is to Paris: an enclave of bourgeois-bohemian chic. Art, culture and architecture abound here. A stroller's paradise, the highlight is the mostly pedestrian old city, **Vieil Aix**. South of cours Mirabeau, **Quartier Mazarin** was laid out in the 17th century, and is home to some of Aix's finest buildings. Central Place des Quatre Dauphins, with its fish-spouting fountain (1667), is particularly enchanting. Further south still is the peaceful **Parc Jourdan**, where locals gather beneath plane trees to play *pétanque*.

From Arles it's a 77km (one-hour) drive down the A54 toll road to Aix-en-Provence. To rejoin the main route take the A51 and A7 for 32km (30 minutes) to Marseille.

Eating & Sleeping

La Rochelle ❶

🛏 Hôtel St-Nicolas   Boutique Hotel €€

(📞05 46 41 71 55; www.hotel-saint-nicolas.com; 13 rue Sardinerie et place de la Solette; d/tr €125/145; 🅿 ❄ 🛜) This stylish hotel, tucked in a peaceful courtyard with delightful summer terrace, has smart comfortable rooms with ultra-modern bathrooms – think giant rain showers, heated towel rails and sweet-smelling welcome products. A handful of rooms are across the courtyard in an equally inviting annexe, and breakfast (€12) is served in an indoor tropical garden. Check its website for excellent-value deals.

St-Émilion ❷

✗ La Terrasse Rouge   French €€

(📞05 57 24 47 05; www.laterrasserouge.com; 1 Château La Dominique; lunch menu €28; ⊙noon-2.30pm & 7-11pm Jun-Sep, noon-2.30pm & 7-11pm Fri & Sat, noon-2.30pm Sun-Thu Oct-May) Foodies adore this spectacular vineyard restaurant. Chefs work exclusively with small local producers to source the seasonal veg, fruit and so on used in their creative cuisine. Oysters are fresh from Cap Ferret, caviar comes from Neuvic in the Dordogne and the wine list is, naturally, extraordinary.

Toulouse ❺

✗ Le Genty Magre   French €€€

(📞05 61 21 38 60; www.legentymagre.com; 3 rue Genty Magre; mains €18-30, menu €38; ⊙12.30-2.30pm & 8-10pm Tue-Sat) Classic French cuisine is the order of the day here, but lauded chef Romain Brard has plenty of modern tricks up his sleeve, too. The dining room feels inviting, with brick walls, burnished wood and sultry lighting. It's arguably the best place in the city to try rich, traditional dishes such as *confit de canard* (duck confit) or *cassoulet* (stew).

🛏 Hôtel Albert 1er   Hotel €€

(📞05 61 21 47 49; www.hotel-albert1.com; 8 rue Rivals; d €65-145; ❄ 🛜) The Albert's central location and eager-to-please staff are a winning combination. A palette of maroon and cream, with marble flourishes here and there, bestows a regal feel on comfortable rooms. Bathrooms are lavished with ecofriendly products. The breakfast buffet is largely organic. Some recently upgraded rooms have mod cons such as USB ports and coffee makers.

Arles ❼

🛏 Le Cloître   Design Hotel €€

(📞04 88 09 10 00; www.hotel-cloitre.com; 18 rue du Cloître; s €105, d €130-185; @ 🛜) Proving you don't need to spend a fortune for originality and imagination, the 19 rooms at this zingy hotel next to the Cloître Ste-Trophime combine history and modern design to winning effect: bold colours, funky patterns and retro furniture abound, and the rooftop terrace is a stunning sundowner spot. The lavish breakfast spread is (unusually) worth the €14 price tag.

Nice ❿

✗ Le Bistrot d'Antoine   Modern French €€

(📞04 93 85 29 57; 27 rue de la Préfecture; menus €25-43, mains €15-25; ⊙noon-2pm & 7-10pm Tue-Sat) A quintessential French bistro, right down to the checked tablecloths, streetside tables and impeccable service – not to mention the handwritten blackboard, loaded with classic dishes like rabbit pâté, pot-cooked pork, blood sausage and duck breast. For classic French food, this is a treat.

🛏 Nice Garden Hôtel   Boutique Hotel €€

(📞04 93 87 35 62; www.nicegardenhotel.com; 11 rue du Congrès; s €75, d €90-123, tr €138; ⊙reception 8am-9pm; ❄ 🛜) Behind heavy iron gates hides this gem: nine beautifully appointed rooms – the work of the exquisite Marion – are a subtle blend of old and new and overlook a delightful garden with a glorious orange tree. Amazingly, all this charm and peacefulness is just two blocks from the promenade. Breakfast €9.

STRETCH YOUR LEGS
BORDEAUX

Start/Finish Cathédrale St-André

Distance 5km

Duration 1½ hours

Good-looking Bordeaux, a Unesco World Heritage site, is one of France's most exciting, vibrant and dynamic cities. With pedestrian-friendly streets, stately architecture and silky-smooth riverside promenades, it is made for exploring on foot. This walking tour reveals the best of downtown Bordeaux.

Take this walk on Trips

1 33

Cathédrale St-André

Lording over the city, the **cathedral** (www.cathedrale-bordeaux.fr; place Jean Moulin; ⊘2-6pm Mon, 10am-noon & 2-6pm Tue-Sun) dates from 1096, but most of what you see today was built in the 13th and 14th centuries. Next door is the gargoyled, 50m-high Gothic belfry, **Tour Pey Berland** (adult/child €5.50/free; ⊘10am-1.15pm & 2-6pm Jun-Sep, 10am-12.30pm & 2-5.30pm Oct-May), erected between 1440 and 1466.

The Walk » Head up rue Elisée Reclus and turn right to enter the small but elegant Jardin de la Mairie, where you'll find the Musée des Beaux-Arts.

Musée des Beaux-Arts

The evolution of occidental art from the Renaissance to the mid-20th century is on view at this fine arts **museum** (www.musba-bordeaux.fr; 20 cours d'Albret; adult/child €4/2; ⊘11am-6pm mid-Jul–mid-Aug, closed Tue rest of year), occupying two wings of the 1770s-built Hôtel de Ville. Highlights include 17th-century Flemish, Dutch and Italian paintings.

The Walk » Continue down cours d'Albret, across place Gambetta and onto cours Georges Clemenceau. At place Tourny turn left onto rue Fondaudège, then take the second right.

Jardin Public

Take a stroll through these gorgeous **gardens** (cours de Verdun). On sunny days it can seem as though half of Bordeaux has come to feed the ducks here.

The Walk » Exit the park via cours de Verdun, then head down cours du Maréchal Foch, turn left onto rue Ferrére and continue to CAPC.

Musée d'Art Contemporain (CAPC)

Built in 1824 as a warehouse for French colonial produce such as coffee, cocoa, peanuts and vanilla, this cavernous building creates a dramatic backdrop for contemporary art at the **CAPC** (www.capc-bordeaux.fr; 7 rue Ferrère; adult/child €4/2; ⊘11am-6pm Tue & Thu-Sun, to 8pm Wed).

The Walk » Follow the river along the quai des Chartrons to the esplanade des Quinconces. Walk through this square, past the Girondins

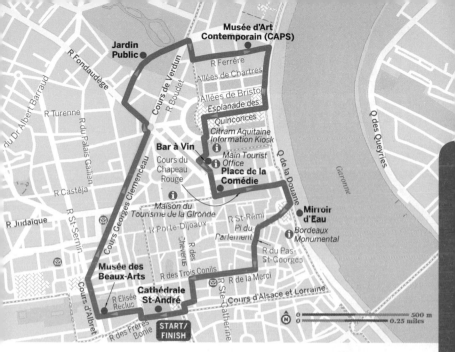

monument, and continue 100m down cours du 30 Juillet to the Maison du Vin de Bordeaux.

Bar à Vin

Time for a drink? In Bordeaux there's only one place to wet the whistle. Winc's holy of holies, the **Bar à Vin** (http://baravin. bordeaux.com; 3 cours du 30 Juillet; 11am-10pm Mon Sat), inside the hallowed **Maison du Vin de Bordeaux**, is the place to come for a tipple with people who really know their wine from their beer.

The Walk » Continue 150m down Bordeaux's swankiest street to people-watching hot spot, place de la Comédie.

Place de la Comédie

One of the city's grandest and busiest squares, place de la Comédie is watched over by Bordeaux's elegant 18th-century opera house, the **Grand Théâtre** (www. opera-bordeaux.com), designed by Victor Louis of Chartres cathedral fame, and legendary **Le Grand Hôtel** (www. ghbordeaux.com), with Gordon Ramsay's Michelin-starred restaurant. But the biggest head-turner is **Sanna** (2013),

a modern sculpture by Spanish artist Jaume Plensa. Grab a cafe terrace pew and enjoy the view.

The Walk » Turn left behind the theatre and walk down attractive cours du Chapeau Rouge. Turn right and head along the waterfront to place de la Bourse.

Miroir d'Eau

Surrounded by magisterial public buildings attesting to Bordeaux's 18th-century wealth is the vast public square, place de la Bourse. Its highlight is the world's largest reflecting pool known as the **Miroir d'Eau** (10am-10pm summer). This 'water mirror' provides hours of entertainment on warm sunny days when the reflections in its thin slick of water are stunning. Every 23 minutes a dense fog-like vapor is ejected for three minutes to add to the fun (and photo opportunities).

The Walk » Head up rue Fernand Philippart to place du Parlement with its numerous cafes, then weave along rue du Pas-St-Georges, rue St-Siméon and rue de la Merci to turn left onto rue de Cheverus and back to the cathedral.

ROAD TRIP ESSENTIALS

France Driving Guide

With stunning landscapes, superb highways and one of the world's most scenic and comprehensive secondary road networks, France is a road-tripper's dream come true.

DRIVING LICENCE & DOCUMENTS

Drivers must carry the following at all times:

➡ passport or an EU national ID card

➡ valid driving licence (*permis de conduire*; most foreign licences can be used in France for up to a year)

➡ car-ownership papers, known as a *carte grise* (grey card)

➡ proof of third-party liability *assurance* (insurance)

An International Driving Permit (IDP) is not required when renting a car but can be useful in the event of an accident or police stop, as it translates and vouches for the authenticity of your home licence.

INSURANCE

Third-party liability insurance *(assurance au tiers)* is compulsory for all vehicles in France, including cars brought from abroad. Normally, cars registered and insured in other European countries can circulate freely. Contact your insurance company before leaving home to make sure you're covered, and to verify whom to call in case of a breakdown or accident.

In a minor accident with no injuries, the easiest way for drivers to sort things out with their insurance companies is to fill out a *Constat Amiable d'Accident Automobile* (accident report), a standardised way of recording important details about what happened. In rental cars it's

Driving Fast Facts

➡ **Right or left?** Drive on the right
➡ **Manual or automatic?** Manual
➡ **Legal driving age** 18
➡ **Top speed limit** 130km/h on *autoroutes* (highways, motorways)
➡ **Signature car** Citroën 2CV

usually in the packet of documents in the glove compartment. Make sure the report includes any proof that the accident was not your fault. If it was your fault you may be liable for a hefty insurance deductible/excess. Don't sign anything you don't fully understand. If necessary, contact the police (⬆17).

French-registered cars have their insurance-company details printed on a little green square affixed to the windscreen (windshield).

HIRING A CAR

To hire a car in France, you'll generally need to be over 21 years old, have had a driving licence for at least a year, and have an international credit card. Drivers under 25 usually have to pay a surcharge *(frais jeune conducteur)* of €25 to €35 per day.

Car-hire companies provide mandatory third-party liability insurance but things such as collision-damage waivers (CDW, or *assurance tous risques*) vary greatly from company to company. When comparing rates and conditions (ie the fine print), the most important thing to check is the *franchise* (deductible/excess), which for a small car is usually around €600 for damage and €800 for theft. With many companies, you can reduce the excess by half, and perhaps to zero, by paying a daily insurance supplement of up to €20. Your credit card may cover CDW if you use it to pay for the rental but the car-hire company won't know anything about this – verify conditions and details with your credit-card issuer to be sure.

Arranging your car hire or fly/drive package before you leave home is usually considerably cheaper than a walk-in rental, but beware of website offers that don't include a CDW or you may be liable for up to 100% of the car's value.

International car-hire companies:

Avis (☎08 21 23 07 60, from abroad 01 70 99 47 35; www.avis.com)

Budget (☎08 25 00 35 64; www.budget.fr)

EasyCar (☎in France 08 26 10 73 23, in the UK 0800 640 7000; www.easycar.com)

Europcar (☎08 25 35 83 58; www.europ car.com)

Hertz (☎01 41 91 95 25, 08 25 86 18 61; www.hertz.com)

Sixt (☎08 20 00 74 98; www.sixt.fr) French car-hire companies:

ADA (☎08 99 46 46 36; www.ada.fr)

DLM (www.dlm.fr)

France Cars (www.francecars.fr)

Locauto (☎04 93 07 72 62; www.locauto.fr)

Renault Rent (☎08 25 10 11 12; www.renault-rent.com)

Rent a Car (☎08 91 700 200; www.renta car.fr)

Deals can be found on the internet and through companies such as the following:

Auto Europe (☎in USA 888-223-5555; www.autoeurope.com)

DriveAway Holidays (☎in Australia 1300 363 500; www.driveaway.com.au)

Holiday Autos (☎in UK 020 3740 9859; www.holidayautos.co.uk)

Rental cars with automatic transmission are very much the exception in France; they usually need to be ordered well in advance and are more expensive than manual cars.

For insurance reasons, it is usually forbidden to take rental cars on ferries, eg to Corsica.

All rental cars registered in France have a distinctive number on the licence plate, making them easily identifiable – including to thieves. *Never* leave anything of value in a parked car, even in the boot (trunk).

BRINGING YOUR OWN VEHICLE

Any foreign motor vehicle entering France must display a sticker or licence plate identifying its country of registration. Right-hand-drive vehicles brought from the UK or Ireland must have deflectors affixed to the headlights to avoid dazzling oncoming traffic.

MAPS

Michelin's excellent, detailed regional driving maps are highly recommended as a driving companion, as they will help you navigate back roads and explore alterna-

Priority to the Right

Under the *priorité à droite* ('priority to the right') rule, any car entering an intersection (including a T-junction) from a road (including a tiny village backstreet) on your right has the right-of-way. Locals assume every driver knows this, so don't be surprised if they courteously cede the right-of-way when you're about to turn from an alley onto a highway – and boldly assert their rights when you're the one zipping down a main road.

Priorité à droite is suspended (eg on arterial roads) when you pass a sign showing an upended yellow square with a black square in the middle. The same sign with a horizontal bar through the square lozenge reinstates the *priorité à droite* rule.

When you arrive at a roundabout at which you do not have the right of way (ie the cars already in the roundabout do), you'll often see signs reading *vous n'avez pas la priorité* (you do not have right of way) or *cédez le passage* (give way).

Road Distances (KM)

	Bayonne	Bordeaux	Brest	Caen	Cahors	Calais	Chambéry	Cherbourg	Clermont-Ferrand	Dijon	Grenoble	Lille	Lyon	Marseille	Nantes	Nice	Paris	Perpignan	Strasbourg	Toulouse
Bordeaux	184																			
Brest	811	623																		
Caen	764	568	376																	
Cahors	307	218	788	661																
Calais	164	876	710	339	875															
Chambéry	860	651	120	800	523	834														
Cherbourg	835	647	399	124	743	461	923													
Clermont-Ferrand	564	358	805	566	269	717	295	689												
Dijon	807	619	867	548	378	572	273	671	279											
Grenoble	827	657	1126	806	501	863	56	929	300	302										
Lille	997	809	725	353	808	112	767	476	650	606	798									
Lyon	831	528	1018	698	439	755	103	820	171	194	110	687								
Marseille	700	651	1271	1010	521	1067	344	1132	477	506	273	999	314							
Nantes	513	326	298	292	491	593	780	317	462	656	787	609	618	975						
Nice	858	810	1429	1168	679	1225	410	1291	636	664	337	1157	473	190	1131					
Paris	771	583	596	232	582	289	565	355	424	313	571	222	462	775	384	932				
Perpignan	499	451	1070	998	320	1149	478	1094	441	640	445	1081	448	319	773	476	857			
Strasbourg	1254	1066	1079	730	847	621	496	853	584	335	551	522	488	803	867	804	490	935		
Toulouse	300	247	866	865	116	991	565	890	890	727	533	923	536	407	568	564	699	205	1022	
Tours	536	348	490	246	413	531	611	369	369	418	618	463	449	795	197	952	238	795	721	593

tive **routes**. Look for both at newsagents, bookshops, airports, supermarkets, tourist offices and service stations along the autoroute.

Institut Géographique National (IGN; www.ign.fr) Publishes regional fold-out maps as well as an all-France volume, *France – Routes, Autoroutes*.

Michelin (www.michelin-boutique.com) Sells excellent, tear-proof yellow-orange 1:200,000-scale regional maps tailor-made for cross-country driving, with precise coverage of smaller back roads.

ROADS & CONDITIONS

France has one of Europe's densest highway networks. There are four types of intercity roads:

Autoroutes (highway names beginning with A) Multilane divided highways, usually (except near Calais and Lille) with tolls (*péages*). Generously outfitted with rest stops.

Routes Nationales (N, RN) National highways. Some sections have divider strips.

Routes Départementales (D) Local highways and roads.

Routes Communales (C, V) Minor rural roads.

The latter two categories, while slower, offer some of France's most enjoyable driving experiences.

Motorcyclists will find France great for touring, with high-quality roads and stunning scenery. Just make sure your wet-weather gear is up to scratch.

Note that high mountain passes, especially in the Alps, may be closed from as early as September to as late as June. Conditions are posted at the foot of each pass ('*ouvert*' on a green background means open, '*ferme*' on a red background means closed). Snow chains or studded tyres are required in wintry weather.

ROAD RULES

Enforcement of French traffic laws (see www.securiteroutiere.gouv.fr for information) has been stepped up considerably in recent years. Speed cameras are common, as are radar traps and unmarked police vehicles. Fines for many infractions are given on the spot, and serious violations can lead to the confiscation of your driving licence and car.

France Playlist

Bonjour Rachid Taha and Gaetan Roussel

Coeur Vagabond Gus Viseur

La Vie en Rose Édith Piaf

Minor Swing Django Reinhardt

L'Americano Akhenaton

Flower Duet from Lakmé Léo Delibes

De Bonnes Raisons Alex Beaupain

Speed Limits

Speed limits outside built-up areas (unless signposted otherwise):

Undivided N and D highways 90km/h (80km/h when raining)

Non-autoroute divided highways 110km/h (100km/h when raining)

Autoroutes 130km/h (110km/h when raining)

Unless otherwise signposted, a limit of 50km/h applies in all areas designated as built up, no matter how rural they may appear. You must slow to 50km/h the moment you come to a white sign with a red border and a place name written on it; the speed limit applies until you pass an identical sign with a horizontal bar through it.

You're expected to already know the speed limit for various types of roads; that's why most speed-limit signs begin with the word *rappel* (reminder). You can be fined for going as little as 10km over the speed limit.

Alcohol

➡ The blood-alcohol limit is 0.05% (0.5g per litre of blood) – the equivalent of two glasses of wine for a 75kg adult.

➡ Police often conduct random breathalyser tests. Penalties can be severe, including imprisonment.

Motorcycles

➡ Riders of any two-wheeled motorised vehicle must wear a helmet.

➡ No special licence is required to ride a motorbike whose engine is smaller than 50cc, which is why rental scooters are often rated at 49.9cc.

Child Seats

A child under 13kg must travel in a backward-facing child seat (permitted in the front seat only for babies under 9kg and if the airbag is deactivated).

➡ Up to age 10 and/or a minimum height of 140cm, children must use a size-appropriate type of front-facing child seat or booster.

➡ Children under 10 are not permitted to ride in the front seat (unless the back is already occupied by other children under 10).

Other Rules

➡ All passengers, including those in the back seat, must wear seat belts.

→ Mobile phones may be used only if equipped with a hands-free kit or speakerphone.

→ Turning right on a red light is illegal.

→ All vehicles driven in France must carry a high-visibility reflective safety vest (stored inside the vehicle, not in the trunk/boot), a reflective triangle, and a portable, single-use breathalyser kit.

PARKING

In city centres, most on-the-street parking places are *payant* (metered) from about 9am to 7pm (sometimes with a break from noon to 2pm) Monday to Saturday, except bank holidays.

FUEL

Essence (petrol), also known as *carburant* (fuel), costs around €1.28 per litre for 95 unleaded (Sans Plomb 95 or SP95, usually available from a green pump) and €1 to €1.30 for diesel (*diesel, gazole* or *gasoil,* usually available from a yellow pump). Check and compare current prices countrywide at www.prix-carburants.gouv.fr.

Filling up *(faire le plein)* is most expensive at autoroute rest stops, and usually cheapest at hypermarkets.

Many small petrol stations close on Sunday afternoons and, even in cities, it can be hard to find a staffed station open late at night. In general, after-hours purchases (eg at hypermarkets' fully automatic, 24-hour stations) can only be made with a credit

---

Driving Problem-Buster

I can't speak French; will that be a problem? While it's preferable to learn some French before travelling, French road signs are mostly of the 'international symbol' variety, and English is increasingly spoken among the younger generation.

What should I do if my car breaks down? Safety first: turn on your flashers, put on a safety vest (legally required, and provided in rental-car glove compartments) and place a reflective triangle (also legally required) 30m to 100m behind your car to warn approaching motorists. Call for emergency assistance (⏃112) or walk to the nearest orange roadside call box (placed every 2km along French autoroutes). If renting a vehicle, your car-hire company's service number may help expedite matters. If travelling in your own car, verify before leaving home whether your local auto club has reciprocal roadside-assistance arrangements in France.

What if I have an accident? For minor accidents you'll need to fill out a *constat amiable d'accident* (accident statement, typically provided in rental-car glove compartments) and report the accident to your insurance and/or rental-car company. If necessary, contact the police (⏃17).

What should I do if I get stopped by the police? Show your passport (or EU national ID card), licence and proof of insurance.

What's the speed limit in France and how is it enforced? Speed limits (indicated by a black-on-white number inside a red circle) range from 30km/h in small towns to 130km/h on the fastest *autoroutes*. If the motorbike police pull you over, they'll fine you on the spot or direct you to the nearest gendarmerie to pay. If you're caught by a speed camera (placed at random intervals along French highways), the ticket will be sent to your rental-car agency, which will bill your credit card, or to your home address if you're driving your own vehicle. Fines depend on how much you're over the limit.

How do French tolls work? Many French *autoroutes* charge tolls. Take a ticket from the machine upon entering the highway and pay as you exit. Some exit booths are staffed by people; others are automated and will accept only chip-and-PIN credit cards or coins.

card that has an embedded PIN chip, so if all you've got is cash or a magnetic-strip credit card, you could be stuck.

SATELLITE NAVIGATION SYSTEMS

Sat-nav devices can be helpful in navigating your way around France. They're commonly available at car-rental agencies, or you can bring your own from home. Accuracy is more dependable on main highways than in small villages or on back roads; in rural areas, don't hesitate to fall back on common sense, road signs and a good Michelin map if your sat nav seems to be leading you astray.

SAFETY

Never leave anything valuable inside your car, even in the boot (trunk). Note that thieves can easily identify rental cars, as they have a distinctive number on the licence plate.

Theft is especially prevalent in the south. In cities like Marseille and Nice, occasional aggressive theft from cars stopped at red lights is also an issue.

RADIO

For news, tune in to the French-language France Info (105.5MHz; www.franceinfo. fr), multilanguage RFI (738kHz or 89MHz in Paris; www.rfi.fr) or, in northern France, the BBC World Service (648kHz) and BBC Radio 4 (198kHz).

Popular national FM music stations include NRJ (www.nrj.fr), Virgin (www.virgin radio.fr), La Radio Plus (www.laradioplus. com) and Nostalgie (www.nostalgie.fr).

In many areas, Autoroute Info (107.7MHz) has round-the-clock traffic information.

France Travel Guide

GETTING THERE & AWAY

AIR

Air France (www.airfrance.com) is the national carrier, with plenty of both domestic and international flights in and out of major French airports.

Smaller provincial airports with international flights, mainly to/from the UK, continental Europe and North Africa, include Paris-Beauvais, Bergerac, Biarritz, Brest, Brive-la-Gaillarde (Vallée de la Dordogne), Caen, Carcassonne, Clermont-Ferrand, Deauville, Dinard, Grenoble, La Rochelle, Le Touquet (Côte d'Opale), Limoges, Montpellier, Nîmes, Pau, Perpignan, Poitiers, Rennes, Rodez, St-Étienne, Toulon and Tours.

CAR & MOTORCYCLE

Entering France from other parts of the EU is usually a breeze – no border checkpoints and no customs – thanks to the Schengen Agreement, signed by all of France's neighbours except the UK, the Channel Islands and Andorra.

Eurotunnel

The Channel Tunnel (Chunnel), inaugurated in 1994, is the first dry-land link between England and France since the last ice age.

High-speed **Eurotunnel Le Shuttle** (✆ in France 08 10 63 03 04, in UK 08443 35 35 35; www.eurotunnel.com) trains whisk bicycles, motorcycles, cars and coaches in 35 minutes from Folkestone through the Channel Tunnel to Coquelles, 5km southwest of Calais. Shuttles run 24 hours a day, with up to three departures an hour during peak periods. LPG and CNG tanks are not permitted, meaning gas-powered cars and many campers and caravans have to travel by ferry.

Eurotunnel sets its fares the way budget airlines do: the further in advance you book and the lower the demand for a particular crossing, the less you pay; same-day fares can cost a small fortune. Fares for a car, including up to nine passengers, start at UK£23/€32.

TRAIN

Rail services link France with virtually every country in Europe. The **Eurostar** (www.eurostar.com) whisks passengers from London to Paris in 2¼ hours.

You can book tickets and get train information from **Rail Europe** (www.raileurope.com). In France ticketing is handled by the national railway company **SNCF** (www.sncf.com). High-speed train travel between France and the UK, Belgium, the Netherlands, Germany and Austria is covered by **Railteam** (www.railteam.co.uk).

Practicalities

➜ **Time** France uses the 24-hour clock and is on Central European Time, which is one hour ahead of GMT/UTC. During daylight saving time, which runs from the last Sunday in March to the last Sunday in October, France is two hours ahead of GMT/UTC.

➜ **DVD** DVDs are set for region 2.

➜ **Weights & Measures** France uses the metric system.

SEA

To get the best fares, check **Ferry Savers** (☑ in UK 0844 371 8021; www.ferrysavers.com).

International Ferry Companies

COMPANY	CONNECTION	WEBSITE
Brittany Ferries	England-Normandy, England-Brittany, Ireland-Brittany	www.brittany-ferries.co.uk; www.brittanyferries.ie
Condor Ferries	England-Normandy, England-Brittany, Channel Islands-Brittany	www.condorferries.co.uk
CTN	Tunisia-France	www.ctn.com.tn
DFDS Seaways	England-Normandy	www.dfdsseaways.co.uk
Irish Ferries	Ireland-Normandy, Ireland-Brittany	www.irishferries.com
Grandi Navi Veloci (GNV)	Morocco-Sète (Languedoc-Roussillon)	www.gnv.it
Manche Îles Express	Channel Islands-Normandy	www.manche-iles-express.com
My Ferry Link	Dover-Calais	www.myferrylink.fr
Norfolk Line (DFDS Seaways)	England-Channel Ports	www.norfolkline.com
P&O Ferries	England-Channel Ports	www.poferries.com
Stena Line Ferries	Ireland-Normandy	www.stenaline.ie
SNCM	Algeria-France, Sardinia-France, Tunisia-France	www.sncm.fr

DIRECTORY A–Z

ACCOMMODATION

Be it a fairy-tale château, a boutique hideaway or floating pod on a lake, France has accommodation to suit every taste and pocket. If you're visiting in high season (especially August), reserve ahead – the best addresses on the coast fill up months in advance.

Categories

As a rule of thumb, budget covers everything from basic hostels to small family-run places; midrange means a few extra creature comforts such as an elevator; while top-end places stretch from luxury five-star palaces with air-conditioning, swimming pools and restaurants to boutique-chic alpine chalets.

Costs

Accommodation costs vary wildly between seasons and regions: what will buy you a night in a romantic *chambre d'hôte* (B&B) in the countryside may get a dorm bed in a major city or high-profile ski resort.

Reservations

Midrange, top-end and many budget hotels require a credit-card number to secure an advance reservation made by phone; some hostels do not take bookings. Many tourist offices can advise on availability and reserve for you, often for a fee of €5 and usually only if you stop by in person. In the Alps, ski-resort tourist offices run a central reservation service for booking accommodation.

Seasons

➡ In ski resorts, high season is Christmas, New Year and the February–March school holidays.

➡ On the coast, high season is summer, particularly August.

➡ Hotels in inland cities often charge low-season rates in summer.

➡ Rates often drop outside the high season – in some cases by as much as 50%.

➡ In business-oriented hotels in cities, rooms are most expensive from Monday to Thursday and cheaper over the weekend.

➡ In the Alps, hotels usually close between seasons, from around May to mid-June and from mid-September to early December; many addresses in Corsica only open Easter to October.

B&Bs

For charm, a heartfelt *bienvenue* (welcome) and solid home cooking, it's hard to beat France's privately run *chambres d'hôte* (B&Bs) – urban rarities but as common as muck in rural areas. By law a *chambre d'hôte* must have no more than five rooms and breakfast must be included in the price; some hosts prepare a meal *(table d'hôte)* for an extra charge of around €30 including wine. Pick up lists of *chambres d'hôte* at tourist offices, or find one to suit online.

Bienvenue à la Ferme (www.bienvenue-a la ferme.com)

Chambres d'Hôtes France (www.chambresdhotesfrance.com)

Fleurs de Soleil (www.fleursdesoleil.fr) Selective collection of 550 stylish *maisons d'hôte,* mainly in rural France

Gîtes de France (www.gites-de-france.com) France's primary umbrella organisation for B&Bs and self-catering properties *(gîtes)*; search by region, theme (charm, with kids, by the sea, gourmet, great garden etc), activity (fishing, wine tasting etc) or facilities (pool, dishwasher, fireplace, baby equipment, etc)

iGuide (www.iguide-hotels.com) Gorgeous presentation of France's most charming and often-times most upmarket B&Bs, organised by region and/or theme (romantic, gastronomic, green, oenological and so forth)

Samedi Midi Éditions (www.samedimidi.com) Country, mountain, seaside...choose your *chambre d'hôte* by location or theme (romance, golf, design, cooking courses)

Camping

Be it a Mongolian yurt, boutique treehouse or simple canvas beneath stars, camping in France is in vogue. Thousands of well-equipped campgrounds dot the country, many considerately placed by rivers, lakes and the sea.

➡ Most campgrounds open March or April to late September or October; popular spots fill up fast in summer so it is wise to call ahead.

➡ 'Sites' refer to fixed-price deals for two people including a tent and a car. Otherwise the price is broken down per adult/tent/car. Factor in a few extra euro per night for *taxe de séjour* (holiday tax) and electricity.

➡ Euro-economisers should look out for local, good-value but no-frills *campings municipaux* (municipal campgrounds).

➡ Many campgrounds rent mobile homes with mod cons like heating, fitted kitchen and TV.

➡ Pitching up 'wild' in nondesignated spots *(camping sauvage)* is illegal in France.

➡ Campground offices often close during the day.

➡ Accessing many campgrounds without your own transport can be slow and costly, or simply impossible.

Hostels

Hostels in France range from funky to threadbare, although with a wave of design driven, up to the minute hostels

---

Sleeping Price Ranges

The following price ranges refer to a double room in high season, with private bathroom (any combination of toilet, bathtub, shower and washbasin), excluding breakfast unless otherwise noted. Breakfast is assumed to be included at a B&B. Where half board (breakfast and dinner) and full board (breakfast, lunch and dinner) is included, this is mentioned with the price.

€ less than €90 (€130 in Paris)

€€ €90–190 (€130–250 in Paris)

€€€ more than €190 (€250 in Paris)

opening in Paris, Marseille and other big cities, hip hang-outs with perks aplenty seem to easily outweigh the threadbare these days.

➡ In university towns, *foyers d'étudiant* (student dormitories) are sometimes converted for use by travellers during summer.

➡ A dorm bed in an *auberge de jeunesse* (youth hostel) costs €20 to €50 in Paris, and anything from €15 to €40 in the provinces, depending on location, amenities and facilities; sheets are always included, breakfast more often than not.

➡ To prevent outbreaks of bed bugs, sleeping bags are not permitted.

➡ Hostels by the sea or in the mountains sometimes offer seasonal outdoor activities.

➡ French hostels are 100% nonsmoking.

Hotels

Hotels in France are rated with one to five stars, although the ratings are based on highly objective criteria (eg the size of the entry hall), not the quality of the service, the decor or cleanliness.

➡ French hotels almost never include breakfast in their rates. Unless specified otherwise, prices quoted don't include breakfast, which costs around €8/12/25 in a budget/midrange/top-end hotel.

➡ When you book, hotels usually ask for a credit card number; some require a deposit.

➡ A double room generally has one double bed (sometimes two singles pushed together!); a room with twin beds *(deux lits)* is usually more expensive, as is a room with a bathtub instead of a shower.

➡ Feather pillows are practically nonexistent in France, even in top-end hotels.

➡ All hotel restaurant terraces allow smoking; if you are sensitive to smoke, you may need to sit inside.

Book Your Stay Online

For more accommodation reviews by Lonely Planet authors, check out http://hotels.lonelyplanet.com. You'll find independent reviews, as well as recommendations on the best places to stay. Best of all, you can book online.

ELECTRICITY

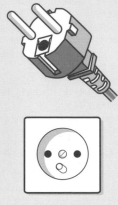

230V/50Hz

FOOD

Few Western cuisines are so envied, aspired to or seminal. The freshness of ingredients, natural flavours, regional variety and range of cooking methods is phenomenal. The very word 'cuisine' was borrowed from the French – no other language could handle all the nuances. The French table waltzes tastebuds through a dizzying array of dishes sourced from aromatic street markets, seaside oyster farms, sun-baked olive groves and ancient vineyards mirroring the beauty of each season. Discovering these varied regional cuisines is an enriching, essential experience.

Restaurants and bistros Range from unchanged for a century to contemporary minimalist; urban dining is international, rural dining staunchly French.

Brasseries Open from dawn until late, these casual eateries are great for dining in between standard meal times.

Cafés Ideal for breakfast and light lunch; many morph into bars after dark.

INTERNET ACCESS

➡ Wi-fi (pronounced 'wee-fee' in French) is available at major airports, in most hotels, and at many cafes, restaurants, museums and tourist offices.

➡ Free public wi-fi hotspots are available in cities and many towns: Paris alone has 400 public hotspots in 26 different locations city-wide (www.paris.fr/wifi), including parks, libraries and municipal buildings. In parks look for a purple 'Zone Wi-Fi' sign near the entrance and select the 'PARIS_WI-FI_' network to connect.

➡ To search for free wi-fi hot spots in France, visit www.hotspot-locations.com.

➡ Tourist offices is some larger cities, including Lyon and Bordeaux, rent out pocket-sized mobile wi-fi devices that you carry around with you, ensuring a fast wi-fi connection while roaming the city.

➡ Alternatively, rent a mobile wi-fi device online before leaving home and arrange for it to be delivered by post to your hotel in France through HipPocketWifi (http://hippocketwifi.com), Travel WiFi (http://travel-wifi.com) or My Webspot (http://my-webspot.com).

➡ Internet cafes are increasingly rare; at least one can usually be tracked down in cities. Prices range from €2 to €6 per hour.

LGBT TRAVELLERS

The rainbow flag flies high in France, a country that left its closet long before many of its European neighbours. *Laissez-faire* perfectly sums up France's liberal attitude towards homosexuality and people's private lives in general, in part because of a long tradition of public tolerance towards unconventional lifestyles.

➡ Paris has been a thriving gay and lesbian centre since the late 1970s, and most major organisations are based there today.

➡ Bordeaux, Lille, Lyon, Montpellier, Toulouse and many other towns also have an active queer scene.

➡ Attitudes towards homosexuality tend to be more conservative in the countryside and villages.

➡ France's lesbian scene is less public than its gay male counterpart and is centred mainly on women's cafes and bars.

Eating Price Ranges

Price indicators refer to the average cost of a two-course meal, be it an *entrée* (starter) and *plat* (main course) or main and dessert, or a two- or three-course *menu* (pre-set meal at a fixed price).

€ less than €20

€€ €20–40

€€€ more than €40

➡ Same-sex marriage has been legal in France since May 2013.

➡ Gay Pride marches are held in major French cities mid-May to early July.

MONEY

ATMs

Automated Teller Machines (ATMs) – known as *distributeurs automatiques de billets* (DAB) or *points d'argent* in French – are the cheapest and most convenient way to get money. ATMs connected to international networks are situated in all cities and towns and usually offer an excellent exchange rate.

Cash

You always get a better exchange rate in-country, but it is a good idea to arrive in France with enough euros to take a taxi to a hotel if you have to.

Credit & Debit Cards

➡ Credit and debit cards, accepted almost everywhere in France, are convenient, relatively secure and usually offer a better exchange rate than travellers cheques or cash exchanges.

➡ Credit cards issued in France have embedded chips – you have to type in a PIN to make a purchase.

➡ Visa, MasterCard and Amex can be used in shops and supermarkets and for train travel, car hire and motorway tolls.

➡ Don't assume that you can pay for a meal or a budget hotel with a credit card – enquire first.

➡ Cash advances are a supremely convenient way to stay stocked up with euros but getting cash with a credit card involves both fees (sometimes US$10 or more) and interest – ask your credit-card issuer for details. Debit-card fees are usually much less.

Moneychangers

➡ Commercial banks charge up to €5 per foreign-currency transaction – if they even bother to offer exchange services any more.

➡ In Paris and major cities, *bureaux de change* (exchange bureaus) are faster and easier, open longer hours and often give better rates than banks.

➡ Some post-office branches exchange travellers cheques and banknotes in a variety of currencies but charge a commission for cash; most won't take US$100 bills.

Tipping

By law, restaurant and bar prices are *service compris* (ie they include a 15% service charge), so there is no need to leave a *pourboire* (tip). If you were extremely satisfied with the service, however, you can – as many locals do – show your appreciation by leaving a small 'extra' tip for your waiter or waitress.

WHERE/WHO	CUSTOMARY TIP
bar	No tips for drinks served at bar; round to nearest euro for drinks served at table
cafe	5-10%
hotel porter	€1-2 per bag
restaurant	10%
taxi	10-15%
toilet attendant	€0.50
tour guide	€1-2 per person

OPENING HOURS

Opening hours vary throughout the year. We list high-season opening hours, but remember that longer summer hours often decrease in shoulder and low seasons.

Banks 9am–noon and 2pm–5pm Monday to Friday or Tuesday to Saturday

Restaurants noon–2.30pm and 7pm–11pm six days a week

Cafes 7am–11pm

Bars 7pm–1am

Clubs 10pm–3am, 4am or 5am Thursday to Saturday

Shops 10am–noon and 2pm–7pm Monday to Saturday

PUBLIC HOLIDAYS

The following *jours fériés* (public holidays) are observed in France:

New Year's Day (Jour de l'An) 1 January

Easter Sunday & Monday (Pâques & Lundi de Pâques) Late March/April

May Day (Fête du Travail) 1 May

Victoire 1945 8 May

Ascension Thursday (Ascension) May; on the 40th day after Easter

Pentecost/Whit Sunday & Whit Monday (Pentecôte & Lundi de Pentecôte) Mid-May to mid-June; on the seventh Sunday after Easter

Bastille Day/National Day (Fête Nationale) 14 July

Assumption Day (Assomption) 15 August

All Saints' Day (Toussaint) 1 November

Remembrance Day (L'onze Novembre) 11 November

Christmas (Noël) 25 December

The following are *not* public holidays in France: Shrove Tuesday (Mardi Gras; the first day of Lent); Maundy (or Holy) Thursday and Good Friday, just before Easter; and Boxing Day (26 December).

Note: Good Friday and Boxing Day *are* public holidays in Alsace.

SAFE TRAVEL

France is generally a safe place in which to live and travel despite crime and terrorism rising dramatically in the last few years. Although property crime is a problem, it is extremely unlikely that you will be physically assaulted while walking down the street. Always check your government's travel advisory warnings.

Because of the threat of terrorism, French police are very strict about security. Do not leave baggage unattended, especially at airports or train stations: suspicious objects may be summarily blown up. In large museums and monuments, it is fairly routine for bags to be checked upon entering.

Hunting season runs from September to February. If you see signs reading *'chasseurs'* or *'chasse gardée'* strung up or tacked to trees, think twice about wandering into the area. As well as millions of wild animals, some 25 French hunters die each year after being shot by other hunters. Hunting is traditional and commonplace in all rural areas in France, especially the Vosges, the Sologne, the southwest and the Baie de Somme.

Natural Dangers

➡ There are powerful tides and strong undertows at many places along the Atlantic Coast, from the Spanish border north to Brittany and Normandy.

➡ Only swim in *zones de baignade surveillée* (beaches monitored by life guards).

➡ Be aware of tide times and the high-tide mark if walking or sleeping on a beach.

➡ Thunderstorms in the mountains and the hot southern plains can be extremely sudden and violent.

➡ Check the weather report before setting out on a long walk and be prepared for sudden storms and temperature drops if you are heading into the high country of the Alps or Pyrenees.

➡ Avalanches pose a significant danger in the French Alps.

Theft

Pickpocketing and bag/phone-snatching (eg in dense crowds and public places) are as prevalent in big French cities – Paris, Marseille and Nice in particular – as in other cities in Europe. There's no need whatsoever to travel in fear. A few simple precautions will minimise your chances of being ripped off.

➡ On trains, avoid leaving smartphones and tablets lying casually on the table in front of you and keep bags as close to you as possible: luggage racks at the ends of carriages are easy prey for thieves; in sleeping compartments, lock the door carefully at night.

➡ Be especially vigilant for bag/phone snatchers at train stations, airports, fast-food outlets, outdoor cafes, beaches and on public transport.

➡ Break-ins to parked cars are a widespread problem. Never, ever leave anything valuable – or not valuable – inside your car, even in the boot (trunk).

➡ Aggressive theft from cars stopped at red lights is occasionally a problem, especially in Marseille and Nice. As a precaution, lock your car doors and roll up the windows.

TELEPHONE

➡ French mobile phone numbers begin with 📞06 or 📞07.

➡ France uses GSM 900/1800, which is compatible with the rest of Europe and Australia but not with the North American GSM 1900 or the system in Japan (though some North Americans have tri-band phones that work here).

➡ Check with your service provider about roaming charges – dialling a mobile phone from a fixed-line phone or another mobile can be incredibly expensive.

➡ It is usually cheaper to buy a local SIM card from a French provider such as Orange, SFR, Bouygues and Free Mobile which gives you a local phone number. To do this, ensure your phone is unlocked.

➡ If you already have a compatible phone, you can slip in a SIM card (from €3.90) and rev it up with prepaid credit, though this is likely to run out fast as domestic prepaid calls cost about €0.50 per minute.

➡ Recharge cards are sold at most *tabacs* (tobacconists/newsagents), supermarkets and online through websites such as Topengo (www.topengo.fr) or Sim-OK (https:// recharge.sim-ok.com).

TOURIST INFORMATION

Almost every city, town and village has an *office de tourisme* (a tourist office run by some unit of local government) or *syndicat d'initiative* (a tourist office run by an organisation of local merchants). Both are excellent resources and can supply you with local maps as well as details on accommodation, restaurants and activities. If you have a special interest such as walking, cycling, architecture or wine sampling, ask about it.

➡ Many tourist offices make local hotel and B&B reservations, sometimes for a nominal fee.

➡ *Comités régionaux de tourisme* (CRTs; regional tourist boards), their *départemental* analogues (CDTs) and their websites are a superb source of information and hyperlinks.

➡ French government tourist offices (usually called Maisons de la France) provide every imaginable sort of tourist information on France.

Useful websites include:

French Government Tourist Office (www.france.fr) The lowdown on sights, activities, transport and special-interest holidays in all of France's regions. Brochures can be downloaded online.

French Tourist Offices (www.tourisme. fr) Website of tourist offices in France, with mountains of inspirational information organised by theme and region.

TRAVELLERS WITH DISABILITIES

While France presents evident challenges for *visiteurs handicapés* (disabled visitors) – cobblestones, cafe-lined streets that are a nightmare to navigate in a wheelchair *(fauteuil roulant),* a lack of kerb ramps, older public facilities and many budget hotels without lifts – don't let that stop you from visiting. Efforts are being made to improve the situation and with a little careful planning, a hassle-free accessible stay is possible. Download Lonely Planet's free *Accessible Travel* guide from http://lptravel.to/AccessibleTravel.

➡ The Paris tourist office runs the excellent 'Tourisme & Handicap' initiative whereby museums, cultural attractions, hotels and restaurants that provide access or special assistance or facilities for those with physical, mental, visual and/or hearing disabilities display a special logo at their entrances. For a list of qualifying places, go to www.parisinfo.com and click on 'Practical Paris'.

➡ Paris metro, most of which was built decades ago (and some of it more than a century ago), is hopeless. Line 14 of the metro was built to be wheelchair-accessible, although in reality it remains extremely challenging to navigate in a wheelchair – unlike Paris buses which are 100% accessible.

➡ Parisian taxi company Horizon, part of Taxis G7 (www.taxisg7.fr), has cars especially adapted to carry wheelchairs and drivers trained in helping passengers with disabilities.

➡ Countrywide, many SNCF train carriages are accessible to people with disabilities. A traveller in a wheelchair can travel in both the TGV and in the 1st-class carriage with a 2nd-class ticket on mainline trains provided they make a reservation by phone or at a train station at least a few hours before departure. Details are available in the SNCF booklet *Le Mémento du Voyageur Handicapé (Handicapped Traveller Summary)* available at all train stations.

Useful resources:

Accès Plus (☑09 69 32 26 26, 08 90 64 06 50; www.accessibilite.sncf.com) The SNCF assistance service for rail travellers with disabilities. Can advise on station accessibility and arrange a *fauteuil roulant* or help getting on or off a train.

Infomobi.com (☑09 70 81 83 85; www.infomobi.com) Has comprehensive information on accessible travel in Paris and the surrounding Île de France area.

Access Travel (☑in UK 01942-888 844; www.access-travel.co.uk) Specialised UK-based agency for accessible travel.

Mobile en Ville (☑09 52 29 60 51; www.mobile-en-ville.asso.fr; 8 rue des Mariniers, 14e, Paris) Association that works hard to make independent travel within Paris easier for people in wheelchairs. Among other things it organises some great family *randonnées* (walks) in and around Paris.

Tourisme et Handicaps (☑01 44 11 10 41; www.tourisme-handicaps.org; 43 rue Marx Dormoy, 18e, Paris) Issues the 'Tourisme et Handicap' label to tourist sites, restaurants and hotels that comply with strict accessibility and usability standards. Different symbols indicate the sort of access afforded to people with physical, mental, hearing and/or visual disabilities.

VISAS

➡ For up-to-date details on visa requirements, see the website of the **Ministère des Affaires Étrangères** (Ministry of Foreign Affairs; www.diplomatie.gouv.fr) and click 'Coming to France'.

➡ Visas are generally not required for stays of up to 90 days (or at all for EU nationals); some nationalities need a Schengen visa.

Language

The sounds used in spoken French can almost all be found in English. There are a couple of exceptions: nasal vowels (represented in our pronunciation guides by o or u followed by an almost inaudible nasal consonant sound m, n or ng), the 'funny' u (ew in our guides) and the deep in the throat r. Bearing these few points in mind and reading our pronunciation guides below as if they were English, you'll be understood just fine.

BASICS

Hello.	*Bonjour.*	bon·zhoor
Goodbye.	*Au revoir.*	o·rer·vwa
Yes./No.	*Oui./Non.*	wee/non
Excuse me.	*Excusez-moi.*	ek·skew·zay·mwa
Sorry.	*Pardon.*	par·don
Please.	*S'il vous plaît.*	seel voo play
Thank you.	*Merci.*	mair·see

You're welcome.
De rien.   der ree·en

Do you speak English?
Parlez-vous anglais?   par·lay·voo ong·glay

I don't understand.
Je ne comprends pas.   zher ner kom·pron pa

How much is this?
C'est combien?   say kom·byun

ACCOMMODATION

Do you have any rooms available?
Est-ce que vous avez   es·ker voo za·vay
des chambres libres?   day shom·brer lee·brer

How much is it per night/person?
Quel est le prix   kel ay ler pree
par nuit/personne?   par nwee/per·son

DIRECTIONS

Can you show me (on the map)?
Pouvez-vous m'indiquer   poo·vay·voo mun·dee·kay
(sur la carte)?   (sewr la kart)

Where's ...?
Où est ...?   oo ay ...

EATING & DRINKING

What would you recommend?
Qu'est-ce que vous   kes·ker voo
conseillez?   kon·say·yay

I'd like ..., please.
Je voudrais ...,   zher voo·dray ...
s'il vous plaît.   seel voo play

I'm a vegetarian.
Je suis végétarien/   zher swee vay·zhay·ta·ryun/
végétarienne.   vay·zhay·ta·ryen (m/f)

Please bring the bill.
Apportez-moi   a·por·tay·mwa
l'addition,   la·dee·syon
s'il vous plaît.   seel voo play

EMERGENCIES

Help!
Au secours!   o skoor

I'm lost.
Je suis perdu/perdue.   zhe swee·pair·dew (m/f)

Want More?

For in-depth language information and handy phrases, check out Lonely Planet's *French Phrasebook*. You'll find it at **shop.lonelyplanet.com**, or you can buy Lonely Planet's iPhone phrasebooks at the Apple App Store.

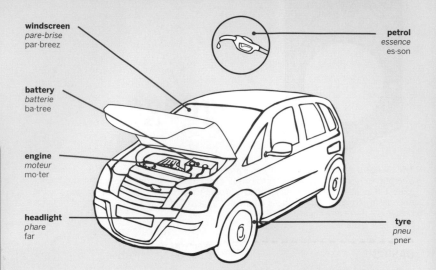

windscreen
pare-brise
par·breez

petrol
essence
es·son

battery
batterie
ba·tree

engine
moteur
mo·ter

headlight
phare
far

tyre
pneu
pner

Signs

Cédez la Priorité	Give Way
Sens Interdit	No Entry
Entrée	Entrance
Péage	Toll
Sens Unique	One Way
Sortie	Exit

I'm ill.
Je suis malade.   zher swee ma·lad

Call the police!
Appelez la police!   a·play la po·lees

Call a doctor!
Appelez un médecin!   a·play un mayd·sun

ON THE ROAD

I'd like to hire a/an ...	*Je voudrais louer ...*	zher voo·dray loo·way ...
4WD	*un quatre-quatre*	un kat·kat
automatic/ manual	*une auto-matique/ manuel*	ewn o·to·ma·teek/ ma·nwel
motorbike	*une moto*	ewn mo·to

How much is it daily/weekly?
Quel est le tarif par jour/semaine?   kel ay ler ta·reef par zhoor/ser·men

Does that include insurance?
Est-ce que l'assurance est comprise?   es·ker la·sew·rons ay kom·preez

Does that include mileage?
Est-ce que le kilométrage est compris?   es·ker ler kee·lo·may·trazh ay kom·pree

What's the speed limit?
Quelle est la vitesse maximale permise?   kel ay la vee·tes mak·see·mal per·meez

Is this the road to ...?
C'est la route pour ...?   say la root poor ...

Can I park here?
Est-ce que je peux stationner ici?   es·ker zher per sta·syo·nay ee·see

Where's a service station?
Où est-ce qu'il y a une station-service?   oo es·keel ya ewn sta·syon·ser·vees

Please fill it up.
Le plein, s'il vous plaît.   ler plun seel voo play

I'd like (20) litres.
Je voudrais (vingt) litres.   zher voo·dray (vung) lee·trer

Please check the oil/water.
Contrôlez l'huile/l'eau, s'il vous plaît.   kon·tro·lay lweel/lo seel voo play

I need a mechanic.
J'ai besoin d'un mécanicien.   zhay ber·zwun dun may·ka·nee·syun

The car/motorbike has broken down.
La voiture/moto est tombée en panne.   la vwa·tewr/mo·to ay tom·bay on pan

I had an accident.
J'ai eu un accident.   zhay ew un ak·see·don

BEHIND THE SCENES

SEND US YOUR FEEDBACK

We love to hear from travellers – your comments help make our books better. We read every word, and we guarantee that your feedback goes straight to the authors. Visit **lonelyplanet. com/contact** to submit your updates and suggestions.

Note: We may edit, reproduce and incorporate your comments in Lonely Planet products such as guidebooks, websites and digital products, so let us know if you don't want your comments reproduced or your name acknowledged. For a copy of our privacy policy visit lonelyplanet.com/privacy.

WRITERS' THANKS

JEAN-BERNARD CARILLET

Big thanks to Christine for joining me for a few days in Beaujolais, and to all the people I met while on the road for their tips and recommendations. Last but not least, a *gros bisou* to my half-Parisian, half-Lorraine daughter Eva.

ALEXIS AVERBUCK

Once again my journey through the Dordogne was made magnificent by the generosity of the gorgeous Janice Bowen. She shared her home, her fantastic knowledge of the region, and her enthusiastic heart. A million thanks to wonderful Alexandra Miliotis for her top tips on travelling the back roads of Brittany. The pink granite coast, walled city of St-Malo and the sumptuous seafood of Brittany wouldn't have been nearly as delicious without my darling Ryan Ver Berkmoes: husband, friend, travel genie and joy.

OLIVER BERRY

For this edition Oliver would like to thank Didier Lafarge, Jean Dubarry, Eloise Guilmard and Agnes Tilleul for help during research and write-up. He would also like to send special thanks to Susie and Gracie Berry for receiving all the postcards, and to Rosie Hillier for love, late-night correspondence, and making the road a lot less lonely.

KERRY CHRISTIANI

I'd like to say a big *merci* to all the wonderful locals I met on my travels, as well as to the tourist boards who made the road to research silky smooth. A special thank you goes to Jeal-Paul de Vries at Romagne 14'-18' for the behind-the-scenes battlefields tour.

GREGOR CLARK

Un grand merci to the countless locals who shared their knowledge of Burgundy and Corsica with me. Special thanks to Claire Beuvrot in Cluny for the cloves that cured my toothache. And big hugs to Gaen, Meigan and Chloe, who always make coming home the best part of the trip.

ANITA ISALSKA

Enormous thanks to the friends and colleagues who shared insider insights, tips and support for this project. Special thank yous go to Thomas

THIS BOOK

This 2nd edition of Lonely Planet's *France's Best Trips* guidebook was researched and written by Alexis Averbuck, Oliver Berry, Jean-Bernard Carillet, Kerry Christiani, Gregor Clark, Anita Isalska, Hugh McNaughton, Catherine Le Nevez, Daniel Robinson, Regis St Louis and Nicola Williams. The previous edition was written by Oliver Berry, Stuart Butler, Jean-Bernard Carillet, Gregor Clark, Donna Wheeler and Nicola Williams. This guidebook was produced by the following:

Destination Editor Helen Elfer

Product Editors Anne Mason, Susan Paterson

Senior Cartographer Valentina Kremenchutskaya

Book Designer Wendy Wright

Assisting Book Designer Wibowo Rusli

Assisting Editors Imogen Bannister, Carolyn Boicos, Kate Chapman, Andrea Dobbin, Bruce Evans, Samantha Forge, Carly Hall, Victoria Harrison, Kate James, Rosie Nicholson, Luna Soo, Fionnuala Twomey, Tracy Whitmey

Cover Researcher Lucy Burke

Thanks to Liz Heynes, Kirsten Rawlings, Alison Ridgway, Ellie Simpson, Lauren Wellicome

Ducloutrier, Bill Lehane, Vanessa Michy, Pascale Suc, Jean-Paul Grimaud, Kate Morgan, Melissa Buttelli, and friendly tourist offices along the Tarn. And Normal Matt, who drove from London to Vichy in a beat-up Toyota just to cheer me on.

CATHERINE LE NEVEZ

Un grand merci to my Paris co-writers Chris and Nicola. *Merci mille fois* to Julian, and everyone in and around Paris and in Languedoc-Roussillon who offered insights and inspiration. In particular, *merci beaucoup* to Laurent for going above and beyond, and to Laurence for the same. Huge thanks also to Helen Elfer, Kate Morgan and everyone at LP. A heartfelt *merci encore* to my parents, brother, *belle-sœur* and *neveu* for sustaining my lifelong love of Paris and France.

HUGH MCNAUGHTAN

Thanks to Helen Elfer and to my ever-understanding family.

DANIEL ROBINSON

Special thanks to (from north to south): Anny Monet (Lille), Virginie Debret (Lens' 14-18 museum), Rodney and Philippe (Arras), Carole Lefebvre and Corinne Vasseur (Parc du Marquenterre Bird Sanctuary), Thapedi Masanabo (South African National Memorial), Lauren Tookey (Amiens and UK) and Madame Thion (Cercil, Orléans). This project would not have been possible without the support, enthusiasm and forbearance of my wife, Rachel, and our sons, Yair and Sasson (Orléans, Tours and New London, Connecticut).

REGIS ST LOUIS

I'm particularly grateful to the tourism officials, innkeepers, booksellers, baristas, priests, hitchhikers and assorted other locals who shared tips and advice along the way. Special thanks to Penny, Thierry and Olivier in Honfleur; Marion and Hans at Florivalier; and the mysterious but kind-hearted vegan galette maker in Foix. Lastly, *gros bisous* to my partner in crime, Cassandra, and daughters Magdalena and Genevieve.

NICOLA WILLIAMS

Un grand merci to the many who aided and abetted in tracking down the very best, including in Nantes, Katia Forte, @Rachelwill and rapidly rising chef Dominic Quirke at neobistro Pickles; Pascale Chaillot in Cognac; and in Bordeaux, wine expert Jane Anson, Kirsty Curtis (Musée du Vin et du Négoce) and Sophie Gaillard (Bordeaux Tourisme). At home, sweet thanks to *belle mère* Christa Luefkens and my highly experienced trilingual 'family travel' research team, Niko, Mischa and Kaya.

ACKNOWLEDGMENTS

Climate map data adapted from Peel MC, Finlayson BL & McMahon TA (2007) 'Updated World Map of the Köppen-Geiger Climate Classification', *Hydrology and Earth System Sciences*, 11, 163344.

Front cover photographs: (top) Carcassonne, Languedoc, Nadia Isakova/AWL ©; (right) Lavender field, Provence, Danita Delimont Stock/AWL ©; (left) Citroen 2CV, Zoonar/Dieter Möbus/Alamy ©

Back cover photograph: Mont St-Michel, Normandy, Susanne Kremer/4Corners ©

INDEX

NICOLA WILLIAMS

British writer Nicola Williams has lived in France and written about it for more than a decade. From her hillside house on the southern shore of Lake Geneva, road trips beckon to Provence, Paris, the Dordogne and onwards to the Atlantic Coast where she has spent endless years revelling in its extraordinary landscapes, architecture and seafaring cuisine. Nicola has worked on numerous Lonely Planet titles, including *Discover France* and *Paris*. Find her on Twitter and Instagram at @Tripalong.

Read more about Nicola at https://auth. lonelyplanet.com/profiles/nicolawilliams

CATHERINE LE NEVEZ

An award-winning, Paris-based travel writer, Catherine first lived in the French capital aged four and has been hitting the road at every opportunity, completing her Doctorate of Creative Arts in Writing, Masters in Professional Writing, and postgrad qualifications in editing and publishing along the way. Over the last dozen-plus years she's written scores of Lonely Planet guides, along with numerous print and online articles, covering Paris, France, Europe and far beyond. Wanderlust aside, Paris remains her favourite city on earth.

Read more about Catherine at https://auth. lonelyplanet.com/profiles/catherine_le_nevez

HUGH MCNAUGHTAN

A former English lecturer, Hugh swapped grant applications for visa applications, and turned his love of travel into a full-time thing. Having done a bit of restaurant-reviewing in his home town (Melbourne) he's now eaten his way across the Alps and Jura, working up an appetite on the slopes at any opportunity. He's never happier than when on the road with his two daughters. Except perhaps on the cricket field...

DANIEL ROBINSON

Co-author (with Tony Wheeler) of Lonely Planet's first *Paris* guide, Daniel has been writing about France for over 25 years. Passionate about history, he is always moved by the grand châteaux of the Loire, the sombre cemeteries of the Somme, and the dramatic and tragic events that both embody. Daniel's travel writing has appeared in the *New York Times, National Geographic Traveler* and many other publications and has been translated into 10 languages. He holds degrees in history from Princeton and Tel Aviv University.

REGIS ST LOUIS

Regis' French ancestry fuelled an early interest in all things francophone, which led to Serge Gainsbourg records, François Truffaut films and extensive travels around France. For his latest journey, Regis walked the drizzly beaches of Normandy, explored Joan of Arc lore in Rouen and idled behind sheep-powered roadblocks in the Pyrenees. A full-time travel writer since 2003, Regis has covered numerous destinations for Lonely Planet, including Montreal, Senegal and New York City. Follow his latest posts on Twitter at @regisstlouis.

Read more about Regis at https://auth. lonelyplanet.com/members/regisstlouis

OLIVER BERRY

Oliver Berry has explored nearly every corner of France for Lonely Planet, travelling all the way from the mountains of Corsica to the beaches of Normandy. He has also photographed and written about France for many newspapers, magazines and online publications. For this trip he returned to the beaches and hilltop villages of the South of France, and practised his *pelota* skills in the French Basque Country. His latest work is published at www. oliverberry.com.

KERRY CHRISTIANI

France was *le coup de foudre* (love at first sight) for Kerry, and she's been travelling there since her school days to brush up her *français*, which she went on to study to MA level. Touring the cellars of Champagne, (over)indulging on Alsatian food and wine on the storybook Route des Vins and striking out into the forested peaks of the Vosges made writing this edition memorable. Kerry authors a number of Lonely Planet's central and southern European titles and tweets @kerrychristiani.

GREGOR CLARK

Gregor Clark's love affair with France started on the midnight streets of Paris at age 14 when, jet-lagged and culture shocked, he successfully ordered a crêpe using his never-before-tested high school French. He's been feeding his France obsession ever since, and writing for Lonely Planet since 2000. Highlights of this research trip included discovering the stunning beauty of Corsica, chasing down Good Friday processions in remote mountain villages and indulging in way too many *beignets de brocciu* (best snack ever!).

ANITA ISALSKA

Anita's passion for France began on childhood ferry rides to Calais and bloomed during an enriching year living in Lille, though she hit peak Francophilia during her European Literature MSt at Oxford. While her enthusiasm for 19th-century French fantastique literature has found few practical applications, Anita loves flexing her language skills on regular travels to France. She writes about travel in Europe, Asia and beyond for a host of websites and magazines; read her stuff on www.anitaisalska.com.

OUR WRITERS

OUR STORY

A beat-up old car, a few dollars in the pocket and a sense of adventure. In 1972 that's all Tony and Maureen Wheeler needed for the trip of a lifetime – across Europe and Asia overland to Australia. It took several months, and at the end – broke but inspired – they sat at their kitchen table writing and stapling together their first travel guide, *Across Asia on the Cheap*. Within a week they'd sold 1500 copies. Lonely Planet was born.

Today, Lonely Planet has offices in Franklin, London, Melbourne, Oakland, Dublin, Beijing and Delhi, with more than 600 staff and writers. We share Tony's belief that 'a great guidebook should do three things: inform, educate and amuse'.

JEAN-BERNARD CARILLET

A Paris-based (and Metz-born) journalist and photographer, Jean-Bernard has clocked up countless trips to all French regions and is a passionate ambassador for his own country. As a hopeless French gourmand and amateur *de bon vins* (wine lover), he was all too happy to research Lyon (pike dumplings, anyone?), La Dombes (that yummy frog pie), Beaujolais (oh, that St-Amour lingers long on the palate) and the Rhône Valley down to the Gorges de l'Ardèche.

Read more about Jean-Bernard at https://auth. lonelyplanet.com/profiles/jbcarillet

ALEXIS AVERBUCK

Alexis Averbuck first came to France when she was four and now visits every chance she gets. Whether browsing markets in the Dordogne, sampling oysters in Brittany, or careening through hilltop villages in Provence (she also contributes to the *Provence & Côte d'Azur* book), she immerses herself in all things French. A travel writer for two decades, Alexis has lived in Antarctica for a year, crossed the Pacific by sailboat, and is also a painter – see her work at www. alexisaverbuck.com.

← MORE WRITERS

Published by Lonely Planet Global Limited
CRN 554153
2nd edition – Mar 2017
ISBN 978 1 7865 7320 9
© Lonely Planet 2017   Photographs © as indicated 2017
10 9 8 7 6 5 4 3 2 1
Printed in China

Although the authors and Lonely Planet have taken all reasonable care in preparing this book, we make no warranty about the accuracy or completeness of its content and, to the maximum extent permitted, disclaim all liability arising from its use.

MIX
Paper from responsible sources
FSC™ C021741

Paper in this book is certified against the Forest Stewardship Council™ standards. FSC™ promotes environmentally responsible, socially beneficial and economically viable management of the world's forests.